THE
100
BEST
STOCKS
TO BUY IN
2013

PETER SANDER
AND
SCOTT BOBO

WITHDRAWN

Aadamsmedia
AVON, MASSACHUSETTS

Published by
Adams Media, a division of F+W Media, Inc.
57 Littlefield Street, Avon, MA 02322. U.S.A.
www.adamsmedia.com

ISBN 10: 1-4405-4183-3
ISBN 13: 978-1-4405-4183-4
eISBN 10: 1-4405-4184-1
eISBN 13: 978-1-4405-4184-1

Printed in the United States of America.

10   9   8   7   6   5   4   3   2   1

This book is available at quantity discounts for bulk purchases.
For information, please call 1-800-289-0963.

Contents

Dedication

We continue to dedicate this book to all of you active investors who have the sense of purpose and independence of thought to make your own investing decisions, or at least to ask the right questions. You continue to be wise enough—and inquisitive enough—to realize that not all the answers can be found in one place, and smart enough to seek the convenience of a good place to start.

Acknowledgments

Peter continues to be thrilled to have research partner and life friend Scott Bobo on board as an official coauthor of this book. He also recognizes the good work of Value Line Inc. and their Investment Survey, which does more than any other known source to turn piles of facts and figures into a simple readable page. Next, no book happens without the added value of exercise to keep a body in shape and a mind clear, and to that end he offers his thanks to his exercise companions. And of course his boys Julian and Jonathan and new fiancée Marjorie get credit for the inspiration to engage in this enterprise.

Scott would like to acknowledge the tireless efforts of his friend and coauthor Peter Sander in setting and keeping a high standard in the research and writing of this series. His diligence is what makes these books and our readers successful. Scott's wife Lorie gets credit for everything Scott knows about the nitty-gritty of financial statements—may her patience with his questions never falter. Scott would also like to acknowledge his mother's fearless spirit as a source of inspiration.

PART I

THE ART AND SCIENCE OF INVESTING IN STOCKS

By Peter Sander

The Art and Science of Investing in Stocks

"While I wasn't expecting a huge overhaul, paying for another book to read about 12 new companies in the list doesn't seem like a bargain at all."

So goes part of the critique of our *100 Best Stocks You Can Buy 2012* by a disgruntled D. Ng on Amazon.com shortly after its release.

We take his critique (as we take all critiques) to heart. We know that no book is perfect, and we know that no investment analysis or list of stocks is perfect.

But the fact is, we think that changing only 12 stocks on a list of 100 "best" stocks in a given year is a pretty good thing. That implies that the list of stocks we decided was "best" in 2011 must have been pretty good. And while the story on the 12 new stocks will no doubt interest Mr. or Ms. Ng, wouldn't it also be of interest, as well as a useful piece of information, that the other 88 stocks were *still* on the list? Wouldn't it be useful to read a refresh, an update, a reiteration of the qualities and attributes of value, with new news thrown in, that made the company great, and *still* great?

We're sure most of our readers hardly expect a list of 100 completely new stocks each year. But you know what? If we published an annual revision that had *no* new stocks—*zero*—all the same as last year, we'd think that we had done a heck of a job. Such a good job that the *100 Best* were *still* the *100 Best*.

We also know the real world doesn't work that way. The economy changes. Technology changes. Markets change. There are no guarantees that the fortunes of a business in Year One will continue just as strong in Year Two. In fact, you can usually bet against it. Furthermore, we're always scanning the business landscape for new ideas, for new companies that might be a *better* fit. (Remember our cardinal rule of selling—sell when there is something else—even cash—that's better to buy.) We also fine-tune the list for balance so as not to have *too* many companies in a hot industry, to have companies that complement each other in a portfolio.

We didn't put 12 new stocks on *this* year's *100 Best Stocks* list. We added 14. We chucked a few losers we probably should have dropped last year. We got rid of some duplicates—don't need two industrial gas suppliers; don't need two suppliers of dental materials. We trimmed the health-care industry from 17 companies down to 15. And we made some changes—well—just because we saw what we thought were better opportunities. Sell when there's something else better to buy.

With that, welcome to the *100 Best Stocks* series, in particular to this 2013 edition of *The 100 Best Stocks to Buy*.

WARNING: If you've read the 2012 book and its predecessors, you'll probably find some of the following familiar.

But here goes, anyway.

Because it is still relevant.

It's Still about the Individual Investor

If you bought this book, you're probably an astute and experienced individual investor who invests in individual stocks in individual companies. Now, that might not seem so profound, but with some 10,000 mutual funds, 8,000 hedge funds, and about 1,500 (and rapidly growing) exchange-traded funds (ETFs) out there, it's conceivable that the individual stock investor is becoming an endangered species.

But that's just not so. For personal profit as well as for the efficient allocation of capital to businesses and ideas that work best, millions still engage in this sort of "pure" investing for all or part of their wealth. Yet much of what we hear about in the financial media these days is still about mutual funds, hedge funds, ETFs, and other investment "products." Are the media catering to your needs or to the needs of the professional fund manager? One wonders sometimes. Either way, we individual investors do exist, but we tend to exist rather quietly. Anyway, off the soapbox. Even if you buy just a few shares of one company, you're an individual investor. You're participating actively in the economy, and you're buying your share of the company with hopes of participating in its success. Like a homeowner choosing to take part in the work of owning a home as a "do-it-yourselfer" you're participating in the individual satisfaction, responsibility, and control that comes with doing it yourself.

If you succeed, you accept the benefits of increased wealth (and reduced fees) along with the satisfaction and sense of accomplishment of doing it yourself. If you fail, true, you'll have no one to blame but yourself. But at least it won't be someone else who lost your money for you. You'll pick yourself up, dust yourself off, learn from the mistakes, and go out and do it again.

Every edition of *The 100 Best Stocks to Buy* is intended to be a core tool for the individual investor. Sure, it's hardly the only tool available. Today's explosion of Internet-based investing tools has made this book one of hundreds of choices for acquiring investing information. With the speed of cyberspace, our book will hardly be the most current source. In fact—we'll admit by way of a disclaimer—because of the typical book publication cycle, we're at least six months out of date. If you check our research, you'll be able to come up with two to as many as four quarters of more current financial information, news releases, and so forth.

So does the delay built into the publishing cycle make our book a poor information source? Not at all. It works because the companies we choose don't change so much, and because they avoid the temptation to manage short-term, quarter-to-quarter performance. We chose these companies *because* they have sustainable performance, so who cares if the latest details or news releases are included? In *100 Best Stocks to Buy in 2013*, as with all of our previous editions, we focus on the *story*—the story of each company—not just the latest facts and figures.

As such, *100 Best Stocks* is intended as a handy guide and core reference for your investing, not as a be-all end-all investing source. Thus, as much as a source of facts and numbers itself, *100 Best Stocks* is intended to present the story for each company and to serve as a model for selecting the best companies and stocks to invest in. By narrowing down the universe to the best and the brightest companies out there, *100 Best Stocks* is designed to serve as a place to start, not to finish, your investment analysis.

To that same point, *100 Best Stocks* goes well beyond just being a stock screen or a "study" of stocks to invest in. Analysis forms the base of *100 Best Stocks*, but it isn't the rigid, strictly numbers-based selection and analysis so often found in published "best stocks" lists. Sure, we look at earnings, cash flow, balance sheet strength, and so forth, but we'll also look far beyond those things. We'll look at the intangible and often subtle factors that make truly great businesses—that is, companies—great. That is, once again, the *story*.

Great companies have good business fundamentals, but what makes them really great is the presence of intangibles and subtleties—the brands, the marketplace successes, the management style, the competitive advantages—that will *keep* them great or make them greater in the future.

So the selection of the *100 Best Stocks* continues to go far beyond being a simple numbers-based stock screen. It's a selection and analysis of really good businesses you would want to buy and own, not just for past results but for future outcomes. Now, does "future" mean "forever?" No, not hardly, not anymore. While the *100 Best Stocks* list correlates well with the notion of "blue chip" stocks, the discussion proceeds with the harsh reality that "blue chip" no longer means "forever."

We feel that the 100 companies listed and analyzed in the pages that follow are the best companies to own for 2013. That said, the word "own" has become a more active concept these days. Gone are the days of "own forever," like the halcyon days when Peter's parents, Jerry and Betty Sander, bought their 35 shares of General Motors, lovingly placed the stock certificate in their safe deposit box, and henceforth bought nothing but GM cars. Today, there is no forever; the economy, technology, and consumer tastes simply change too fast, and the businesses that participate in the economy by necessity change with it. Ownership is a more active concept than it was even 10 or 20 years ago.

So going forward, we offer the 100 best companies to own now and in 2013, those that have the best chances of not only surviving but evolving with—or even ahead of—the economy based on their current market position and approach to doing business. But as we all found out, especially during the past five years, 2008–2013, nothing is sacred in the business world and companies and entire industries can fall apart with astounding speed. What does that mean?

Simply this: You can't take anything you read in the following pages as "investment advice" or as hard, unwavering truths. The world simply changes too fast, and the analysis of a business and especially the *value* of a business are not a precise science, it is inherently a combination of science and art. True business value is subject to different interpretations and different opinions, and further, we must layer in the pace and effects of change.

And as we see over and over, change sometimes happens faster than we expect. It can really sneak up on us. The digital photography example is classic. But here we are, in 2012, scolding ourselves for hanging on to Hewlett-Packard too long as mobile and tablet computing undermines the PC space and printing anything suddenly becomes passé. Here we are scolding ourselves for hanging on to Best Buy for too long as consumer electronic stores recede from prominence in favor of Walmart, Costco, Target, and online alternatives, and are no longer a favorite family destination for a Saturday afternoon. It's a good thing we didn't latch on to the solar industry, for it has tanked as cheap supply has outstripped demand and government subsidies go away. And what about natural gas? Even some of the steadiest industries go through upheaval and change.

What this all means is simple and straightforward: You'll have to take the information presented, do your own assessment, reach your own conclusions, and take your own actions. Anything else would go beyond our intentions, and more importantly, stop short of the mark for you.

With that in mind, make the most of what follows, and good luck with your investing!

What's New for 2013

Really, for 2013, we've charted the same course. No changes to the author team of Scott and Peter. No revolutionary changes in content or format to report. No big market events or surprises (for a change) to take into account. The year 2013 is a mildly evolutionary, certainly not a revolutionary, continuation of the *100 Best Stocks* series.

Of course, there's always something to report, so here is a short summary of tweaks and changes (aside from the stock list itself) to report.

- *Dividends, dividends, and more dividends.* As we'll explore further below under "Yield Signs" we continue to think dividends are important. This year we measure another characteristic of dividends—not just yield or size of the dividend, but the *persistency* of dividend increases. We have companies that have raised their dividends for 50 straight years. As a long-term investor, nothing is better than watching your dividend double, triple, or increase even more over time, providing a substantial return particularly when regarded against your original investment. We have started measuring and including in the write-ups the number of dividend raises in the past 10 years and have also identified a "dividend aggressors" list for companies that go the distance to reward their shareholders with persistently strong and increasing dividends.

- *Total shareholder return.* We've always, of course, shined a light on shareholder returns, which come directly from a company through dividends and share repurchases. This year, more than ever, we consider dividends and dividend raises and planned and actual repurchases in our choices, and make comments on both in the write-ups as we can.

- *Back to one book.* Last year, we expanded the series to four books: *The 100 Best Stocks You Can Buy 2012*, *The 100 Best Aggressive Stocks You Can Buy 2012*, *The 100 Best Technology Stocks You Can Buy 2012*, and *The 100 Best ETFs You Can Buy 2012*. The idea was to expand the "100 Best" thought process into new territory and to give you some additional investment options. Unfortunately, due in part to the book retail channel collapse led by Borders Group, these books didn't pencil out for a 2013 redo. But we both, and particularly Scott with his technology background, stay tuned to what's happening in the aggressive, technology, and ETF spaces, and are currently seeking out possible new ways to share our findings. That leads us to:

- *Your comments, please.* Up until now, your authors have kept a pretty low profile. We do the books and keep working in background to provide the very best recommendations for the next year. But this is an interconnected world, isn't it? We would enjoy—and benefit from—your feedback and questions by seeing what's on your mind and understanding how well our recommendations "click," and we realize that Amazon.com and similar comment spaces aren't really the right way to do this. We would also like to keep the door open to sharing information—somehow to be determined—on aggressive, technology, ETF, and eventually other investments as they make sense. As such, we now offer contact points. You can contact us, and view and participate in the discussion of the 100 Best Stocks at *www.facebook.com/100BestStocks*.

About Your Authors

Peter Sander

Peter is an independent professional researcher, writer, and journalist specializing in personal finance, investing, and location reference, as well as other general business topics. He has written 35 books on these topics—the latest of which, *The 25 Habits of Highly Successful Investors*, expands on the ideas and methods outlined in this introduction—has done numerous financial columns and independent privately contracted research and studies. He came from a background in the corporate world, having experienced a 21-year career with a major West Coast technology firm.

He is, and has been, most emphatically an individual investor, and has been since the age of twelve, when his curiosity at the family breakfast table got the better of him. He started reading the stock pages with his parents. He had an opportunity during a one-week "project week" in the seventh grade to read about, and learn about, the stock market. He read Louis Engel's *How to Buy Stocks*, then the pre-eminent book—and one of the only books —about investing available at the time. He read Engel, picked stocks, and made graphs of their performance by hand with colored pens on real graph paper. He put his hard-earned savings into buying five shares of each of three different companies. He watched those stocks like a hawk and salted away the meager dividends to reinvest. He's been investing ever since.

Yes, he has an MBA from Indiana University in Bloomington, but it isn't an MBA in finance. He also took the coursework and certification exam to become a Certified Financial Planner (CFP). By design and choice, he has never held a job in the financial profession. His goal has always been to share his knowledge and experience in an educational way, a way helpful for the individual as an investor and a personal financier to make his or her own decisions.

He has never earned a living giving direct investment advice or managing money for others, nor does he intend to.

A few years ago, it dawned on Peter that he has really made his living finding value, and helping or teaching others to find value. Not just in stocks, but other things in business and in life. And what does he mean by value? Simply, the current and potential *worth* of something (or someone) as compared to its price or cost. As it turns out, he's made a career out of assessing the value of people, places, and companies.

His last assignment at the high-tech firm was to find value in customers. *People*. His title: customer valuation manager. At the time, around the turn of the millennium, his team was building a "customer relationship management" platform, and his job was to segment millions of customers by value, and to assign values to each one to help target messaging and so-called "one-to-one" marketing campaigns. A tricky enterprise, no doubt, because no company can really know what a customer is truly worth, down to the penny, especially going forward. It became an exercise in looking at previous buying behavior, considering other known customer attributes internal and external to the business, assessing the customer's cost (marketing and support costs), making some assumptions, and testing results.

At the time, he did not really grasp that the same exact process really applied to investing, too. But a sharp editor at John Wiley & Sons' "Dummies" division put two and two together and hired him to write *Value Investing for Dummies*. The light went on. Whether it's people or stocks, the thought process is the same. Take what you know (fundamentals), add some intuition (intangibles), make some assumptions, proceed carefully, and evaluate the results.

The same publisher—different division—gave him another chance two years later, this time to write a complete reference guide to places to live. Hundreds of places to live appraised for value and ranked top to bottom, best to worst. Value is extremely important in deciding where you would want to live. Sure, the "best" places to live might include Greenwich, Connecticut; Jupiter, Florida; or Palo Alto, California. But most of us can't afford them. So the true "best places" for most of us are the places that deliver the most value for the money, now and in the future. The resulting book, *Cities Ranked & Rated—More Than 400 Metropolitan Areas Evaluated in the U.S. and Canada*, and the sister publication *Best Places to Raise Your Family*, finally went beyond the "study" and short list to truly answer the question most of us have—what's the best place to live *for my money*. The same value approach works in the world of business and stock investing. It isn't just the biggest or the richest corporations that we should be putting our hard-earned money into. If that were the case, we'd simply buy GE or ExxonMobil and move on. But do these companies represent the best *value* for your investing dollar? Maybe, but maybe not.

Just like customers or places to live, we want companies that produce the greatest return, the highest value, *per dollar invested*. And *for the amount of risk taken*. The amount of risk taken translates into additional dollars that an investment might cost, analogous to living in a great place rampant with crime or with questionable schools that might cost you more in the long term. The companies we will identify as among the *100 Best* have, in our assessment, the greatest long-term *value*, and if you can buy these companies at a *reasonable price* (a factor which we leave out of this analysis because this is a book and prices can change considerably), then these investments deliver the best prospects.

Later we'll come back to describe some of the attributes of value that we look for.

SCOTT BOBO

Peter and Scott have been friends and colleagues since, roughly, tenth grade (a long time!). Scott has been part of the team for three years, and has been huge not only in identifying the *100 Best Stocks* but also analyzing them and explaining their pros and cons crisply and in plain English so that you can make the best use of the list. Having Scott on the team allows you to get the combined wisdom and observations of two people, not just one, in an arena where one plus one almost always equals something greater than two.

Scott has been an investor since age 14, when he made the switch from analyzing baseball box scores to looking at the numbers and charts in the business section. In his 20-plus years in engineering and technology management, he's learned that a unique product value proposition is important to the success of any company. He has also learned (the hard way) that proper financial fundamentals are critical. From a development manager's perspective, comprehending a new product's risk/reward proposition is one of the keys to a company's success. From an investor's perspective, it's also one of the keys to successful value investing in a dynamic, innovation-driven market.

Scott adds a strong analytical touch. But he is most at home as an applications engineer, explaining how a company's products work and how they apply to a customer's needs. Consequently, and in addition to analytical legwork, Scott really adds an extraordinary and very real-world sense of how a company's products "fit" in the marketplace. Determining whether a company's products are relevant, best-in-class, and have a competitive advantage over others is an oft-overlooked core skill for a value investor. Scott brings this skill to the table in a big way.

Scott is the cocreator and the driving force behind our *100 Best Aggressive Stocks* and *100 Best Technology Stocks* books published for 2012.

The Roller Coaster Ride Continues

With our arrival on the scene in 2010 and the wild ride our markets gave us in 2008–2009, the *100 Best* book series went through some pretty major changes—not revolutionary, perhaps, but strongly evolutionary. As described above, that "strong" evolution has evolved into more of an annual fine-tuning, and annual pruning of the small branches done while carefully leaving the larger limbs intact. This is as it should be, if we're doing the right things and making prudent picks in the first place.

In our first year, 2010, we struck some 26 companies from the prevailing 2009 list, as we felt that there were too many commodity producers, defense contractors, and others with relatively weak competitive advantages and thus weren't comfortably placed in an era of volatile markets and public sector cutbacks. That storm blew through in 2010; in 2011, we made more moderate changes, deleting 14 stocks from the list as we became more focused on current returns—dividends. For the 2012 list, we pruned out only 12 stocks—four of them to move over to the *100 Best Aggressive* list. Now it appears we may not have pruned as aggressively as we should have, leaving the likes of Hewlett-Packard and Best Buy on the list perhaps a year or two too long. So in 2013, we're back up to 14 changes, pruning some of 2012's dead wood, plus eliminating some duplicates, diversifying a little more out of health care, and other adjustments. Tables 3, 4, and 5 detail the 14 deletions and additions to the 2013 list.

The methodology used for analysis and selection of the *100 Best Stocks* remains largely unchanged. We continue to focus on "fundamentals that really count," like cash flow; profit margins and balance sheet strength; and those intangibles such as brand, market share, channel and supply-chain excellence, and management quality that really determine success *going forward*. We continue to place more focus on dividends. More and more, especially in today's volatile markets, we feel that investors should get paid something to commit their precious capital to a company; it's a sign of good faith to investors and provides at least some return while waiting for a larger return in the future—or if things happen to go south later on. So, as it turns out, some 96 of the *100 Best* picked pay at least some dividends—that's up from 95 last year and 91 on the 2011 list. Those that don't, like Apple, CarMax, or Itron, were on the list because of other excellence factors; we can turn our heads the other way on the dividend for a while, but would expect some dividends eventually as the business models "matured," or in Apple's case, as the timing became right (which it did, to the effect of a $10.60 per share annual dividend, starting in mid 2012).

Additionally, for dividend-paying stocks, we've formalized our increasing preference for companies with a track record for regular dividend *increases*. We have started tracking, for each company, the number of dividend increases or *raises* (yes, you can think of them as comparable to a raise in your own wage or salary) in the past 10 years. We are proud to report that of the 96 *100 Best* stocks paying dividends, some 86 of them raised their dividend from 2011 to 2012. Of those 96, fully 67 of them have raised their dividend in at least six of the past 10 years, and 40 of them have raised dividends in each of the past 10 years.

As in the 2012 edition, we will give you a performance report on our 2012 picks, which for this year, turned out to be a success story—if not a particularly exciting one. Finally, we will continue with our "stars" lists identifying the best stocks in five different categories:

1. Yield Stars (stocks with solid dividend yields—Table 6)
2. Dividend Aggressors (a new idea, companies with strong and persistent records and policies toward dividend *growth*—Table 6.1)
3. Safety Stars (solid performers in any market—Table 7)
4. Growth Stars (companies positioned for above average growth—Table 8)
5. Recovery Stars (companies that cut costs and are otherwise positioned well for an economic recovery—Table 9)
6. Moat Stars (companies with significant sustainable competitive advantage—Table 10)

So, if you're an investor partial to any of these factors, like Safety, these lists are for you.

The Markets: Up, Down, and Sideways

For what seems like forever, the markets have been on a roller coaster ride, starting the year with optimism only to fall off into a chasm midyear, then recover. We don't need to repeat the story of 2008–2010, where the Dow Jones Industrial Average sunk to a ten-year low of 6,547 by March 9 of 2009, then recovered some 68 percent by April 2010. That high point turned out to be brief, as the BP Gulf disaster, the first notions of the Greek debt crisis, and the nerve-wracking May 6, 2010, "flash crash" all plagued the markets. The markets dipped through the summer of 2010, only to come back when those stories wound down, and the economic reports really started to point toward recovery. But then by late summer 2011, the re-emergence of the Greek contagion, this time with reports of similar trouble in Spain, Italy, and other countries, and a persistence of good but not great economic data caused the markets to dip again, almost 18 percent as measured by the S&P 500 Index—quite similar to the 16 percent decline of the previous year. Again the markets got accustomed to the Europe problem, and economic statistics and in particular, spending by businesses started to look good again, and all the while the Fed maintained its accommodating stance. The markets made a gradual climb to about their previous April level by February 2012.

As we'll see shortly, the market indices drifted slightly higher from there, but many of our *100 Best* picks, tied more to the global economy, went flat at that point. Through the first half of 2012, the markets continue to gyrate to good and bad European news, and to good and bad U.S. economic news and especially employment and housing indicators. Not surprisingly, we advocate staying the course with really good businesses that have a strong global footprint and sufficient cash flow to pay investors while gaining a stronger foothold in the fragile global economy.

Now mind you, this book isn't supposed to be about the past—it's supposed to be about the *future*, specifically the future of your investments. We know that. But we feel that it's important to set the climate and context for this and next year's performance, and would feel derelict in our duties if we didn't drive home the challenges—particularly the challenges of news-driven and trading-driven volatility. We continue to think the markets will experience large swings in sentiment but relatively short cycles of upside and downside performance over the next few years. Short-term trading, particularly driven by adjustments in ETFs and other funds (ETFs must buy or sell stocks according to fund inflows and outflows, and do this almost instantaneously and without consideration of market conditions) will continue to make markets volatile, as will the headlines of excessive European debt and debt elsewhere. Headline risk, in today's nervous world of fear and instantaneous headlines, will also add to volatility. Probably the biggest *real* fear, outside of some major news event like a political crisis, is that inflationary forces might really take hold resulting from the flood of easy money encircling the globe—indeed there are already signs of that in the form of rising commodity prices, although we feel that at least some of that is a trading-driven cycle much like we saw in 2008. Nevertheless, investors, particularly in companies that buy a lot of commodity materials, need to stay alert. The kind of volatility we've seen recently can actually provide some buying opportunities, so even those really pricey stocks that *everyone* thinks are best to own can be had if the time is right.

Remember that investing in stocks is still about buying shares of a business, and just because there's a "flash crash" or a $2 billion trading loss by JP Morgan Chase doesn't mean that IBM or Johnson & Johnson or Abbott Laboratories are any worse off as companies. It simply means that the market has taken a different approach, probably an irrational one, to evaluating them. It is imperative, as an investor, that you invest in good businesses. If you do, the price of the shares will come out okay in the long term. And if you want to sleep at night, businesses with steady results will tend to be less volatile. Finally, for further insulation against the ups and downs of the markets, we're favoring stocks that pay dividends, because no "flash crash" can take away money you've received and socked in the bank, right?

Now it's time to uphold tradition and see how we did with last year's picks.

Report Card: Recapping Our 2012 Picks

There are many ways to evaluate the performance of a group of stocks over time. Some are simplistic, such as simply averaging the percent gain in each share price. But such a method may not weight a portfolio very realistically, for it assumes you buy the same number of shares of Apple at $530 as you would Southwest Airlines at $11. We continue to feel it's better to take the approach of an investor with $100,000 to invest—who invested $1,000 in each of the *100 Best Stocks* across the board, regardless of share price. Sure, you end up with some weird quantities of shares in your portfolio, but the portfolio, and thus the performance metrics, isn't weighted in favor of more expensive stocks.

The Bottom Line

Okay, we'll cut to the chase this year. Our investment performance, compared to a buyable basket of S&P 500 companies, was mediocre. For this year, anyway, we didn't justify your purchase of this book! If we were eighth graders, we would have earned a "C."

We don't like getting Cs, but we think it's important to be honest, and we think it's important to understand why.

If you had invested $100,000 in our *100 Best Stocks 2012* list, $1,000 in each of the 100 stocks, on April 1, 2011, you would have had $103,213.33 on April 1, 2012, not including dividends paid during that period. The return is just 3.2 percent. Including dividends of some $2,327, you would have had $105,540.48. The S&P as measured by the buyable "SPDR" S&P 500 Trust was ahead 5.4 percent ($105,400 implied return)—a virtual dead heat.

What was frustrating is that up until just two months before our April 1 cutoff date, we were sizably ahead of the averages, up 11 percent compared to the benchmark 4.4 percent. A premium of several percentage points—more than double the benchmark—much more what we're used to. What happened?

As mentioned earlier, we held on to a few losers, like HP and Best Buy, too long, and the news at those companies during the first few months of 2012 only made their bad situations worse. We also lost out on Southwest Airlines mainly because of an upward reversal in fuel prices. More universally, we lost ground because of our tendency to favor companies with a strong international presence, which has served us well as U.S. economic growth has lagged behind international and especially developing country growth. We think companies that are competitive overseas will participate in growth and are more likely to have a sustained competitive advantage in *all* markets. We also prefer investing in U.S. companies with a strong overseas presence to investing in foreign companies, whose fortunes are harder to track and understand. Finally, in a weaker dollar environment, which has persisted for years, international sales are relatively more valuable.

But the revised concerns in Europe and a falling euro hurt a lot of companies that we had picked—the Caterpillars and Deeres and Fluors and Medtronics (and the HPs, for that matter). These companies really faded in the last two months of our measurement period. Will we take these companies off the list for 2013? For the most part, no. While we do fear the European financial problems, we feel that these companies will survive that and be well-positioned to flourish in other parts of the world, particularly emerging markets. Needless to say, we expect better performance of these—and all *100 Best* companies—by the end of our 2013 measurement period.

Winners and Losers

The full list of the *100 Best Stocks 2011* and how they did through the comparison period can be found in Appendix A. At this point, we'll give a short overview of what really worked and what didn't within the list. First, the winners:

▼ Table 1: Performance Analysis: Winners

TOP WINNERS, ONE YEAR GAIN/LOSS, APRIL 1, 2011–APRIL 1, 2012

Company	Symbol	Price 4/1/2011	Price 4/1/2012	% change	Dollar gain, $1,000 invested
Apple	AAPL	$350.13	$605.23	72.9%	$728.59
Starbucks	SBUX	$36.20	$61.67	70.4%	$703.59
Ross Stores	ROST	$36.85	$59.06	60.3%	$602.71
Tractor Supply	TSCO	$61.87	$98.38	59.0%	$590.11
Visa	V	$78.12	$123.16	57.7%	$576.55
Grainger, W.W.	GWW	$151.60	$213.18	40.6%	$406.20
NIKE	NKE	$82.32	$108.80	32.2%	$321.67
McDonald's	MCD	$76.09	$96.97	27.4%	$274.41
Lubrizol	LZ	$106.68	$134.97	26.5%	$265.19
Bed, Bath & Beyond	BBBY	$56.13	$69.41	23.7%	$236.59
Church & Dwight	CHD	$41.24	$50.11	21.5%	$215.08
CVS/Caremark	CVS	$36.22	$43.43	19.9%	$199.06
Allergan	AGN	$79.56	$94.65	19.0%	$189.67
IBM	IBM	$170.58	$202.80	18.9%	$188.88
UnitedHealth Group	UNH	$49.23	$58.05	17.9%	$179.16
Target	TGT	$49.10	$57.43	17.0%	$169.65
Ecolab	ECL	$52.76	$61.61	16.8%	$167.74
FMC	FMC	$79.89	$92.68	16.0%	$160.10
Aetna	AET	$41.38	$47.82	15.6%	$155.63
Amgen	AMGN	$56.85	$65.59	15.4%	$153.74

This year, the winners list really reflects companies with excellent and timely business models, such as Apple, Starbucks, Visa, and Ross Stores. These are companies that dominate their niches and have accelerated their earnings, margins, and cash flow growth considerably. Although you could consider Starbucks and Aetna as "turnaround" situations, they aren't doing the kind of turnaround International Paper and some of the industrial giants of the 2011 list did. Many of our strongest performers such as Ross, Tractor Supply, Grainger, Aetna, and CVS have relatively limited international footprints. And of course we wonder where we would be if we hadn't chosen Apple—which, by the way, accounts for some 10 percent of the S&P 500's total gains for the past couple of years. The winners list isn't as diverse as it was in 2011, and we had fewer winners overall (in fact, we had only 56 winners out of the 100 stocks) but nothing here indicates a wholesale change in our approach. Now, for the losers:

▼ Table 2

TOP LOSERS, ONE YEAR GAIN/LOSS, APRIL 1, 2011–APRIL 1, 2012

Company	Symbol	Price 4/1/2011	Price 4/1/2012	% change	Dollar loss, $1,000 invested
Medtronic	MDT	$41.75	$37.51	-10.2%	$(101.56)
United Technologies	UTX	$89.58	$79.80	-10.9%	$(109.18)
Nucor	NUE	$46.96	$41.57	-11.5%	$(114.78)
3M	MMM	$97.21	$85.69	-11.9%	$(118.51)
Becton, Dickinson	BDX	$85.94	$74.79	-13.0%	$(129.74)
Harris	HRS	$53.13	$44.42	-16.4%	$(163.94)
Fluor	FLR	$69.94	$58.10	-16.9%	$(169.29)
Archer Daniels Midland	ADM	$37.02	$30.75	-16.9%	$(169.37)
Deere	DE	$97.50	$79.47	-18.5%	$(184.92)
Johnson Controls	JCI	$41.00	$32.57	-20.6%	$(205.61)
Oracle	ORCL	$35.96	$28.50	-20.7%	$(207.45)
Schlumberger	SLB	$89.75	$68.38	-23.8%	$(238.11)
Suburban Propane	SPH	$56.21	$42.79	-23.9%	$(238.75)
Total S.A.	TOT	$64.23	$47.77	-25.6%	$(256.27)

TOP LOSERS, ONE-YEAR GAIN/LOSS, APRIL 1, 2011–APRIL 1, 2012
(continued)

Company	Symbol	Price 4/1/2011	Price 4/1/2012	% change	Dollar loss, $1,000 invested
Staples	SPLS	$21.14	$15.53	-26.5%	$(265.37)
St. Jude Medical	STJ	$53.44	$38.58	-27.8%	$(278.07)
Best Buy	BBY	$31.22	$22.04	-29.4%	$(294.04)
Apache	APA	$133.37	$93.65	-29.8%	$(297.82)
Southwest Airlines	LUV	$11.75	$7.94	-32.4%	$(324.26)
Hewlett-Packard	HPQ	$40.37	$24.57	-39.1%	$(391.38)

Out of 100 stocks, we had 44 losers in 2012, as compared to only 17 in 2011. Needless to say, this is a disappointing performance from a relatively strong April 2011 starting point. As we've mentioned a few times, we held HP and Best Buy too long. Some of the other issues, such as Apache and perhaps Schlumberger and St. Jude, were just plain overpriced, which may make them better opportunities for this year. Some, such as Total S.A., Oracle, and some of the industrials and pharma companies, were hurt by Europe. We dropped HP, Best Buy, Apache, Staples, and other big losers this year, but will continue to take our chances with Southwest and some of the industrials that could benefit from an international turnaround and whose business models remain attractive.

Sustainable Investing

With the recent volatility and the speed of change becoming an increasingly permanent characteristic of today's markets, many financial journalists and pundits have recently announced the demise of long-term investing, specifically the so-called "buy-and-hold" strategy. Indeed, one wonders when such stalwarts as Citigroup and AIG and such long-term growth and income favorites as General Electric and BP run into trouble. The speed of change—change in technology and consumer tastes (think, tablets and the PC industry), news-driven change (think BP or JP Morgan Chase), or change in market structure and business models (think Netflix or Blockbuster)—does indeed bring some concern to the idea of buying shares and locking them away in your safe deposit box. More than ever, you need to stay on your toes and watch for change.

What it really means is that you need to select companies that adapt well to change and can stay in front of changing markets. It also means that a periodic review of your investments—all of your investments—is more important than ever. Every stock you own should be evaluated from scratch—as though you were going to buy it again—at least once a year.

But that doesn't mean that long-term investing is dead. Great companies respond to change and find ways to continue to satisfy customers and make money, regardless of the mood and change of the day. Companies such as Procter & Gamble reinvent themselves constantly, not with a big housecleaning (pardon the pun) and restructuring every few years. They get into cosmetics like Olay as the population ages and people become more conscious of their appearance, and as competitive pressure and lack of consumer interest drives profit margins on peanut butter steadily downward. (They did something about this, too, selling their Jif brand to *100 Best Stocks* member J. M. Smucker, which knows a thing or two about both peanut butter and jelly.) As aging men become more concerned about their appearance, Procter developed Olay lines for men. You get the idea.

Some companies respond better to changes in the wind than others. Starbucks sailed in front of a huge tailwind, opening store after store until they had so many stores that they cannibalized each other and, worse, lost their agility and brand cachet. We now see that they learned from this mistake, and once again are a perennial favorite as well as a *100 Best Stocks* member based on brand strength, management excellence, balance sheet strength, and core business profitability. A fault once in a while is okay, but we tend to avoid companies that seem to be "restructuring" or "reinventing themselves" continuously.

Value—Now More Than Ever

The bottom line is this: For intelligent investors, chasing the latest fad doesn't work; neither does buying something and locking it away forever. Investors must make intelligent choices based on true value and follow those choices through time and change. It all points to taking a "value"-oriented approach to investing and to staying modestly "active" with your investments.

The next obvious task is to define what we mean by a "value" approach. Essentially, it is to think of buying shares in a company as buying the company itself; it is about putting yourself in an entrepreneurial frame of mind, not just an investment frame of mind. Would you want to own that business? Why or why not?

Fundamentally, whether or not you want to own the business depends on two factors: first, the returns you expect to receive on your investment in the near- and long-term future and second, the risk you'll take in generating those returns. Fortunately, the third factor the prospective entrepreneur must consider—"do I have the time for this?"—isn't typically a consideration.

So you are looking for tangible value—tangible worth—for your precious, scarce, and hard-earned investment capital. Now, that return doesn't have to be immediate in the form of dividends or a share of the assets, as many in the traditional "value school" suggest. It can come in the form of growth for the longer term. If you realize your return in the form of owning a share of a larger company eventually, that's still a legitimate return. Cash flow received later in the form of a higher share price or a takeover is still cash return, it is just less certain because of the forces of change that may take place in the interim. It is also theoretically worth less because of the nature of discounting—a dollar received tomorrow is worth more than a dollar received 20 years in the future.

The point: Many investment experts distinguish between "value" and "growth" investing; in fact, mutual funds are often classified as being one or the other. We dismiss this separation; growth can be an essential component of a firm's value.

Value also implies safety. The safety comes in three forms. First is the fundamental quality and soundness of the firm's financial fundamentals—that is, income, cash flow, and the balance sheet. Value companies have plenty of reserves, a large enough *margin of safety*, to weather downturns and unforeseen events in the marketplace. Second, they have strong enough intangibles—brands, market position, supply-chain strength, etc.—to maintain their position in that marketplace and generate future returns.

Thirdly, if you're really practicing value investing principles, you buy these companies at reduced prices, when the markets are down, when the company is out of favor. You're looking for situations where the price is less than what you perceive to be the value, although calculating the value that precisely is elusive. When you "buy cheap" you provide another margin of safety; that margin makes it less likely that the stock will drop further. It gives you room for error if you turn out to be wrong about a choice. Again, it's much like buying a business of your own—you want to pay as little as possible in case things don't turn out as you'd expect.

So taking a value approach provides greater confidence and safety and is more likely to get you through today's volatile business and investing cycles.

Stay Active

And what do we mean by "active?" "Active" means that you should stay abreast of your investments, and like any business you own, keep an eye on its performance. Periodically review it as you would your own finances to see if it is making money and generally doing what you think it should be doing. You may watch the stock price daily, and you may also watch for news bulletins affecting the company, and you should keep track of earnings announcements.

Time permitting, you should listen in on investor conference calls (usually at earnings announcements) to see what management has to say about the business. In addition, you should watch your business in the marketplace—see how many people are going to your local Starbucks and whether they are enjoying the experience, and look for other signs of excellence. So, we're not talking about constant monitoring of the "twitter" of the stock price. Instead, we're suggesting a remote oversight of the business as though it were one of a portfolio of businesses you happen to own and, while professionally managed, requires an occasional glance to make sure everything is still acting according to your best interests. We also recommend a periodic review—at least annually—of whether your investments are still your best investments. Evaluate each investment against its alternatives. If you still perceive it to be the best value out there, keep it. If not, consider a swap for something new.

YOU DON'T NEED TO BE A MATH GENIUS

Calculating "value" can be a daunting task, especially if one goes into the nuances of compounding, discounting, and all that business school stuff. Today's value investor doesn't ignore the numbers, but shuns complex mathematical formulas, which in the recent bust, tended not to work anyway; greater forces overtook almost all statistical and mathematical models for stock analysis, leaving many a "quant" scratching his or her head.

Buying companies is not a math-driven process, just as you can't evaluate a school based on its test scores alone. Warren Buffett and Charlie Munger have made this clear over the years and came back to the point with emphasis in the 2009 Berkshire Hathaway shareholders meeting. Buffett mused: "If you need to use a computer or a calculator to make the calculation, you shouldn't buy it." Reading between the lines: The story should be simple and straightforward enough to be obvious without detailed calculations.

Munger, Buffett's relatively more intrepid sidekick, added: "Some of the worst business decisions I've ever seen are those with future projections and discounts back. It seems like the higher mathematics with more false precision should help you, but it doesn't. They teach that in business school because, well, they've got to do something."

No need to read between the lines there.

Indeed, while the numbers are important, savvy value investors try to see where the puck is going. And that means a clear-eyed assessment of the intangible things that make companies great.

The 100 Best for 2013: A Few Comments

With continued worldwide economic malaise, excessive debt, and political turmoil in certain parts of the world, the environment going forward is as uncertain as ever. We don't think the American economy will ever be quite the same, the best example being Apple's statement that they could never move iPad or iPhone production to the United States if they wanted to because of the lack of supply chain, real-time manufacturing infrastructure, and skills on this side of the Pacific. It isn't just a matter of labor costs.

While this may be true, and while we think the excessive health-care cost burden is an additional detractor for all but the 15 health-care companies on our list, we do foresee a rebound in U.S. manufacturing and value-add economic activity. Many companies have found out that moving stuff overseas isn't the good-times panacea they had all anticipated. Foreign companies continue to invest in the United States because of good supply chains and skills for building things like automotive transmissions and electronics here. We believe that we are undergoing a long-term, semi-subconscious adjustment away from financial services and other low-value-add industries to a back-to-basics, let's-make-things-that-people-need mentality. We are slowly moving back toward the thinking that factories and research labs are better places to put capital than housing and real estate; that should bode well for the longer term.

Now, on to 2013. We still think that companies that have a good business model, produce high value-add things that people (or companies) need, and do it efficiently and generate a lot of cash will do well. Good businesses. Not just companies that make a lot of money, but good businesses. This year, as noted earlier in the introduction, we've replaced 14 companies, two more than last year. A few really bad performers were removed from the list, but most of the changes could be counted as "adjustments." We eliminated some duplicates like Dentsply and Air Products & Chemicals, cut a couple of health-care companies (to get from 17 to 15) and made some other adjustments that, well, just felt better.

▼ **Table 3: Companies Removed from 2012 List**

Company	Symbol	Category	Sector
Air Products	APD	Aggressive Growth	Materials
Alexander & Baldwin	ALEX	Growth and Income	Transportation
Apache	APA	Aggressive Growth	Energy
Best Buy	BBY	Aggressive Growth	Retail
CR Bard	BCR	Conservative Growth	Healthcare
Dentsply	XRAY	Conservative Growth	Healthcare
Ecolab	ECL	Conservative Growth	Materials
Google	GOOG	Aggressive Growth	Information Technology
Harris	HRS	Aggressive Growth	Information Technology
Hewlett-Packard	HPQ	Aggressive Growth	Information Technology
Lubrizol	LZ	Growth and Income	Materials
Northern Trust	NTRS	Conservative Growth	Financials
Oracle	ORCL	Aggressive Growth	Technology
Staples	SPLS	Aggressive Growth	Retail

We weren't sure how Alexander & Baldwin would fare after splitting its shipping and Hawaiian sugar and real estate businesses, and they've had a good run anyway. As we've said, HP, Best Buy, and probably Staples have business models that, if they aren't broken, simply aren't going anywhere fast. Apache was too expensive and may still be. Harris's technology seems outdated and they are expensive too. Oracle perhaps shouldn't have gotten into the hardware business, and, while solid as a company, we just don't see much upside in any of the IT companies (we've shifted to those that sell the picks and shovels to those companies, like Seagate, Intel, and Molex; see the next section). We cautiously removed Google from the list because we can't figure out their strategic direction or business model; they appear to be investing in everything, whether it goes with the core business or not. That kind of behavior can run into a wall eventually. Ecolab is good but expensive, Northern Trust seems to have joined the dustbin of financial services companies that can't really find its way, and Lubrizol was acquired by Berkshire Hathaway.

Table 4 shows additions to the *100 Best Stocks* list to arrive at the current 2013 version (which can be seen in its entirety at the beginning of Part II).

▼ **Table 4: New Companies for 2013**

Company	Symbol	Category	Sector
Eastman Chemical	EMN	Conservative Growth	Materials
Harman International	HAR	Aggressive Growth	Consumer Discretionary
Intel	INTC	Conservative Growth	Information Technology
Itron	ITRI	Aggressive Growth	Information Technology
Macy's	M	Aggressive Growth	Retail
Molex Inc.	MOLX	Conservative Growth	Industrials
Mosaic	MOS	Aggressive Growth	Materials
Seagate Technology	STX	Aggressive Growth	Information Technology
Tiffany	TIF	Aggressive Growth	Retail
Time Warner Inc.	TWX	Conservative Growth	Entertainment
United Parcel Service	UPS	Conservative Growth	Transportation
Valero	VLO	Aggressive Growth	Energy
Waste Management	WM	Growth and Income	Business Services
Whirlpool	WHR	Conservative Growth	Consumer Durables

This year's additions represent an interesting mix of companies we've considered for a long time but in some cases have considered too aggressive (seven came from our *100 Best Aggressive* list) or play a background role to more established companies from Intel and Seagate to IBM and HP. Many of these names, such as Molex, Mosaic, Eastman, Itron, and even Valero, aren't household names but dominate their niches like crazy. A few others, such as Tiffany, Macy's, and Intel, *are* household names and—guess what—also dominate their niches. We wanted to add an entertainment company, and we see Time Warner as a player that's learned its lessons and is offering healthy current returns. Healthy current and future cash returns—dividends and buybacks—also hooked us on Waste Management, Seagate, UPS, and Intel. As is usually the case, there is no one reason why any of these companies made the grade; it is a combination of fundamentals, intangibles, and shareholder returns.

To give a bit of a "big picture" view of our changes, Table 5 gives our annual summary of what changed by sector. Other than lightening up a bit on health care (from 17 to 15 companies) there is no real shift in sector balance implied with these numbers. Most of our 2013 changes tend to replace companies in a sector with other players in the same sector. For example, in the IT sector we cut HP and Oracle but added Intel, Seagate, and Itron, a move that we think puts us closer to where the money is being made in this sector. Ditto for Mosaic and Eastman, stronger niche players in the Materials sector. In retail, niche strength again directs us toward Tiffany and Macy's and away from Staples and Best Buy.

▼ Table 5: Sector Analysis and 2013 Change by Sector

NUMBER OF COMPANIES:

Sector	On 2012 List	Added for 2013	Cut from 2012	On 2013 List
Business Services	1	1		2
Consumer Discretionary	3	1		4
Consumer Staples	14			14
Consumer Durables		1		1
Energy	8	1	-1	8
Entertainment		1		1
Financials	3		-1	2
Health Care	17		-2	15
Heavy Construction	1			1
Industrials	12	1		13
Information Technology	9	3	-4	8
Materials	8	2	-3	7
Restaurant	2			2
Retail	9	2	-2	9
Telecommunications Services	3			3
Transportation	5	1	-1	5
Utilities	5			5

Yield Signs

In late 2011, we hit an unusual milestone in the annals of investing. The average dividend yield of the S&P 500 exceeded the yield of the ten-year T-note for the first time since 1958. In fact, the S&P 500 yield hit 3.3 percent, some 0.6 percent higher than the T-Notes yield of 2.7 percent.

For those of you investors needing or desiring current yield from your investments, this is a significant milestone. It signals that stocks may be where it is really "at," not just for growth investing but for income investing too.

Sure, dividends and dividend-paying stocks are riskier, for the stock price can go up and down with the fortunes of the economy, not to mention the fortunes of individual companies. But don't forget—the price of bonds can go down too, especially longer-term bonds such as the ten-year note in question. Inflation is a constant risk, and interest rate hikes could jeopardize the price of your bond investment in the short term.

On the other hand, dividend-paying stocks can—and many do—raise their dividends over time. So not only do you get an attractive yield from the day you buy the stock, but you may also get handsome raises over time. And as we reported earlier, some 86 of the 96 dividend-paying stocks on the 2013 *100 Best* list raised their dividends in 2011, and some 40 of those have raised their dividends in each of the past 10 years. We like this. We like it a lot. A company that raises its dividend 10 percent will roughly double the payout in just 7 years. (Calculation? Rule of 72—divide the percent increase into 72, you'll get the number of years it takes to double: 72/10 equals 7.2 years.) You could end up with twice the income in addition to any gains or growth in the price of the stock.

This year, we'd like to focus even more on those healthy companies willing to not only share a portion of their profits, but also to give you, the investor, a periodic raise to recognize the value of your commitment of precious investment capital. We show the number of dividend increases in the past 10 years in the header right after "current yield."

We've also put together a still-experimental "Dividend Aggressors" list. Dividend aggressors are companies with substantial payouts that are also growing those payouts at a persistent and substantial rate. They have indicated through both words and performance that they continue to do so and have the resources to do it. So it isn't enough to raise the dividend each year by just a penny; it must be substantial. It also isn't enough to raise the dividend each year, but still only be yielding 0.5 percent. There are lists of "Dividend Achievers" floating around on the Internet; and there are even a few funds constructed around a "dividend achievers" index. Our Aggressors are—well—a bit more aggressive.

The climate for dividend growth continues to be favorable. Standard & Poor's estimates that some 401 of the S&P 500 companies pay a dividend, the highest in over a decade, and that 2012 dividends will be fully 16 percent ahead of 2011. Companies are swimming in cash, and rather than commit to expensive wages or business investments that might not pan out, are simply returning cash to previously starved shareholders. Actually, we believe that in most instances, companies have gotten so whipped into shape by recession that they have enough to invest in their businesses *and* return cash to shareholders. The risks in the bond markets and the persistence of favorable dividend tax treatment for investments (which we think will continue to persist, but maybe not to as great an advantage down the road) contribute to this story.

The growing-dividend-plus-growing-stock scenario continues to be one of our favored retirement-planning and retirement-investing scenarios. While we do expect markets overall, and our selected stocks in particular, to appreciate over time as good businesses capture more markets, become more efficient, and get better in general, stock price growth has become less dependable than in the past. The decades-long record of 10 to 11 percent annual growth, we think, will become more difficult to match. As a result, we think the more solid play is to invest for dividends, and particularly for dividend growth—and hey, if the stock price happens to grow too, so much the better.

Appendix B shows dividend yields for all *100 Best Stocks* for 2013. For this year, we added a column showing the number of dividend raises in the past 10 years. Appendix C shows all *100 Best* companies, sorted by percentage yield, with the highest yielders at the top of the list. We continue developing and sharing our "star" categories—groups of stocks, essentially the "best of the best" in five categories we chose to highlight—yield stars, safety and stability stars, growth stars, recovery stars, and "moat" stars. This year we keep the same categories, while adding the experimental "Dividend Aggressors" as a subset Table 6.1. As usual, we kick it off as we did last year with "yield stars."

Table 6 shows the top 20 stocks on our *100 Best* list by percentage yield as of mid-2012.

▼ **Table 6: Yield Stars**

TOP 20 DIVIDEND-PAYING STOCKS

Company	Symbol	Dividend	Yield %	Dividend raises, past 10 years
Suburban Propane	SPH	$3.41	7.8%	10
Total S.A.	TOT	$2.61	6.2%	5
AT&T	T	$1.76	5.7%	9
Cincinnati Financial	CINF	$1.61	5.7%	10
Verizon	VZ	$2.00	5.5%	6
Otter Tail Corporation	OTTR	$1.19	5.4%	5
Duke Energy	DUK	$1.00	4.8%	6
Southern Company	SO	$1.96	4.3%	10
PayChex	PAYX	$1.28	4.2%	8
Waste Management	WM	$1.42	4.2%	8
Dominion Resources	D	$2.11	4.1%	8
Kimberly-Clark	KMB	$2.96	4.0%	10
Johnson & Johnson	JNJ	$2.44	3.8%	10
NextEra Energy	NEE	$2.40	3.8%	10
ConocoPhillips	COP	$2.64	3.7%	10
Heinz	HNZ	$1.92	3.6%	8
Molex	MOLX	$0.80	3.6%	10
Nucor Corp.	NUE	$1.46	3.6%	8
Sysco	SYY	$1.08	3.6%	10
Campbell Soup	CPB	$1.16	3.5%	9

Table 6.1 shows our list of Dividend Aggressors for 2013:

▼ **Table 6.1: Dividend Aggressors**

COMPANIES WITH STRONG DIVIDEND TRACK RECORDS

Company	Symbol	Dividend	Yield %	Dividend raises, past 10 years
3M Company	MMM	$2.36	2.6%	10
Abbott Laboratories	ABT	$2.04	3.4%	10
Automatic Data Processing	ADP	$1.58	2.9%	10
Chevron	CVX	$3.60	3.0%	10
Clorox Company	CLX	$2.40	3.5%	9
Coca-Cola	KO	$2.04	2.8%	10
Heinz	HNZ	$1.92	3.6%	8
Intel	INTC	$0.84	3.0%	8
Johnson & Johnson	JNJ	$2.44	3.8%	10
Kimberly-Clark	KMB	$2.96	4.0%	10
McDonald's	MCD	$2.80	2.9%	10
NextEra Energy	NEE	$2.40	3.8%	10
Norfolk Southern	NSC	$1.88	2.8%	10
PepsiCo	PEP	$2.15	3.1%	10
Procter & Gamble	PG	$2.25	3.1%	10
Seagate	STX	$1.00	3.3%	4
J. M. Smucker	SJM	$1.92	2.4%	10
Southern Company	SO	$1.96	4.3%	10
Sysco	SYY	$1.08	3.6%	10
Waste Management	WM	$1.42	4.2%	8

REMEMBER, THERE ARE NO GUARANTEES

While dividends and especially high yields are attractive, investors must remember that corporations are under no contractual or legal obligation to pay them! Interest payments on time deposits and bonds are much more clearly defined, and failure to pay can represent default. But with dividends, there is no such safety net. Companies can—and do—reduce or eliminate dividends in bad times, as most strikingly observed with BP in the wake of the Deepwater Horizon Gulf spill disaster and most bank stocks after the 2008 dive. Dividend investors should therefore keep an eye out for changes in a company's business prospects—and shouldn't put too many eggs in a single high-yielding basket. On the flip side, as investors become more conscious of returns—and as corporate management teams become more conscious of such investor consciousness—we've seen a lot of companies trumpet their recent dividend increases rather loudly to their investors and the investing public. It's a nice sound that we hope to continue to hear.

Dancing with the Stars

Readers have frequently asked us: "Out of your 100 Stocks, what are the best ones? What are your top 10 picks?" Well, we don't actually rank our *100 Best Stocks* as one through 100. Why? Because different stocks serve different interests, needs, and risk tolerances, among other things, in a stock portfolio. And we're sure that if we name a "number one," everyone will follow our lead into it and some dumb thing will happen like the Gulf oil spill or some other more subtle unforeseen change in business conditions. The art and science of stock picking simply do not lend themselves to choosing an overall number one. Smart investors should buy groups of stocks to build a portfolio, much as a diner in an à la carte restaurant picks several dishes to make a meal rather than looking for the single best dish on the menu.

With that in mind, we do believe we can create some value and interest by identifying the top 10 stocks by certain attributes typically of common interest to investors, especially value-oriented investors. So this year we once again offer top-ten lists in four categories. We call them our "stars" list, bringing the idea forward from our "Yield Stars" list above. The four categories are Safety Stars, Growth Stars, Recovery Stars, and Moat Stars.

Safety Stars

Safety stars are companies we think will hold up well in volatile and negative stock markets as well as recessionary economies. They have stable products and customer bases, and long traditions of being able to manage well in downturns. This list is mostly unchanged from last year, although we replaced Ecolab, removed from the *100 Best* list altogether, with food and restaurant supplier Sysco. It wouldn't have been hard to pick a few more candidates like Colgate Palmolive or General Mills or Southern Company from the remainder of the *100 Best* list.

▼ **Table 7: Safety Stars**

TOP 10 STOCKS FOR SAFETY AND STABILITY

Company	Symbol	Dividend	Yield%
Becton, Dickinson	BDX	$1.80	2.1%
Campbell Soup	CPB	$1.16	3.5%
Clorox Company	CLX	$2.20	3.5%
General Mills	GIS	$1.22	3.1%
Heinz	HNZ	$1.92	3.6%
Johnson & Johnson	JNJ	$2.44	3.8%
Kimberly-Clark	KMB	$2.46	4.0%
McCormick & Co.	MKC	$1.24	2.3%
J. M. Smucker	SJM	$1.96	2.4%
Sysco	SYY	$1.08	3.6%

Growth Stars

Looking at the other side of the coin, we picked 10 stocks we feel are especially well positioned to grow, even in a negative economy and especially in a positive one. We changed three companies here, two (Google, Apache) because they were removed from the *100 Best* completely, and one (Teva) because it is going through a bit of a strategic redirection that may put its growth story on pause. Not surprisingly, we added three of the former *100 Best Aggressive* stocks as replacements—Harman, Itron, and Mosaic.

▼ **Table 8: Growth Stars**

TOP 10 STOCKS FOR GROWTH

Company	Symbol	Dividend	Yield%
Apple Inc	AAPL	$-	0.0%
Carmax, Inc	KMX	$-	0.0%
Harman International	HAR	$0.03	0.6%
Itron	ITRI	$-	0.0%
Mosaic	MOS	$0.50	1.0%
NIKE, Inc.	NIKE	$1.44	1.3%
Nucor Corp.	NUE	$1.46	3.6%
Perrigo	PRGO	$0.32	0.3%
St. Jude Medical	STJ	$0.92	2.4%
Tractor Supply Company	TSCO	$0.80	0.5%

Recovery Stars

As we continue to emerge from the 2008–2010 recession (assuming a normal course of economic recovery) we feel that certain companies will do especially well. The assessment is based both on top-line revenues and their ability to cut costs during bad times. As good times return, these companies are well positioned to turn recovery into bottom-line returns. The 2013 list is mostly unchanged, only replacing Alexander & Baldwin with Eastman Chemical.

▼ **Table 9: Recovery Stars**

TOP 10 STOCKS FOR AN ECONOMIC RECOVERY

Company	Symbol	Dividend	Yield%
3M Company	MMM	$2.36	2.6%
Caterpillar	CAT	$1.84	1.7%
Deere & Co.	DE	$1.84	2.3%
Eastman Chemical	EMN	$1.04	2.0%
Fluor Corporation	FLR	$0.60	1.1%

TOP 10 STOCKS FOR AN ECONOMIC RECOVERY (continued)

Company	Symbol	Dividend	Yield%
Int'l Paper	IP	$1.05	3.2%
Johnson Controls	JCI	$0.72	2.3%
Norfolk Southern	NSC	$1.88	2.8%
PayChex	PAYX	$1.28	4.2%
Wells Fargo	WFC	$0.88	0.6%

Moat Stars

Finally, we get back to one of the basic tenets of value investing—the ability of a company to build a sustainable and unassailable competitive advantage. Value investing aficionados call such an advantage a "moat," for it represents a barrier to entry for competitors that is likely to preserve advantage for some time. The moat can come in the form of technology, the use of technology, a brand, enduring customer relationships, channel relationships, size or scale, or simply a really big head start into a business, making it hard or even impossible for competitors to catch up. The appraisal of a "moat" is hardly an exact science; here we give our top-ten picks based on the size and strength (width?) of the moat.

This year we left the picks largely unchanged (and they won't change much if we've correctly identified the moat). We took Valmont off the list although we think they still have a strong moat in the form of leadership in most of their businesses. We just liked the moat created by the strength and panache of the Tiffany brand a bit better.

▼ **Table 10: Moat Stars**

TOP 10 STOCKS FOR SUSTAINABLE COMPETITIVE ADVANTAGE

Company	Symbol	Dividend	Yield%
Apple Inc	AAPL	$-	0.0%
Carmax, Inc	KMX	$-	0.0%
Fair Isaac	FICO	$0.08	0.2%
Iron Mountain	IRM	$1.00	3.0%
McCormick & Co.	MKC	$1.24	2.3%

TOP 10 STOCKS FOR SUSTAINABLE COMPETITIVE ADVANTAGE (continued)

Company	Symbol	Dividend	Yield%
Starbucks	SBUX	$0.68	1.1%
Sysco	SYY	$1.08	3.6%
Tiffany	TIF	$1.16	1.7%
Visa	V	$0.88	0.7%
W.W. Grainger	GWW	$3.20	1.5%

Tenets, Anyone? The Essentials of Successful Investing

Warning: What follows for the rest of Part I is likely to look familiar to those who have purchased and read recent editions of this book. Is that a bad thing? No. Because the fundamental tenets of investing we advocate and deploy don't change much. Read on . . . *The 100 Best Stocks to Buy in 2013* is designed to help you get started with picking stocks suitable for you. But rather than simply giving you fish (which may not be the freshest fish by the time they reach you), we feel it is also important to give you some investing groundwork to use in your own investing practice, as well as to help explain some of our guiding principles.

We do not intend to give a complete course in investing, or value investing, here. That probably wasn't the purpose you had in mind when you bought this book, and there isn't space here for a complete discussion anyway. For a more complete treatment of the topic, refer to Peter's title *Value Investing for Dummies* (second edition, Wiley, 2008).

At the risk of sounding "corporate," what makes sense here is to give a high-level overview of key investing "tenets" to keep top of mind and back of mind as you sift through the thousands of investment choices. By absorbing these principles, you'll gain a better understanding of the *100 Best Stocks* list and take away ideas to help with your own investment choices outside the list.

Buy Like You're Buying a Business

Already covered this one, but it's worth repeating: By buying shares of a corporation, you are really buying a share of a business. The more you can approach the decision as if you were buying the entire business yourself, the better.

Buy What You Know and Understand

Two of the most widely followed investment "gurus" of our age, Peter Lynch and Warren Buffett, have stressed the idea of buying businesses you know about and understand. This idea naturally follows the entrepreneurial idea of buying stocks as if you were buying a business; if you didn't understand the business, would you be comfortable buying it?

Peter Lynch, former manager of the enormous Fidelity Magellan fund and author of the well-known 1989 bestseller *One Up on Wall Street*, gave us the original notion of buying what you know. He suggests that the best investment ideas are those you see—and can learn about and keep track of—in daily life, on the street, on the job, in the mall, in your home. A company like Starbucks makes sense to Lynch because you can readily see the value proposition and how it extends beyond coffee, and can follow customer response and business activity at least in part just by hanging around your own neighborhood edition. And we hardly need to bring up the subject of iPods and iPads, and their use—and how they've turned Apple into the most valuable company in the world.

Buffett has famously stuck with businesses that are easy to understand—paint, carpet, electric utilities. He has famously shunned technology investments because he doesn't understand them, and more than likely, because their value and consumer preference shift too fast for him to keep up.

Both approaches make sense, and especially in hindsight, would have kept us farther from trouble in the 2008–2009 crash. Many, many investors didn't understand financial firms as well as they should have; the preponderance of evidence suggests that those financial firms didn't even understand themselves!

Clearly, you won't understand everything about the businesses you invest in—there's a lot of complexity and detail even behind the cooking and serving of hamburgers at McDonald's! Further, a sizeable amount of good knowledge is confidential so you likely won't ever get your hands on it. So you need to go with what you know and realize that a lot of the devil is in the details. When you analyze a company, if you can say "the more you know the better" instead of "the more you know the more you don't know," you'll be better off.

Greater Trends Are Important

We already covered the notion that technologies and consumer tastes change, and with them so do businesses—at least the good ones. Add to this the idea of change brought on by demographic trends (the aging of the population, for instance) and changes in law and policy (toward "green," toward universal health care, toward lower or higher interest rates, for instance) and you end up with a wide assortment of influences that can affect your stock picks.

Sector analysis is employed by many investors as a starting point. Where sector analysis does make sense is in capturing and correctly assessing the larger trends in that sector or industry. The sector thus becomes the arena in which to appraise those trends, often by reading sector analyses published in the media or in trade publications in that sector. One can, and should, learn about the construction industry or health-care industry before investing in a company in that industry.

Once the sector trends are understood, a selection of a company, or companies, in that sector can make more sense. A good example is offered by PC makers Hewlett-Packard (a former *100 Best Stocks* choice) and Dell Computer. Dell was the darling of the sector for years, achieving high margins and return on equity, market share growth, and popular marketplace preference for years. The direct sales model seemed unbeatable as a way to reduce costs and avoid obsolescence, and the just-in-time supply chain model, using accounts payable as a primary financing mechanism, all seemed strategically right.

But change was in the air for the PC industry. Lower prices, greater standardization, and the migration to laptops all pointed to HP's retail-centric model. No longer was it necessary, or even advantageous, for customers to order direct from Dell. With more standardized computing applications and inexpensive technology, there was less need to customize computers. With laptops, displays, size, and the look and feel are more important than simple "speeds and feeds," and people wanted to see what they were buying. Finally, as costs came down, a PC, laptop or otherwise, was simply something to pick up at a local store. We predicted PCs would soon sell in Walgreens, and if you don't believe that, consider that VCRs and DVD players also followed that thought-to-be-impossible path.

So, for a time, HP ended up in the right place with their emphasis on the retail channel and further, was strategically correct in their emphasis on printers and high-margin consumables that go with them, and in their emphasis on international markets. Dell fell by the wayside on counts—hence their 80 percent price drop from 2000 and 70 percent drop from their 2005 price peaks, respectively.

Now, was that the end of the story? Up until about two years ago, it was. Now the tablet and almost everything Apple makes has upended the PC space. The miniaturized "netbook" came and went in about two years, ousted by the tablet and shrinking traditional laptop sizes. Printing has diminished both because of tablet displays and because of the cloud. Who needs to print what can be stored and accessed from anywhere? Add to that the headline-worthy ineptitude of HP's management, a complete absence of innovation, and a bloated cost structure, and we now can easily see that we waited too long to take this company off our list.

The upshot is that you must understand a company's marketplace position for what it really is today, and be able to project it forward a few years as well. Perhaps both HP and Dell will learn how to coexist with, even supply parts of, the cloud. But for now, these recent high flyers look to be in a struggle to keep up with, not lead, their industries, and may eventually be washed out to sea with many other lesser high flyers, such as Gateway and Lotus Development and perhaps even someday Microsoft, that simply can't regain their industry leadership positions as the currents continue to change and the tide washes them out farther and farther.

So again the lesson, or tenet, is to understand the greater trends in the economy, in the market, in the sector, and in the industry. If you buy a business, you want to know about the industry, right? Who the competitors are, how they compete, about the market and customer needs and customer tastes, and how companies do business in that market. Right? You want to understand the *future* of that industry and market. It's no different when you buy shares.

One more thing to add: Most of the time we try to buy what we think to be the best company in the sector—best based on past, current, and expected future performance. But sometimes it makes sense, from an opportunity viewpoint, to "play the Avis game," that is, to buy a more nimble, more aggressive, less arrogant or complacent number-two competitor. Such a company is leaner, meaner, hungrier, and likely sells for a more reasonable price. Sometimes we'll buy both if we feel the industry or sector is large enough to support two strong competitors, and if there are large enough or strong enough niches available so they won't become cutthroat competitors.

Niche and Get Rich

In understanding sectors, industries, and markets, it's important to consider success opportunities for niche players. A "niche" is a small captive market segment, usually too small for the biggest competitors to profitably consider, but still lucrative for a smaller, more nimble player. Niche players can define and play smaller markets based on product, location or geography, distribution channels, or other differentiators like language. Caribou is an example, capturing the franchising niche. Or McCormick & Co. (a *100 Best* stock) capturing the spice niche in a larger food and beverage industry. Or Pall Corporation, another *100 Best* stock, capturing the market for filtration systems in a variety of manufacturing industries.

Stick to the Real Stuff

If you're familiar with the accounting profession, you know that contrary to public perception, accounting for business assets and activity is not always a precise science. In fact, there can be quite a bit of art involved in accounting, especially for business assets and business income.

Why? Because, while the purchase *price* for most "physical" assets is known, the *value* of those assets over time is a subjective calculation. And there are many assets, like intellectual property, that elude precise evaluation altogether. How much is a patent worth? How much is an acquired business worth? Just like a stock you buy, you know what you paid for it, but how much is it really worth in terms of future returns to the acquiring company? It's a subjective number.

Likewise, reported net income can be fairly subjective, too. How much depreciation expense was taken against assets, and thus against income? How much "expense" was taken to write down intangible assets like patents and other intellectual property? How much "restructuring" expense was incurred? The rules give the accountants and corporate management quite a bit of flexibility to "manage" reported earnings, and asset values as well: What you see may not always be what you get.

The bottom line is this: While assets and income have at least some subjectivity in their valuation, debts are quite real, and so is cash. Debts must be paid sooner or later; there is no subjectivity or "art" to their valuation. Likewise, cash is cash, the stuff in the proverbial drawer, and is a take-it-or-leave-it, like-it-or-not fact of life or death for a business.

Thus, as value investors, we look at assets and income as important measures of business activity, but know that there's some subjectivity in those measures. At the same time, we look at debts, cash, and cash flow in and out of the business as absolute; neither cash nor debt lie. So we hang our valuation hats on cash and debt where we can.

Now, in particular, cash isn't an absolute measure of business success, either, for there are timing issues. Suppose you are running an airline and decide this is the year to buy an airplane. A huge cash outflow, possibly matched by a cash inflow from borrowing. Are this year's cash flow statements fully representative of the firm's success or failure? No, because the airplane will be used over a number of years, and the cost of the airplane must be divvied up among those years and matched to airfares collected and other costs to truly understand performance. That's where conventional income accounting comes in—it helps to do that.

All that said, sharp value investors learn to look for companies that, over time, *produce* capital, in contrast to companies that *consume* it. As judged by the statement of cash flows, a company that produces more cash from operations than it consumes in investing activities (capital equipment purchases mainly) and in financing activities (repaying debt, dividends, etc.) is producing capital. When a company must always go to the capital markets to make up for a deficit in operating or investing cash flow, that's a sign of trouble, which is incidentally borne out by the other absolute measure—debt. If debt is high and increasing and especially if it is increasing faster than the business is growing—look out. Or at least, look for a story, like company XYZ is going through a known, and rational, expansion that needs to be funded. Going to the capital markets to fund operational cash deficits is an especially bad thing to do.

Thus, as an investor, you should always pay attention to assets and income, but even closer attention to cash and debt. This tenet was used in identifying the *100 Best Stocks*.

What Makes a *Best Stock* Best?

So now we get down to brass tacks. What is it that defines excellence—sustainable excellence—among companies? That's been a topic of considerable debate for years, and with all the study that's gone into it, it's amazing that nobody has hit upon a single formula for deciphering undeniable excellence in a company.

That's largely because it isn't as scientific as most of us would like or expect it to be. It defies mathematical formulas. Take the square of net profits, multiply by the cosine of the debt-to-equity ratio, add the square root of the revenue-per-employee count, and what do you get? Some nice numbers, but not a clear picture of how it works together or how a company will sell its products to customers and prosper going forward.

Fundamentals such as profitability, productivity, and asset efficiency tell us how well a company has done and, by proxy, how well it is managed and how well it has done in the marketplace. Fundamentals are about what the company has already achieved and where it stands right now, and if a company's current fundamentals are a mess, stop right now—there isn't much point in going any further.

In most cases, what really separates the great from the good are the intangibles, the "soft" factors of market position, market acceptance, customer "love" of a company's products, its management, its aura. These features create competitive advantage, or "distinctive competence," as an economist would put it, that cannot be valued. Furthermore, and most importantly, they are more about what a company is set up to achieve in the future.

Buffett put it best: Give me $100 billion, and I could start a company. But I could never create another Coca-Cola.

What does that mean? It means that Coke has already established a worldwide brand cachet; the distribution channels, customer knowledge, and product development expertise cannot be duplicated at any cost. When companies have competitive advantages that cannot be duplicated at any cost, they have an enduring grip on their markets. They can charge more for their products. They have a "moat" that insulates them from competition, or makes it much more expensive for competitors to participate. They're perceived by loyal customers as being top-line products worth paying more for.

A company with exceptional intangibles can control price and in many cases, can control its costs.

LUV—A GREAT EXPERIENCE. BUT IS IT A GOOD INVESTMENT?

One way to learn a principle is to examine what happens when the principle does not apply. One industry where most of the fundamentals and almost all the intangibles work against it is the airline industry. Airlines cannot control price, because of competition, and because an airplane trip is an airplane trip. Aside from serving different snacks or offering better schedules, there is little an airline can do to differentiate their product, and almost nothing they can do to justify charging a higher price. Further, they have no control over costs—like fuel prices, union contracts, and airport landing fees. While some airlines offer good service, there is almost nothing they can do to distinguish themselves as excellent companies or excellent investments.

With these ills in mind, for two years we resisted the temptation to put Southwest, one of the most efficient, customer-focused, and best-managed businesses we know of on our *100 Best* list. Great company, bad industry. But then, last year we decided to add them to the list anyway, as their business model and the continued floundering of their competitors should give them an edge that we feel investors may finally be willing to reward. We also think they've been so good for so long that many of their customers will be willing to pay somewhat higher prices to stick with their offering. Indeed, there's recent evidence that their average revenue per ticket has risen substantially. They've also introduced some effective revenue enhancers, like priority check-in, a much more customer-friendly revenue booster than the annoying baggage fees charged by other carriers. These guys still get it, and we feel that their approach will put them farther ahead of the competition and allow them to overcome some of the industry's worst ills. Did it work out? No. We got blindsided by another round of higher fuel prices. So we'll take that bump of unexpected turbulence in stride and continue our flight plan, at least for now, and keep our seat belts loosely fastened in case of more unexpected turbulence....

Strategic Fundamentals

Let's examine a list of "strategic fundamentals" that define, or keep score of, a company's success. This list can be used as a checklist, although it's hard to find a company that shows excellence in all of these areas.

Are Gross and Operating Profit Margins Growing?

We like profitable companies; who doesn't? But what really counts is the size of the margin and especially the growth. If a company has a gross margin (sales minus costs of goods sold) exceeding that of its competitors, that shows that it's doing something right, probably with its customers and/or with its costs. But competitive analysis is elusive; there is no dependable source of "industry" gross margins, and comparing competitors can be difficult because no two companies are exactly alike; it's easy to mix apples and oranges.

We like to see what direction gross margin is moving in—up or down. A growing gross margin also signals that the company is doing something right. That isn't perfect either; as the economy moved from boom to bust many excellent companies reported declines in gross and especially operating margins (sales – cost of goods sold – operating expenses) as they laid off workers and used less capacity. Still, in a steady-state environment, it makes sense to favor companies with growing margins. In a declining market, companies that can *protect* their margins will come out ahead.

Does a Company Produce More Capital Than It Consumes?

Make no mistake about it—we like cash. And pure and simple—we like it when a company produces more cash than it consumes.

At the end of the day, cash generation is the simplest measure of whether a company is being successful, especially over the long term. Sure, if a company buys an airplane or opens a factory or a bunch of stores in a given quarter, it will be cash-flow negative. But that should be a temporary thing; over the long haul, it should produce, not consume cash. Companies that continually have to borrow or sell shares to raise enough cash to stay in business are on the wrong track.

So how do you determine this? You'll have to become familiar with the Statement of Cash Flows or equivalent in a company's financial reports. "Cash flow from operations" is usually positive and represents cash booked from sales less cost of goods sold, with adjustments for noncash items like depreciation and for increases or decreases in working capital. In simple terms, is the cash going into the cash register from the business?

"Cash used for investing purposes" or similar is a bit of a misnomer and represents net cash used to "invest" in the business—usually for capital expenditures, but also for short-term noncash investments like securities and a few other smaller items usually beyond scope. This figure is typically negative unless the company sells some part of its infrastructure. Over the long haul, cash generated from operations should well exceed cash used to invest in the business.

Companies in expansion mode may not show this surplus, and that's where "cash from financing activities" comes in. That's the cash generated from issuing debt or selling securities—or paying off debt or repurchasing shares, if things are going well, and dividends are included here as well. Again, a successful company will produce more cash—capital—from the business than it consumes, just as a successful household does the same, or else it goes into debt. Smart investors track this surplus over time.

Are Expenses Under Control?

Again, just like your household, company expenses should be under control, and anything else, especially without explanation, is a yellow flag.

The best way to test this is to check whether the "Selling, General and Administrative" expenses (SG&A) are rising, and more to the point, rising faster than sales. If so, that's a yellow, not necessarily a red, flag, but if it continues, it suggests that something is out of control, and it will catch up with the company sooner or later. In the recent downturn, companies that were able to reduce their expenses to match revenue declines scored more points, too.

Is Noncash Working Capital Under Control?

Working capital is a hard concept to grasp—even for small entrepreneurs who live with its ups and downs on a daily basis. Insufficient working capital is one of the biggest causes of death for small businesses, and working capital and especially changes in working capital can signal success or trouble.

Using a simplistic analogy, working capital is the circulatory lifeblood of the business. Money comes in, money goes out; working capital is what circulates in the veins in between. In its purest sense, it is cash, receivables, and inventory, less short-term debts. It's what you own less what you owe aside from fixed assets like plant, stores, and equipment.

If receivables are increasing, that sounds like a good thing—more people owe you more money. But if receivables are rising and sales aren't, that suggests that people aren't paying their bills, or worse, the business has to finance more to achieve the same level of sales. Similarly, a rise in inventory without a rise in sales means that it costs the business more money—more working capital—to do the same amount of business. That costs twice, because unless the firm is lucky, more inventory means more obsolescence and potentially more deep-discount sales or more write-offs down the road.

So a sharp investor will check to see that major working capital items—receivables and inventory—aren't growing faster than sales; indeed, a company that generates more sales with a decrease in working capital is becoming more productive.

Is Debt in Line with Business Growth?

Like many other "fundamentals" items, you can tear your hair out looking at debt figures and trying to decide whether they're in line with asset levels, equity levels, and industry norms. A simpler test is to check and see whether long-term debt is increasing or decreasing, and in particular, whether it is increasing faster than business growth. Gold stars go to companies with little to no debt, and to companies able to grow without issuing mountains of long-term debt.

Is Earnings Growth Steady?

We enter the danger zone here, because the management of many companies have learned to "manage" earnings to provide a steady improvement, always "beating the street" by a penny or two. So stability is a good thing for all investors, and companies that can manage toward stability get extra points, and it's worth checking for, but with the proverbial grain of salt.

Still, a company that is able to manage its sales, earnings, cash flow, and debt levels more consistently than competitors, and perhaps more consistently than what would be suggested by the ups and downs of the economy, is desirable—or at least more desirable than the alternatives.

Is Return on Equity Steady or Growing?

Return on equity (ROE) is another of those hard-to-grasp concepts and another measure subject to subjectivity in valuing assets and earnings. But at the end of the day, it's what all investors really seek, that is, returns on their capital investments.

And like many other figures derived from income statements and balance sheets, a pure number is hard to interpret—does a 26.7 percent ROE mean, in itself, that a company is excellent? The figure sounds healthy, to be sure—it's a heck of a lot better than investing your money in a CD or T-Bill. But because earnings and asset values are subjective, it may not represent true success. In fact, a company can increase ROE simply by borrowing money (yes!) and investing it into the business, even if it isn't invested as productively as other previous funds were invested. The math is complicated; we won't go into it here.

So the true test of ROE success is to check whether it is steady or increasing. Increasing—that makes sense. Why *steady*? Because if a company makes profits in a previous period and reinvests them in the business, that amount of money becomes part of equity (retained earnings). If the company reinvests productively, it will produce more returns, and ROE will at least keep up. If the company can't reinvest those earnings productively, ROE will drop—and perhaps it should be paying the earnings to you as dividends instead of investing them unproductively in the business. So if ROE is steady, the company still has good investments to make, and management is probably doing the right thing.

Does the Company Pay a Dividend?

Different people feel differently about dividends, and as shown earlier, we're placing a greater emphasis on dividend-paying stocks this year. After all, save for the eventual sale of the company to someone else, a dividend is the only true cash that an investor will realize from buying a stock in a corporation, other than by selling the stock. And, at least in theory, investors should receive some compensation for their investments once in a while.

Yet, many companies don't pay dividends or don't pay dividends that compete very effectively with fixed-income yields. Why do investors put up with this? Because, in theory anyway, a company in a good business should be able to reinvest profits more effectively than the investor can (or else why would the investor have bought the company in the first place?). And investors trust that reinvested profits will eventually bring the growth in company value that will be reflected in the share price, or eventual takeover or an eventual payment of a dividend or, better yet, growth in that dividend.

That's the theory, anyway. But there are still lots of companies that get away with paying no dividend at all. Can we tolerate this? Yes, if a company is really doing a great job with their retained profits, like Apple or Bed, Bath & Beyond. But we favor companies that offer at least something to their investors in the short term, some return on their hard-earned and faithfully committed capital. If nothing else, it keeps management teams honest, and shows that management understands that shareholder interests are up there somewhere on the list of priorities.

A dividend is a plus. Lack of a dividend isn't necessarily a deal breaker, but it suggests a closer look. A dividend reduction—and there were many in the past year—suggests poor financial and operational health, because the dividend is usually the last thing to go, but in some cases, reflects management prudence and conservatism. Best question to ask yourself: Would you have reduced the dividend if you were running the company? And down the road, does the company bring back the dividend as times get better? A "no" to either of these questions is troubling.

Finally, dividend payouts should be examined over time. We've seen, and included in our lists, a number of companies that have steadily increased dividends—many for each of the 10 previous years. We like this; it's just like getting an annual raise, and if you hold the stock long enough, the percentage return against your original investment can get quite large, even approaching 100 percent per year if the stock is held long enough and the dividend is raised persistently enough. Getting an ever-increasing dividend—and owning a stock that has most likely appreciated because the dividend has increased—is like having your cake and eating it too—a true favorite among investors.

ARE VALUATION RATIOS IN LINE?

One of the most difficult tasks in investing is determining the true value—and per share value—of a company. If this were easy, you'd just determine a value, compare it to the price, and if the price were lower than the value, push the buy button.

Professional investors try to determine what they call the "intrinsic value" of a company, which is usually the sum of all projected future cash flows of a company, discounted back to the present (remember, money received tomorrow is both less predictable and less valuable than money received now). They use complex math models, specifically, "discounted cash flow" or DCF models, to project, then discount, earnings flows. But those models—especially for the individual investor, depend too much on the crystal-ball accuracy of earnings forecasts, and the so-called discount rate is a highly theoretical construct beyond the scope of most individual investors. DCF models require a lot of estimates and number crunching, especially if multiple scenarios are employed as they should be. They take more time than it's worth for the individual investor. If you're an institutional investor buying multimillion-share stakes, we would conclude otherwise.

Valuation ratios are a shorthand way to determine if a stock price is acceptable relative to value. By far and away the most popular of these ratios is the so-called "price-to-earnings" (P/E) ratio, a measure of the stock price usually compared to "TTM," or trailing twelve months' earnings, but also sometimes compared to future earnings.

The P/E ratio correlates well to your expected return on an investment you might make in the company. For instance, if the P/E is 10, the price is 10 times the past, or perhaps expected, annual earnings of the company. Take the reciprocal of that—1 divided by 10—and you get 0.10, or 10 percent. That's known as "earnings yield," the theoretical yield you'd get if all earnings were paid to you as dividends as an owner. 10 percent is pretty healthy compared to returns on other investments, so a P/E of 10 suggests success.

But of course, the earnings may not be consistent or sustainable, or there may be substantial risk from factors intrinsic to the company, or there may be exogenous risk factors, like the total meltdown of the economy. The more risk, the more instability, the lower the expected P/E should be, for the earnings stream is less stable. If you think the earnings stream is solid and stable in the face of the risk, then the stock may be truly undervalued. Look for P/Es that (1) suggest strong earnings yield and (2) are favorable compared to competitors and the industry.

Apart from P/E, the price-to-sales ratio (P/S), price to cash flow (P/CF), and price to free cash flow (P/FCF) are often used as fundamentals yardsticks. Like P/E, these measures also have some ambiguities, and it's best to think about them in real-world, entrepreneurial terms. Would you pay three times annual sales for a business and sleep well at night? Probably not—unless its profit margins were exceptionally high. So if a P/S ratio is 3 or above, look out; and opt for a business with a P/S of 1 or less if you can. Similarly, the price-to-cash-flow ratios can be thought of as true return going into your pocket for your investment; is it enough? Is it enough given the risk? And about the difference between "cash flow" and "free cash flow"? The difference is mostly cash laid out for capital expenditures, so it's worth making this distinction, although the lumpiness of capital expenditures makes consistent application of this number elusive. Incidentally, we don't regard price-to-book value (P/B) ratios as that helpful, because the book value of a company can be very elusive and arbitrary unless most of a company's assets are in cash or other easy-to-value forms.

Companies with high P/E, P/S, P/B, and P/CF ratios aren't necessarily bad investments, but you need to have good reasons to look beyond these figures if they suggest truly inadequate business results.

Strategic Intangibles

When you look at any company, perhaps the bottom-line question follows the Buffett wisdom: If you had a hundred billion in cool cash to spend (and we'll assume the genius intellect to spend it right), could you recreate that company?

If the answer is "yes," it may still be a great company, but it may not be great enough to fend off competition and keep its customers forever. If the answer is "no," the company truly has something unique to offer in the marketplace, difficult to duplicate at any cost. That distinctive competence, that sustainable competitive edge—whatever it is, a brand, a trade secret, a lock on distribution or supply channels, may be worth more than all the factories and high-rise office buildings and cash in the bank a company could ever have.

What we're talking about are the intangibles, the "soft" factors that make companies unique, that add up to more than the sum of their parts, the factors that ultimately drive future revenues. Intangibles not only define excellence, they define the future, while fundamentals mainly define the past. Seven key intangibles follow, although you'll think of more, and some industries may have some unique ones of their own, like intellectual property in the technology sector.

DOES THE COMPANY HAVE A MOAT?

A business "moat" performs much the same role as the medieval castle equivalent—it protects the business from competition. Whatever factors, some discussed below, create the moat, ultimately those are the factors that prevent you, with your $100 billion, from taking their business. Moats are usually a combination of brand, product technology, design, marketing and distribution channels, and customer loyalty all working together to protect a company. A moat doesn't just protect the existence of a company, it helps it command higher prices and earn higher profits.

Whether a company has a "narrow" moat, a "wide" moat, or none at all is a subjective assessment for you to make. However, you can get some help at Morningstar (*www.morningstar.com*) whose stock ratings include an assessment of the moat.

Coca-Cola has a moat because of the sheer impossibility of surpassing its brand and brand recognition worldwide. CarMax has a moat because it is farther along in putting retail-style dealerships on the ground and applying management information technologies to its business than anyone else is; it would take years for a competitor to catch up. Tiffany has a moat because of its immediately recognized brand and elegantly simple, stylish brand image, and the enduring and timeless panache around that. The "Moat Stars" list presented earlier identifies the top 10 stocks with a solid and sustainable competitive advantage.

Does the Company Have an Excellent Brand?

It's hard to say enough about brand, especially in today's fast-moving, highly packaged, highly national and international marketplace. A strong brand means consistency and a promise to consumers, and consumers sold on a brand will prefer it over any other, almost regardless of price. People still buy Tide; Starbucks is still synonymous with high quality and ambience. Good brands command higher prices, and foster loyalty and identity and even customer "love."

Ask yourself if a company has a sought-after brand, a brand customers would pay extra to buy or align with, a brand that would be difficult to duplicate at any cost. Would customers rather fight than switch? Think about Starbucks, Coca-Cola, Heinz, Tiffany, NIKE, or the brands within a house, like Frito-Lay (Pepsi) or Tide (P&G) or Teflon (DuPont).

Is the Company a Market Leader?

Market leadership usually—but not always—goes hand in hand with brand. The trick is to decide whether a company really leads in its industry. Often—but not always—that's a factor of size. The market leader usually has the highest market share, and the important point is that it calls the shots with regard to price, technology, marketing message, and so forth—other companies must play catch-up and often discount their prices to keep up. Apple is a market leader in digital music, Intel is the market leader in microprocessors, and, despite a few setbacks, Toyota is emerging as the market leader in automobiles.

Excellent companies tend to be market leaders, and market leaders tend to be excellent companies. But this relationship doesn't always hold true—sometimes the nimble but smaller competitor is the excellent company—and will likely assume market leadership eventually. Examples like CarMax, Nucor, Perrigo, Valero, and Southwest Airlines can be found on our list.

DOES THE COMPANY HAVE CHANNEL EXCELLENCE?

"Channel" in business parlance means a chain of players to sell and distribute a company's products. It might be stores, it might be other industrial companies, it might be direct to the consumer. If a company is considered a top supplier in a particular channel, or a company has especially good relations with its channel, that's a plus.

Excellent companies develop solid channel relationships and become the preferred supplier in those channels. Companies such as Patterson, Fair Isaac, McCormick, NIKE, Pepsi, Procter & Gamble, Sysco, and Whirlpool could all have excellent relationships with the channels through which they sell their product.

DOES THE COMPANY HAVE SUPPLY-CHAIN EXCELLENCE?

Like distribution channels, excellent companies develop excellent and low-cost supply channels. They are seldom caught off guard by supply shortages and tend to get favorable and stable prices for whatever they buy. This is often not an easy assessment unless you know something about a particular industry. Nike and Target are good examples of companies that have done a good job managing their supply chain.

DOES THE COMPANY HAVE EXCELLENT MANAGEMENT?

Well, it's not hard to grasp what happens if a company *doesn't* have good management; performance fails and few inside or outside the company respect the company. It's not easy for an investor to determine if a management team does a good job or acts in shareholder interests. Clues can include candor and honesty and the ability of company management to speak in accessible, easily understood terms about the company and company performance (it's worth listening to conference calls as a resource). A management team that admits errors and eschews other forms of arrogance and entitlement (i.e., luxury perks, office suites, aircraft) is probably tilting his or her interests toward shareholders, as is the management team that can cough up some return to shareholders once in a while in the form of a dividend.

This may be the most subjective and elusive assessment of all, as few investors work with these folks on a daily basis. Still, over time, you can garner a strong hunch about whether a management team is effective and on your side.

ARE THERE SIGNS OF INNOVATION EXCELLENCE?

This question seems pretty obvious, but it's not just about the products that a company sells. True, if the company is leading the industry in innovation, that's usually a good thing, for "first to market" definitely offers business advantages.

The less obvious part of this question is whether the company makes the best *use* of technology to make operations and customer interfaces as efficient and effective as possible. Southwest Airlines may have missed our list in the past because of the difficulty of achieving excellence in an industry where players can't control prices or costs. But they do make our list today, not only because of brand and management excellence, but also innovation excellence. Why? Simply because, after all these years, amazingly, they still have the best, simplest, easiest-to-use flight booking and check-in in the industry. Sometimes these sorts of innovations mean a lot more than bringing new, fancy products and bells and whistles to the market. And one can also look to Apple, CarMax, FedEx, Itron, UPS, and Visa on our list for more obvious examples of companies that have deployed technology and innovative customer interfaces to achieve sustainable competitive advantage.

Choosing the 100 Best

So with all of this in mind, just how was this year's *100 Best Stocks* list actually chosen? It's probably about time to get to that.

The answer is a little more subtle than you might think. If we could give you a precise formula, you wouldn't need this book. You'd be able to do it yourself. In fact, every investor would be able to do it on his or her own. Our book would simply be the result of yet another stock screener. And every investor would invest in the same stocks. Is that a feasible or practical solution? Hardly. Everyone would scramble to buy the same *100 Best Stocks*. The prices would be sky high, and the price of other stocks would melt to nothing.

SIGNS OF VALUE

Following are a few signs of value to look for in any company. Not an exhaustive list by any means, but a good place to start:

- » Gaining market share
- » Can control price
- » Loyal customers
- » Growing margins
- » Producing, not consuming, capital (free cash flow)
- » Steady or increasing ROE
- » Management forthcoming, honest, understandable

SIGNS OF UNVALUE

. . . and signs of trouble, or "unvalue":

- » Declining margins
- » No brand or who-cares brand
- » Commodity producer, must compete on price
- » Losing market dominance or market share
- » Can't control costs
- » Must acquire other companies to grow
- » Management in hiding, off message, making excuses, difficult to understand, or in the news for all the wrong reasons

Fortunately or unfortunately, however you want to look at it, it isn't that simple. There are so many fundamentals, so many intangibles, and so many unknown and unknowable weighting factors to combine the fundamentals and intangibles that—well—it just wouldn't work. No screener could recreate the subtle judgment that gets applied to the cold, hard facts. It's that judgment, the interpretation of the facts and intangibles that makes it worth spending money on a book like this.

While we didn't apply a specific formula or screener to the universe of stocks, we did take a few measurable factors into account to narrow the list from thousands to a few hundred issues. Those factors came from several sources, but at this point, we must tip our cap to Value Line and the research and database work they do as part of the Value Line Investment Survey. If you aren't familiar with Value Line, it's worth a look for any savvy individual investor, either online at *www.valueline.com* or, in many cases, at your local library. It is an excellent resource.

Here are six metrics we use as a starting point to select and sort stocks for further review:

- *S&P Rating* is a broad corporate credit rating reflecting the ability to cover indebtedness, in turn reflecting business levels, business trends, cash flow, and sustained performance. It's a bit like the credit score you might use or might have used to determine your personal credit risk.
- *Value Line Financial Strength Rating* is used much like the S&P rating except that it goes further into overall balance sheet and cash flow strength. It should be noted that several companies with "B" ratings were selected; these are typically newer companies that will grow into A companies or that may have been hit harder by the recession than others.
- *Value Line Earnings Predictability* is what it sounds like, a calculated tendency of companies to deliver consistent and predictable earnings without surprises.
- *Value Line Growth Persistence* is again what it sounds like—the company's ability to consistently grow even in weaker economic times.
- *Value Line Price Stability* reflects the stability and relative safety of a company. Again, we did not reject a company out of hand due to volatility; rather, if stability was low, we tried to make a case that the business, business model, and intangibles were worth the risk.
- *Dividends and Yield.* Companies that pay something are held in higher regard; however, again, it is not by any means an absolute criterion.

With these facts and figures in mind, the evaluation proceeded with a close eye on the "signs of value" and intangibles mentioned above. Some consideration was also given to diversification; we did not want to overweight any sector or industry, but rather to give you a healthy assortment of stocks to pick from across a variety of industries.

With these thoughts in mind, you can make more sense of the companies we picked. And of course, full disclosure and full disclaimer—we didn't do *all* the analysis. We couldn't have. It wouldn't have made any sense anyway, for things would have changed from the time we did it, and it might not match your preferences anyway. So it is of utmost importance for you to take our selections and analysis and make them yours—that is, do the due diligence to further qualify these picks as congruent with your investment needs.

Strategic Investing

Although this book is designed to help you pick the best stocks to buy, investing, by nature, goes well beyond simply buying stocks, just like owning an automobile goes far beyond buying it. Just as clearly, this book isn't about investing strategy, or about the personal financial strategies necessary to ensure retirement or a prosperous future. That said, we think a few words are in order.

We find that a lot of investors lose the forest in the trees, spending all of their energy trying to find individual stocks or funds without putting enough consideration into their overall investing framework. If they look at the big picture at all, they look at the formulaic covenants of asset allocation, a favorite subject of the financial planning and advisory community, as though the difference between 50 percent equities and 60 percent equities makes all the difference in the world. Sure, it might in the world of pension funds and other institutional investments, where a 10 percent adjustment could move millions into or out of a particular asset class and more or less toward safety, but what about a $100,000 portfolio? Does $10,000 more or less in stocks, bonds, or cash make that much difference?

Perhaps not. And of course there's more to that story—doesn't it matter more which equities you invest in than just the fact that you're 60 percent in equities? So while asset allocation models make for nice pie charts, we prefer to approach big-picture portfolio constructs differently.

Start with a Portfolio in Mind

We're assuming you are not a professional investor. You have other things to do with your time, and time is of the essence. You cannot spend 40, 50, or 60 hours a week glued to a computer screen analyzing your investments.

To that assumption, we'll add another: that, as an individual investor, you're looking to beat the market. Not by a ton—20 percent sustained returns simply aren't possible without taking outlandish risks. But perhaps if the market is up 4 percent in a year, you'd like to achieve, 5, 6, perhaps 7 percent without taking excessive risks. Or if the market is down 20 percent, perhaps you cut your losses at 5 or 10 percent. You're looking to do *somewhat* better than the market.

Because of time constraints, and owing to your objective to do slightly better than average, we suggest taking a tiered approach to your portfolio. The tiers aren't based on the type of assets; they're based on the amount of activity and attention you want to pay to different parts of your portfolio. It's a strategic portfolio approach you would probably take if you were managing a small business—put most of your focus on the products and customers who might bring the greatest new return to your business; let the rest of your slow steady customer base function as it has for the long term.

We suggest breaking up your portfolio into three tiers or segments. This can be done by setting up specific accounts; or less formally by simply applying the model as a thought process.

Active Portfolio Segmentation

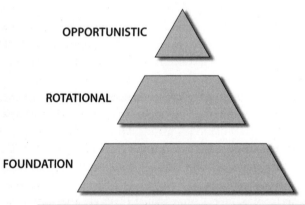

	CLASSIC	CONSERVATIVE	AGGRESSIVE
OPPORTUNISTIC	10-20%	5-10%	20-40%
ROTATIONAL	10-30%	5-10%	10-30%
FOUNDATION	50-80%	80-90%	30-70%

We can't go much further without defining the three segments:

The Foundation Portfolio

In this construct, each investor defines and manages a cornerstone foundation portfolio, which is long term in nature and requires relatively less active management. Frequently, the foundation portfolio consists of retirement accounts (the paradigmatic long-term investment) and may include your personal residence or other long-lived personal or family assets, such as trusts, collectibles, and so forth. The typical foundation portfolio is invested to achieve at least average market returns through index funds, quality mutual funds, and some income-producing assets like bonds held to maturity. A foundation portfolio may contain some long-term plays in commodities or real estate to defend against inflation, particularly in such commodities as energy, precious metals, and real estate trusts. The foundation portfolio is largely left alone, although as with all investments it is important to check at least once in a while to make sure performance—and managers if involved—are keeping up with expectations.

The Rotational Portfolio

You manage the rotational portfolio fairly actively to keep up with changes in business cycles and conditions. It is likely in a set of stocks or funds that might be rotated or remixed occasionally to reflect business conditions or to get a little more offensive or defensive. More than the other portfolios, this portfolio follows the rotation of market preference among different kinds of businesses and business assets. The portfolio is managed to redeploy assets among market or business sectors, between aggressive and defensive business assets, from "large cap" to "small cap" companies from companies with international exposure to those with little of the same, from companies in favor versus out of favor, from stocks to bonds to commodities, and so forth. Sector-specific exchange-traded funds are a favorite component of these portfolios, as are cyclical and commodity-based stocks like gold mining stocks.

Is this about "market timing"? Let's call it "intelligent" or "educated" market timing. Studies telling us that it is impossible to effectively time market moves have been around for years. It is impossible to catch highs and lows in particular investments, market sectors, or even the market as a whole. Nobody can find exact tops or bottoms. But by watching economic indicators and the pulse of business and the marketplace, long-term market performance can be boosted by well-rationalized and timely sector rotation. The key word is "timely." The agile active investor has enough of a finger on the pulse to see the signs and invest accordingly.

While the idea isn't new, the advent of "low-friction" exchange-traded funds and other index portfolios makes it a lot more practical for the individual investors. What does "low-friction" mean? They trade like a single stock—one order, one discounted commission. You don't have to liquidate or acquire a whole basket full of investments on your own to follow a sector. We should note that it's been possible to rotate assets in mutual fund families for years with a single phone call, but most funds in these families are less "pure" plays in their sector, and most families do not cover all sectors.

THE OPPORTUNISTIC PORTFOLIO

The opportunistic portfolio is the most actively traded portion of an active investor's total portfolio. The opportunistic portfolio looks for stocks or other investments that seem to be notably under- or overvalued at a particular time. The active investor looks for shorter-term opportunities, perhaps a few days, perhaps a month, perhaps even a year, to wring out gains from undervalued situations.

The opportunistic portfolio also may be used to generate short-term income through covered option writing. Options are essentially a cash-based risk transfer mechanism whereby a possible, but low-probability investment outcome is exchanged for a less profitable but more certain outcome. A fee or "premium" is paid in exchange for transferring the opportunity for more aggressive gain to someone else. You collect this fee. Effectively, you as the owner of a stock can convert a growth investment into an income investment, paying yourself a dividend for the ownership of the stock by selling an option. Is this risky? Actually, it is less risky than owning the stock without an option.

Curiously, the main objective of this short-term portfolio is to generate income, or cash. Most traditional investors look at the long-term, more conservative components of a portfolio to generate income through bonds, dividend-paying stocks, and so forth. In this framework, the short-term opportunistic portfolio actually does the "heavy lifting" in terms of generating cash income. An active investor might look to trade those stocks with varying degrees of frequency or to sell some options to generate cash. These "swing" trades usually run from a few days to a month or so, and may be day trades if things work out particularly well and move particularly fast. It should be emphasized again that day trades are not the active investor's goal or typical practice.

ARE RETIREMENT ACCOUNTS ALWAYS PART OF THE FOUNDATION?

The long-term objectives and nature of retirement accounts suggest normal inclusion as part of the foundation portfolio. In fact, retirement assets can be deployed as part of either the rotational or opportunistic portfolio. In fact, it might make a lot of sense. Why? Because returns generated are tax free, at least until withdrawn. Tax-free returns can compound much faster. Because of the importance of these assets, one should only commit a small portion to an actively managed opportunistic portfolio, but it can be a good way to "juice" the growth of this important asset base.

100 Best Stocks and the Segmented Portfolio

The next natural question is—"So how do I use the *100 Best Stocks* to construct my portfolio tiers?" The answer is really that selections from the *100 Best* list can be used in all tiers, depending on your time horizon and current price relative to value. If you see a stock on the *100 Best* list take a nosedive, and feel that nosedive is out of proportion to the real news and near-term prospects of the company, it may be a candidate for the opportunistic portfolio. If the stock makes sense as a long-term holding (as many on our list do) it's a good candidate for the foundation portfolio. Likewise, if you feel that, say, health-care stocks are, as a group, likely to be in favor and are undervalued now, you can pick off the health-care stocks on the *100 Best* list as a rotational portfolio pick. Similarly, if you feel that large-cap dividend-paying stocks will do well, again you can use the *100 Best* list to feed into this hunch.

Not surprisingly, we feel the *100 Best* stocks are of the highest quality, and can be used with relatively less risk than most other stocks to achieve your objectives.

When to Buy? Consider When to Sell

If it's hard to figure out when to buy a stock, it's even harder to figure out when to sell. People "get married" to their investment decisions, feeling somehow that if it isn't right, maybe time will help, and things will get better. Or they're just too arrogant to admit that they made a mistake. There are lots of reasons why people hold on to investments for too long a time. Here's the fundamental truth: Buying and selling should be much the same process. Let's look at it from the point of view of selling. When should you sell? Simply, when there's something else better to buy. Something else better for future returns, something else better for safety, something else better for timeliness or synchronization with overall business trends. That something else can be another stock, a futures contract, or a house. It can also be cash— sell that stock when . . . when what? When cash is a better investment. Or when you need the money, which is another way of saying that cash is a better investment.

Similarly, if you think of a buy decision as a best possible deployment of capital, as a buy because there's no better way to invest your money, you'll also come out ahead. It really isn't that hard, especially if you've done your homework. And it's also made easier if you avoid rash overcommitments; that is, you avoid buying all at once in case you've made a mistake or in case better prices come later down the road.

Investing for Retirement

Most of us don't invest just for the sake of investing. We're not so much like players at a poker table who not only enjoy winning money but also the process of winning. We're more interested in the result of investing than the process. We may like to invest, like to do research, like to see things come out the way we had in mind. But the main reason we do it is to make money.

And why do we want to make money? Well, for some of us, it's about buying homes, paying for college, or just having a little extra spending money. But for a great many of us, especially those of us for whom there's no defined-benefit pension awaiting us when we retire, we invest because we want a more secure, comfortable retirement years down the road.

So how should you invest for retirement? Should you invest any differently than you would for any of the other objectives we just mentioned? Mostly, investing is investing, and the goal is to make money over the intended period of time one invests. Retirement investing isn't that much different, except there is a greater emphasis on the long term, and for many, a greater need for safety.

The retirement planning process starts with creating a goal, that is, estimating what you will need during retirement to live on. The "what you'll need" is referred to euphemistically as your "number"—an amount that will, with carefully planned withdrawals, service your needs beyond what government (Social Security) and other pensions can cover until you and your spouse die. There are many ways to calculate this "number," and financial advisers have a bag of tricks and fancy spreadsheets. We like to use a permanent withdrawal rate rule of thumb—that is, you can draw down 4 percent of your asset base each year in retirement. So if you need $2,000 a month to live, in addition to amounts furnished by Social Security and pensions, that's $24,000 a year; $24,000 a year is 4 percent of what number (multiply by 25)—that's $960,000 you'll need in your retirement account on Retirement Day 1. This number, however, assumes that market returns are steady and there won't be any severe market corrections during your retirement. The reality is that you can keep withdrawing a constant percentage; it may just be that the base amount, and thus your income, fluctuates. If you must keep your income steady, the 4 percent rule can be jeopardized in down or very volatile markets. You can see how complex the calculation can become.

But that's not the point of reading *100 Best Stocks*—the point is to get some tips on where and how to invest to achieve the number. We offer the following:

- *Stay diversified.* You've read about how Enron shareholders had their entire retirement tied up in company stock. If the company fails, you fail twice. It's probably best to not even invest most of your retirement assets in the same industry you work in. A good portfolio of stocks or funds (seven or so different stocks, three or so different funds) is probably optimal. But don't over-diversify—you can achieve the same returns at a lot less cost by simply buying an index fund.

- *Think long term.* Obvious, right? Well, today's market can bring some serious surprises to those who think they can simply buy and hold forever and capitalize on the growth of the American Way. The trick here is to buy individual companies that you think will not only be around when you retire, but will also be better than they are today. Try to visualize your company 10, 20, or 30 years from now. And be prepared to bail out when things start to not look like you expected. There are a lot of GM shareholders and bondholders who wish they had done just that. The key word is "think."

- *Get at least some dividends.* Future appreciation is nice for retirement, but I believe that a bird in hand is worthwhile, especially if you can reinvest it in the stocks or funds held in your retirement accounts.

And as we've already discussed, dividend raises are important for not only keeping up with inflation but for increasing your total cash returns over time.

- *Dollar cost average.* If you keep reinvesting dividends and/or adding funds to your accounts consistently, you'll buy more shares when prices are low, bringing your average cost down. For most people, it's best to keep retirement contributions—and investments—as consistent as possible.

- *Use a portfolio strategy.* Like the one outlined above—create a strong, steady "foundation" and add some opportunistic investments. The opportunistic investments can be used to stretch returns a bit, and they work better in retirement accounts because capital gains taxes are deferred or avoided altogether. That said, you should opportunistically invest only what you can afford to lose. Most of the *100 Best* stocks are suitable for foundation investments, and a few of the "aggressive growth" entries are good for opportunistic investments as well. Make some rules and stick by them.

When and How to Use an Adviser

To use a professional adviser or not to use a professional adviser. That is the question almost all individual investors ask themselves at one time or another.

Individual investors are independent, self-starting, self-driven folks largely capable of accepting responsibility for their own decisions and actions. That's good, and I assume that if you're reading this book, you have at least some of that character. However, the world isn't so simple, and your time isn't so plentiful, and maybe business and investing stuff just isn't your cup of tea, anyway. You don't want to throw everything over the wall to a professional adviser (and pay the fees and lose control and all that) but you may want some help from time to time.

Just remember this—you, you alone, and ultimately you are responsible for your own finances, just like a pilot flying an airplane is ultimately responsible for what happens to that airplane and its passengers. You are in charge. You are in charge whether or not you have someone else, like a broker or professional adviser, helping you out. You can (and should) think of an adviser as more like a copilot, navigator, or air traffic controller—who will give you information and suggestions and help you interpret the information and remind you of the rules when necessary—but ultimately you're in charge.

Financial advisers come in many forms, and we won't go into the details here. What's important is to realize that no matter how much you outsource, you're still at the helm. You need to develop a good, two-way relationship with the adviser, who can then bring value and help you bring value to the investment decisions and investment strategy. An adviser should neither tell you what to do nor just be the "yes man" for everything you want to do. A lively, point-counterpoint discussion of any financial move with an adviser is healthy; two heads are better than one. Remember, if two people think the exact same way, you don't need one of them.

Don't be snowed by fancy terminology and concepts. Find an adviser who speaks your language—that is, plain English. Smart, experienced people make things simple, not complex, for others.

Also be clear what you want and what you expect from an adviser. Say that you want help constructing your portfolio and learning about, say, the tech and health-care sectors, which you don't know enough about. Ask the adviser to help you understand the headlines and what's important about them for the banking industry. And so forth.

And of course—as Bernard Madoff has made so clear for so many— make sure you understand what they're doing if they're managing anything on your behalf. There is nothing worse than thinking everything is okay when in fact it's completely off in the weeds.

Bottom line, an investment adviser should be a great partner, someone you'd hire into your business if you were trying to create a partnership in the investing business. Look for common sense, look for the adviser to help you most with the things you're least comfortable with. Learn what the adviser does (and has done) with other clients; if it sounds too good to be true, it probably is.

Individual Stocks versus Funds and ETFs

As long as we're sharing opinions on things like financial advisers and other help you can get with your investing, it makes sense to take a short detour into the world of managed investments. What are managed investments? Simply, they are individual investments where some intermediary buys and repackages individual investments, and sells you pieces of that package.

Intermediaries can be investment companies with professional managers choosing specific investments and otherwise looking after the portfolio. They can also be indexes, where groups of like stocks are accumulated into an index according to some sort of generally fixed formula. Either way, by buying into one of these intermediaries, you're giving up picking individual investments in favor of a packaged and sometimes professionally managed approach.

Of course, like any value proposition, you're giving up something in the interest of gaining something else. The "something else" you're trying to gain by using the packaged approach is usually a combination of the following:

- *Time*—you don't have the time to research individual stocks or to research individual stocks for 100 percent of your portfolio.
- *Expertise*—in the case of managed funds, you're getting a trained, experienced, investment professional. Some also prefer to hire others to do the work to take the emotion out of investing decisions.
- *Diversification*—by definition, both managed and index funds spread your investments so that you don't have too much wrapped up in a single company; this is generally good unless they diversify away any chance of outperforming the markets. Funds and ETFs also allow you to play in markets otherwise difficult to play in for lack of knowledge or time, e.g., Asian stocks, networking technology companies, and so on.
- *Convenience*—it takes work to build and manage an investment portfolio. With funds you can move in and out of the markets with a single transaction; the administrative work is taken care of.

Of course, with any value proposition comes a downside, and the downsides of fund and index investing are often underappreciated by prospective clients:

- *Fees*—Not surprisingly, funds, and especially managed funds, charge money for the packaging and services they provide. Actively managed funds can take a half to over 2 percent of your asset value each year, whether they do well or not. If you understand compounding, you know that the difference between a 6 percent return and a 4 percent *net* return over time is huge. Index funds and ETFs are better in this regard, usually charging 0.10 to 0.50 percent, but it still puts a drag on your outcomes.
- *Tax efficiency*—When ordinary mutual funds sell shares, any gains flow through to you (unless you hold them in a tax-free or tax-deferred retirement account). You cannot control when this happens,

and many "active" funds may roll their portfolios frequently, producing adverse tax consequences. Also, you need to watch when you enter the fund—you should buy in after capital gains are paid out, not before, or else you'll be paying for someone else's gains. Index funds and ETFs are far less likely to produce "unwanted" gains, for they tie their investments to the indexes, which don't change much.

- *Control*—With funds of any sort, you lose control, and there are few things more painful than having someone else lose your money for you. Particularly with managed funds, it is almost impossible to know what they are really doing with your money except in hindsight. We would support any initiative requiring funds to give you a more real-time accounting of what they do with *your* funds.

- *Tendency toward mediocrity.* One of the biggest criticisms of funds over time is the tendency for managers to follow each other and to follow standard business-school investing and risk management formulas. The result you tend to get in practice is a herd instinct, known in the trade as an "institutional imperative." You can see this in many funds—pick almost any fund and the top 10 holdings are GE, Microsoft, ExxonMobil—you get the idea. Worse—and this is the biggie from our perspective—when you buy a fund and especially an index fund, you're getting *all* the companies in the industry—the mediocre players, the weak hands—not just the best ones.

So we suggest using funds where it makes sense to get some exposure to an industry or a segment of the market otherwise difficult to access or outside your expertise. Use funds to round out a portfolio or build a foundation or rotational portfolio, and to save yourself the time and bandwidth to focus more closely on other more "opportunistic" investments.

Part II

THE 100 BEST STOCKS TO BUY

The 100 Best Stocks to Buy

Index of Stocks by Category

Company	Symbol	Industry	Sector
—A—			
3M	MMM	Conservative Growth	Industrials
Abbott	ABT	Growth and Income	Health Care
Aetna	AET	Conservative Growth	Health Care
Allergan	AGN	Aggressive Growth	Health Care
Amgen	AMGN	Conservative Growth	Health Care
Apple	AAPL	Aggressive Growth	Consumer Discretionary
Archer Daniels Midland	ADM	Conservative Growth	Consumer Staples
AT&T	T	Growth and Income	Telecommunications Services
Automatic Data Processing	ADP	Conservative Growth	Information Technology
—B—			
Baxter	BAX	Aggressive Growth	Health Care
Becton, Dickinson	BDX	Conservative Growth	Health Care
Bed, Bath & Beyond	BBBY	Aggressive Growth	Retail
—C—			
Campbell Soup	CPB	Conservative Growth	Consumer Staples
CarMax	KMX	Aggressive Growth	Retail
Caterpillar	CAT	Aggressive Growth	Industrials
Chevron	CVX	Growth and Income	Energy
Church & Dwight	CHD	Aggressive Growth	Consumer Staples
Cincinnati Financial	CINF	Income	Financials
Clorox	CLX	Conservative Growth	Consumer Staples
Coca-Cola	KO	Conservative Growth	Consumer Discretionary
Colgate-Palmolive	CL	Conservative Growth	Consumer Staples
Comcast	CMCSA	Aggressive Growth	Telecommunications Services
ConocoPhillips	COP	Growth and Income	Energy
Costco Wholesale	COST	Aggressive Growth	Retail
CVS/Caremark	CVS	Conservative Growth	Retail
—D—			
Deere	DE	Aggressive Growth	Industrials
Dominion Resources	D	Growth and Income	Utilities
Duke Energy	DUK	Income	Utilities
DuPont	DD	Growth and Income	Materials

Index of Stocks by Category (continued)

Company	Symbol	Industry	Sector
—E—			
Eastman Chemical*	EMN	Conservative Growth	Materials
ExxonMobil	XOM	Growth and Income	Energy
—F—			
Fair Isaac	FICO	Aggressive Growth	Business Services
FedEx	FDX	Aggressive Growth	Transportation
Fluor	FLR	Aggressive Growth	Heavy Construction
FMC	FMC	Aggressive Growth	Materials
—G—			
General Mills	GIS	Growth and Income	Consumer Staples
Grainger, W.W.	GWW	Conservative Growth	Industrials
—H—			
Harman International*	HAR	Aggressive Growth	Consumer Discretionary
Heinz	HNZ	Growth and Income	Consumer Staples
Honeywell	HON	Aggressive Growth	Industrials
—I—			
Illinois Tool Works	ITW	Conservative Growth	Industrials
Intel*	INTC	Conservative Growth	Information Technology
IBM	IBM	Conservative Growth	Information Technology
International Paper	IP	Conservative Growth	Materials
Iron Mountain	IRM	Aggressive Growth	Information Technology
Itron*	ITRI	Aggressive Growth	Information Technology
—J—			
Johnson & Johnson	JNJ	Growth and Income	Health Care
Johnson Controls	JCI	Conservative Growth	Industrials
—K—			
Kellogg	K	Growth and Income	Consumer Staples
Kimberly-Clark	KMB	Growth and Income	Consumer Staples
—M—			
Macy's*	M	Aggressive Growth	Retail
Marathon Oil	MRO	Aggressive Growth	Energy
McCormick	MKC	Conservative Growth	Consumer Staples
McDonald's	MCD	Aggressive Growth	Restaurants
McKesson	MCK	Conservative Growth	Health Care
Medtronic	MDT	Aggressive Growth	Health Care

Index of Stocks by Category (continued)

Company	Symbol	Industry	Sector
Molex Inc.*	MOLX	Conservative Growth	Industrials
Monsanto	MON	Aggressive Growth	Industrials
Mosaic*	MOS	Aggressive Growth	Materials
—N—			
NextEra Energy	NEE	Growth and Income	Utilities
NIKE	NKE	Aggressive Growth	Consumer Discretionary
Norfolk Southern	NSC	Conservative Growth	Transportation
Nucor	NUE	Aggressive Growth	Materials
—O—			
Otter Tail	OTTR	Growth and Income	Energy
—P—			
Pall Corporation	PLL	Aggressive Growth	Industrials
Patterson	PDCO	Aggressive Growth	Health Care
Paychex	PAYX	Aggressive Growth	Information Technology
Pepsi	PEP	Conservative Growth	Consumer Staples
Perrigo	PRGO	Aggressive Growth	Health Care
Praxair	PX	Conservative Growth	Materials
Procter & Gamble	PG	Conservative Growth	Consumer Staples
—R—			
Ross Stores	ROST	Aggressive Growth	Retail
—S—			
Schlumberger	SLB	Aggressive Growth	Energy
Seagate Technology*	STX	Aggressive Growth	Information Technology
Sigma-Aldrich	SIAL	Aggressive Growth	Industrials
J. M. Smucker	SJM	Growth and Income	Consumer Staples
Southern Co.	SO	Growth and Income	Utilities
Southwest Airlines	LUV	Conservative Growth	Transportation
St. Jude Medical	STJ	Aggressive Growth	Health Care
Starbucks	SBUX	Aggressive Growth	Restaurant
Stryker	SYK	Aggressive Growth	Health Care
Suburban Propane	SPH	Income	Utilities
Sysco	SYY	Conservative Growth	Consumer Staples
—T—			
Target	TGT	Aggressive Growth	Retail
Teva Pharmaceuticals	TEVA	Aggressive Growth	Health Care
Tiffany*	TIF	Aggressive Growth	Retail

Index of Stocks by Category (continued)

Company	Symbol	Industry	Sector
Time Warner Inc*	TWX	Conservative Growth	Entertainment
Total S.A.	TOT	Growth and Income	Energy
Tractor Supply	TSCO	Aggressive Growth	Retail
—U—			
Union Pacific	UNP	Conservative Growth	Transportation
UnitedHealth Group	UNH	Aggressive Growth	Health Care
United Parcel Service*	UPS	Conservative Growth	Transportation
United Technologies	UTX	Conservative Growth	Industrials
—V—			
Valero*	VLO	Aggressive Growth	Energy
Valmont	VMI	Aggressive Growth	Industrials
Verizon	VZ	Growth and Income	Telecommunications Services
Visa	V	Aggressive Growth	Financials
—W—			
Waste Management*	WM	Growth and Income	Business Services
Wells Fargo	WFC	Growth and Income	Financials
Whirlpool*	WHR	Conservative Growth	Consumer Durables

* New addition to the list

CONSERVATIVE GROWTH

3M Company

Ticker symbol: MMM (NYSE) □ S&P rating: AA– □ Value Line financial strength rating: A++ □ Current yield: 2.6% □ Dividend raises, past 10 years: 10

Company Profile

The 3M Company, originally known as the Minnesota Mining and Manufacturing Co., is now a $30 billion diversified manufacturing technology company with leading positions in industrial, consumer and office, health care, safety, electronics, telecommunications, and other markets. The company has operations in more than 60 countries and serves customers in nearly 200 countries. The company has such a broad reach that it is often looked to as a general indicator for the health of the world economy and has served that role well during the roller coaster ride of the past 5 years.

3M's operations are divided into 6 segments, approximate revenue percentages in parentheses:

- The Industrial and Transportation segment (32 percent) produces industrial tapes, a wide variety of abrasives, adhesives, specialty materials, filtration products, and products for the separation of fluids and gases. They supply markets such as paper and packaging, food and beverage, electronics, automotive (OEM), and the automotive aftermarket.
- The Health Care segment (17 percent) serves markets that

include medical clinics and hospitals, pharmaceuticals, dental and orthodontic practitioners, and health information systems. Products and services include medical and surgical supplies, skin health and infection prevention products, drug delivery systems, dental and orthodontic products, health information systems, and antimicrobial solutions.

- The Safety, Security, and Protection Services segment (12 percent) serves a broad range of markets that increase the safety, security, and productivity of workers, facilities, and systems. Major product offerings include personal protection, safety and security products, energy control products, building cleaning and protection products, track and trace solutions, and roofing granules for asphalt shingles.
- The Consumer and Office segment (14 percent) serves markets that include retail, home improvement, building maintenance, and other markets. Products in this segment include office supply products such as the familiar tapes and Post-it notes, stationery products, construction and home improvement

products, home care products, protective material products, and consumer health-care products. This segment will grow considerably with the acquisition of the Avery-Dennison office products line, noted below.

- The Display and Graphics segment (15 percent) serves markets that include electronic display, traffic safety, and commercial graphics. This segment includes optical film solutions for electronic displays, computer screen filters, reflective sheeting for transportation safety, commercial graphics systems, and projection systems, including mobile display technology and visual systems products.
- The Electro and Communications segment (11 percent) serves the electrical, electronics, and communications industries, including electric utilities. Products include electronic and interconnect solutions, microinterconnect systems, high-performance fluids, high-temperature and display tapes, telecommunications products, electrical products, and touch screens and touch monitors.

The company has been on an acquisition tear recently, capped off by its early January 2012 announcement of the acquisition of the Avery-Dennison office and consumer products business for $550 million, to close out the second half of 2012. The well-known "Avery labels" are the flagship product of this group, but it markets a broad range of products for the office and education markets. The group should fit well with—and bring scale to—the existing Consumer and Office segment. Other acquisitions during 2011: Alpha Beta Enterprise Co. Ltd., a manufacturer of box sealing tape and masking tape; Hybrivet Systems Inc., a provider of instant-read products to detect lead and other contaminants and toxins; Original Wraps Inc., a company specializing in the creative business development, technology, and design of personalization platforms for vehicles and vehicle accessories; and GPI Group, a manufacturer and marketer of home improvement products such as tapes, hooks, insulation, and floor protection products.

Financial Highlights, Fiscal Year 2011

The company reported revenue of $29.611 billion in fiscal 2011, a bit softer than some analysts had hoped for due mostly to generally soft world economic conditions and some softness in the highly competitive electronics and communications segment. That said, earnings slightly exceeded expectations at $5.90/share. Acquisitions, notably of the Avery-Dennison business, and management's projected 2–5 percent organic growth estimates bring FY2012 estimates close to $31 billion in sales and $6.25 to $6.50 per share in earnings. The 2–5 percent growth is down somewhat from previous years, but it is still healthy for a company of this size and could go higher if the economic recovery picks up steam.

Reasons to Buy

3M manufactures a broad line of products for end user markets—and for other manufacturing activities. We like the combination of manufacturing reach, innovation, and international presence (two-thirds of sales are overseas). The company makes many steady-selling products essential to manufacturing and day-to-day operations of other companies and organizations, and seemingly essential to most of us, e.g., Post-it notes and Scotch tape.

Aside from the attraction of the business itself, 3M offers a good combination of stability and innovation; financials are solid while adding a better than average growth prospect through its own innovations and expansion in overseas markets.

The company just announced a dividend increase to $0.59 quarterly; such increases have happened in each of the past 10 years, and the size of those increases is growing. If you look at the chart, the stock price has not kept up with the steady march forward in dividends and earnings; we think there is some potential left on the table with a Post-it note saying, "Buy me, stupid!"

Reasons for Caution

3M is somewhat exposed to business cycles, and slowdowns in global manufacturing activity have tended to lead to down cycles in the share price. For the most part, these dips have proven to be buying opportunities. There is a risk that 3M may continue to acquire aggressively if internal growth stalls.

SECTOR: **Industrials**
BETA COEFFICIENT: **.87**
10-YEAR COMPOUND EARNINGS PER SHARE GROWTH: **9.0%**
10-YEAR COMPOUND DIVIDENDS PER SHARE GROWTH: **6.0%**

	2004	2005	2006	2007	2008	2009	2010	2011
Revenues (Mil)	20,011	21,167	22,293	24,462	25,269	23,123	26,662	29,611
Net Income (Mil)	2,403	3,111	3,851	4,096	3,460	3,193	4,189	4,250
Earnings per share	3.75	3.98	5.06	5.6	4.89	4.52	5.75	5.90
Dividends per share	1.44	1.68	1.84	1.92	2.00	2.04	2.10	2.20
Cash flow per share	5.07	5.55	6.71	7.29	6.65	6.15	7.43	7.85
Price: high	90.3	87.4	88.4	97	84.8	84.3	91.5	96.2
low	73.3	69.7	67	72.9	50	40.9	68.0	63.6

3M Center
St. Paul, MN 55144–1000
(651) 733-8206
Website: *www.3m.com*

GROWTH AND INCOME

Abbott Laboratories

Ticker symbol: ABT (NYSE) ❑ S&P rating: AA ❑ Value Line financial strength rating: A++ ❑ Current yield: 3.4% ❑ Dividend raises, past 10 years: 10

Company Profile

For many years "A Promise for Life" has been the slogan of Abbott Laboratories, founded in 1888 and one of the most diverse health-care manufacturers in the world. Abbott is the third-largest producer of pharmaceuticals in the United States, behind Johnson & Johnson and Pfizer, and is the largest company in the nutritional products market. The company's products are sold in more than 130 countries, with about 40 percent of sales derived from international operations. Abbott's major business segments include Pharmaceutical Products (particularly in immunology, cardiology, and infectious diseases), Diagnostic Products (laboratory and molecular diagnostics, diabetes and vision care), Vascular Products (stents and closure devices), and Nutritional Products (infant, adult, and special needs). Pharmaceuticals accounted for about 56.5 percent of FY2010 sales.

But that's all about to change. We're not sure what will happen with the slogan, but by 2013 Abbott will be split into two companies—one to produce and market proprietary pharmaceuticals, and the other to produce and market the broad line of medical products and supplies made up of the current Diagnostic, Vascular, and Nutritional products businesses. The latter segment will retain the Abbott name.

The idea is to unlock shareholder value mainly by bringing more attention to the less glamorous diversified medical products business and insulating it from the ups and downs of the pharma business. The two businesses have different growth, financial, and marketing profiles; independence should help them along. It's not unlike what's happening with some integrated oil companies, like ConocoPhillips and Marathon (both on our *100 Best Stocks* list), separating out R&D-intensive exploration and production components into separate companies.

Currently, Abbott's leading brands include Freestyle (diabetes monitoring), Ensure (nutritional supplements for adults), Humira (rheumatoid arthritis), and Similac (infant formula).

The company has widespread respect among the medical and financial community as one of the most solid and diversified health-related names, as well as one of the most innovative in the industry.

Financial Highlights, Fiscal Year 2011

Abbott turned in solid results for 2011 with another low double-digit growth revenue performance, with solid gains in operating margins, earnings, cash flow, and dividends. The company announced another dividend increase, to $0.48 quarterly, in early 2012. Interestingly, the relatively smaller Diagnostics (10.8 percent of FY10 sales), Nutritional (15.7 percent), and Vascular (9.1 percent) segments have been the real growth drivers recently, while the pharmaceuticals business has been dominated by a few lower-growth giants like Humira. Growth in some of those blockbusters is slowing, while at the same time the medical products segments are doing well, especially in overseas markets. The planned split will bring more attention to these segments.

Reasons to Buy

Our Abbott write-up used to be pretty simple to update. Feather in the latest growth figures, all else was fairly steady-state. True, the company continues to be a solid performer and is well diversified

both in product line and in geography. Now we have the planned split, and while the split requires some attention, it should only serve to unlock value while keeping fundamental return components like earnings, cash flow, and dividends intact. The company continues to invest over 10 percent of sales in R&D and appears to get good results from those investments. Not only does Abbott bring an attractive combination of income and growth potential, but it is almost recession-proof and carries a sleep-at-night beta of only 0.31, meaning it largely ignores market gyrations. ABT has paid consecutive quarterly dividends since 1924 and has raised the dividend in each of the past 10 years.

Reasons for Caution

Major reorganizations and restructurings often bring some complexities and doubt; we'll see what happens here. Also to watch are the expirations of patents, for instance, Humira in 2016. One must always watch politics and belt-tightening efforts in the health-care sector. Finally, recent price performance may have already reflected some of the benefits of the split, so investors should look for favorable entry points.

SECTOR: **Health Care**
BETA COEFFICIENT: **.31**
10-YEAR COMPOUND EARNINGS PER SHARE GROWTH: **8.0%**
10-YEAR COMPOUND DIVIDENDS PER SHARE GROWTH: **9.0%**

	2004	**2005**	**2006**	**2007**	**2008**	**2009**	**2010**	**2011**
Revenues (Mil)	19,680	22,337	22,476	25,914	29,528	30,764	35,167	39,000
Net Income (Mil)	3,522	3,908	3,841	4,429	4,734	5,745	6,500	7,290
Earnings per share	2.27	2.50	2.52	2.84	3.03	3.69	4.17	4.65
Dividends per share	1.04	1.10	1.18	1.30	1.44	1.60	1.76	1.88
Cash flow per share	3.05	3.42	3.51	4.05	4.32	5.00	5.90	6.60
Price: high	47.6	50.0	49.9	59.5	61.1	57.4	56.8	56.4
low	38.3	37.5	39.2	48.8	45.8	41.3	44.6	45.1

Abbott Laboratories
100 Abbott Park Road
Abbott Park, IL 60064–6400
(847) 937-6100
Website: *www.abbott.com*

CONSERVATIVE GROWTH

Aetna Inc.

Ticker symbol: AET (NYSE) ❑ S&P rating: A+ ❑ Value Line financial strength rating: A ❑ Current yield: 1.5% ❑ Dividend raises, past 10 years: 2

Company Profile

Founded in 1853, Aetna is one of the nation's longest-lived insurers. However, that by itself doesn't qualify the company for our *100 Best Stocks* list. Today's Aetna, a product of a 1996 merger between Aetna Life and Casualty and U.S. Healthcare, is one of the largest and most important diversified health-care, insurance, and benefits companies in the United States.

Today, the company has three businesses operated in three divisions. Health Care provides a full assortment of health benefit plans for corporate, small business, and individual customers, including PPO, HMO, point of service, vision care, dental, behavioral health Medicare/Medicaid, and pharmacy benefits plans. The Group Insurance business provides group term life, disability, and accidental death and dismemberment insurance products primarily to the same sort of businesses that might sign up for its health plans. The Large Case Pensions business administers pension plans for certain existing customers. The health-care business is by far the largest segment and the focal point of our selection of this

company. The business insures some 35 million individuals. Now with impending health-care reforms, many of which are targeted at the insurance side of the industry, it would normally be hard to recommend such a company because of the uncertainty going forward and the general public dislike of health insurers. However, Aetna has proven itself to be a pacesetter among insurance providers, mainly through its support and innovations in the area of consumer-directed health care.

For example, with Aetna's consumer-directed HealthFund plans, subscribers become responsible for a portion of their own health-care costs and are given the tools to shop for health-care alternatives and maximize preventive care. Aetna originally led the way with some of the first Health Savings Account–compatible products in 2001. Since then the company has led the industry in developing tools, such as the Aetna Navigator price transparency tool designed to help patients evaluate the cost and outcomes of procedures in different geographies. The company also has championed patient- and doctor-accessible medical records and other techniques for making health care delivery more efficient. These initiatives are meant not only to save money for end users, but also the businesses purchasing insurance plans; the company estimates a savings of $21.5 million per 10,000 customers over five years. Aetna has made a series of small acquisitions to broaden its offering and streamline processes, including Medicity, Inc. a health information exchange company (January 2011); Prodigy Health Group, a third-party administrator of self-funded health-care plans (June 2011); Genworth Financial, Inc.'s Medicare Supplement business; and PayFlex Holdings, Inc., an independent account-based health plan administrator, the last two in October 2011.

Financial Highlights, Fiscal Year 2011

Improved "utilization"—that is, the reduction of the amount and cost of health care provided per subscriber—has taken hold over the past few years, probably both as a result of direct management, process improvements, and a general pattern of cost consciousness among both consumers and providers. That improved utilization reduces costs and drops straight to the bottom line, allowing Aetna to earn $5.15 a share, a 36 percent increase over FY2010 and the first time the company has exceeded even $4.00 a share. Besides utilization, one factor was a drop of almost 10 percent of outstanding shares to 350 million through repurchases. Financially the company is clicking on all cylinders, and while share repurchases will continue, the company is cautious about the sustained rally, calling for FY2012 EPS of $5.00.

Reasons to Buy

We feel that Aetna is ahead of the pack in terms of both business and technology innovation. Not only has this edge started to pay off in terms of increased utilization and profitability, it will also serve the company well going forward as it aligns the business to upcoming health-care reforms. Many of the innovations the company has championed will also get a favorable ruling in the court of public opinion, which should help. The company has a solid brand and financials. Relatively recently it has committed to paying a healthier dividend, indicated at 70 cents for 2012, and the company expanded its share buyback program again, having already reduced its share count from 610 million in 2003 to 350 million recently. Shareholder returns are in clear focus.

Reasons for Caution

Public and governmental scrutiny of health insurers has never been higher, and the burgeoning of health-care costs is difficult for even a company of Aetna's caliber to manage. It may become more difficult to pass cost increases on, and the cost of health insurance is simply knocking many potentially lucrative subscribers out of the market. Aetna investors will have to pay attention to ongoing and occasionally disruptive industry change.

SECTOR: **Health Care**
BETA COEFFICIENT: **1.26**
10-YEAR COMPOUND EARNINGS PER SHARE GROWTH: **16.0%**
10-YEAR COMPOUND DIVIDENDS PER SHARE GROWTH: **NM**

	2004	2005	2006	2007	2008	2009	2010	2011
Revenues (Mil)	19,904	22,492	25,146	27,600	30,951	34,765	34,246	33,700
Net income (Mil)	1,215	1,344	1,602	1,842	1,922	1,236	1,555	1,850
Earnings per share	1.76	2.23	2.82	3.49	3.93	2.75	3.68	5.15
Dividends per share	.01	.02	.04	.04	.04	.04	.04	0.45
Cash flow per share	2.38	2.73	3.63	4.36	5.07	3.83	5.20	6.25
Price: high	31.9	49.7	52.5	60.0	59.8	34.9	36.0	46.0
low	16.4	29.9	30.9	40.3	14.2	16.7	25.0	30.6

Aetna, Inc.
151 Farmington Avenue
Hartford, CT 17405–0872
(860) 273-0123
Website: *www.aetna.com*

AGGRESSIVE GROWTH

Allergan, Inc.

Ticker symbol: AGN (NYSE) ❑ S&P rating: A+ ❑ Value Line financial strength rating: A+ ❑ Current yield: 0.2% ❑ Dividend raises, past 10 years: 1

Company Profile

Allergan is a health-care products company making pharmaceutical, over-the-counter, and medical device items for the ophthalmic, neurological, dermatological, and urologic fields as well as for use in an assortment of aesthetic medical procedures such as breast aesthetics and obesity intervention, and other specialty medical markets. The company was founded in 1977 and originally marketed ophthalmic products for contact lens wearers and other products for eye inflammation and other disorders.

The company operates in two segments. The Specialty Pharmaceuticals segment markets the ophthalmic products, including contact lens products, glaucoma therapy, artificial tears, and allergy- and infection-fighting products. Brand names include Restasis, Lumigan, Refresh, Alphagan, and Acuvail among others.

Specialty Pharmaceuticals also sells Botox for a variety of medical conditions and for aesthetic use. Botox is used not only for the familiar skin wrinkle therapies, but also for neuromuscular disorders; recently it has been approved for use in treating chronic migraines, a new market with substantial potential. It has also been approved for an overactive bladder condition. In total, with these approvals, the "therapeutic" side of the Botox business (in contrast to the "cosmetic") is quite healthy; total Botox-related revenues are expected to grow at least 10 percent in FY2012 and perhaps more as these treatments become mainstream. The segment also offers a number of popular skincare and acne medications for both acute care and aesthetic use, including acne care, psoriasis, and eyelash enhancement. Brand names include Aczone and Tazorac for acne and psoriasis, Vivite for aging skin care, and Latisse for eyelashes.

The Medical Devices Segment makes and markets breast implants for augmentation, revision, and reconstructive surgery. Obesity intervention products include the "lap-band" system and the Orbera Intragastic Balloon System. The segment also markets other skin and tissue regenerative products for aesthetic and reconstructive purposes for burn treatment and other traumas.

The approximate FY2011 business breakdown by revenue, almost unchanged from FY2010, is 47 percent eye care, 30 percent neuromuscular including Botox, 11 percent breast and facial implants, 6 percent obesity implants, 1 percent urological, and 5 percent other. Foreign sales account for about 39 percent of the total, up from 35 percent in FY2010.

Financial Highlights, Fiscal Year 2011

The company reported broad sales gains in FY2011, with revenues up approximately 10 percent to $5.3 billion and per share earnings up about 8 percent to $3.41 per share. Excluding one-time charges, earnings would have been about $3.65 per share, a 16 percent gain. The only "soft" spot in the company report was the obesity control Lap Band devices, which are facing some public opinion headwinds as well as—like many Allergan treatments—being excluded from insurance coverage. The Botox and eye-care businesses look particularly strong for FY2011, boosted by an aggressive international expansion (overseas sales are on a double-digit growth trajectory in all regions). Sales are projected at about $5.8 billion, with per share earnings in the $4.13–$4.19 range, a 22 percent gain based on the midpoint.

Reasons to Buy

Allergan tends to be more economically sensitive and cyclical than other pharmaceutical and medical products companies because much of what they sell supports cosmetic, thus elective, and thus cash-paid (in contrast to insurance-paid) procedures. Of course, this is a negative when the economy is soft, although the company sells enough regularly required products such as eye-care products to not be hurt too much by bad times. We like the issue because it will do especially well in good times. Further, with aging and demographics we see a greater trend toward taking care of personal aesthetics through cosmetic procedures. At the same time, new technologies such as a "cohesive-gel" breast implant and others means that taking care of such issues is becoming safer, easier, and more mainstream, a trend that should make the business stronger going forward. New uses for Botox, such as the migraine treatments, overactive bladder symptoms, and others are also promising. We also like the prospects in overseas markets as treatments become available for a growing (and aging) middle class.

Reasons for Caution

All pharmaceutical and medical device products come with an inherent risk of short- and long-term failure with painful financial and brand-image consequences. Cosmetic devices could be even more vulnerable—witness what happened to Dow Corning with breast implants in the 1970s. Among pharmaceutical companies, Allergan is unique; that is what we like about it, but it could also end up being what we don't like about it, if a protracted legal battle is encountered or its treatments fall out of favor. We also think the time will come soon, if not already, to give more back to the shareholders in terms of dividend and/or share repurchases; the stock price has continued strong and may have outpaced the company's prospects; at recent prices the company doesn't have much room for error. In fact, as a new *100 Best* stock for the 2012 list, it had a pleasing 19.2 percent gain for the year, but we considered removing it from the list based on its success and questions about whether it can continue. We don't like to remove companies from the list after only one year—especially because of good news. Upshot: Pick your buying opportunities carefully.

SECTOR: **Health Care**
BETA COEFFICIENT: **.82**
10-YEAR COMPOUND EARNINGS PER SHARE GROWTH:**14.5%**
10-YEAR COMPOUND DIVIDENDS PER SHARE GROWTH: **2.5%**

		2004	2005	2006	2007	2008	2009	2010	2011
Revenues (Mil)		2,046	2,318	3,063	3,939	4,403	4,503	4,883	5,347
Net income (Mil)		371	477	452	575	786	850	975	1,057
Earnings per share		1.39	1.78	1.51	1.86	2.57	2.78	3.16	3.41
Dividends per share		0.18	0.20	0.20	0.20	0.20	0.20	0.20	0.20
Cash flow per share		1.67	2.07	1.98	2.58	3.46	3.65	4.03	4.29
Price:	high	46.3	56.3	61.5	68.1	70.4	64.1	74.9	89.3
	low	33.4	34.5	46.3	52.5	29.0	35.4	56.3	68.0

Allergan, Inc.
2525 Dupont Drive
Irvine, CA 92612
(714) 246-4500
Website: *www.allergan.com*

Amgen Inc.

Ticker symbol: AMGN (NASDAQ) ▫ S&P rating: A+ ▫ Value Line financial strength rating: A++ ▫ Current yield: 2.1% ▫ Dividend raises, past 10 years: 2

Company Profile

Founded in 1980, Amgen is the world's largest and one of the first independent biotech medicines company. The company develops medicines and therapeutics based on advances in cellular and molecular biology, mainly for grievous or chronic illnesses such as cancer, kidney disease, rheumatoid arthritis, bone disease, inflammation, nephrology, and others.

Interestingly, the company generates most of its approximately $15 billion in revenues each year with nine major products, most of which you won't have heard of unless you have one of these diseases or are in the medical profession: Aranesp, Enbrel, Epogen, Neulasia, Neupogen, Nplate, Prolia, Sinsipar, and Vectibix. The explanations of these products are far too technical for most of us to comprehend. Witness, per company literature describing its products, "Neulasta (pegfulgrastim), a pegylated protein based on the Filgrastim molecule, and Neupogen (Filgrastim) a recombinant-methionyl human granulocyte colony-stimulating factor, (G-SCF),

both [of which] stimulate the production of neutrophils (a type of white blood cell that helps the body fight infection)."

Get that? We didn't either, really. Ordinarily we'd be reluctant to recommend a company with only nine major products—products we don't really understand—in such an R&D-intensive business and changing technology. But Amgen is an exception—maybe an exception for biotech in general—because it has turned these products into a cash machine. The company earned about $4.6 billion on that $15 billion in sales with about $6 billion in cash flow and $18 billion in cash on the balance sheet—not bad for a limited product assortment.

While the company continues to invest heavily—almost 20 percent of revenues—in R&D, it has also in the past few years shifted its focus to shareholder returns. Dividends were initiated in FY2011 at $1.12 per share annually; that figure was just increased to $1.44 annually. Share buybacks have reduced share counts from 1.224 billion in 2005 to a present-day 870 million.

Financial Highlights, Fiscal Year 2011

FY2011 revenues came in at just over $15.5 billion, 3 percent higher than FY2010 and matching the previous year's increase. Earnings came in at $5.20 per share, again just slightly ahead of FY2010. Both figures were affected by the new health-care reform legislation. Those numbers sound modest, but management now projects FY2012 revenues in the $16.1 to $16.5 billion range, with earnings in the $5.90 to $6.15 range, both healthy increases. These increases reflect a few modest acquisitions and development partnerships and greater acceptance of their major product offerings. They also reflect growth in developing markets. The company has several new products in late-stage development, mainly in oncological, inflammatory, and metabolic disease categories.

Reasons to Buy

Amgen is regarded as the dominant player in this biotech niche, and has had success with R&D and approval processes thus far. Even with recent share price increases, the P/E is hovering in the 11 to 13 range, and with a net profit margin of 30 percent, the company generates huge volumes of cash, especially when bulges of late-stage R&D expense pass as is happening now. As mentioned earlier, the company is placing much more emphasis on current shareholder return through dividends and share buybacks. Not only does this juice up total returns, but it also reduces the temptation to make costly acquisitions. Amgen is an unusual example of current value combined with a technology expertise and leadership giving strong growth potential for a next leg upward.

Reasons for Caution

With so much R&D and other expense going into a handful of products, any failure or FDA rejection can be very costly. The company is huge, but as with any biotech, fortunes can change quickly and in ways that may be difficult for lay investors to comprehend. The company, as mentioned, faces some impact from the new health-care reform legislation, and initiatives to reduce health-care costs could affect Amgen. And, we normally shy away from companies whose products we don't understand.

SECTOR: **Health Care**
BETA COEFFICIENT: **0.44**
10-YEAR COMPOUND EARNINGS PER SHARE GROWTH: **17.0%**
10-YEAR COMPOUND DIVIDENDS PER SHARE GROWTH: **NA**

	2004	2005	2006	2007	2008	2009	2010	2011
Revenues (Mil)	10,550	12,420	14,268	14,771	15,093	14,642	15,053	15,500
Net income (Mil)	2,885	3,710	4,181	3,761	4,196	4,931	4,941	4,680
Earnings per share	2.19	2.95	3.51	3.31	3.90	4.83	5.12	5.20
Dividends per share	—	—	—	—	—	—	—	1.12
Cash flow per share	2.87	3.72	4.41	4.57	5.03	6.01	6.39	6.60
Price: high	66.9	86.9	81.2	76.9	86.5	64.8	61.3	61.5
low	52.0	56.2	63.5	46.2	39.2	45.0	50.3	47.7

Amgen Inc.
One Amgen Center Drive
Thousand Oaks, CA 91320
(805) 447-1000
Website: *www.amgen.com*

Apple Inc.

Ticker symbol: AAPL (NASDAQ) ❑ S&P rating: not rated ❑ Value Line financial strength rating: A++ ❑ Current yield: Nil ❑ Dividend raises, past 10 years: NM

Company Profile

Riddle: I am a 35-year-old American corporation. I was worth $3 billion in total market value in 1997. I grew through and beyond the dot.com bust at a healthy clip, tripling in value to almost $10 billion in 2003. Not bad, you say. But paltry by comparison to what I've done since. In the 9 years since 2003, my market value has increased some 56-fold to $560 billion, well over $150 billion larger than my nearest rival, ExxonMobil.

Who am I?

The figures may surprise, but you probably guessed it anyway: Apple, Inc. Apple designs, manufactures, and markets personal computers, tablet computers, portable music players, cell phones, and related software, peripherals, downloadable content, and services. It sells these products through its own retail stores, online stores, and third-party and value-added resellers. The company also sells a variety of third-party compatible products such as printers, storage devices, and other accessories through its online and retail stores, and digital content through its iTunes store.

The company's products have become household names: the iPhone, iPod, iPad, and MacBook are just some of the company's hardware products. And while the software may be less well known, iTunes, QuickTime, OSX, and the emerging iCloud are important segments of the business, each with their own revenue streams.

The company was incorporated in 1977 as Apple Computer but has since changed its name to simply Apple. The name change in 2007 was the last step in a 10-year retooling that had already changed the company from a personal computer also-ran into one of the most recognizable and profitable consumer electronics brands in the world.

It's hard to imagine the current consumer tech landscape without Apple's presence at the top of the heap. Their product line, while comparatively narrow, is focused on areas where the user interface is highly valued. Apple has leveraged this focus on the user experience into a business that is far and away the most profitable in the industry.

Enhancing the user experience is the industrial design. The Apple design ethic is extraordinarily well executed and is a large part of the value proposition for every product they release. Many of Apple's customers are uncomfortable with any tech product *not* designed around Apple's common content management interface, and those interfaces are becoming more mainstream and more ubiquitous among loyal audiences everywhere.

Apple has become a case study in creating extraordinary value through innovation, innovative leadership, and marketing excellence. But while wildly successful, the company has come upon a test anticipated for some time, the passing of Steve Jobs in October 2011. Steve was clearly the driving and leading force in Apple's innovation, style, and success (for more on this leadership style, we refer you to co-author Peter Sander's recent book *What Would Steve Jobs Do?*). It remains to be seen if the momentum can be maintained in the absence of this unique guiding light.

Financial Highlights, Fiscal Year 2011

Apple continued to be successful on all fronts in FY2011. The rapid adoption of the iPad, the iPad2, and the iPhone 4 and 4S models drove a massive 66 percent revenue increase in 2011 with an 83 percent EPS increase to $27.89 per share. Operating margins increased again

to 32.9 percent, some 10 full percentage points higher than in 2009. While there was a minor slowing in earnings during the FY2011 fourth quarter (ending September), it appears this was largely due to postponement of iPhone purchases anticipating the iPhone 4S rollout—not a decrease in demand. Such bumps will occur occasionally and were repeated with the recent iPad3 release as well. The size and growth in these numbers go a long way toward justifying the high stock valuation, so long as things continue along this path. In fact, Apple's 10-year earnings growth has risen to 43 percent, a stunning figure when you consider the size of the company and the power of compounding. Sales and earnings growth are expected to moderate somewhat in 2012, back to a 30 percent range more typical prior to 2011.

Reasons to Buy

It's hard to argue with the kind of success Apple has experienced, and it looks like the formula continues to be in place. The stock touched $600 in March 2012, high but not excessive given the implied P/E in the 15 to 20 range and the growth rates. Not to mention customer acceptance, growing margins, and so forth. The big question is, "What's next?" The iPod, iPhone, and iPad were revolutionary new product platform launches creating or dominating whatever markets existed at the time. Can Apple repeat these successes? Or is its destiny tied to refinements and enhancements of these products, with the usual evolution to cost-cutting "strategies" and overloaded bureaucracies that typically follow? It only remains to be seen what other markets, like home TV and home theater, it chooses to get into. If it redefines digital video the way it redefined digital audio, look out.

Finally, back to basics, the company has accumulated a huge cash hoard, and in early 2012 it finally started to pay some of it out in the form of a $2.65 per share dividend and a stock buyback. How they carry these cash disbursements forward remains to be seen.

Reasons for Caution

When you're the biggest, the brightest, and the best, and you lose your leader, there's always room for caution. Steve Jobs was vehemently on the side of the customer, vehemently against the usual risk-averse bureaucracies that eventually strangle almost all businesses, and vehemently for clean, innovative designs for his products. On top of that, he was an extremely tough act to follow as a spokesperson. Can Tim Cook and his team measure up to the task? The demise of Jobsian leadership—and the long price run-up—are the biggest risk factors going forward.

SECTOR: **Consumer Discretionary**
BETA COEFFICIENT: **1.25**
10-YEAR COMPOUND EARNINGS PER SHARE GROWTH: **43%**
10-YEAR COMPOUND DIVIDENDS PER SHARE GROWTH: **Nil**

		2004	2005	2006	2007	2008	2009	2010	2011
Revenues (Mil)		8,279	13,931	19,315	24,006	32,479	36,537	65,225	108,249
Net Income (Mil)		276	1,254	1,989	3,496	4,834	5,704	14,013	25,992
Earnings per share		0.36	1.44	2.27	3.93	5.36	6.29	15.15	27.89
Dividends per share		0	0	0	0	0	0	0	0
Cash flow per share		0.54	1.72	2.59	4.37	5.97	7.12	16.42	29.85
Price:	high	34.8	75.5	93.2	203.0	200.3	214	326.7	426.7
	low	10.6	31.3	50.2	81.9	79.1	78.2	190.3	310.5

Apple Inc.
1 Infinite Loop
Cupertino, CA 95014
(408) 996-1010
Website: *www.apple.com*

Archer Daniels Midland Co.

Ticker symbol: ADM (NYSE) ❑ S&P rating: A ❑ Value Line financial strength rating: A ❑ Current yield: 2.2% ❑ Dividend raises, past 10 years: 10

Company Profile

ADM is one of the largest food processors in the world. It buys corn, wheat, cocoa, oilseeds, and other agricultural products and processes them into food, food ingredients, animal feed and ingredients, and biofuels. It also resells grains on the open market. Rather than the finished consumer products most food processors are known for, ADM produces and distributes intermediate components for food product manufacture and is the largest publicly traded company in this business by far. Among the more important products are vegetable oils, protein meal and components, corn sweeteners, flour, biodiesel, ethanol, and other food and animal feed ingredients. Foreign sales make up about 47 percent of total revenue.

The company is highly vertically integrated and owns and maintains facilities used throughout the production process. It sources raw materials from 60 countries on 6 continents, transports them to any of their 230 processing plants via their own extensive sea/rail/road network, and then transports the finished products to the customer.

The company operates in three business segments: Oilseeds Processing (33 percent of FY2011 sales), Corn Processing (12 percent), and Agricultural Services (47 percent). The Oilseeds Processing unit processes soybeans, cottonseed, sunflower, canola, peanuts, and flaxseed into vegetable oils and protein meals for the food and feed industries. Crude vegetable oils are sold as is or are further refined into consumer products, while partially refined oils are sold for use in paints, chemicals, and other industrial products. The solids remaining from this processing are sold for a number of applications, including edible soy protein, animal feed, pharmaceuticals, chemical, and paper.

The Corn Processing segment milling operations (primarily in the United States) produce food products too numerous to list, but include syrup, starch, glucose, dextrose, and other sweeteners. Markets served include animal feeds and the vegetable oil market. Fermentation of the dextrose yields ethanol, amino acids, and other specialty food and feed products. The ethanol is processed for beverage stock or industrial use as the base for ethanol-blended gasoline and other fuels.

The Agricultural Services segment is the company's storage and transportation network. This business is primarily engaged in buying, storing, cleaning, and transporting grains to/from ADM facilities and for export. It also resells raw materials into the animal feed and agricultural processing industries.

Financial Highlights, Fiscal Year 2011

Fueled by worldwide demand for food products and biofuels, leading to increases in both prices and volumes, ADM has been on a roll for the past five years, with revenues, earnings, dividends, cash flows, and book value all turning in healthy double-digit increases. FY2011 was particularly strong on the revenues front, reflecting price increases and a few acquisitions. Due to increased input costs, earnings growth lagged behind both the previous year and the strong 20.5 percent 10-year earnings growth average. Most estimates continue to suggest a P/E ratio in the range of 9 to 11 and a price to cash-flow ratio between 6 and 7, solid figures for a strong player in this key agricultural business.

Reasons to Buy

Core businesses are strong and growing, and China, India, Eastern Europe, and other emerging market growth will be particularly strong. The company is and has been a strong player in the biofuels industry. While there are some uncertainties (discussed below) the company's experience and scale in ethanol and biodiesel are strong positives. The federal government recently paved the way to raising ethanol content in motor fuel from 10 percent to 15 percent. This business tends to do well when energy prices escalate, as they have recently. We like the solid track record for growth in dividends and overall shareholder value, which appears to be lagged by the growth in share price.

ADM continues to make small acquisitions, most in the emerging markets of Asia, South America, and Eastern Europe. Sales growth outside the United States has far outpaced domestic growth, and ADM's presence and extensive transportation capability give it a decided advantage over its smaller competitors, many of which are focused only in certain markets or certain industries. ADM's market and geographic breadth reduce its exposure to both climatic and political variables, and overall, we think solid plays in the "food chain" are a good place to be.

Reasons for Caution

ADM is heavily invested in the corn-ethanol-fuel processing chain. Federal government policy toward ethanol subsidies and ethanol imports (primarily sugar-based ethanol from Brazil) both bear watching, especially in the wake of the 2012 election. While ethanol prices have strengthened moderately, corn and other commodity prices have risen and become more volatile, adding some risk to the business. An increase in the beta from the sleep-at-night 0.24 to 0.48 in the past year reflects some of this volatility; that said, ADM is still a relatively safe issue.

SECTOR: **Consumer Staples**
BETA COEFFICIENT: **0.48**
10-YEAR COMPOUND EARNINGS PER SHARE GROWTH: **20.5%**
10-YEAR COMPOUND DIVIDENDS PER SHARE GROWTH: **12.5%**

	2004	2005	2006	2007	2008	2009	2010	2011
Revenue (Mil)	36,151	35,944	36,596	44,018	69,816	69,207	61,692	80,676
Net Income (Mil)	744	921	1,312	1,561	1,834	1,970	1,959	1,970
Earnings per share	1.16	1.40	2.00	2.38	2.84	3.06	3.06	3.13
Dividends per share	0.27	0.32	0.37	0.43	0.49	0.54	.58	.62
Cash flow per share	2.20	2.44	3.00	3.51	3.97	4.21	4.49	4.54
Price: high	22.5	25.5	46.7	47.3	48.9	33.0	34.0	38.0
low	14.9	17.5	24	30.2	13.5	23.1	24.2	23.7

Archer Daniels Midland Co.
4666 Faries Parkway, Box 1470
Decatur, IL 62525
(217) 424-5200
Website: *www.admworld.com*

AT&T Inc.

Ticker symbol: T (NYSE) □ S&P rating: A- □ Value Line financial strength rating: A+ □ Current yield: 5.7% □ Dividend raises, past 10 years: 9

Company Profile

Measured by revenue, AT&T continues to be the world's largest telecommunications holding company. Although known for years as the center of the wireline local and long distance telecom service, it has evolved to be the largest provider of wireless, commercial broadband, and wi-fi services in the United States and has become a large player in IP (Internet-based) television. At 54 percent of total revenues, the AT&T Wireless subsidiary has emerged as the largest business segment and is still probably the leading and probably the most progressive cell phone service provider in the country although with a significant challenge from Verizon.

Beyond these consumer and commercial products, the company's servers and trunk lines constitute a major part of the global Internet. Data and data services now account for 23 percent of the sales mix.

Its traditional wireline subsidiaries account for another 20 percent of revenues and offer services in 13 states, and the wireless business provides voice coverage primarily for traveling U.S. customers and U.S. businesses in 220 countries. The company has long been focused on offering "one-stop-shop" services—wireline, data, wireless, and other services with one price on one bill. These efforts have had varying success, but the latest venture, called U-verse, an IP-based bundling of TV, data, and voice services turning the TV, the PC, and the cell phone into integrated display and transaction devices, is a particularly important development.

FY2011 was a year full of news and competitive challenges. The company announced a huge deal to acquire wireless rival T-Mobile, only to drop the offer late in the year due to antitrust pressures. T-Mobile would have given AT&T a stronger position in the low-end, budget-conscious wireless space, as well as much-needed wireless spectrum. As the result of the dropped bid, the company now is left with a $3 billion breakup fee obligation to parent Deutsche Telecom and a payment in the form of valuable wireless spectrum. At the same time, Verizon brought the Apple iPad and iPhone on line in late 2010, and Sprint followed suit in 2011.

The wireless space continues to be ultracompetitive. The company's strategy appears to center on the idea of migrating its customer base to smartphones, which while bringing a solid future revenue stream, carry a lot of upfront cost in the form of device subsidies and marketing/advertising expenses.

Financial Highlights, Fiscal Year 2011

The aforementioned smartphone marketing expenses resulted in a slight decrease in FY2011 earnings to $2.20 per share, and earnings in Q4, ending in December 2011, were off more sharply to 42 cents per share, due mainly to smartphone subsidies. Revenues have moderated to around a 2 percent growth rate annually, although that still results in increases of about $2 to $3 billion annually for a company of this size. Earnings should resume a mid-single-digit growth path as smartphone revenue streams come on line.

Reasons to Buy

AT&T has built a strong wireless base, especially going forward as millions use—and pay for—data access anywhere, anytime. We think a company that can charge $20 for 200 MB of data is positioned well for the future, given the gobs of data used by nearly everyone and especially younger folks getting into the game. Beyond that, AT&T has made the most of its early-game distributorship of Apple products, and continues to milk the wireline "cash cow" successfully. For now at least, the company continues to be perceived as having the best wireless coverage and service in the industry. We see modest earnings growth, and that growth appears to be destined for shareholder pockets in the form of one of the best dividend payouts for a quality company available today.

Reasons for Caution

Wireless continues to be one of the most competitive businesses around—which is why you see so many ads and offers everywhere. That competition increases marketing spend, moderates prices, and hurts profitability, and the loss of the iPhone/iPad monopoly will also hurt a bit. We continue to be concerned that the company is banking too much on smartphones, leaving a vast market of "ordinary" wireless customers behind, especially in the wake of the T-Mobile unwinding. The company is challenged by limits in physical spectrum, as well as capital investments, to handle all this data consumed, but has met those challenges so far. This is a well-managed company with a solid earnings and dividend base, but even the best-managed companies can't change the laws of physics or gradual shifts in consumer preference.

SECTOR: **Telecommunications Services**
BETA COEFFICIENT: **0.61**
10-YEAR COMPOUND EARNINGS PER SHARE GROWTH: **4.2%**
10-YEAR COMPOUND DIVIDENDS PER SHARE GROWTH: **5.5%**

	2004	2005	2006	2007	2008	2009	2010	2011
Revenues (Mil)	40,787	43,862	63,055	118,928	124,028	123,018	124,399	126,723
Net Income (Mil)	4,884	5,803	9,014	16,950	12,867	12,535	13,612	13,103
Earnings per share	1.47	1.72	2.34	2.76	2.16	2.12	2.29	2.20
Dividends per share	1.25	1.29	1.22	1.42	1.60	1.64	1.68	1.72
Cash flow per share	3.77	3.42	4.63	5.36	5.56	5.46	5.60	5.31
Price: high	27.7	26.0	36.2	43.0	41.9	29.5	29.6	31.9
low	23.0	21.8	24.2	32.7	20.9	21.4	23.8	27.2

AT&T Inc.
208 S. Akard Street
Dallas, TX 75202
(210) 821-4105
Website: *www.att.com*

Automatic Data Processing, Inc.

Ticker symbol: ADP (NYSE) ❑ S&P rating: AAA ❑ Value Line financial strength rating: A++ ❑ Current yield: 2.9% ❑ Dividend raises, past 10 years: 10

Company Profile

"The Business behind Business" is the rather apt slogan employed by Automatic Data Processing, or ADP, as it is more widely known. ADP is the nation's largest provider of outsourced employer payroll, tax processing, employee benefits, and other automated and nonautomated human resources (HR) and other business services.

The Employer Services unit accounts for about 70 percent of revenues and is engaged in payroll, tax, and other transaction processing for about 570,000 employers worldwide. These transactions include paychecks, direct deposit, FICA withholding tax payments, retirement and other benefits services, and reporting. About 80 percent of this business is in the United States, 13 percent in Europe, 5 percent in Canada, and 2 percent in Asia and Latin America.

The Professional Employer Organization Services unit provides a more complete, seamless HR back-end solution, branded as "TotalSource," for about 5,600 clients, including personal HR consultation for employees and retirement plan administration. There are 47 TotalSource offices in 22 states. This unit accounts for about 18 percent of the business.

The remainder of ADP's business is primarily made up of the Dealer Services unit. Dealer Services provides a comprehensive and integrated dealership management solution (DMS), with bundled hardware and software designed to manage all dealership operations including sales management, inventory, HR, procurement, factory communications, warranty, accounting, and other functions. This DMS product is used by auto, truck, marine, motorcycle, and heavy equipment dealers, among others.

Recently the company has made a series of small acquisitions to expand into other vertical industries. A good example is AdvanceMD, a privately held provider of practice management and electronic health records systems for small and mid-sized medical practices. Another is Byte Software House S.p.A., an Italian payroll and HR software and service provider. Others include Cobalt; Workscape, Inc.; DO2 Technologies; OneClick HR; and others in the HR and office processing space.

Financial Highlights, Fiscal Year 2011

ADP's products and services are directly tied to the level of employment, so while business flattened (but didn't decline) at the height of the recession, FY2011 provided a nice comeback with total revenues advancing 10.7 percent, well ahead of forecasts. That said, earnings didn't keep up, with FY2011 EPS only 5.4 percent ahead of FY2010. One big reason for the subpar earnings performance was low interest rates. How does that figure? Typically, ADP earns a lot on payroll "float," that is, cash held in reserve waiting for dispersal and check cashing by employees. These lower returns are only partially offset by increases in account balances. Operating margins dropped about 1 percent to 21 percent as a result. For 2012, earnings growth is forecast to return to a more normal trajectory with an increase to about $2.75 per share.

Reasons to Buy

While not an exceptional growth business, ADP continues to be a good safe and steady way to play the normal growth in the economy, with a bit of a short-term kicker in the form of the economic recovery. The company has a good brand in the business, and with the exception of PayChex (another *100 Best* stock), it has little substantial competition and should own, or co-own, this niche for a long time to come. Outsourcing trends should push more business their way, while acquisitions make the offering more complete and achieve international expansion. In a way, ADP is really a "cloud" play as companies turn more of their IT over to centralized outsourced services. The dividend is solid and the company continues to raise it regularly and has been aggressive in buying back shares, reducing share count by 100 million to 490 million shares in the past 10 years. The company is almost debt free, with debt less than 1 percent of total capital.

Reasons for Caution

Aside from not being a growth star, the company is also somewhat vulnerable to economic downturns. That said, the most recent one didn't hurt them much. Low interest rates continue to hurt, but that is also an opportunity, as rates should revert to their mean sooner or later.

SECTOR: **Information Technology**
BETA COEFFICIENT: **.68**
10-YEAR COMPOUND EARNINGS PER SHARE GROWTH: **6.5%**
10-YEAR COMPOUND DIVIDENDS PER SHARE GROWTH: **14.5%**

	2004	2005	2006	2007	2008	2009	2010	2011
Revenues (Mil)	7,754	8,499	8,881	7,800	8,776	8,867	8,927	9,879
Net income (Mil)	936	1,055	1,072	1,021	1,162	1,208	1,207	1,254
Earnings per share	1.56	1.79	1.85	1.83	2.20	2.39	2.39	2.52
Dividends per share	0.54	0.61	0.68	0.83	1.04	1.24	1.34	1.42
Cash flow per share	2.12	2.34	2.42	2.30	2.74	2.85	2.92	3.07
Price: high	47.3	48.1	49.9	51.5	46.0	44.5	47.3	55.1
low	38.6	40.4	42.5	43.9	30.8	32.0	28.5	44.7

Automatic Data Processing, Inc.
1 ADP Boulevard
Roseland, NJ 07068
(973) 974-5000
Website: *www.adp.com*

AGGRESSIVE GROWTH

Baxter International, Inc.

Ticker symbol: BAX (NYSE) ❑ S&P rating: A+ ❑ Value Line financial strength rating: A++ ❑ Current yield: 2.4% ❑ Dividend raises, past 10 years: 5

Company Profile

Baxter International develops, manufactures, and markets bio-pharmaceuticals, drug delivery systems, and medical equipment. Their products are used to treat patients with hemophilia, immune deficiencies, infectious diseases, cancer, kidney disease, and other chronic and acute disorders. Based in the United States, Baxter has operations in over 100 countries and operates in two primary segments: Medical Products and Bioscience.

The Medical Products segment (56 percent of FY2011 revenues) produces and markets a wide range of medication delivery equipment used to apply, inject, infuse, and otherwise deliver fluids and medications to the patient. Products include intravenous administration sets, premixed drugs and drug-reconstitution systems, and pre-filled vials, syringes for injectable drugs, IV nutrition products, infusion pumps, inhalation anesthetics, and pharmacy compounding and packaging technologies. The Medical Products segment also markets Baxter's industry-leading line of renal care products, including home-based kidney care products,

primarily for the dialysis and end-stage kidney disease market. That segment was formerly broken out separately and makes up about 19 percent of Baxter's total revenue.

The Bioscience segment (44 percent) included pharmaceuticals mainly derived from blood plasma for treatment of hemophilia and other bleeding disorders, immune deficiencies, burns and shock, and other chronic and acute blood-related conditions. It also includes biosurgery products and vaccines.

International sales are about 59 percent of the total, with Europe accounting for about 32 percent, Asia Pacific 15 percent, and Latin America 12 percent.

Financial Highlights, Fiscal Year 2011

Baxter had a solid FY2011, with a 6.4 top-line increase and about a 5 percent increase in the bottom line. Thanks to share buybacks, which have been executed at a steady pace, per-share earnings actually rose 8.2 percent to $4.31, and the company has allocated another $1 billion to buybacks for FY2012. The company has increased its dividend in each of the past 5 years after holding it steady for eight years prior to that, and the current dividend rate has doubled in 5 years. For FY2012, the company has guided for a 4–5 percent revenue increase before currency translation (which may bring it down to 2–3 percent and earnings per share in the $4.49 to $4.57 range.

Reasons to Buy

Baxter is a solid play on medical supplies for recurring or chronic diseases and will do well as the population ages and as medication of these diseases expands into overseas and especially emerging markets. Baxter has been a strong player in its niches, particularly the Bioscience and renal products, and has enjoyed profit margins stronger than the industry average as a result. The net profit margin of 18.3 percent is higher than 10 other companies we looked at in this business, yet its P/E ratio is one of the lowest. The company has an ambitious and successful R&D program, with some 7 percent of sales being invested in R&D. In recent years the company has placed more emphasis on shareholder returns through buybacks and dividend increases, and we expect this practice to continue.

Reasons for Caution

Health-care reform and related spending slowdowns may cut into demand for some of Baxter's products. International exposure can create growth but may also create a near-term drag from the strengthening of the dollar.

SECTOR: **Health Care**
BETA COEFFICIENT: **0.49**
10-YEAR COMPOUND EARNINGS PER SHARE GROWTH: **10.5%**
10-YEAR COMPOUND DIVIDENDS PER SHARE GROWTH: **6.0%**

	2004	2005	2006	2007	2008	2009	2010	2011
Revenues (Mil)	9,509	9,849	10,378	11,263	12,348	12,562	13,056	13,893
Net Income (Mil)	1,040	958	1,464	1,826	2,155	2,330	2,368	2,471
Earnings per share	1.68	1.52	2.23	2.79	3.38	3.8	3.98	4.31
Dividends per share	0.58	0.58	0.58	0.72	0.91	1.07	1.18	1.27
Cash flow per share	2.66	2.46	3.13	3.8	4.52	5.02	5.25	5.50
Price: high	34.8	41.1	48.5	61.1	71.5	61	61.9	62.5
low	27.1	33.1	35.1	46.1	47.4	45.5	40.3	47.6

Baxter International, Inc.
1 Baxter Parkway
Deerfield, IL 60015
Website: *www.baxter.com*

Becton, Dickinson and Company

Ticker symbol: BDX (NYSE) □ S&P rating: A+ □ Value Line financial strength rating: A++ □ Current yield: 2.4%

Company Profile

Becton, Dickinson is a global medical technology company broadly focused on improving drug delivery, enhancing the diagnosis of infectious diseases and cancers, and advancing medical lab work and drug discovery. The company develops, manufactures, and sells medical supplies, devices, laboratory instruments, antibodies, reagents, and diagnostic products through its three segments: BD Medical, BD Diagnostics, and BD Biosciences. These products are sold to health-care institutions, life science researchers, clinical laboratories, the pharmaceutical industry, and the general public. International sales account for about 56 percent of the total. BD is a familiar brand both for observant patients in clinics, medical offices, and hospitals and for the nursing and medical community.

The company operates in three worldwide business segments: Medical (51 percent of FY 2011 sales), Biosciences (32 percent), and Diagnostics (17 percent).

The Medical segment produces a variety of drug delivery devices and supplies, including hypodermic needles and syringes, infusion therapy devices, intravenous catheters, insulin injection systems, regional anesthesia needles, and pre-fillable drug-delivery systems for pharmaceutical companies.

BD Diagnostics offers system solutions for collecting, identifying, and transporting blood and other specimens, as well as instrumentation for analyzing these specimens. Testing systems include those for sexually transmitted diseases, microorganism identification and drug susceptibility, and certain types of cancer screening. The business also provides customer training and business management services.

BD Biosciences provides research tools and reagents to accelerate the pace of biomedical discovery. Clinicians and researchers use BD Biosciences' tools to study genes, proteins, and cells to understand disease, improve technologies for diagnosis and disease management, and facilitate the discovery and development of new therapeutics.

Recently the company has been making small to medium-sized acquisitions in the lab automation space, most notably the Dutch-based KIESTRA Lab Automation.

Financial Highlights, Fiscal Year 2011

FY2011 was a decent year for BDX despite the soft economy and the 2010 divestiture of its ophthalmic and surgical supplies businesses, which accounted for some $200 million in revenues and $0.20 in earnings previously. Revenues grew about 6.2 percent to $7.8 billion, while per-share earnings grew about 13.8 percent to $5.62. With the combined headwinds of acquisition costs, unfavorable currency translation and economic softness, FY2012 estimates both by the company and analysts are mostly flat. That said, cash flows and cash flow growth remain strong, and the company announced both a dividend increase and the intent to continue share buybacks, so shareholder rewards should grow even during this lackluster period.

Reasons to Buy

Becton, Dickinson continues to be as recession-proof as any stock on our list, while also offering decent growth potential, especially in earnings, cash flow, and dividends. The company has achieved double-digit growth in earnings, cash flow, dividends, and book value for the past 10 years, and revenue growth has only slightly missed that mark. Operating margins have steadily improved from about 25 percent 10 years ago to about 30 percent currently. The company is well branded and well established in all of its markets, and it offers a solid way to play the long-term "health" of the health-care industry. Planned share repurchases are on the increase, and the company has already bought back some 20 percent of outstanding shares since 2005. The yield, as a percentage of share price, continues to inch higher. As of mid-2012, the share price has lagged the market and the company's long-term earnings and cash return potential, making it a relatively good buy compared to some other names on our *100 Best* list.

Reasons for Caution

Continued uncertainty surrounding the health-care issue in the United States has to be considered when looking at any stock in this sector. Due to the basic and necessary nature of the bulk of their product line, we feel BD is well positioned to sail though these waters without getting swamped, but a re-evaluation of BD would make sense once the policy issues have been settled. There is also a general softening in elective and postponable medical procedures in response to the recession; it is still unclear when these procedures will return to full volume. While recent acquisitions are interesting, we would hope the company doesn't go on too much of an acquisition tear simply to buy growth.

SECTOR: **Health Care**
BETA COEFFICIENT: **.59**
10-YEAR COMPOUND EARNINGS PER SHARE GROWTH: **13.0%**
10-YEAR COMPOUND DIVIDENDS PER SHARE GROWTH: **15.0%**

	2004	**2005**	**2006**	**2007**	**2008**	**2009**	**2010**	**2011**
Revenues (Mil)	4,935	5,415	5,835	6,560	7,156	7,160	7,372	7,828
Net Income (Mil)	582	692	841	978	1,1128	1,220	1,185	1,272
Earnings per share	2.21	2.66	3.28	3.84	4.46	4.95	4.94	5.61
Dividends per share	0.6	0.72	0.86	0.98	1.14	1.32	1.48	1.64
Cash flow per share	4.13	4.60	5.08	5.82	6.60	7.13	7.25	8.27
Price: high	58.2	61.2	74.2	85.9	93.2	80.0	80.6	89.4
low	40.2	49.7	58.1	69.3	58.1	60.4	66.5	72.5

Becton, Dickinson and Company
1 Becton Drive
Franklin Lakes, NJ 07417–1880
(201) 847-5453
Website: *www.bd.com*

Bed, Bath & Beyond Inc.

Ticker symbol: BBBY (NASDAQ) ❑ S&P rating: BB+ ❑ Value Line financial strength rating: A++ ❑ Current yield: Nil

Company Profile

Founded in 1971, Bed, Bath & Beyond (BB&B) and its subsidiaries sell a wide assortment of goods, primarily domestics merchandise and home furnishings, but including food, giftware, health and beauty care items, and infant and toddler merchandise. The approximate business breakdown is 59 percent home furnishings, which include kitchen and tabletop items, basic housewares, bath hardware and soft lines, lighting, consumables, and certain juvenile products; 12 percent bed linens; and 29 percent general merchandise.

With over 1,100 stores in the United States, Canada, and Mexico, the company has strong geographic coverage and a growing web presence—their goal is to be the customer's first choice for the merchandise categories offered. BB&B competes on the breadth and depth of its product offerings, its focus on the home and personal care, its customer service, new merchandise offerings, and low prices.

The company also owns (through acquisition) and operates three other retail chain concepts. Its CTS (Christmas Tree Shops) chain counts 68 stores in 18 states. There are 46 Harmon stores in 3 states, and 45 buybuy BABY stores in 21 states. Additionally, the web presence has grown through BB&B's own website and emerging separate sites for buybuy BABY and Harmon FaceValues Discount Health & Beauty sites. The latter in particular is worth a glance at *www.facevaluesonline.com*.

The buybuy BABY stores offer over 20,000 products for infants and toddlers, including cribs, dressers, car seats, strollers, and highchairs; feeding, nursing, bath supplies, and everyday consumables; as well as toys, activity centers, and development products. The stores are equipped with private feeding and changing rooms and offer home delivery and setup on everything they sell.

Founded on Cape Cod in 1970, Christmas Tree Shops is a value-priced retailer of home décor, giftware, housewares, food, paper goods, and seasonal products. The stores specialize in low-cost merchandise with frequent changes in mix to generate continued interest.

These specialty stores thus far account for only a small portion of revenue and profits, although company documents don't break the percentage down specifically. The company is also dabbling in international markets, with stores in Canada and Puerto Rico. In addition, the company is a partner in a joint venture that operates two stores in the Mexico City market under the name Home & More.

Financial Highlights, Fiscal Year 2011

BB&B continues to hit on all cylinders. The FY2011 top line grew almost 8 percent to $9.44 billion. Gross, operating, and net profit margins continue to exceed those in most of the industry, at 44.5 percent, 18.5 percent, and 10.1 percent respectively. This reflects both strength in its niches and effective management. Sales should exceed $10 billion in FY2012 with an EPS projected at $4.45 per share, a healthy gain even from FY2011's $3.90. Cash flows are strong, and the company continues to buy back shares aggressively—the share count has been reduced 20 percent since 2003—although we'd like to see a dividend at some point.

Reasons to Buy

Occasionally a retailer hits on a formula that works, and this one works well in its market and among other market participants. On the upper end are specialty shops like Restoration Hardware and Williams-Sonoma, competing on "fancy" with strong merchandising and shopping experiences but with high prices, relatively limited selection, and difficult mall access; at the low end lies Walmart and others with assortments of name-brand goods at low prices, but perhaps not such a complete assortment. BB&B fills the gap, stocking more products per category than its competitors, and arranges its stores so as to emphasize the number of products per category. The BB&B format has not yet reached saturation levels, as there appears to be room for another 500 stores in the United States and Canada. The company's move into other formats, buybuy BABY in particular, comes along at just the right time, as BB&B is generating more than enough cash to fund its own expansion. International opportunities look attractive, and the company continues to benefit from the greater dominance of its niche resulting from the exit of Linens 'N Things in 2009. Finally, company finances are strong; there is no long-term debt, and the Value Line "A++" financial strength rating is unusual for a retailer and a company with BB&B's growth potential.

Reasons for Caution

Two cautions that dog all specialty retailers: First, the concept may tire and get stale; consumers are fickle and may move on to something else. Second, a new competitor, not present on the horizon, may emerge to facilitate this process, much as Lowe's did to Home Depot several years back. Additionally, these and other chains are starting to stock items like cleaning products and decorative rugs that enter into BB&B's turf. Investors should consistently reaffirm this company's dominance in its niche and the ability to translate that dominance into financial results.

SECTOR: Retail
BETA COEFFICIENT: 1.08
10-YEAR COMPOUND EARNINGS PER SHARE GROWTH: 17.5%
10-YEAR COMPOUND DIVIDENDS PER SHARE GROWTH: Nil

	2004	2005	2006	2007	2008	2009	2010	2011
Revenues (Mil)	5,147	5,810	6,617	7,049	7,208	7,829	8,759	9,440
Net Income (Mil)	505	573	611	563	425	600	791	955
Earnings per share	1.65	1.92	2.15	2.10	1.64	2.30	3.07	3.90
Dividends per share	—	—	—	—	—	—	—	—
Cash flow per share	2.05	2.43	2.68	2.78	2.31	2.98	3.65	4.70
Price: high	44.4	47	41.7	43.3	34.7	40.2	50.9	63.8
low	33.9	35.5	30.9	28	16.2	19.1	26.5	44.8

Bed, Bath, and Beyond Inc.
650 Liberty Avenue
Union, NJ 07083
(908) 688-0888
Website: *www.bedbathandbeyond.com*

CONSERVATIVE GROWTH

Campbell Soup Company

Ticker symbol: CPB (NYSE) ❑ S&P rating: A- ❑ Value Line financial strength rating: B++ ❑ Current yield: 3.5% ❑ Dividend raises, past 10 years: 9

Company Profile

Campbell Soup Company is the world's largest "maker of convenience foods." To most of the free world, that still translates to "soup" and the ubiquitous pop-culture-iconic Campbell's Soup can. But there is a lot else to this story.

While there are 20 such brands under the Campbell roof, the original Campbell soup is still far and away the most important. The three top soups make up three of the top 10 grocery products sold in the United States every week. Approximately 80 percent of U.S. households purchase the soup, and the average inventory on hand is six cans. Few brands have enjoyed such penetration and loyalty.

The company has reorganized and now has five reporting segments. To highlight the company's own vision of breadth beyond soup, they now house the former U.S. Soup division, along with U.S. Sauces, in the Simple Meals division, reflecting a stronger targeting and message around the concept of convenience. Other divisions include U.S. Beverages; Global Baking and Snacking; International Simple Meals and Beverages; and North America

Foodservice. Within each segment reside the many familiar brands that constitute the business: Swanson, Prego, Pace, V8, Pepperidge Farm, Arnott's, Wolfgang Puck, and, of course, Campbell's.

Campbell's products are distributed to 120 countries worldwide and are sold through its own sales force and through distributors. U.S.-based operations continued to account for 81 percent of revenue and 88 percent of earnings in FY2011, unchanged from FY2010. Products are manufactured in 20 principal facilities within the United States and in 14 facilities outside the country, primarily in Australia, Europe, and Asia/Pacific. The vast majority of these facilities are company owned.

Campbell's product strategy continues to center on three large, global categories—simple meals, baked snacks, and healthy beverages—which they feel are well aligned with broad consumer trends. The company's growth strategy has evolved toward greater innovation in product marketing and brand recognition and new packaging designed to broaden use in today's fast-paced economy, as well as a healthy dose of internationalization. New store displays and branding offer soups in four easily recognized categories: Classic Favorites, Healthy & Delicious, Taste Sensations, and Healthy Kids. As FY2012 unfolds, the company has announced plans to step up R&D and innovation to enhance its product offerings. There is a new Pepperidge Farm Innovation Center under construction to come on line in FY2013. We feel that all of these activities will move the brand forward while maintaining core values and the core customer base. "Nourishing Peoples' Lives Every Day" should play well in the international space, a frontier the company is just beginning to capitalize on.

Financial Highlights, Fiscal Year 2011

Campbell has not been by any means a "growth star" for the past 10 years. Sales growth continues to be unexciting, with an increase of less than 1 percent in FY2011 after taking a pretty good hit for this type of company in the 2009 recession. Margins have improved, however, more than a full percentage point to 21 percent, a healthy gain in this type of business especially in an environment of increased input costs. The resulting profitability, however, has been invested in innovation and marketing, resulting

in essentially flat earnings over the past few years. As CPB is one of the few companies we select that hasn't been buying back shares recently, earnings per share have also flattened out—although the company did announce a $1 billion buyback plan in mid FY2011. The company is exposed, however, to commodity price increases.

Reasons to Buy

Brand strength is a key reason to stock a few shares of Campbell in your investment pantry. Campbell owns the number one or number two position in each of the product categories in which it participates. It dominates the $4 billion U.S. soup market with a 60-plus percent market share.

Beyond that, we look at FY2011 and FY2012 as investment years. We like the new focus on innovation, and think this company could kick-start growth with a few product category and packaging winners, not to mention the still largely untapped international opportunity. While these growth opportunities may or may not pan out, this is a fairly defensive stock with one of the lowest beta coefficients on our list at 0.29; noncyclical, nonfinancial, low debt, and with a respectable yield well covered by cash flow. It's a good place to be if you're building a core of safe, well-established businesses that grow conservatively and occupy the top positions in their markets, and a good stock to buy for the long term on what seems like regular annual price dips.

Reasons for Caution

Even with the recent emphasis on innovation, the company's brands and core customer base are aging, and adoption of new products may prove slow, especially among the younger set. As others, like Coca-Cola, have found out over the years, there are risks inherent with tinkering with a long-established brand such as Campbell's. We would hope that Campbell's succeeds with its new ventures without pulling the rug out from under the old ones. We still like a good ol' can of Beans with Bacon occasionally for lunch.

SECTOR: Consumer Staples
BETA COEFFICIENT: .29
10-YEAR COMPOUND EARNINGS PER SHARE GROWTH: 2.5%
10-YEAR COMPOUND DIVIDENDS PER SHARE GROWTH: 1.0%

	2004	2005	2006	2007	2008	2009	2010	2011
Revenues (Mil)	7,109	7,548	7,343	7,867	7,998	7,586	7,676	7,715
Net income (Mil)	652	707	681	771	798	771	842	805
Earnings per share	1.58	1.71	1.66	1.95	2.09	2.15	2.45	2.42
Dividends per share	0.64	0.69	0.74	0.82	0.88	1.00	1.05	1.15
Cash flow per share	2.24	2.42	2.41	2.78	3.07	2.87	3.25	3.29
Price: high	30.5	31.6	40	42.7	40.8	35.8	37.6	35.7
low	25	27.3	28.9	34.2	27.3	24.8	24.6	29.7

Campbell Soup Company
1 Campbell Place
Camden, NJ 08103–1799
(856) 342-6428
Website: *www.campbellsoup.com*

AGGRESSIVE GROWTH

CarMax, Inc.

Ticker symbol: KMX (NYSE) ▫ S&P rating: not rated ▫ Value Line financial strength rating: B+ ▫ Current yield: Nil ▫ Dividend raises, past 10 years: NA

Company Profile

"The Way Car Buying Should Be." That's the slogan used by this clean-cut chain of used vehicle stores and superstores and its new big-box retail-like model for selling cars. CarMax buys, reconditions, and sells cars and light trucks at 103 retail centers in 49 metropolitan markets, mainly in the Southeast, Midwest, and California. The company specializes in selling cars that are under six years old with less than 60,000 miles and in excellent condition; the cars are sold at a competitive price for their condition in a no-haggle environment. The price is the price; the emphasis is on the condition of the vehicles and on a helpful and friendly sales and transaction process. Sales representatives are compensated for cars they sell, but not in such a way that drives them to push the wrong car on a customer. The company sold some 396,181 used vehicles in FY2011, up 11 percent from the previous year, and most reports suggest they are gaining market share in the markets they serve with a high degree of customer satisfaction. Further, the health of the economy and consumer spending have swung car buying into a higher gear—but with newfound consumer prudence. Many of these purchases are heading to the one-to-six-year-old used car sector of the business. In addition to "retail" used car sales, CarMax is a big player in auto wholesaling, having moved about 200,000 units mostly taken in trade. The company also earns income through its financing unit, known as CarMax Auto Finance, or CAF.

CarMax also has service operations and web-based and other tools designed to make the car selection, buying, and ownership experience easier. The offering continues to be unique in the industry, and competitors would have a long way to go to catch up.

During FY2011 the company resumed its geographic expansion and now plans outlets in important markets not served to date, including Colorado and Pennsylvania. In total the company plans 10 new stores in FY2012, with that figure or more per year through 2016.

Financial Highlights, Fiscal Year 2011

FY2011 saw a continuation of the recovery begun in FY2010. Sales jumped more than 10 percent to almost $10 billion, reflecting increased unit volumes mentioned above. Modest increases in average selling price and gross margins delivered a 9 percent increase in net profit, although the company felt some pressure from tight used car supplies and increased wholesale prices, which were partially offset by increases in cars purchased directly from consumers, new efficiencies in presale refurbishment, and better inventory management.

Reasons to Buy

Quite simply, CarMax continues to be a stock to buy if you believe the traditional dealer model is broken, and if you believe people will continue to see value in late-model used vehicles.

Additionally, CarMax brings the latest in business intelligence and analytic models to the car marketing process, in procurement, merchandising, pricing, and selling the vehicles. Do green Jeep Commanders sell well in Southern California? Then let's find some, and put them on the lot there, and set a market-based price. KMX is well ahead of the industry in making analysis-based supply and selling decisions and has quite successfully deployed analytic tools to adjust prices and inventories quickly to market conditions, a competency that bodes well for the future.

CarMax is clearly taking market share from "trad" used car dealers. There are close to 70,000 new and used car dealerships in the United States; that number will shrink over the next few years while CarMax builds brand strength and reputation in this important market and gains operational strength and experience to support it. The company is positioned well both for organic growth through market share and for geographic growth; additionally, earnings growth will be aided by increased market dominance, which should help both pricing and per-vehicle cost. CarMax is already the largest used car buyer in the world.

Reasons for Caution

CarMax will always be somewhat vulnerable to economic cycles, the availability of credit, and of quality used vehicles to resell. Used car supply has been a concern, especially with the downturn in new car sales and the scaling back in vehicle leasing seen in recent years. In addition, while international markets are a golden opportunity for most of our *100 Best* stocks, it isn't clear how this company can grow internationally, although it is far from out of the question. Finally, as this company is still in the growth phase, and new dealerships involve putting lots of new cars on the ground, working capital needs are extensive, and we don't see KMX paying a dividend for quite some time.

SECTOR: **Retail**
BETA COEFFICIENT: **1.35**
10-YEAR COMPOUND EARNINGS PER SHARE GROWTH: **9.0%**
10-YEAR COMPOUND DIVIDENDS PER SHARE GROWTH: **NA**

		2004	2005	2006	2007	2008	2009	2010	2011
Revenues (Mil)		5,260	6,560	7,466	8,200	6,974	7,400	8,975	9,900
Net Income (Mil)		112.9	148.1	198.6	182	59.2	281.7	380.9	415
Earnings per share		0.54	0.7	0.92	0.83	0.27	1.26	1.67	1.90
Dividends per share		0	0	0	0	0	0	0	0
Cash flow per share		0.64	0.83	1.08	1.05	0.52	1.52	1.95	2.10
Price:	high	18.5	17.4	27.6	29.4	23	24.8	30.0	37.0
	low	9	12.3	13.8	18.6	5.8	6.9	18.6	22.8

CarMax, Inc.
12800 Tuckahoe Creek Parkway
Richmond, VA 23238
(804) 747-0422
Website: *www.carmax.com*

AGGRESSIVE GROWTH

Caterpillar, Inc.

Ticker symbol: CAT (NYSE) ❏ S&P rating: A ❏ Value Line financial strength rating: A+ ❏ Current yield: 1.7% ❏ Dividend raises, past 10 years: 10

Company Profile

Headquartered in Peoria, Illinois, Caterpillar is the world's largest manufacturer of construction and mining equipment, diesel and natural gas engines, and industrial gas turbines. It is a *Fortune* 50 industrial company, now with more than $60 billion in sales in today's reasonably healthy and global economy. The company is a true global player in construction, mining, infrastructure development and repair, forestry, railroad, and other markets, with some 68 percent of sales coming from overseas.

Caterpillar's broad product line ranges from the company's line of compact construction equipment to hydraulic excavators, backhoe loaders, track-type tractors, forest products, off-highway trucks, agricultural tractors, diesel and natural gas engines, industrial gas turbines, and diesel-electric railroad locomotives. Cat products are used in the construction, road building, mining, forestry, energy, transportation, and material-handling industries.

Caterpillar products are sold, rented, and serviced through a notably loyal and effective dealer network. Products and components are manufactured in 41 plants in the United States and 43 more plants worldwide.

Caterpillar's largest segment, the Construction Industries segment, makes the company's well-known yellow-painted grading and earthmoving equipment, including bulldozers, graders, excavators, backhoes, skid-steer loaders, pipelayers, and other medium- to large-sized construction machinery for the general and heavy construction markets. The Resource Industries segment makes very specialized heavy excavating equipment for the mining and quarry industries, as well as machinery for agriculture, forestry, waste processing, and other industries.

The Power Systems segment makes diesel, turbine, and other types of engines for its own construction, mining, and rail as well as for the electric power industry and other end users. The Financial Products segment provides financing to Caterpillar dealers and customers. Financing plans include operating and finance leases, installment sales contracts, working capital loans, and wholesale financing plans.

Caterpillar's end markets are very cyclical and competitive. Demand for Caterpillar's earth-moving equipment is driven by the health of global economies, commodity prices, interest rates, and foreign exchange. Competition from foreign companies—Kubota, Komatsu, and Hitachi in particular—can be strong in world markets, especially if the dollar is strong. Energy prices also affect demand in two ways: Naturally, these big machines use a lot of energy, but they are also used in energy and other natural resource recovery. The company recently acquired Electromotive, the world's largest maker of diesel-electric railroad locomotives, and Bucyrus International, a competing heavy equipment maker.

Financial Highlights, Fiscal Year 2011

Cyclical as Caterpillar is, it took a huge hit during the recession, with sales dropping some 37 percent in 2009 from previous levels. In FY2011 and as FY2012 unfolds, a combination of machinery replacement and healthy foreign end market demand in construction and mining, combined with acquisitions, drives revenues from the FY2009 cyclical low of $32.3 billion to $60.1 billion in FY2011. Margins are also at an all-time high, helped by manufacturing

efficiencies and foreign manufacture in some key markets. Not surprisingly, these factors helped earnings and cash flows, with earnings up to $7.19 per share from $1.43 in the lean times of FY2009.

Reasons to Buy

Caterpillar continues to be a strong player in international business and exports, the expansion of mining and the rebuilding of U.S. infrastructure, and the building of new infrastructure, particularly in Latin America and Asia. The company continues to enjoy a solid brand strength and reputation worldwide. Stated goals to increase earnings to $10 per share seem on track, assuming the economy stays reasonably healthy. The strength and loyalty of the dealer network, coupled with the in-house financing business, are pluses. We like the combination of brand excellence, management excellence, and continued growth prospects in infrastructure creation and replacement. We should also note the company's track record of dividend increases despite the 2009 downturn.

Reasons for Caution

Caterpillar is irretrievably tied to the economic cycle, although as we've seen in the last recession, economic downturns can lead to greater spending on infrastructure, which can help Cat even during these lean times. While foreign markets are a strength, we are also concerned about foreign competition from companies like Kubota and Komatsu, makers of mainly smaller, more compact equipment that is cheaper to acquire and operate. The share price has responded well to the recovery; new investors would be encouraged to wait and buy on dips. While the company has a solid track record of dividend raises, these raises and the size of the dividend itself are relatively small compared to earnings and cash flow—characteristic of a well-managed cyclical company.

SECTOR: **Industrials**
BETA COEFFICIENT: **1.88**
10-YEAR COMPOUND EARNINGS PER SHARE GROWTH: **8.5%**
10-YEAR COMPOUND DIVIDENDS PER SHARE GROWTH: **10.5%**

		2004	2005	2006	2007	2008	2009	2010	2011
Revenues (Mil)		30,251	36,339	41,517	44,958	51,234	32,396	42,588	60,138
Net income (Mil)		2,035	2,854	3,537	3,541	3,557	895	2,700	5,202
Earnings per share		2.88	4.04	5.17	5.37	5.71	1.43	4.15	7.81
Dividends per share		0.78	0.96	1.2	1.32	1.62	1.68	1.72	1.80
Cash flow per share		5.00	6.46	8.03	8.64	9.25	5.17	7.82	11.98
Price:	high	49.4	59.9	82	87	86	61.3	116.6	114.6
	low	34.3	41.3	57	58	32	50.5	67.5	92.8

Caterpillar, Inc.
100 N. E. Adams Street
Peoria, IL 61629–5310
(309) 675-4619
Website: *www.cat.com*

Chevron Corporation

Ticker symbol: CVX (NYSE) □ S&P rating: AA □ Value Line financial strength rating: A++ □ Current yield: 3.0% □ Dividend raises, past 10 years: 10

Company Profile

Chevron is the world's fourth-largest publicly traded, integrated energy company based on oil-equivalent reserves and production. It is engaged in every aspect of the oil and gas industry, including exploration and production, refining, marketing and transportation, chemicals manufacturing and sales, and power generation.

Active in more than 180 countries, Chevron, formerly Chevron-Texaco from the 2001 merger, has reserves of 7.2 billion barrels of oil and 25.9 trillion cubic feet of gas, with a daily production capacity of 1.9 million barrels of oil and about 4 billion cubic feet of gas. In addition, it has global refining capacity of more than 2 million barrels per day (bpd) and operates more than 22,000 retail outlets (including 4,093 of their own) around the world. The company also has interests in 30 power projects now operating or being developed. The "upstream" capacity is concentrated in North America, Africa, Asia, and the Caspian Sea area, with less exposure to the Middle East than some competitors. The company is more concentrated in oil (less in

gas) than some of its competitors, although the company has invested in new shale gas developments. The emphasis on oil has been a strength recently as oil prices have climbed, while gas prices have fallen to levels not seen in 50 years.

Its downstream (refining/retailing) businesses include four refining and marketing units operating in North America, Europe, West Africa, Latin America, Asia, the Middle East, and southern Africa. Downstream also has five global businesses: aviation, lubricants, trading, shipping, and fuel and marine marketing.

The company's global refining network comprises 23 wholly owned and joint-venture facilities that process more than 2 million barrels of oil per day. Gasoline and diesel fuel are sold through more than 22,000 retail outlets under three well-known consumer brands: Chevron in North America; Texaco in Latin America, Europe, and West Africa; and Caltex in Asia, the Middle East, and southern Africa.

Chevron is the number one jet fuel marketer in the United States and third worldwide, marketing 550,000 barrels per day in 80 countries. The company's fuel and marine marketing business is a leading global supplier and marketer of fuels, lubricants, and coolants to the marine and power markets, with about 500,000 barrels of sales per day.

Financial Highlights, Fiscal Year 2011

Chevron has recovered from a fairly substantial 2009 recession-related dip, and higher 2011 oil prices (average $101/barrel in 2011 vs. $76 in 2010) drove revenues up 24 percent even with a slight decline in volume. The only negative was a small loss in the refining segment—due to the high cost of oil input feedstock. The company expects another record year in 2012, which will be especially easy to attain if natural gas prices reverse their downtrend. Strong prices and margin improvements led to a net profit of some $26.8 billion, easily a new record.

Reasons to Buy

Chevron has benefited from favorable trends in all aspects of this business—and so have investors. The company is most exposed to some of the best sectors and geographies in the business and has established a good brand and track record for discovery, production, and downstream operations. The company may cut back its refining base some, but we also think refining is a good business in the long term. The company has a solid record of earnings, cash generation, and cash distribution, and shareholders should be rewarded in the long term.

Reasons for Caution

The risks of being in the oil business are well known, and the recent BP disaster in 2010 reminded us all once again. The company gets about 10 percent of its production from the Gulf. A double-dip recession would also slow things down for Chevron, but no more than for anyone else, and the company's financial strength would go a long way to mitigate any impact on investors.

SECTOR: Energy
BETA COEFFICIENT: .77
10-YEAR COMPOUND EARNINGS PER SHARE GROWTH: 15.0%
10-YEAR COMPOUND DIVIDENDS PER SHARE GROWTH: 8.0%

	2004	2005	2006	2007	2008	2009	2010	2011
Revenues (Bil)	150.9	198.2	210.1	220.9	273	172.6	204.9	253.7
Net income (Bil)	13	14.1	17.1	18.7	23.9	10.5	19.0	26.9
Earnings per share	6.14	6.54	7.8	8.77	11.67	5.24	8.48	13.44
Dividends per share	1.53	1.75	2.01	2.32	2.53	2.66	2.84	3.09
Cash flow per share	8.67	8.96	10.09	12.11	16.69	10.95	15.99	19.98
Price: high	56.1	66	76.2	95.5	104.6	79.8	92.4	111.0
low	41.6	49.8	53.8	65	55.5	56.1	66.8	102.1

Chevron Corporation
6001 Bollinger Canyon Road
San Ramon, CA 94583–2324
(925) 842-5690
Website: *www.chevron.com*

Church & Dwight

Ticker symbol: CHD (NYSE) ❑ S&P rating: BBB ❑ Value Line financial strength rating: A ❑ Current yield: 2.0% ❑ Dividend raises, past 10 years: 6

Company Profile

Church & Dwight is the world's largest producer of sodium bicarbonate, but that hardly tells the whole story. The story is really about how this company built a brand and series of products based on sodium bicarbonate, known to most of us as baking soda. These well-known products are marketed under the Arm & Hammer brand, a brand that is deployed across several product categories. The company has sold this iconic product continually since its founding in 1846—the product's longevity owing to its versatility. Sodium bicarbonate is used in the chemical industry, baking, cleaning, agriculture (as both a soil and feedstock amendment), medicine, and the paper industry. It's an abrasive, a deodorizer, a leavening agent, a water purifier, an antacid, a dialysate (treatment for kidney failure), a blowing agent for plastics . . . the list goes on.

Church & Dwight is a fairly quiet, low-profile company that has gradually learned the ropes of contemporary consumer staple marketing. Sodium bicarbonate is not the company's only product, but it is at the core of most of its businesses. Most of the bicarbonate products are sold under the well-known and iconic Arm & Hammer brand, a brand that the company has learned to leverage into a number of product categories beyond ordinary cleaners, including toothpaste, deodorant, carpet and room deodorizers, cat litter, detergents, and others. It is an excellent brand extension story. About 40 percent of the company's U.S. consumer products are sold under the brand name Arm & Hammer and derivative trademarks, such as Arm & Hammer Dental Care Toothpaste and Arm & Hammer Super Scoop Clumping Cat Litter. But fueled by acquisitions mostly since 2001, the brand portfolio extends well past Arm & Hammer. The other seven are Trojan, Oxiclean, Spinbrush, First Response, Nair, Orajel, and XTRA.

In 2003, the company acquired the former Unilever oral care business in the United States and Canada, comprising the Mentadent, Pepsodent, and Aim Toothpaste brands, and exclusive licensing rights to Close-Up Toothpaste. Late in 2005, the company expanded its oral-care business with the acquisition of the

Spinbrush battery-operated toothbrush business from Procter & Gamble. In August 2006, the company expanded its household brand portfolio with the acquisition of the net assets of Orange Glo International.

The company claims the Arm & Hammer brand appears in more grocery aisles than any other brand, and that the brand appears in over 90 percent of American homes. Most of the company's brands, Arm & Hammer and XTRA in particular, are marketed as "value" selections at attractive price points. In today's more frugal environment, this goes a large way toward explaining the company's recent success.

Financial Highlights, Fiscal Year 2011

FY2011 was a success, particularly on the earnings front. The company turned a 5 percent growth in sales into an 11 percent gain in earnings, largely driven by higher volumes and margins and success in international markets, mostly Canada, Mexico, and Australia. These figures also point to the benefits of a diverse product portfolio, pricing strength even in a "value" segment, and effective management. Sales, earnings, and cash flow have all increased at double-digit rates over the past 10 years, a sparkling performance in this type of industry. The company also raised its dividend substantially, doubling the yield.

Reasons to Buy

Ten years ago, Church & Dwight had one iconic consumer brand and its net sales were just over $1 billion. They now have more than 80 brands and $2.7 billion in annual sales. The growth in their base of core brands has accelerated over the past five years, and the company is in terrific position for further acquisitions. They've done an excellent job of integrating the acquired brands into the core business, as well as leveraging their core brand into new products. We like the steady growth in an extremely competitive industry, and the recent dividend raise makes the company more attractive from a total return viewpoint. Another way to look at it is the $6.5 billion market cap makes this company a good value—one to own if, say, we had $6.5 billion to invest—and that may get some of its larger rivals thinking about owning it too.

Reasons for Caution

While core brand expansion has been very successful, and while recent acquisitions have been successful, we tend to be cautious about companies that tend to overly rely on acquisitions as a growth strategy. It's easy to make a mistake, even though the company has had an excellent track record so far. The company is also exposed to raw material and commodity price increases, but seems to have been able to pass them on so far.

SECTOR: **Consumer Staples**
BETA COEFFICIENT: **0.34**
10-YEAR COMPOUND EARNINGS PER SHARE GROWTH: **18.5%**
10-YEAR COMPOUND DIVIDENDS PER SHARE GROWTH: **21.1%**

	2004	**2005**	**2006**	**2007**	**2008**	**2009**	**2010**	**2011**
Revenues (Mil)	1,462	1,737	1,946	2,221	2,422	2,521	2,589	2,715
Net Income (Mil)	88.8	123	143	169	201	249	286	315
Earnings per share	0.69	0.92	1.04	1.23	1.43	1.74	1.98	2.20
Dividends per share	0.12	0.12	0.13	0.13	0.17	0.23	0.31	0.68
Cash flow per share	1.01	1.32	1.49	1.70	1.94	2.37	2.51	2.75
Price: high	16.8	19.8	21.8	28.6	32.5	31.2	35.5	46.3
low	12.8	16.1	16.3	21.2	23.8	22.7	29.5	33.8

Church & Dwight Co., Inc.
469 North Harrison Street
Princeton, NJ 08543
(609) 683-5900
Website: *www.churchdwight.com*

INCOME

Cincinnati Financial

Ticker symbol: CINF (NASDAQ) □ S&P rating: BBB □ Value Line financial strength rating: B++ □ Current yield: 4.7% □ Dividend raises past 10 years: 10

Company Profile

Cincinnati Financial Corporation (CFC), founded in 1968, is engaged primarily in property casualty insurance marketed through independent insurance agents in 37 states. The company, one of the 25 largest property and casualty insurers in the nation, operates in four segments: Commercial Lines Property Casualty Insurance, Personal Lines Property Casualty Insurance, Life Insurance, and Investments. Commercial lines account for about 70 percent of premium revenues; personal lines about 30 percent, and all insurance products are sold through independent agencies.

Cincinnati Financial fully or partially owns a series of subsidiary companies, which actually provide and manage the insurance products marketed by the company and its agents. Its standard market property casualty insurance group includes two subsidiaries: the Cincinnati Casualty Company and the Cincinnati Indemnity Company. This group writes a range of business, homeowner, and auto policies.

The two noninsurance subsidiaries of Cincinnati Financial are CSU Producer Resources, which offers insurance brokerage services to CFC's independent agencies so their clients can access CFC's excess and surplus lines insurance products; and CFC Investment Company, which offers commercial leasing and financing services to CFC's agents, their clients, and other customers.

Financial Highlights, Fiscal Year 2011

FY2011 continued the story from the last few years: high casualty losses (Hurricane Irene in the United States) and low interest rates, leading to lower than normal returns on invested assets. Underwriting income continues to be negative, showing a deficit of $3.28 per share; resulting earnings were only $0.74 per share, a steep drop from $1.68 a year earlier. Early projections for FY2012, however, call for only a $0.80 per share underwriting deficit and per-share earnings once again up to the $1.45 level. A strengthening pricing environment, improved business conditions for business customers, and a hopeful lack of major catastrophes will get the company back on its track. Investment income remains strong at $3.30 per share despite the weak interest rate environment. All told, a recovery in underwriting and in interest rates could produce some impressive earnings results; in the meantime the company has relatively low debt for this industry and should be able to keep paying the healthy dividend for the foreseeable future.

Reasons to Buy

CINF enjoys both a loyal customer base and a loyal agency base. Measured by premium volume, the company is ranked as the number one or number two carrier among 75 percent of the agencies that have represented them for the past five years. Working to improve that measure further, during 2009 the company rolled out three major new technology platforms for their writers, with the goal of improving efficiency in quoting, billing, and payment across all business and personal lines.

The company is on firm financial footing with a dividend covered by investment income and cash flow and a relatively low 13 percent long-term debt as a percentage of total capital. Despite the recent financial storm, dividend payouts have increased slowly and steadily each year, and at an average 9.5 percent rate over the past 10 years, a nice bonus. Any return to normal investment return rates, and resurgence in policy writing and pricing will figure well for this solid insurance play, and may add some growth to the already attractive yield.

Reasons for Caution

Interest rates on the industry's traditional investment instruments look to be weak for some time. Competition is stiff, and continued substantial casualty losses could hurt. While the dividend is covered for now, a sustained negative environment could bring its viability into question.

SECTOR: Financials
BETA COEFFICIENT: 0.79
10-YEAR COMPOUND EARNINGS PER SHARE GROWTH: 4.5%
10-YEAR COMPOUND DIVIDENDS PER SHARE GROWTH: 9.5%

	2004	2005	2006	2007	2008	2009	2010	2011
Total Assets (Mil)	16,107	16,003	17,222	16,637	13,369	14,440	15,095	15,668
Net Income (Mil)	386	562	496	610	344	215	273	121
Earnings per share	2.94	3.17	2.82	3.54	2.10	1.32	1.68	0.74
Dividends per share	1.00	1.21	1.34	1.42	1.53	1.57	1.59	1.61
Loss/Prem Earned	.63	.63	.64	.59	.73	.77	.74	.83
Price: high	53.5	45.9	49.2	48.4	40.2	29.7	32.3	34.3
low	36.6	38.4	41.2	36.0	13.7	17.8	25.3	23.7

Cincinnati Financial Corporation
6200 S. Gilmore Road
Fairfield, OH 45014
(513) 870-2000
Website: *www.cinfin.com*

CONSERVATIVE GROWTH

The Clorox Company

Ticker symbol: CLX (NYSE) ❑ S&P rating: BBB+ ❑ Value Line financial strength rating: B++ ❑ Current yield: 3.5%

Company Profile

A leading manufacturer and marketer of consumer cleaning and other household products, Clorox markets some of consumers' most trusted and recognized brand names, including its namesake bleach and cleaning products; Green Works natural cleaners; Fresh Step and Scoop Away cat litter; Kingsford charcoal; Hidden Valley and K C Masterpiece dressings and sauces; Brita water-filtration systems; Glad bags, wraps, and containers; and Burt's Bees natural personal care products. By sales, the more mundane liquid bleach products, trash bags, and charcoal dominate sales, contributing 14, 13, and 11 percent of sales respectively. International sales continue to account for about 21 percent of the total.

The company's home-care cleaning products are primarily comprised of disinfecting sprays and wipes, toilet bowl cleaners, carpet cleaners, drain openers, floor mopping systems, toilet and bath cleaning tools, and premoistened towelettes.

Clorox also provides professional products for institutional, janitorial, and foodservice markets, including bleaches, disinfectants, food-storage bags, and bathroom cleaners. The company's Lifestyle Division offers food products, including salad dressings, seasonings, sauces, and marinades. The company was founded in 1913 as Electro-Alkaline Company. It has been known as the Clorox Company since 1957.

Financial Highlights, Fiscal Year 2011

Fiscal year 2011 operating earnings, ending June 2011, fell off just a bit from 2010 due to higher advertising, logistics, and commodity costs, to $545 million from $603 million the previous year. That figure does not include a $258 million impairment charge related to the $925 million Burt's Bees personal care products acquisition in 2007. On a per-share basis, that works out to $4.16, and a continuation of existing trends has the company estimating FY2012 to come in at $4.10, but it is roughly in line with the previous year's trajectory. Energy prices, and particularly for plastics used in containers and Glad trash bags, are a factor. Revenues have been largely flat.

Reasons to Buy

Even in a slowing consumer market, Clorox, due to its strong brand position (number one or two positions in the market with 88 percent of its products) has proven itself able to increase prices in the past. That said, many consumers have switched away from name-brand products; just how many remains to be seen. Clorox has proven itself to be a strong and shareholder-oriented defensive player. During the 2008–09 recession, the company increased its dividend by 25 percent, and has raised its dividend for 30 straight years. The stock has tended to trade in a very tight range even with negative news; it is a safety and stability play.

There may be some shareholder value yet to unlock, as Carl Icahn recently reminded us by buying a stake (since mostly disposed) and threatening a proxy fight. Such situations are both good and bad, as they can stir things up and lead to acquisitions or favorable divisions of assets, but they also can be a distraction. As Mr. Icahn has largely departed from the scene, the distraction is mostly gone, but the message is still clear.

Finally, the company's brands remain strong, and we especially like the emerging Green Works brand, which, unlike many "green" products, seems to actually work and to have become a standard on store shelves.

Reasons for Caution

We continue to be concerned about the lack of international exposure, although that could also be viewed as a positive in light of events in Europe and slowing China growth. The company is exposed to higher commodity prices, although thus far has been able to recover them with price increases. With Burt's Bees, the company has also learned a lesson about overreaching with acquisitions; the beauty care maker may turn out to have been a fad not worth chasing, but we are concerned that the company could be tempted again into poor acquisitions to spur growth. It's just too hard to grow demand and market share for bleach, trash bags, and charcoal. While we considered dropping Clorox from the list, we feel that core brand strength, good management, and orientation toward shareholder returns continue to earn it its stripes.

SECTOR: **Consumer Staples**
BETA COEFFICIENT: **.39**
10-YEAR COMPOUND EARNINGS PER SHARE GROWTH: **7.5%**
10-YEAR COMPOUND DIVIDENDS PER SHARE GROWTH: **10.0%**

	2004	2005	2006	2007	2008	2009	2010	2011
Revenues (Mil)	4,324	4,388	4,644	4,847	5,273	5,450	5,534	5,231
Net Income (Mil)	546	517	443	496	461	537	603	258
Earnings per share	2.43	2.88	2.89	3.23	3.24	3.81	4.24	2.07
Dividends per share	1.08	1.1	1.14	1.31	1.66	1.88	2.05	2.25
Cash flow per share	3.49	4.66	4.17	4.55	4.82	5.22	5.68	3.51
Price: high	59.4	66	66	69.4	65.3	65.2	69.0	75.4
low	46.5	52.5	56.2	56.2	47.5	59	59.0	60.6

The Clorox Company
1221 Broadway
Oakland, CA 94612
(510) 271-2270
Website: *www.clorox.com*

The Coca-Cola Company

Ticker symbol: KO (NYSE) □ S&P rating: A+ □ Value Line financial strength rating: A++ □ Current yield: 2.8% □ Dividend raises, past 10 years: 10

Company Profile

The Coca-Cola Company is the world's largest beverage company. For more than 100 years, the company has mainly produced concentrates and syrups, which it then sells to independent bottlers worldwide. These bottlers add water (still or carbonated, depending on the product), sugar, and other (often local) ingredients, then bottle and distribute the products to restaurants, retailers, and other distributors. The company owns the brand and is responsible for consumer brand marketing initiatives, while the distributors handle all downstream merchandising. The company operates in over 200 countries and markets nearly 500 brands of concentrate. These concentrates are then used to produce over 3,000 different branded products, including Coca-Cola.

In 2010, the company took a big step toward full integration of its supply chain, with the purchase of the North American operations of Coca-Cola Enterprises (CCE), the largest of its network of bottlers in orders to streamline distribution and marketing, give greater control

of pricing, and cut about $350 million in redundant costs. At the same time, Coke sold distribution in Norway, Sweden, and a future in Germany back to CCE, reaffirming the third-party bottler model in international, or at least European, markets.

The company continues to strive to expand its beverage offerings beyond the traditional carbonated soda drinks. Major brands besides Coke include Minute Maid juices, Dasani and Evian bottled water, Powerade and Full Throttle sports beverages, and Nestea iced teas.

The total numbers are staggering: 500 brands, 620 billion servings per year, 1.7 billion beverages consumed per day, 19,675 servings per second, processed through over 300 bottlers, and all handled through the world's largest beverage distribution system. Some 70 percent of the company's sales are overseas.

Financial Highlights, Fiscal Year 2011

FY2011 was a strong year for Coke, although due to the Coca-Cola

Enterprises acquisition, the numbers are somewhat hard to follow. With CCE, revenues grew some 32 percent for the year; without CCE and some currency effects, the figure is more like 5 percent, still a healthy top-line growth for a company of this size. Net earnings were up some 12 percent.

FY2012 looks a bit softer in view of exposure to international currency fluctuations and higher commodity prices, especially for sweeteners. Although some analysts have dropped their earnings projections, most still expect high single-digit to nearly 10 percent growth.

Reasons to Buy

The reasons to buy Coke continue to be solid. The company has category leadership, especially globally, in soft drinks, juices, and juice drinks, and ready-to-drink coffees and teas. They're number two globally in sports drinks, and number three in packaged water and energy drinks. In Coca-Cola, Diet Coke, Sprite, and Fanta, they own four of the top five brands of soft drink in the world.

Although the company has lagged the market in terms of non-CSD (carbonated soft drink) product offerings, the growth of those products in Coke's developing markets is very encouraging. Coke has targeted double-digit growth

moving forward, particularly in the growing economies of India, Indonesia, and China. The growth in the consumption of nonalcoholic ready-to-drink beverages tracks the per-capita growth in disposable income, and the company has identified key cities with the most promising demographics for its marketing efforts. If Coke could realize the success in China—which is currently at about 20 per capita consumption (PCC), or beverages consumed per capita per year—that it has in Mexico (660 PCC), the effects would be huge.

The Coca-Cola name is probably the most recognized brand in the world, and is almost beyond valuation. Warren Buffett once uttered the classic line about brand strength and intangibles in reference to Coke: "If you gave me $100 billion and said take away the soft drink leadership in the world from Coke, I'd give it back to you and say it can't be done."

Coke has traditionally been a steady hedge stock, and offers a solid dividend with a steady track record of dividend growth. The company boasts—quite rightly—about having raised dividends in each of the past 49 years. It is also as close to a pure play on international business as you'll find in a U.S. company, which may once again be the best place to be for 2013.

Reasons for Caution

U.S. sales, in part affected by greater concerns about obesity and health, continue to be flat (no pun intended). The newly acquired CCE business is a lower-margin business, and while having everything together under one roof may produce some synergies and supply-chain simplification, it is a complex business and may be somewhat distracting to management.

As Coke consumers ourselves, we continue to be concerned at the erosion of Coke products in favor of Pepsi in many restaurants and fast food chains. We realize that PepsiCo owns a number of fast food chains and has a captive market there, but we wonder how and why Coke is losing this important distribution and brand recognition channel, especially as far more people seem to specify Coke than Pepsi when ordering their cola. It makes us wonder whether there are larger elephants in their sales and marketing room. It also serves as an example of what you, as an astute individual investor, can yourself observe about your companies in the course of daily life.

SECTOR: **Consumer Discretionary**
BETA COEFFICIENT: **0.53**
10-YEAR COMPOUND EARNINGS PER SHARE GROWTH: **8.5%**
10-YEAR COMPOUND DIVIDENDS PER SHARE GROWTH: **10.0%**

	2004	2005	2006	2007	2008	2009	2010	2011
Revenues (Mil)		23,104	24,088	28,857	31,944	30,990	35,123	46,600
Net Income (Mil)	5,014	5,196	5,568	5,981	7,050	6,824	8,144	8,770
Earnings per share	2.06	2.17	2.37	2.57	3.02	3.05	3.49	3.85
Dividends per share	1	1.12	1.24	1.36	1.52	1.64	1.76	1.88
Cash flow per share	2.45	2.59	2.81	3.08	3.58	3.6	4.18	4.55
Price: high	53.3	45.3	49.3	64.3	65.6	59.4	65.9	71.8
low	38.3	40.3	39.4	45.6	40.3	37.4	37.4	61.3

The Coca-Cola Company
One Coca-Cola Plaza
Atlanta, GA 30313
(404) 676-2121
Website: *www.coca-cola.com*

Colgate-Palmolive Company

Ticker symbol: CL (NYSE) ◻ S&P rating: AA- ◻ Value Line financial strength rating: A++ ◻ Current yield: 2.5% ◻ Dividend raises, past 10 years: 10

Company Profile

Colgate-Palmolive is the second-largest global producer of detergents, toiletries, and other household products. The company manages its business in two straightforward segments: Oral, Personal, and Home Care; and Pet Nutrition. The Oral, Personal, and Home Care division produces and markets a number of familiar brands and products: Ajax, Palmolive, Irish Spring, Softsoap, Mennen, and SpeedStick, as well as the familiar Colgate brand of oral care products. These brands are strong with substantial market share in most markets: Colgate owns 43 percent of the worldwide oral care market and 22 percent each of the Personal Care and Home Care markets. Colgate is also one of the leaders in the pet nutrition market; its Hill's pet food brand represents 17 percent of its total sales.

Colgate is also strong in the global consumer products market, with a presence in more than 200 countries and territories. About 80 percent of its business is international, and about 50 percent of *that* business is in emerging markets.

Financial Highlights, Fiscal Year 2011

Fiscal year 2011 brought a bright smile to Colgate investors, with revenues up some 10.5 percent and earnings per share up 14.6 percent over the prior year. Strong market share, especially in more profitable emerging markets, plus innovations and operational improvements offset higher commodity costs and some negative currency effects to deliver these gains; a further 3 percent reduction of outstanding shares helped too. For 2012, the company projects EPS of $5.40 on sales in the $17.3 billion range, and just announced a 7 percent dividend increase.

Reasons to Buy

Colgate has strong, globally accepted brands and healthy and growing market share in most markets, especially overseas, where such items as toothpaste are still rapidly growing markets. Analysts suggest that worldwide, consumer oral care products are barely at 50 percent market penetration. Given this healthy potential for market growth, along with the improving demographics of a health-conscious and appearance-conscious pool of consumers especially in more profitable emerging markets, globalization gives a Colgate investor a lot to smile about.

Looking at the bigger picture, Colgate is probably a safer, steadier alternative in this consumer staple marketplace than Procter & Gamble (another *100 Best* stock), as it is less prone to reach for new, rapidly changing markets, like cosmetics, and less apt to try to grow through acquisitions. This company is about slow, steady returns with little risk and little market volatility in bad times. We like the fact that Colgate has been able to grow earnings and

dividends faster than sales; the focus on operational efficiency has paid off. The company touts not just 10, but *50* consecutive years of dividend increases. We also like the company's orientation toward international and especially emerging markets, although currency adjustments create another source of volatility.

Reasons for Caution

Colgate participates in an increasingly competitive market, requiring more frequent new product rollouts and related marketing expenses just to keep up. Also, the Colgate business will not stimulate aggressive investors.

SECTOR: **Consumer Staples**
BETA COEFFICIENT: **.44**
10-YEAR COMPOUND EARNINGS PER SHARE GROWTH: **10.5%**
10-YEAR COMPOUND DIVIDENDS PER SHARE GROWTH: **12.0%**

	2004	2005	2006	2007	2008	2009	2010	2011
Revenues (Mil)	10,584	11,397	12,238	13,790	15,330	15,327	15,564	16,734
Net Income (Mil)	1,327	1,351	1,353	1,737	1,957	2,291	2,203	2,431
Earnings per share	2.33	2.43	2.46	3.2	3.66	4.37	4.31	4.94
Dividends per share	0.96	1.11	1.28	1.44	1.56	1.72	2.03	2.27
Cash flow per share	3.18	3.42	3.71	4.21	4.54	5.29	5.14	5.94
Price: high	59	57.2	67.1	81.3	82	87.4	86.1	94.9
low	42.9	48.2	53.4	63.8	54.4	54.5	73.1	74.9

Colgate-Palmolive Company
300 Park Avenue
New York, NY 10022–7499
(212) 310-2291
Website: *www.colgate.com*

Comcast Corporation

Ticker symbol: CMCSA (NASDAQ) ❏ S&P rating: BBB+ ❏ Value Line financial strength rating: B+ ❏ Current yield: 2.2% ❏ Dividend raises, past 10 years: 3

Company Profile

Comcast is one of the nation's leading providers of communications services and information and entertainment content passed through those services. The core business is Comcast Cable, the familiar cable TV network that has evolved into a "pipe" for delivering bundled high-speed Internet services, phone services, and on-demand content. This business serves some 23 million subscribers in 39 states.

The company has been evolving its information and entertainment business over the years through its ownership of regional sports networks and national channels such as the Golf Channel, E! (an entertainment channel), fandango.com, and others. The company took a major leap forward as a content provider with the early 2011 closing of the acquisition of 51 percent of NBC Universal (GE still owns the other 49 percent), almost instantly turning the company into not only a connectivity powerhouse but a media powerhouse as well through its ownership of Universal Pictures among other assets. With that acquisition, Comcast is now regarded as the largest integrated content development and distribution business in the United States.

Most likely in an attempt to evolve and to overcome the legacy of negative public opinion about cable operators, the company has been building its "Xfinity" Internet portal brand to compete with satellite operators and such offerings as AT&T U-verse and Verizon FiOS. Customers can buy bundles of service including TV, with 200,000 selections of on-demand video and, as an emerging offering, on-demand TV. (The company owns a stake in the leading free TV website Hulu, a new on-demand TV service that bears watching.) With Xfinity, customers can also get up to 105 mbps Internet service, probably the best service for downloading large chunks of video content. Through the Xfinity package and brand, Comcast also announced a new "Internet 2go" wireless Internet service through a 4G network. In short, Comcast has evolved from being a lackluster cable TV service to a full-scale communications utility with some of the highest performance products on the market. The company is adroitly using the Xfinity platform to draw customers in for the rest of its service bundle. In fact the company added 1.2 million Internet subscribers in 2011 alone. The company is now also rolling out an on-demand "Streampix" platform to compete with Netflix video on demand for customers not on the Xfinity platform.

The vast majority of Comcast customers are residential, although the company also offers a "Business Class" service to meet the needs of small and mid-sized organizations. The company also owns the Philadelphia 76ers and Flyers and a series of Universal theme parks through the NBC Universal subsidiary.

Financial Highlights, Fiscal Year 2011

The NBC Universal partnership gave a big boost to revenues to almost $56 billion in FY2011, compared to $38 billion in FY2010 and $22 billion back in 2005. The company has clearly solidified its base as a complete content provider beyond the simple cable TV operator it was just seven years ago and is leveraging that combination. Per-share earnings have almost quintupled from the 33 cents per share in 2005, and margin improvements and volume gains will add to earnings momentum, projected to be up some 17 percent, or $1.85 per share, for FY2012. In that time frame, the company has also emphasized shareholder returns, starting a dividend in 2008 and raising it to 65 cents recently to deliver a respectable 2-plus percent return. Notably, the NBC Universal acquisition added to revenues but did not add to share count. A projected $3 billion share repurchase (up from $2.1 billion in FY2010) will reduce the share count by 100 million to 2.6 billion. There were 3.2 billion shares outstanding in 2005.

Reasons to Buy

Comcast is one of those companies that has spent years building its product and infrastructure, and is now finally figuring out how to utilize it more profitably while at the same time offering a better value proposition to customers. Although there are some risks in entering the oft-fickle media business, we generally like Comcast's efforts to make the most of its network. What really intrigues us at this point is the on-demand services for both video and TV. While Netflix and others are bringing such services to market, because of bandwidth and other considerations, they probably make the most sense to deliver through the extremely high bandwidths of a cable system. Comcast owns the largest such system and is putting it to use—and starting to question whether the competitors should be able to use its network. While such restrictive thinking can annoy customers and bring out the antitrust regulators, it should serve to build business, and the Xfinity offering makes this much more consumer friendly. In short, Comcast is doing a lot of the right things both in the marketplace and financially. In addition and moreover, the results of those successes are being paid back to shareholders in a big way.

Reasons for Caution

There are a number of factors that could cause a little heartburn, and should be taken into account, although the company has dealt with them well so far. First is public opinion—in most people's minds, Comcast is still a cable company, and people don't like cable companies. If the company becomes too aggressive in the media content market, and particularly if it restricts others from using its "last mile" of cable, that could bring some grief in the court of public opinion, not to mention regulation. The company faces extreme competition in most of its markets, although it may have at least a temporary bandwidth advantage at present. The company must continue to invest in its technologies and delivery. Programming costs are likely to escalate, although the company is now also a producer of programming content. The high share count may still be a drag; for all the improvements the company has made the share price hasn't been that exciting—of course, therein may lie the opportunity. Finally, scenarios where the top two executives make over $50 million combined and have a controlling interest in the voting Class B shares can turn out to be a negative.

SECTOR: **Telecommunications**
BETA COEFFICIENT: **1.05**
10-YEAR COMPOUND EARNINGS PER SHARE GROWTH: **18.5 percent**
10-YEAR COMPOUND DIVIDENDS PER SHARE GROWTH: **10.0%**

		2004	2005	2006	2007	2008	2009	2010	2011
Revenues (Mil)		20,307	22,255	24,966	30,895	34,256	35,756	37,937	55,842
Net income (Mil)		970	1,098	2,235	2,287	2,701	3,638	3,535	4,377
Earnings per share		0.29	0.33	0.47	0.74	0.91	1.26	1.29	1.58
Dividends per share		—	—	—	—	0.25	0.27	0.38	0,45
Cash flow per share		1.69	1.84	1.48	2.82	3.10	3.57	3.89	4.44
Price:	high	23.6	22.8	28.7	29.6	22.5	17.3	21.2	27.2
	low	17.3	17.0	16.2	17.3	12.1	10.3	14.3	19.2

Comcast Corporation
One Comcast Center
Philadelphia, PA 19103
(215) 665-1700
Website: *www.comcast.com*

ConocoPhillips

Ticker symbol: COP □ Listed: NYSE □ S&P rating: A □ Value Line financial strength rating:
A++ □ Current yield: 3.7% □ Dividend raises, past 10 years: 10

Company Profile

In its current form, ConocoPhillips is the third-largest U.S-based integrated energy company and the sixth-largest worldwide based on market capitalization. It is also the second-largest petroleum refiner in the United States and the fifth-largest refiner in the world. The company does business throughout the hydrocarbon value chain from wellhead through refining, marketing, transportation, and chemicals.

Headquartered in Houston, Texas, ConocoPhillips operates in more than 40 countries with about 30,000 employees worldwide and annual revenues approaching $250 billion.

The company has four core activities worldwide:

- Petroleum exploration and production. This segment, approximately 23 percent of FY2011 revenues, primarily explores for, produces, transports, and markets crude oil, natural gas, and natural gas liquids on a worldwide basis. The company's E&P operations are geographically diverse, producing in the United States, including a large presence in Alaska's Prudhoe Bay; Norway; the United Kingdom; western Canada; Australia, offshore Timor-Leste in the Timor Sea; Indonesia; China; Vietnam; Libya; Nigeria; Algeria; and Russia.

- Petroleum refining, marketing, supply, and transportation. This segment, approximately 73 percent of revenues, purchases, refines, markets, and transports crude oil and petroleum products, mainly in the United States, Europe, and Asia. In the U.S. marketplace, COP products are mainly marketed under the familiar Phillips 66, Conoco, and 76 brand names.

- Midstream. This segment, about 4 percent of revenues, gathers, processes, and markets natural gas produced by ConocoPhillips and others, and fractionates and markets natural gas liquids, predominantly in the United States and Trinidad.

- Chemicals/Emerging Businesses/other. This 1 percent segment manufactures and markets petrochemicals and plastics on a worldwide basis. The Chemicals segment consists of a 50 percent equity investment in Chevron Phillips Chemical Company LLC (CPChem). There are also investments in power generation, waste hydrocarbon recovery, and other energy technologies.

The company is in the midst of a multiyear restructuring and right-sizing of its businesses. First, a split into two separate companies, one in the E&P business, one in refining and marketing, is in the works. Such splits, also taken on recently by Marathon Oil on our *100 Best* list, tend to unlock value and make it easier for both new companies to operate in their markets. Second, the company has been getting rid of nonstrategic assets, including some of its pipeline business and, as reported last year, its interest in the Russian energy conglomerate LUKOIL. Third, the $10–$15 billion obtained from asset sales is being returned to shareholders in the form of stock buybacks; the company plans to buy back some 11 percent of its outstanding shares in FY2012. All three of these developments will benefit shareholders, in our opinion.

Financial Highlights, Fiscal Year 2011

Continued strength in oil prices drove a substantial increase in FY2011 revenues and earnings. Revenues jumped 29 percent to $244 billion, while per-share earnings, aided by a substantial reduction in share count, jumped 47 percent to $8.70. Forecasts call for a relatively flat 2012 due to restructuring costs and, to a lesser extent, low natural gas prices.

Reasons to Buy

Oil and gas stocks have historically been cyclical with long-term growth as a trend. We like COP's business mix and track record, and we applaud the "rightsizing," a refreshing change from the usual pedal-to-the-metal growth strategies we see in place around the industry. The company has solid financials with an excellent earnings, cash flow, and dividend track record, in fact, a rare "quintuple play" with sales, earnings, cash flow, dividends, and book value all growing in double digits over the past 10 years. This and the share buybacks suggest a focus on shareholder value not always found in the energy industry. We also think the companies—and shareholders—will do well after the announced split.

Reasons for Caution

The split may bring some risk and cost with it, but we think it will be a smooth transition, as it was for Marathon. Refining margins always bear watching, but have been adequate lately. Like most energy companies, the ambiguities of exploration and geopolitics add a bit more uncertainty to the risk profile.

SECTOR: **Energy**
BETA COEFFICIENT: **1.15**
10-YEAR COMPOUND EARNINGS PER SHARE GROWTH: **13.5%**
10-YEAR COMPOUND DIVIDENDS PER SHARE GROWTH: **11.5%**

	2004	2005	2006	2007	2008	2009	2010	2011
Revenues (Bil)	135.1	179.4	183.7	187.4	240.8	149.3	189.4	244.8
Net Income (Bil)	8.11	13.64	15.55	11.89	15.86	5.35	9.8	12.2
Earnings per share	5.79	9.55	9.66	9.14	10.66	3.59	5.92	8.76
Dividends per share	0.9	1.18	1.44	1.64	1.88	1.91	2.16	2.64
Cash flow per share	8.28	10.27	14.19	14.86	16.8	9.85	12.50	15.65
Price: high	45.6	71.5	74.9	90.8	96	57.4	68.6	77.4
low	32.2	41.4	54.9	61.6	41.3	34.1	48.5	68.0

ConocoPhillips
600 North Dairy Ashford
Houston, TX 77079–1175
(212) 207-1996
Website: *www.conocophillips.com*

AGGRESSIVE GROWTH

Costco Wholesale Corporation

Ticker symbol: COST (NASDAQ) ❑ S&P rating: A+ ❑ Value Line financial strength rating: A+ ❑ Current yield: 1.1% ❑ Dividend raises, past 10 years: 8

Company Profile

Costco Wholesale Corporation operates a multinational chain of membership warehouses, mainly under the Costco Wholesale name, that carry brand-name merchandise at substantially lower prices than are typically found at conventional wholesale or retail sources. The warehouses are designed to help small to medium-sized businesses reduce costs in purchasing for resale and for everyday business use, but as most know, the individual consumer has been their big growth driver. The company capitalizes on size and operational efficiencies, like "cross-docking" shipments directly from manufacturers to stores, to achieve attractive pricing to its customers. Costco is the largest membership warehouse club chain in the world based on sales volume and is the fifth-largest general retailer in the United States.

Costco carries a broad line of product categories, including groceries, appliances, television and media, automotive supplies, toys, hardware, sporting goods, jewelry, cameras, books, housewares, apparel, health and beauty aids, tobacco, furniture, office supplies, and office equipment. The company also operates self-service gasoline stations at a number of its U.S. and Canadian locations. Approximately 52 percent of sales come from food, beverages, alcohol, sundries, and snacks. Another 17 percent come from "hardlines"—electronics, appliances, hardware, automotive, office supplies, and health and beauty aids—and 10 percent from "softlines"—primarily clothing, housewares, media, jewelry, and domestics—and the rest, including gasoline, pharmacy, optical and other services, form a catchall "other" category. The emergence of Costco as a grocer of choice cannot be missed.

Additionally, Costco Wholesale Industries, a division of the company, operates manufacturing businesses, including special food packaging, optical laboratories, meat processing, and jewelry distribution.

Costco is open only to members of its tiered membership plan. As of 2011 Costco has 566 locations, 426 in the United States and Puerto Rico, 80 in Canada, 32 in Mexico, 22 in the UK, 22 in Asia, and one in Australia. The company plans to open 20 more warehouse clubs overseas in 2012, primarily in Spain, France, and Asia.

Financial Highlights, Fiscal Year 2011

Like all retailers, Costco rebounded from the worldwide recession and felt the effects of its recovery during FY2011. Sales were up a heady 14 percent from FY2010, with a 7 percent same-store sales gain in the fourth quarter of that year, from a combination of increased traffic (5 percent) and increased per-ticket sales (2 percent). Both trends bode well for the future. Earnings advanced only 12.6 percent, lagging the sales increase due to heightened price competition, primarily with Walmart and other heavy discounters, and from an increased reliance on food sales (56 percent of total in FY2011 vs. 52 percent in FY2010).

Reasons to Buy

Costco is in an attractive best-of-both-worlds niche: They are a price leader consistent with the attitudes of today's more frugal consumer, yet they enjoy a reputation for being more upscale than their competition. We also continue to like the international expansion and think the formula will play well overseas. Anyone who has hosted a visitor from abroad knows that Costco is a favored destination during the visit.

We expect international expansion will be one of the company's primary growth drivers over the next 10 years. The company has a strong brand in a highly competitive sector, is gaining market share, and has a strong management track record. Although the 1.1 percent yield isn't that much of an attraction, the company has raised it each year since initiating it in 2004. The company also dramatically increased its stock repurchase authorization to $4 billion during FY2011.

Reasons for Caution

One concern is the dependence on low-margin food and sundry lines. With the ramp-up of Walmart and Target groceries and stiff competition elsewhere, Costco may not always be the food source of choice. That said, food does get customers into the store. We are also concerned about the company's not surprisingly razor-thin net profit margins—which dropped in FY2011 from 1.7 percent to 1.6 percent—even a small change in supply/demand economics or cost structure can wipe out profitability. Most retail concepts run out of steam eventually, as they run out of opportunities to expand, although Costco's international expansion attenuates this concern somewhat. With these concerns in mind, recent share prices may, once again, be a bit rich.

SECTOR: **Retail**
BETA COEFFICIENT: **.65**
10-YEAR COMPOUND EARNINGS PER SHARE GROWTH: **8.5%**
10-YEAR COMPOUND DIVIDENDS PER SHARE GROWTH: **NM**

	2004	**2005**	**2006**	**2007**	**2008**	**2009**	**2010**	**2011**
Revenues (Mil)	48,107	52,935	60,151	64,400	72,483	71,422	77,946	88,915
Net Income (Mil)	882	989	1,103	1,083	1,283	1,086	1,307	1,462
Earnings per share	1.85	2.03	2.3	2.37	2.89	2.57	2.93	3,30
Dividends per share	0.2	0.45	0.49	0.55	0.61	0.68	0.77	.89
Cash flow per share	2.03	2.31	2.63	2.89	2.89	4.16	4.85	5.34
Price: high	50.5	51.2	57.9	72.7	75.2	61.3	73.2	88.7
low	35	39.5	46	51.5	43.9	38.2	53.4	69.5

Costco Wholesale Corporation
999 Lake Drive
Issaquah, WA 98027
(425) 313-8203
Website: *www.costco.com*

CVS/Caremark Corporation

Ticker symbol: CVS (NYSE) □ S&P rating: BBB+ □ Value Line financial strength rating: A □ Current yield: 1.5% □ Dividend raises, past 10 years: 10

Company Profile

Stanley and Sid Goldstein were distributing health and beauty products in the early 1960s when they decided to branch out into retailing, opening their first Consumer Value Store in Lowell, Massachusetts, in 1963. The CVS chain had grown to 40 outlets by 1969, the year they sold the business to Melville Shoes. Melville underwent a restructuring in the mid-1990s, spinning off CVS and other retail units.

CVS Corporation is now the largest pharmacy health-care provider in the United States. Its flagship domestic drugstore chain operates 7,300 retail and specialty pharmacy stores in 41 states and the District of Columbia. The company holds the leading market share in 32 of the 100 largest U.S. drugstore markets, more than any other retail drugstore chain. Over time, it has expanded through acquiring other players in the category—Osco, Sav-On, Eckerd, and Long's Drugs. CVS's purchase of Long's Drugs in 2008 vaulted the company into the lead position in the U.S. drug retail market, ahead of Walgreen's.

Stores are situated primarily in strip shopping centers or free-standing locations, with a typical store ranging in size from 8,000 to 12,000 square feet. Most new units being built are based on either a 10,000 square foot or 12,000 square foot prototype building that typically includes a drive-thru pharmacy. The company says that about one-half of its stores were opened or remodeled over the past five years.

The Caremark acquisition in 2007 transformed CVS from strictly a retailer into the nation's leading manager of pharmacy benefits, the middlemen between pharmaceutical companies and individuals with drug benefit coverage. The Caremark acquisition forms the core of the company's Pharmacy Benefits Management (PBM) operations, which have some 65,000 pharmacy outlets including hospitals and clinics as well as the above-mentioned stores. The company dispenses some 775 million prescriptions a year, and the Pharmacy Services segment now makes up about 65 percent of sales.

MinuteClinic is especially interesting in today's climate of examining health-care costs, now with 657 clinics in 25 states offering basic health services like flu shots and such in a convenient retail environment. All but twelve of these clinics are located in CVS stores, naturally serving to drive traffic into the stores and vice versa. The company also operates mail order and online pharmacies for regular and chronically ill patients.

Financial Highlights, Fiscal Year 2011

The 2010 softness in the Pharmacy Benefits segment, which caused an overall sales decline in that year, is now behind the company. Aided by a new PBM contract signed with Aetna, CVS recorded a "healthy" 11 percent increase in sales. Earnings, however, languished a bit as the company continues to digest its acquisitions and seek efficiencies in the lower margined PBM business. Helped along by share buybacks, the company expects to earn $3.18 to $3.28 per share in FY2012, which would be a 15 percent increase over FY2011. Although the dividend isn't large, the company seems dedicated to raising it regularly, and has been fairly aggressive in share repurchases since making its big acquisitions in the mid 2000s.

Reasons to Buy

People who shop CVS regularly can see the difference between these stores and the ubiquitous competitors, especially Walgreen's. These stores are essentially big-box convenience stores, but we think the company does a notably good job of merchandising, offering a good mix of convenience merchandise, food, and health-care products to truly capitalize on its convenient retail format.

That goes beyond the typical positives seen for this industry: the graying of the population, the rather effortless spending on health care that still goes on. The company continues to feel that its leadership in sun-belt states will capitalize on this megatrend. The recent federal health-care overhaul left Medicare Part D basically untouched, which at the end of 2009, provided prescription coverage to 27 million Americans who would otherwise not be eligible. Medicare Part D also encourages caregivers to use generic drugs whenever possible, and generics, while cheaper overall, generate higher margins for the pharmacy. Over the next five years, more than $50 billion in branded drugs will lose patent protection, creating further opportunities for generics and driving pharmacy margins even higher.

Finally, the company has scored a quintuple play over the past 10 years with double-digit compounded sales, earnings, cash flow, dividend, and book value growth over the period. That said, the dividend yield remains modest.

Reasons for Caution

The PBM business continues to be challenging from both a sales and profitability standpoint. Like all players in the health-care industry, increased focus on cost control could hurt CVS, although we think both the PBM and retail store concepts are fairly recession-proof.

SECTOR: **Retail**
BETA COEFFICIENT: **0.80**
10-YEAR COMPOUND EARNINGS PER SHARE GROWTH: **13.0%**
10-YEAR COMPOUND DIVIDENDS PER SHARE GROWTH: **10.5%**

	2004	2005	2006	2007	2008	2009	2010	2011
Revenue (Mil)	30,594	37,006	43,814	76,330	87,472	98,729	98,413	107,273
Net Income (Mil)	847	1,225	1,369	2,637	3,589	3,662	3,700	3,770
Earnings per share	1.15	1.45	1.6	1.92	2.44	2.63	2.67	2.80
Dividends per share	0.13	0.14	0.16	0.24	0.26	0.3	0.35	0.50
Cash flow per share	1.75	2.15	2.5	2.59	3.37	3.73	3.75	4.10
Price: high	23.7	31.6	36.1	42.6	44.3	38.3	37.8	39.5
low	16.9	22	26.1	30.5	23.2	23.7	26.8	31.3

CVS/Caremark Corporation
One CVS Drive
Woonsocket, RI 02895
(914) 722-4704
Website: *www.cvs.com*

AGGRESSIVE GROWTH

Deere & Company

Ticker symbol: DE (NYSE) ❏ S&P rating: A ❏ Value Line financial strength rating: A++ ❏ Current yield: 2.3% ❏ Dividend raises, past 10 years: 10

Company Profile

Founded in 1837, Deere & Company grew from a one-man blacksmith shop into a worldwide corporation that today does business in more than 160 countries and employs more than 40,000 people around the globe. Deere has a diverse base of operations reporting into three segments: Agriculture and Turf Equipment, Construction and Forestry, and Credit.

Deere has been the world's premier producer of agricultural equipment for nearly 50 years. The Agriculture and Turf segment produces and distributes tractors, loaders, combines, harvesters, seeding, mowers, hay baling, tilling, crop care and application, snow removal, and other equipment. If it's used on a farm and requires an engine, Deere likely offers it. With the Construction and Forestry segment, Deere is also the world's leading manufacturer of forestry equipment, and a major manufacturer of heavy construction equipment (Caterpillar being the market leader in this segment). They're also the world leader in premium turf-care equipment and utility vehicles in both the commercial and consumer markets.

The Credit segment includes John Deere Credit, which is one of the largest equipment finance companies in the United States, with more than 1.8 million accounts and a managed asset portfolio of nearly $16 billion. It provides retail, wholesale, and lease financing for agricultural, construction, and forestry equipment; commercial and consumer equipment, including lawn and ground care; and revolving credit for agricultural inputs and services. These services are available in all of Deere's largest markets, including Argentina, Australia, Brazil, Canada, France, and Germany. Overall, international sales continue to account for about 42 percent of the total.

Financial Highlights, Fiscal Year 2011

Global economic recovery and strong agricultural commodity prices made FY2011 a very strong "harvest" for Deere. Revenues jumped some 24 percent to $29.5 billion, while earnings, strengthened by restructuring moves made during 2009, plowed ahead some 50 percent to $2.8 billion, or $6.63 per share. The company raised the dividend 31 percent and bought back almost 4 percent of its stock—all in all a pretty good year. FY2012 is off to a good start, and the company is quite confident in its abilities to earn $3 billion for their year (actually, almost $3.2 billion) on sales of $39.2 billion.

Reasons to Buy

"Nothing runs like a Deere" is the company's apt slogan, and as far as industrial companies go, Deere has achieved almost unparalleled excellence over the years. They have an outstanding brand (and one of the most popular logos for hats, jackets, and so on, worn by people who have never seen a farm field!) and reputation in the agriculture industry, and we see the ag industry as strong and strategic far into the future as global living standards improve and emerging markets develop. Farm incomes continue to rise worldwide. The company is making good progress in developing markets, particularly in Brazil and India. The business cycle is also turning positive for the smaller Construction and Forestry segment.

Beyond its products, Deere has established an almost unassailable brand leadership with its services and customer-centered innovations. Deere, more than others, puts its people in the field (literally) to figure out what agriculture professionals really need, and they work with their customers closely to sell their products through a solid dealer network, not unlike Caterpillar in the construction market.

Finally, as evidenced by dividend increases and share buybacks, the company seems to have total shareholder returns in mind.

Reasons for Caution

The company is, and always will be, vulnerable to business cycles and particularly cycles in the farm sector. While agricultural commodities are once again on the rise, that can turn on a dime. Farmers, sensing price declines, will change their attitudes about buying new equipment on that same dime. The company's 1.53 beta reflects this long-term volatility. Recent public-sector belt tightening both at the federal and state level may hurt the farming business, as will any protracted rise in energy prices. Many analysts feel Deere may have already seen the best of this cycle.

SECTOR: **Industrials**
BETA COEFFICIENT: **1.53**
10-YEAR COMPOUND EARNINGS PER SHARE GROWTH: **22.0%**
10-YEAR COMPOUND DIVIDENDS PER SHARE GROWTH: **11.0%**

		2004	2005	2006	2007	2008	2009	2010	2011
Revenues (Mil)		17,673	19,401	19,884	21,489	25,804	20,756	23,573	29,644
Net income (Mil)		1,406	1,447	1,453	1,822	2,053	1,198	1,865	2,799
Earnings per share		2.78	2.94	3.08	4.01	4.7	2.82	4.35	6.534
Dividends per share		0.53	0.61	0.78	0.91	1.06	1.12	1.16	1.52
Cash flow per share		3.54	3.85	4.09	5.12	6.01	4.05	5.72	8.34
Price:	high	37.5	37.4	50.7	93.7	94.9	56.9	84.9	89.7
	low	28.4	28.5	33.5	45.1	28.5	24.5	46.3	78.8

Deere & Company
One John Deere Place
Moline, IL 61265
(309) 765-4491
Website: *www.deere.com*

Dominion Resources, Inc.

Ticker symbol: D (NYSE) ❑ S&P rating: A- ❑ Value Line financial strength rating: B++ ❑ Current yield: 4.1% ❑ Dividend raises, past 10 years: 10

Company Profile

Dominion is one of the nation's largest producers and distributors of energy, with 27,000 megawatts of regulated and nonregulated power generation; 6,000 miles of electric transmission lines; and 11,000 miles of natural gas transmission, gathering, and storage pipeline. Included in these assets is the nation's largest underground natural gas storage system with about 947 billion cubic feet of storage capacity serving retail energy customers in twelve states. Dominion's strategy is to be a leading provider of electricity, natural gas, and related services to customers in the energy-intensive Midwest, Mid-Atlantic, and Northeast regions of the United States, a potential market of 50 million homes and businesses where 40 percent of the nation's energy is consumed.

The company has several operating subsidiaries, which group into three primary segments: Dominion Generation, which operates independent generation assets and produces about 49 percent of FY2011 profits; Dominion Virginia Power (25 percent of profits), the regulated retail arm, distributing electricity in Virginia and parts of North Carolina; and Dominion Energy, (26 percent of profits), which operates in the regulated gas distribution and unregulated transmission and storage businesses. More detailed descriptions:

- Dominion Generation includes the independent generation operations of Dominion's merchant fleet and regulated electric utility, as well as energy marketing and price risk management activities for its generation assets. Their utility generation operations primarily serve the supply requirements for the Dominion Virginia Power segment's utility customers. Their generation mix is diversified and includes coal, nuclear, gas, oil, and renewables. The mix currently is 31 percent coal, 28 percent nuclear, 10 percent gas, 2 percent "other," and 29 percent purchased, and the operation has another coal- and a natural gas–fired plant coming on line.
- Dominion Energy includes Dominion's Ohio regulated

natural gas distribution company, regulated gas transmission pipeline and storage operations, regulated liquefied natural gas (LNG) operations, and Appalachian natural gas Exploration & Production (E&P) business. Dominion Energy also includes a producer services business line, which aggregates natural gas supply, engages in natural gas trading and marketing activities and natural gas supply management, and provides price-risk management services to Dominion affiliates. The gas transmission pipeline and storage business serves gas distribution businesses and other customers in the Northeast, Mid-Atlantic, and Midwest.

■ Dominion Virginia Power is responsible for all regulated electric distribution and electric transmission operations in Virginia and North Carolina. It is also responsible for Dominion Retail and all customer service, as well as its nonregulated retail energy marketing operations. DVP's electric transmission and distribution operations serve residential, commercial, industrial, and governmental customers in Virginia and northeastern North Carolina.

Financial Highlights, Fiscal Year 2011

The Virginia-based Dominion Resources endured an earthquake and a hurricane in FY2011. Yes, indeed, the Virginia earthquake was of 5.6 magnitude, centered 110 miles from one of its Virginia nuclear units, and Hurricane Irene, just three days later, knocked out about half its customers' power at least briefly. These events, combined with unusually mild weather conditions, led to a 5 percent revenue decrease and a 15-cent hit to per-share earnings, which dropped about 4.5 percent to $2.76 per share. Ample cash flow and reserves enabled the company to continue increasing its dividend by some 7.6 percent, and another 7 percent increase is slated for FY2012. Payout ratios are low at 70 percent of earnings, and the payout as a percentage of the cash flow is even healthier; it was encouraging to see how easily the company handled these combined events. FY2012 projections call for per-share earnings to rise about 14 percent, essentially resuming the growth track prior to the "perfect storm" of 2011.

Reasons to Buy

Dominion's core businesses are healthy and located in areas of solid recovery and growth potential, particularly in the Eastern Seaboard areas. The company is resilient and dedicated to shareholder returns, as evidenced by the events of 2011. The size of dividend increases has been growing, and the regulatory environment, so far, has been cooperative.

Reasons for Caution

The company has a larger nuclear exposure than most at 28 percent of generating capacity; that can be good in times of rapidly increasing fossil fuel prices but bad when unforeseeable events occur and/or when natural gas appears to be the bargain fuel of the day. Last year nearby Duke Energy acquired Progress Energy, meaning that acquisitions may be in the air once again; it's hard to predict how that might affect Dominion.

SECTOR: **Utilities**
BETA COEFFICIENT: **.46**
10-YEAR COMPOUND EARNINGS PER SHARE GROWTH: **9.0%**
10-YEAR COMPOUND DIVIDENDS PER SHARE GROWTH: **3.0%**

	2004	**2005**	**2006**	**2007**	**2008**	**2009**	**2010**	**2011**
Revenues (Mil)	13,972	17,971	16,482	15,674	16,290	15,131	15,197	14,379
Net Income (Mil)	1,425	1,033	1,704	1,414	1,781	1,585	1,724	1,604
Earnings per share	2.13	1.5	2.4	2.13	3.04	2.64	2.89	2.76
Dividends per share	1.3	1.34	1.38	1.46	1.58	1.75	1.83	1.97
Cash flow per share	4.18	3.71	4.91	5.08	5.07	4.82	5.10	5.05
Price: high	34.5	43.5	42.2	49.4	48.5	39.8	45.1	53.6
low	30.4	33.3	34.4	39.8	31.3	27.1	36.1	42.1

Dominion Resources, Inc.
P.O. Box 26532
Richmond, VA 23261–6532
(804) 819-2156
Website: *www.dom.com*

Duke Energy

Ticker symbol: DUK (NYSE) ❑ S&P rating: A- ❑ Value Line financial strength rating: A ❑ Current yield: 4.8% ❑ Dividend raises, past 6 years: 6

Company Profile

Duke Energy Corporation is a utility provider and operator working primarily in the Southeast and Midwest but with operations outside those areas. The company has three segments: U.S. Franchised Electric and Gas, Commercial Power, and International Energy. The company was reformed into a new company in 2007 after spinning off most of its gas business into a new company called Spectra Energy.

The Franchised Electric and Gas segment generates, transmits, distributes, and sells electricity as a regulated utility in central and western North Carolina, western South Carolina, southwestern Ohio, Indiana, and northern Kentucky including the Greater Cincinnati area; and transports and sells natural gas in southwestern Ohio and northern Kentucky. This segment supplies electric service to approximately 4 million residential, commercial, and industrial customers with approximately 151,600 miles of distribution lines and a 20,900-mile transmission system. The company is relatively heavily invested in nuclear power, with some 33 percent of its power

provided this way (56 percent coal, 10 percent other).

The Commercial Power segment's main business is to generate power to sell into the unregulated wholesale market, with about 7,500 megawatts of generating capacity located mainly in the Midwest. The Duke Energy Generating Services subsidiary within this segment develops and operates renewable energy projects, including some newly acquired solar arrays in North Carolina and Arizona. One subsidiary within this segment also offers onsite energy solutions and utility services for large customers, including municipalities and large factory complexes.

The International Energy segment operates and manages power generation facilities and sells and markets electric power, natural gas, and other energy products outside the United States, mainly in Latin America.

In early 2011, Duke announced a $13.7 billion takeover of Progress Energy, which operates in adjacent markets. The combined company would be the largest public utility in the United States. Aside from direct impacts on the company and its operations, the acquisition is viewed as a referendum on public regulator acceptance of a new round of "mega" mergers in the utility industry. If approved, the deal is expected to close sometime in mid-2012.

Financial Highlights, Fiscal Year 2011

Revenues and earnings both advanced modestly and in line with expectations in FY2011. Recent rate increase approvals in the Carolinas have the company guiding for earnings in the $1.40–$1.45 range for FY2012, slightly up from FY2011's $1.38. Notably, the company continues to generate cash flow almost double reported earning, and the dividend is well covered for now. The Progress deal will add about 770 million new shares to the existing 1.33 billion, a hefty jump that shouldn't change things much but may bear watching.

Reasons to Buy

Duke has always been a well-managed utility operating in solid markets with a growing customer base. The North Carolina customer base is diverse and especially attractive as more companies and individuals move there to enjoy lower costs of living and costs of doing business. The company should

also stand to benefit, perhaps more than its peers, from an economic recovery.

We actually like its nuclear exposure, as we do think nuclear power will return to the electricity generating stage in a bigger way. Duke will have the advantage of experience and existing infrastructure, and is gaining experience with other renewables as well, perhaps paving the way to a less fossil-fuel–driven future. Because it's a relatively new concern in its current form, and perhaps because of its nuclear exposure, the dividend is about 1 percent higher than the average for similar companies.

Reasons for Caution

For many, nuclear power is a reason for caution, and we certainly would want to diversify utility holdings to avoid overexposure to utilities with nuclear facilities. Like most utilities, Duke depends on regulatory rate relief to grow revenues, and so the regulatory environment is critical. The Progress acquisition would create size and critical mass but may also consume a lot of cash and make the company too big and perhaps too reliant on acquisitions to fuel growth. That said, the company seems well enough managed to take on such an endeavor.

SECTOR: **Utilities**
BETA COEFFICIENT: **0.35**
10-YEAR COMPOUND EARNINGS PER SHARE GROWTH: **NA**
10-YEAR COMPOUND DIVIDENDS PER SHARE GROWTH: **NA**

	2004	**2005**	**2006**	**2007**	**2008**	**2009**	**2010**	**2011**
Revenues (Mil)	—	—	10,607	12,720	13,207	12,731	14,272	14,529
Net Income (Mil)	—	—	1,080	1,522	1,279	1,461	1,771	1,848
Earnings per share	—	—	.92	1.20	1.01	1.13	1.34	1.38
Dividends per share	—	—	—	.86	.90	.94	.97	.99
Cash flow per share	—	—	2.62	2.70	2.45	2.53	2.70	2.95
Price: high	—	—	21.3	20.6	17.9	17.5	18.6	22.1
low	—	—	16.9	13.5	11.7	15.9	15.5	20.9

Duke Energy Corporation
526 South Church Street
Charlotte, NC 28202–1803
(704) 594-6200
Website: ***www.duke-energy.com***

GROWTH AND INCOME

E. I. DuPont De Nemours

Ticker symbol: DD (NYSE) ❑ S&P rating: A ❑ Value Line financial strength rating: A++ ❑ Current yield: 3.1% ❑ Dividend raises, past 10 years: 4

Company Profile

"The miracles of science" is the slogan and rallying cry of this $30 billion-plus science and technology juggernaut originally founded in 1802 to make gunpowder. Although the company is known to many as a cyclical "diversified chemical" company making a host of rather lifeless chemical products and ingredients, many by the tank-car load, today's DuPont is reawakening as a world leader in science and technology with important end product ingredients in a range of disciplines, including biotechnology, electronics materials and science, safety and security, and synthetic fibers. The company has always been a technology leader with such well-known inventions as Nylon and Rayon in earlier years, and Teflon and Kevlar more recently, but at least until recently has been taken in more as a commodity producer than an innovator. We see signs of change in that reputation, toward its own "market-driven science" business vision.

The company continues to operate in an eight-segment alignment established in 2009. Admittedly, in our 2012 edition of *100 Best Stocks*, we could have done a better job of explaining these businesses; here is our 2013 attempt:

- The Agriculture segment (15 percent of revenues) delivers a portfolio of products and services specifically targeted to achieve gains in crop yields and productivity, including Pioneer brand seed products and well-established brands of insecticides, fungicides, and herbicides. Pioneer develops, produces, and markets corn hybrid and soybean varieties and sells wheat, rice, sunflower, canola, and other seeds under the Pioneer and other brand names. DuPont also sells a line of crop protection products for field and orchard agriculture.
- Electronic and Communications (7 percent) makes a line of high-tech materials for the semiconductor industry, including ceramic packages and LCD materials. E&C supplies differentiated materials and systems for photovoltaics (solar), consumer electronics, displays, and advanced printing.

- Nutrition and Health (7 percent) consists of the recently acquired Danisco's specialty food ingredients business and Solae, a majority-owned venture with Bunge Limited, which is engaged in developing soy-based technologies. The segment is a provider of solutions for specialty food ingredients, health, and safety. Products include cultures, emulsifiers, gums, natural sweeteners, and soy-based foods.
- Industrial Biosciences (4 percent) is engaged in developing and manufacturing a wide range of enzymes, the biocatalysts that enable chemical reactions, on a large scale. The segment's enzymes add value and functionality to a broad range of products and processes, such as animal nutrition, detergents, food manufacturing, ethanol production, and industrial applications.

These first four businesses are relatively new and growing, and add on to the traditional core businesses:

- Performance Chemicals (23 percent) delivers a range of industrial and specialty chemical products like fluorochemicals (refrigerants, Teflon) and titanium-based pigments to a variety of industrial customers, including plastics and coatings, textiles, mining, pulp and paper, water treatment, and health-care manufacturers.
- Performance Materials (13 percent) supplies high-performance polymers, films, plastics, and substrates to a variety of industries from automotive to aerospace and consumer durable goods manufacturers and many others.
- Performance Coatings (19 percent) primarily supplies motor vehicle paints and coatings. The company recently announced an "auction" of its auto paint business, and expects to fetch somewhere around $4 billion from it.
- Safety and Protection (11 percent) makes protective fibers and clothing, including bulletproof apparel; disinfectants; and protective building surfaces—Tyvek house wrap is one of the bigger brands here.

The company has operations in 90 countries worldwide, and about 70 percent of consolidated net sales are made to customers outside the United States. Worldwide subsidiaries and affiliates of DuPont conduct manufacturing, seed production, or selling activities, and some are distributors of products manufactured by the company.

DuPont has one of the largest R&D budgets of any company in the world and operates more than 75 R&D centers worldwide. DuPont's core research is concentrated at its Wilmington, Delaware, facilities. DuPont's modern research is focused on renewable bio-based materials, advanced bio-fuels, energy-efficient technologies, enhanced safety products, and alternative energy technologies.

Financial Highlights, Fiscal Year 2011

A few years ago, the company projected 2012 earnings at $3.50 per share, up from the mid-$1 range. That promise was greeted with skepticism, but hey, guess what? The company achieved $3.68 per share in FY2011, a year ahead of schedule, and now projects $4.20 to $4.40 per share going forward for FY2012, a 7 to 12 percent increase. Revenues, aided by the Danisco acquisition, advanced some 21 percent. Core businesses are rebounding with the rebound in the auto industry and others, and the newer businesses and products are growing and making a steadily larger contribution. Agriculture is strong, and other "new" businesses are gaining traction.

Reasons to Buy

DuPont continues to succeed in reinventing itself (and remarketing itself) as an innovation leader, and to capitalize equally on innovation and product leadership in established categories. Not that this company doesn't have experience with innovation—quite the opposite, in fact, the problem seems to be in getting recognized for its innovation. The product pipeline continues to be full, individual product margins remain strong, and the company's biggest money-makers still dominate their markets.

The company now visualizes itself as a "fast growing science company" set to capitalize on "global megatrends"—population growth, alternative energy production, and so forth. The improvement of worldwide food production is at the center of its new growth initiatives. Alternative energy will also get the spotlight: The Danisco acquisition is, among other things, a major play in the synthetic cellulosic biofuels market with its Genencor industrial enzymes business. The U.S. government has mandated some 30 billion gallons of annual cellulosic biofuel production by 2017.

In short, this company is clicking on all cylinders, especially in terms of capitalizing on existing brands and technology leadership. The 3.6 percent dividend yield provides an added measure of safety and opportunity to wait for things to really come together. When things do, look for more frequent dividend increases, share buybacks and all of those other shareholder goodies.

Reasons for Caution

For whatever reason—anemic marketing may be one of them—the company has seldom been able to capitalize on its "science and technology" positioning, and is viewed as a commodity producer instead. We'll see if it's any different this time. The stock price has woken up to these brighter prospects, and has been relatively strong, particularly in comparison to its 2009 low of $16. Buyers should look for dips—like the one in late 2011 as manufacturer inventory "destocking" caused a brief sales slump.

SECTOR: **Materials**
BETA COEFFICIENT: **1.53**
10-YEAR COMPOUND EARNINGS PER SHARE GROWTH: **0.5%**
10-YEAR COMPOUND DIVIDENDS PER SHARE GROWTH: **1.5%**

	2004	**2005**	**2006**	**2007**	**2008**	**2009**	**2010**	**2011**
Revenues (Mil)	27,340	26,639	28,982	30,653	30,529	26,109	31,505	38,000
Net Income (Mil)	2,390	2,100	3,148	2,988	2,477	1,769	3,032	3,670
Earnings per share	2.38	2.32	2.88	3.22	2.73	2.04	3.28	3.68
Dividends per share	1.4	1.46	1.48	1.52	1.64	1.64	1.64	1.64
Cash flow per share	3.75	3.97	4.4	4.89	4.25	3.4	4.80	5.65
Price: high	49.4	54.9	49.7	53.9	52.5	35.6	50.2	57.0
low	39.9	37.6	38.5	42.3	21.3	16	31.9	37.1

E. I. DuPont De Nemours
1007 Market Street
Wilmington, DE 19898
(800) 441-7515
Website: *www.dupont.com*

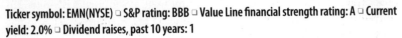

CONSERVATIVE GROWTH

NEW
FOR 2013

Eastman Chemical

Ticker symbol: EMN(NYSE) □ S&P rating: BBB □ Value Line financial strength rating: A □ Current yield: 2.0% □ Dividend raises, past 10 years: 1

Company Profile

When you open a bottle of your favorite carbonated beverage, do you think about the little plastic seal inside the cap designed to preserve the fizz? Without changing the taste. Through all climate conditions—120-degree beer trucks in summer to the inside of your refrigerator. For 13 billion bottles annually for Anheuser-Busch alone. Those are the kinds of things that Eastman Chemical thinks about, in fact, the "plasticizer" additives designed to increase the flexibility and durability of any beverage container liner—without using phthalates. Phthalates? Remember that one for your next spelling bee.

Eastman is one of those "better living through chemistry" companies with a history of solving problems and providing standard, high-tech, and high-precision materials to industries ranging from food and beverage to toys to medical equipment to computers and electronics. The company was spun off from Eastman Kodak (which now probably wishes they had kept it) in 1993.

The company is organized into four product groups, all of which

have something more or less to do with petrochemicals:

- Performance Chemicals and Intermediates ("PCI," 36 percent of sales) produces "acetyl and olefin streams" that eventually become strategic ingredients for agricultural chemicals, fibers, food and beverage ingredients, laundry-care products, pharmaceuticals, and medical devices and other specialty applications.
- Coatings, Adhesives, Specialty Polymers, and Inks ("CASPI," 27 percent of sales) produces resins and other components designed to improve the appearance and performance of paints, coatings, inks, adhesives, and similar products.
- Fibers (27 percent) produces materials and finished fibers for everything from cigarette filters to clothing and home furnishings.
- Specialty Plastics (18 percent) produces specialty materials and films for, among other things, liquid crystal displays (LCDs).

Obviously there could be considerably more detail in these descriptions, but it would probably only be meaningful to those with a strong chemistry or materials background. The upshot: Eastman makes a lot of strategically important materials that support a lot of manufacturing processes for common and fairly high-volume items, like beer bottles, for example. Additionally, these materials are used in considerable amounts in overseas manufacturing. Eastman has adapted by setting up plants in 10 countries and driving foreign sales to 52 percent of the total.

Financial Highlights, Fiscal Year 2011

Eastman is tied closely to manufacturing cycles, and the 2008–09 recession took its toll. As the economy has improved and international manufacturing activities in particular expanded, Eastman has seen strength in sales, product prices, and profit margins. FY2011 sales advanced 23 percent to $7.2 billion, a level consistent with the boom years prior to the recession. Operating margins have improved to 18–20 percent in the past two years compared to 10–15 percent in most years before that. Per-share earnings, thus, advanced over 30 percent to $4.56, a level well ahead of the boom years, thanks to

strengthening margins and a substantial reduction of share count from 167 million in 2006 to 137 million at the end of 2011.

Reasons to Buy

Although Eastman lies on the edge of the "buy businesses you understand" test, it's obvious from the numbers and especially the improving margins that the company really does produce things vitally important to manufacturing today's products. The company has become much more profitable and has done so quietly; it's not a company that most people have heard of. The strategy of establishing a global manufacturing presence seems to be working, and greater profitability combined with expanding volumes over time should bode well. Additionally, Eastman acquired Solutia, another complementary specialty chemicals maker for $2 billion; this acquisition is expected to drive FY2012 EPS to $5.00 from the relatively flat $4.56 forecast initially, and $6.00 the following year—showing the hallmarks of a good acquisition. While shareholder returns have come in the form of aggressive buybacks, we would expect the cash dividend to rise once the acquisition is complete.

Reasons for Caution

Eastman will never be immune to manufacturing cycles and energy (feedstock) prices. While product pricing has been strong recently, weakening global demand may force price reductions, as competition is strong for many of Eastman's products. We would also hope that Eastman doesn't get too aggressive with acquisitions and instead focuses on expanding its own product portfolio organically.

SECTOR: **Materials**
BETA COEFFICIENT: **1.95**
10-YEAR COMPOUND EARNINGS PER SHARE GROWTH: **5.5%**
10-YEAR COMPOUND DIVIDENDS PER SHARE GROWTH: **1.0%**

	2004	2005	2006	2007	2008	2009	2010	2011
Revenues (Mil)	6,580	7,059	7,450	6,830	6,720	5,047	5,842	7,178
Net income (Mil)	195	485	416	423	342	265	514	653
Earnings per share	1.25	2.97	2.50	2.53	2.25	1.82	3.48	4.56
Dividends per share	.88	.88	.88	.88	.88	.88	.88	.97
Cash flow per share	3.63	4.94	4.33	4.71	4.20	3.72	5.62	6.76
Price: high	29.1	30.9	30.6	39.2	39.1	31.0	42.3	55.4
low	19.0	22.0	23.7	28.8	12.9	8.9	25.9	32.4

Eastman Chemical Corporation
200 South Wilcox Drive
Kingsport, TN 37662
(423) 229-2000
Website: *www.eastman.com*

GROWTH AND INCOME

ExxonMobil Corporation

Ticker symbol: XOM (NYSE) ❏ S&P rating: AAA ❏ Value Line financial strength rating: A++ ❏ Current yield: 2.2% ❏ Dividend raises, past 10 years: 10

Company Profile

ExxonMobil is the world's largest publicly traded oil company, with annual sales approaching half a trillion dollars. The company is engaged in all parts of the hydrocarbon value chain, including the exploration, production, manufacture, transportation, and sale of crude oil, natural gas, and petroleum products. They also have a stake in the manufacture of petrochemicals, packaging films, and specialty chemicals.

Divisions and affiliated companies of ExxonMobil operate or market products in the United States and some 200 other countries and territories. Their principal business is energy, involving exploration for and production of crude oil and natural gas, manufacture of petroleum products, and transportation and sale of crude oil, natural gas, and petroleum products.

The company is a major manufacturer and marketer of basic petrochemicals, including olefins, aromatics, polyethylene, and polypropylene plastics and a wide variety of specialty products. It also has interests in electric power generation facilities.

ExxonMobil conducts oil and gas exploration, development, and production in every major accessible producing region in the world. They have the largest energy resource base of any nongovernment company and are the largest nongovernment natural gas marketer and reserves holder. They're the world's largest fuels refiner and manufacture of base stocks used for making motor oils. The company is also involved in producing "synthetic" crude from crude bitumen extracted from open pit mines, mostly in Canada. They have refining operations in 26 countries, 42,000 retail service stations in more than 100 countries, and lubricants marketing in almost 200 countries and territories. They market petrochemical products in more than 150 countries, and 90 percent of the company's petrochemical assets are in businesses that are ranked number one or number two in market position.

The XTO acquisition, completed in 2010, is a strong indication of Exxon's shift toward more profitable upstream operations, as well as a play in the likely future upside in natural gas prices. Since then, the company has been relatively quiet on the acquisition front, but we may see more activity, especially in the natural gas business.

Financial Highlights, Fiscal Year 2011

The numbers are just enormous, and getting larger as energy prices escalate. Revenues for FY2011 were up some 27 percent to $433.5 billion, although about $10 billion of that owes to the XTO acquisition. (Take XTO out, and the growth rate is still 24 percent!) Profits—this is profits, not revenue—grew 34.5 percent to $41 billion. It is hard to comprehend numbers of this magnitude. Moving forward, earnings per share came in at $8.42, up from $6.42 in FY2010. The company clearly fired on all cylinders in FY2011 but expects growth to slow as high prices temper demand and reduce refining profits. Among other pluses: They report a healthy 121 percent reserve replacement rate. The company also retired 186 million of its 4.7 billion shares and has retired almost 2 billion shares since 2004.

Reasons to Buy

ExxonMobil used to vie with Apple, Inc. for the number one and number two spots in total market capitalization, that is, the total value of shares outstanding. Apple pulled way ahead due to its stellar growth

and market position but still has "only" $25 billion in profits to show annually versus the $41 billion produced by XOM. Yes, valuation is also based on growth, and Apple indeed is on a faster growth trajectory, but XOM could be viewed as a company that has already gotten there. A decision to buy ExxonMobil over a company such as Apple is essentially the decision to own a company with 25 billion barrels of oil equivalent in the ground and the means to bring them to market as high value-add products, in contrast to owning a company with outstanding products, market acceptance, and innovation. It's an interesting choice.

Exxon is the largest publicly traded oil company in the world, and in the oil business, there are strategic advantages that accrue to size. Having the resources to bring to bear on an opportunity can mean the difference between winning and losing an exploration or development award. Despite the company's enormous size, it has managed to return double-digit growth over the past 10 years in sales, earnings, and cash flow, although these might be tied more to energy prices than operational excellence. Finally, Exxon's track record of returning cash to shareholders has been good, and we might well see the yield increase over time (which is far from certain with Apple!).

Reasons for Caution

ExxonMobil is the biggest and the best at a lot of things in a key strategic industry. But there can be such a thing as too big, and if any integrated energy company is to suffer for being too big, this may be the one. Additionally and not surprisingly, XOM tends to be a lightning rod for criticism of oil company profits, and may be square in the sights of tax reform and tax preference legislation. While we applaud the share buybacks, we would like to see a higher dividend payout, although the recent low yields reflect a resurgence in the stock price—also not a positive for entering investors. We don't expect XOM to outperform the market to any great extent, but it should continue to be a solid cornerstone holding.

SECTOR: **Energy**
BETA COEFFICIENT: **0.50**
10-YEAR COMPOUND EARNINGS PER SHARE GROWTH: **12.5%**
10-YEAR COMPOUND DIVIDENDS PER SHARE GROWTH: **7.0%**

	2004	2005	2006	2007	2008	2009	2010	2011
Revenues (Bil)	264	328	335	359	425	276	342	434
Net Income (Bil)	25.3	36.1	39.1	40.6	45.3	19.3	30.4	41
Earnings per share	3.89	5.71	6.62	7.28	8.69	3.98	6.22	8.42
Dividends per share	1.06	1.14	1.28	1.37	1.55	1.66	1.74	1.85
Cash flow per share	5.48	7.19	8.82	9.82	11.58	6.60	9.08	11.97
Price: high	52	66	79	95.3	96.1	82.7	73.7	88.2
low	39.9	49.2	56.4	69	56.5	61.9	55.9	67.0

ExxonMobil Corporation
5959 Las Colinas Boulevard
Irving, TX 75039–2298
(972) 444-1538
Website: *www.exxonmobil.com*

Fair Isaac Corporation

Ticker symbol: FICO (NYSE) □ S&P rating: not rated □ Value Line financial strength rating: B++ □ Current yield: 0.2% □ Dividend raises, past 10 years: 2

Company Profile

Fair Isaac Corporation provides decision support analytics, software, and solutions to help businesses improve and automate decision making and risk management. The most well-known and best example of these solutions is the "FICO score"—an analytic single-figure estimate of a consumer's creditworthiness used in the credit industry and for other purposes such as employment and insurance.

FICO provides its analytic solutions and services to a variety of financial and other service organizations, including banks, credit-reporting agencies, credit card processing agencies, insurers, retailers, marketers, and health-care organizations. It operates in three segments: Applications, Scores, and Tools. The Applications segment provides decision and risk management tools, market targeting products, and fraud detection tools and associated professional services. The Scores segment includes the business-to-business scoring solutions; myFICO solutions, delivering FICO scores for consumers; and associated professional services. The Tools segment provides software products and consulting services to help organizations build their own analytic tools.

Financial Highlights, Fiscal Year 2011

FICO is well past the crunch of the 2008–09 financial crisis, which saw a sharp slackening of demand as financial services firms reduced spending and as credit and loan activity diminished altogether. The demand for traditional credit scoring products has resumed, though not to previous levels. What has emerged as a stronger growth driver is the analytics provided by the Applications segment, primarily in fraud prevention and in marketing analytics, predicting consumer behavior and so forth. Revenues in that segment are on a 13 percent annual growth trajectory. The company has also been performing well in overseas markets, where its analytics are more of a new idea. Its scoring products are now available to the Spanish-speaking market as well.

For FY2011, total revenues advanced a rather modest 1.9 percent, although FY2012 Q1 rose a stronger 9 percent. As a company that provides software and information, most of its cost structure is relatively fixed in the form of staff—cost of goods sold is almost insignificant—so, as such, is driven by volumes. Higher volumes on the same overhead base bring large earnings increases, and indeed, FY2011 earnings per share rose 26 percent to $1.79, and are guided by management to rise into the $2.45–$2.55 range for FY2012.

Reasons to Buy

There are a number of companies, large and small, in the analytics business. But few have the brand reputation and leadership enjoyed by FICO. FICO is the gold standard for this type of product, and has built its leadership, and really a pretty large moat, on its brand. We also think a stabilizing financial industry with new rules, fewer workers, and a greater recognition for risk and risk management will bode well for the FICO product suite. FICO products offer a good combination of streamlining and sophistication to financial and other decision making. Long term, we can easily see their modeling approaches being further extended

to analyzing customer behavior and providing decision support for insurability, employability, acceptance into schools, and other areas well beyond a consumer's ability to repay extended credit. International demand for FICO's products continues to grow.

The dividend remains inconsequential, but we should note that share counts have dropped from almost 70 million in 2004 to 37 million at present—this drop in fact has amplified the earnings per share performance considerably but also represents real return to remaining shareholders.

Reasons for Caution

Most of the changes afoot in the credit card and financial services industry bode well for FICO, but we wonder if credit demand will ever be what it was in 2004–07. The company's business is still heavily tied to transaction volumes. There is some public concern that scoring models oversimplify lending and insurability decisions and should not be used or relied on so heavily. And as we've seen, the company is vulnerable to economic downturns.

SECTOR: **Information Technology**
BETA COEFFICIENT: **1.45**
10-YEAR COMPOUND EARNINGS PER SHARE GROWTH: **8.0%**
10-YEAR COMPOUND DIVIDENDS PER SHARE GROWTH: **13.0%**

	2004	2005	2006	2007	2008	2009	2010	2011
Revenues (Mil)	706.2	798.7	825.4	822.2	744.8	630.7	605.6	619.7
Net Income (Mil)	108.9	134.5	103.5	104.7	81.2	65.1	64.5	71.6
Earnings per share	1.49	1.86	1.5	1.82	1.64	1.34	1.42	1.79
Dividends per share	0.08	0.08	0.08	0.08	0.08	0.08	0.08	0.08
Cash flow per share	2.24	2.91	2.57	3.03	2.49	2.15	2.36	2.58
Price: high	41.5	48.5	47.8	41.8	32.2	24.5	27.0	38.5
low	23.7	32.3	32.5	32.1	10.4	9.8	19.5	20.0

Fair Isaac Corporation
901 Marquette Avenue, Suite 3200
Minneapolis, MN 55402–3232
Phone: (612) 758-5200
Website: *www.fairisaac.com*

FedEx Corporation

Ticker symbol: FDX (NYSE) ❑ S&P rating: BBB ❑ Value Line financial strength rating: B++ ❑ Current yield: 0.6% ❑ Dividend raises, past 10 years: 9

Company Profile

FedEx Corporation is the world's leading provider of guaranteed express delivery services, and is a major player in the overall small shipment and small package logistics market. The corporation is organized as a holding company, with four individual businesses that compete collectively and operate independently under the FedEx brand, offering a wide range of express delivery services for the time-definite transportation of documents, packages, and freight. The familiar FedEx Express operation offers overnight and deferred air service to 57,000 drop-off locations, operating 688 aircraft and approximately 50,000 ground vehicles to support this business. The company also offers freight services for less time-sensitive items and small or less than truckload (LTL) shipments under the FedEx Ground and FedEx Freight brands. FedEx Ground offers overnight service for up to 400 miles anywhere in the United States for packages weighing up to 150 pounds, while FedEx Freight offers standard and priority LTL service across North America mainly for business supply-chain operations. Finally, the company has ventured into more comprehensive FedEx Services, which offers specialized logistics services and customer support, and also includes the former Kinko's copy and office centers, now operating under the FedEx/Kinko's brand.

The company's operations include:

- The world's largest express transportation company (FedEx Express).
- North America's second-largest ground carrier for small-package business shipments (FedEx Ground).
- The largest U.S. regional less-than-truckload freight company (FedEx Freight).
- A 24/7 option for urgent shipments, providing nonstop, door-to-door delivery in the contiguous United States, Canada, and Europe (FedEx Custom Critical).
- The largest-volume customs filer in the United States, providing freight forwarding, advisory services, and trade technology (FedEx Trade Networks).

In total, the company operates an enormous logistics network of 688 aircraft, 170,000 ground vehicles, over 700 World Service Centers, over 1,800 FedEx Office locations, nearly 7,000 authorized ShipCenters, and over 43,000 Drop Boxes. They serve over 375 airports in over 200 countries. In FY2011, the Express segment accounted for 62 percent of revenues, Ground 21 percent, Freight 12 percent, and Services 5 percent, the same mix as FY2010.

Financial Highlights, Fiscal Year 2010/2011

As the economy emerged from the recession and commerce and manufacturing resumed toward full scale, FedEx did quite well in FY2011. Revenues advanced 13 percent to $39.3 billion, while earnings per share took to the skies a full 30 percent to $4.90 per share. Not surprisingly, e-commerce is creating considerable single-shipment volume, and the new economy-minded "Smart-Post" offering, which uses the U.S. Postal Service for end customer delivery, has gained a lot of traction. Margins have also improved with firmer pricing and fuel cost recovery, and with higher capacity utilization. All of these factors lead to a guided FY2012 EPS in the $6.35–$6.50 range, the midpoint of which would represent another 30 percent growth in earnings.

Reasons to Buy

FedEx has a strong brand and offers a diverse set of services, really a complete logistics solution, for a large group of customers. The continued resurgence in the economy and growth in online shopping and delivery will certainly help volumes and pricing, and the continuing shift to e-commerce gives a boost to this recovery. The resumption of strong U.S. exports not only helps volume but also helps fill up planes traveling from the United States. The logistics business is always ripe for innovation, and FedEx has long been an innovator in the transportation and small-package shipment business, not only with new transportation services but also with new tools to help customers track shipments and manage their supply chains in real time; we expect this to continue. The accelerating earnings rate and very strong cash flows, more than double per-share earnings, are also an attraction, and some of that is cautiously being paid back to shareholders.

Reasons for Caution

FedEx is obviously vulnerable to fuel price increases, and the same economic factors that create business growth can lead to growth in costs, so efficiency is Job Number One. The company has recently been investing in its ground businesses, which to a large degree compete head-to-head with UPS. These are relatively low-margin businesses that we feel will succeed the most if effectively integrated—and marketed—with other services into a total solution. FedEx/Kinko's hasn't worked out as well financially as the company had hoped, although some of the integration we just spoke of has happened. Yes, you can have a FedEx Ground shipment held at FedEx/Kinko's for you to pick up, but too few people know about such services. Most still perceive FedEx/Kinko's as a good place to get copies. FedEx could do a better job of marketing what they really do to the general public, and perhaps, to businesses.

The company is always vulnerable to fuel prices, particularly if cost increases come faster than they can be recovered in rates and fuel surcharges—as is often the case. Finally, while cash flows are strong, this company must occasionally purchase or lease aircraft; this and other "capex" can put a big dent in cash flows.

SECTOR: **Transportation**
BETA COEFFICIENT: **1.26**
10-YEAR COMPOUND EARNINGS PER SHARE GROWTH: **6.5%**
10-YEAR COMPOUND DIVIDENDS PER SHARE GROWTH: **8.0%**

		2004	2005	2006	2007	2008	2009	2010	2011
Revenues (Mil)		24,710	29,363	32,294	35,214	37,953	35,497	34,734	39,204
Net Income (Mil)		838	1,449	1,885	2,073	1,821	1,173	1,184	1,554
Earnings per share		2.76	4.82	5.98	6.67	5.83	3.76	3.76	4.90
Dividends per share		0.24	0.29	0.33	0.37	0.40	0.44	0.44	.48
Cash flow per share		8.15	9.74	11.13	12.39	12.13	10.09	10.01	11.13
Price:	high	100.9	105.8	120	121.4	99.5	92.6	97.8	98.7
	Low	64.8	76.8	96.5	89.5	53.9	34	69.8	64.1

FedEx Corporation
942 South Shady Grove Road
Memphis, TN 38120
(901) 818-7200
Website: *www.fedex.com*

Fluor Corporation

Ticker symbol: FLR (NYSE) ◻ S&P rating: A- ◻ Value Line financial strength rating: A++ ◻ Current yield: 1.1% ◻ Dividend raises, past 10 years: 2

Company Profile

Fluor is one of the world's largest publicly owned engineering, procurement, construction, maintenance, and project management companies. They provide a diverse portfolio of large-scale infrastructure and infrastructure services, primarily for five industry segments:

- Oil and Gas (34 percent of revenue, 26 percent of gross profit in 2010) where they serve all facets of the traditional energy industry, including upstream, downstream, and petrochemical markets, including oilfields, refineries, and pipelines.
- Industrial and Infrastructure (34 percent of revenue, 37 percent of profits) is their most diverse organization, which includes transportation, mining, life sciences, telecom, manufacturing, and commercial and institutional projects. This segment also covers the emerging alternative energy projects, including major windmill farm developments.
- Government (15 percent of revenue, 14 percent of profits)

addresses the U.S. Departments of Energy, Defense, and Homeland Security.

- Global Services (7 percent of revenue, 15 percent of profits) provides operations and maintenance, supply chain, equipment services, and contract staffing.
- Power (8 percent of revenue, 8 percent of profits) designs, builds, commissions, and retrofits electric generation facilities using coal, natural gas, and nuclear fuels.

Financial Highlights, Fiscal Year 2011

The essential nature of this company—and its opportunities and cycles—is seen in how the different sectors of the business fluctuate from year to year. In 2010, the Oil & Gas segment garnered 34 percent of total revenues and 55 percent of total profits, while the Industrial & Infrastructure unit brought 33 percent of revenues but (–27) percent of the profits. Infrastructure, in the form of factory and mining construction has recovered, and the company got two large charges related to major infrastructure projects behind it. Now, most all of its end customers are doing well, and the company booked record revenues of $23 billion in 2011, up some 12 percent from 2010, Earnings have recovered to $698 million, or $3.40 per share, and are expected to advance to $3.75 per share in 2012. The balance sheet remains strong with long-term debt only 5 percent of capital—and that was from a recent debt sale to take advantage of low interest rates. The company raised its dividend 28 percent in early 2012.

Reasons to Buy

For investors tolerant of some economic risk, Fluor's shares represent a solid way to play an economic recovery, as well as the continued need to replace old infrastructure. General large-scale construction should regain health across all industries including oil and gas as the construction cycle becomes more favorable. In our view, the company has two growth "kickers" not to be ignored: one is their presence in the alternative energy industry; the other is their presence in the utility infrastructure industry. Both will see waves of new investment to capitalize on new energy technologies; in addition, there are thousands of miles of old water pipes, electric lines, and other infrastructure that is due, or overdue, for replacement. These two megatrends will boost Fluor's business for quite some time to come. Top-line revenue projections call for healthy growth of 10 percent plus for the next two years, and the company's conservative financial management will likely reap the best results from this increased activity.

Reasons for Caution

Fluor is more cyclical and more responsive to economic trends than most companies, as is clear from its relatively high beta of 1.35. There is a lot of competition in this industry, and the slightest blip on the economic radar drives down bids—and thus revenues and profits—pretty quickly. Also, due to long cycle times, this company tends to lag the economy—the full effects of the recession weren't felt until 2010—but that effect also works in reverse. All that said, Fluor is more steady than many peers in this industry.

SECTOR: **Industrials**
BETA COEFFICIENT: **1.35**
10-YEAR COMPOUND EARNINGS PER SHARE GROWTH: **13.0%**
10-YEAR COMPOUND DIVIDENDS PER SHARE GROWTH: **1.5%**

	2004	2005	2006	2007	2008	2009	2010	2011
Revenues (Mil)	9,380	13,161	14,079	16,691	22,326	21,990	20,849	23,381
Net Income (Mil)	178	227	264	410	673	685	357.5	698
Earnings per share	1.08	1.31	1.48	2.25	3.67	3.75	1.98	3.40
Dividends per share	0.32	0.32	0.32	0.4	0.5	0.5	0.50	0.50
Cash flow per share	1.58	1.9	2.21	3.14	4.61	4.85	3.11	5.31
Price: high	27.6	39.6	51.9	86.1	101.4	50.5	67.3	75.8
low	18	25.1	36.8	37.6	28.6	41.7	41.2	44.2

Fluor Corporation
6700 Las Colinas Blvd.
Irving, TX 75039
Tel: (469) 398-7000
Website: *www.fluor.com*

AGGRESSIVE GROWTH

FMC Corporation

Ticker symbol: FMC (NYSE) □ S&P rating: A- □ Value Line financial strength rating: A □ Current yield: 0.7% □ Dividend raises, past 10 years: 5

Company Profile

FMC Corporation is a diversified chemical company serving global agricultural, industrial, and consumer markets. The company, founded in 1883, operates its businesses in three segments: Agricultural Products, Specialty Chemicals, and Industrial Chemicals. The company is one of the world's largest producers of strategic materials like phosphorus, hydrogen peroxide, and lithium compounds.

FMC Agricultural Products (43 percent of revenues) provides crop protection and pest control products for worldwide markets. The business offers a solid portfolio of insecticides and herbicides, and is considered an industry leader for its innovative packaging.

In the Specialty Chemicals Group, which represents 20 percent of the business, FMC BioPolymer is the world's leading producer of alginate, carrageenan, and microcrystalline cellulose, which are key thickening, texturing, stabilizing, and fat substitute ingredients used in the food industry. Not too closely related, but of strategic importance is FMC Lithium, one of the world's leading producers of lithium-based products and recognized as the technology leader in specialty organolithium chemicals and related technologies. Among other things, lithium is a key ingredient in emerging battery technologies.

In the Industrial Chemicals Group, FMC Alkali Chemicals (31 percent of revenues) is the world's largest producer of natural soda ash and is the market leader in North America. Downstream products include sodium bicarbonate, sodium cyanide, sodium sesquicarbonate, and caustic soda. FMC Hydrogen Peroxide is the market leader in North America with manufacturing sites in the United States, Canada, and Mexico. FMC Active Oxidants is the world's leading supplier of persulfate products and a major producer of peracetic acid and other specialty oxidants. You may not have heard of many of these products, which typically are used to manufacture things like glass, paper, detergents, tires, and electronic components, among other things—and ship by the rail tank car load—but they are vital ingredients to a number of key industries worldwide.

Speaking of which, about 63 percent of the company's overall business comes from overseas.

Financial Highlights, Fiscal Year 2011

As the first-half 2012 boom in the share price might tell you, FMC had a banner FY2011 and kept the momentum going during FY2012. Sales grew 8.4 percent to $3.4 billion, while earnings per share, helped along by share repurchases and margin improvements, jumped ahead 29 percent to $5.98 per share. The company has enjoyed the boom in agriculture and firmer prices in many of its specialty chemical segments; advantages in scale and market share are likely playing a big part. For FY2012, the company recently raised guidance to $6.60–$7.05 per share, the midpoint of that range representing another 15 percent improvement, and just announced another share repurchase and a 20 percent dividend increase, although the yield remains low due to the higher share price.

Reasons to Buy

FMC is well positioned in several areas of relative strategic importance in the chemical industry, in particular the agriculture, peroxygen (hydrogen peroxide, etc.), biopolymer, and lithium compounds businesses. The strength of the economic rebound combined with these leadership positions in specialty markets bode well for the company. Pricing strength, improving margins, and strong international sales (65 percent of sales in 2011) all add to a promising picture.

As an example of FMC's strategic portfolio, the company is well positioned as the leading supplier of lithium-based compounds used in the lithium-ion battery industry. Lithium batteries are used extensively in technology products such as laptops, music players (you know which ones we're referring to), tablets (again, you know), and soon, electric cars. Every hybrid car currently in production uses nickel metal hydride (NiMH) battery chemistry, but lithium batteries appropriate for automobile usage are not far off. Lithium's unparalleled power-to-weight ratio and rapid recharge cycle time make cars lighter and more amenable to typical usage patterns.

FMC is a key player in a broad consortium of U.S.-based companies working to establish a dominant domestic lithium battery industry. Lithium battery technology is the key to the future of the automotive industry, and some have said that the country that makes the batteries will make the cars.

Reasons for Caution

While the company occupies a leadership position in several important chemical and ingredient markets, FMC can't get away completely from its role as a commodity producer, particularly in such compounds as soda ash. As such, competition and business cycles will always play a role in growth and stability. Additionally, while

the company did start paying dividends in 2006, the cash return rate could really be better. Additionally, recent share prices seem to already include a lot of the good news; waiting for good entry points would be advisable.

SECTOR: **Materials**
BETA COEFFICIENT: **1.07**
10-YEAR COMPOUND EARNINGS PER SHARE GROWTH: **6.5%**
10-YEAR COMPOUND DIVIDENDS PER SHARE GROWTH: **NM**

	2004	2005	2006	2007	2008	2009	2010	2011
Revenues (Mil)	2,051	2,150	2,347	2,633	3,115	2,826	3,116	3,378
Net Income (Mil)	135.2	171.9	216.4	132.4	351	305	353	429
Earnings per share	1.60	2.20	2.74	3.40	4.63	4.15	4.83	5.98
Dividends per share	—	—	0.36	0.42	0.48	0.50	.50	.60
Cash flow per share	3.64	4.00	4.54	5.25	6.55	6.00	6.81	7.95
Price: high	25.3	31.9	39	59	80.2	63.3	82.0	93.0
low	16.5	21.6	25.9	35.6	28.5	34.9	50.8	63.8

FMC Corporation
1735 Market Street
Philadelphia, PA 19103
(215) 299-6000
Website: *www.fmc.com*

GROWTH AND INCOME

General Mills, Inc.

Ticker symbol: GIS (NYSE) ❑ S&P rating: BBB+ ❑ Value Line financial strength rating: A+ ❑ Current yield: 3.1% ❑ Dividend raises, past 10 years: 7

Company Profile

General Mills is the second-largest domestic producer of ready-to-eat breakfast cereals and the sixth-largest food company in the world. Their sales are broken out into three major segments: U.S. Retail (69 percent of revenues), International (19 percent), and Bakery and Food-stuffs (12 percent).

Major cereal brands, most of which bear the Big G label, include Cheerios, Wheaties, Lucky Charms, Total, and Chex. The company owns Pillsbury, which it acquired in 2001. Other consumer packaged food products include baking mixes (Betty Crocker and Bisquick); meals (Betty Crocker dry packaged dinner mixes); Progresso soups; Green Giant canned and frozen vegetables; Hamburger Helper; snacks (Pop Secret microwave popcorn, Bugles snacks, and grain and fruit snack products); Pillsbury refrigerated and frozen dough products, including Pillsbury Doughboy, frozen breakfast products, and frozen pizza and snack products; organic foods; and other products, including Nature Valley, Yoplait, Go-gurt, and Colombo yogurt. The company's holdings include many other brand names, such as Häagen-Dazs ice cream and a host of joint ventures.

In the International sector, General Foods sells numerous local brands, in addition to internationally recognized brands such as Häagen-Dazs ice cream, Old El Paso Mexican foods, and Green Giant vegetables. Those international businesses have sales and marketing organizations in 33 countries.

Financial Highlights, Fiscal Year 2011

For momentum-oriented investors, FY2011 was a boring one. Revenues increased less than 1 percent to 14.9 billion. The company is feeling the effects of commodity inflation. Management estimates a 10 to 11 percent increase in the cost of ingredients, which the company tries to pass on, but doesn't always do so successfully. Consumers switch to private brands or consume a little less, and sales go flat. Earnings per share did, however, increase 4.3 percent, helped along by a 2 percent decrease in share count. Management has guided for $2.50–2.55 per share in FY2012—again not stellar growth, but healthy cash flow, which turns into a healthy dividend, and stock repurchases make this sort of a "health food" company for conservative investors.

Reasons to Buy

General Mills continues to enjoy solid brand strength and a strong position in a very competitive cereal and packaged food market. Recent trends have pointed to brand leveraging (e.g., Chocolate Cheerios, Wheaties Fuel), and the results have been encouraging. There's evidence that the recession "taught" more people to eat at home, and those folks are starting to return to more premium brands found on store shelves. Finally, while the company has developed some international markets, notably in Latin America and the Caribbean, and generates about 24 percent of its sales overseas, we feel that additional international expansion may bring some opportunity.

Earnings, operating margins, and cash flows have all followed a slow but steady and cash-rich track upward and in tune with management guidance. The company has continued its policy of share repurchase. Since 2004 the company has reduced its share count from 758 million to about 640 million. The company also raised the dividend 10 percent in 2010 and another 17 percent in 2011 and has generally boosted its dividend "raises" in recent years. Finally, General Mills is a notably safe and stable stock with a beta of 0.18, one of the lowest on our list.

Reasons for Caution

As noted, recent uptrends in commodity prices have posed some challenges to the company, especially as not all costs can be passed on to discerning consumers. As a result of these trends, U.S. retail sales fell almost 7 percent in the quarter ended November 2011. While this will almost certainly moderate as commodity inflation moderates, the trend bears watching.

SECTOR: **Consumer Staples**
BETA COEFFICIENT: **.18**
10-YEAR COMPOUND EARNINGS PER SHARE GROWTH: **8.5%**
10-YEAR COMPOUND DIVIDENDS PER SHARE GROWTH: **6.0%**

	2004	2005	2006	2007	2008	2009	2010	2011
Revenues (Mil)	11,070	11,244	11,640	12,442	13,652	14,691	14,796	14,880
Net Income (Mil)	1,055	1,100	1,090	1,144	1,288	1,367	1,571	1,652
Earnings per share	1.43	1.37	1.45	1.59	1.78	1.99	2.30	2.48
Dividends per share	0.55	0.62	0.67	0.72	0.79	0.86	0.96	1.12
Cash flow per share	1.97	2.09	2.13	2.30	2.50	2.78	3.09	3.29
Price: high	25.0	26.9	29.6	30.8	36.0	36.0	39.0	40.8
low	21.5	22.3	23.5	27.1	25.5	23.2	33.1	34.5

General Mills, Inc.
Post Office Box 1113
Minneapolis, MN 55440–1113
(763) 764-3202
Website: *www.generalmills.com*

CONSERVATIVE GROWTH

W. W. Grainger, Inc.

Ticker symbol: GWW (NYSE) □ S&P rating: AA+ □ Value Line financial strength rating: A++ □ Current yield: 1.5% □ Dividend raises, past 10 years: 10

Company Profile

If you're running a production operation and have a sudden and urgent need for a hand truck, a "Keep Out" sign, a positive displacement pump, or a pair of safety glasses, who do you call? You certainly can't afford to send someone out to Home Depot or some such store, and no "big-box" retailer would stock even a small fraction of the 1 million items that W.W. Grainger stocks anyhow.

Grainger is North America's largest supplier of maintenance, repair, and operating supply (MRO) products. They sell more than a million different products from more than 3,500 suppliers through a network of over 600 branches (400 in the United States), 15 distribution centers, and several websites, with a catalog containing some 307,000 items (a fascinating read if you like this sort of thing). Grainger also offers repair parts, specialized product sourcing, and inventory management supplies. Grainger sells principally to industrial and commercial maintenance departments, contractors, and government customers. The company has nearly 2 million customers, mostly in North America, and achieves overnight delivery to approximately 98 percent of them.

Their Canadian subsidiary is Canada's largest distributor of industrial, fleet, and safety products. They serve their customers through 172 branches and five distribution centers, and they offer bilingual websites and catalogs. Grainger, S.A. de C.V. is Mexico's leading facilities maintenance supplier, offering customers more than 84,000 products. The company also has important operations, through joint ventures, in Japan, China, and India and does business in 157 countries worldwide.

Grainger's customer base includes governmental offices at all levels; heavy manufacturing customers (typically textile, lumber, metals, and rubber industries); light manufacturing; transportation (shipbuilding, aerospace, and automotive); hospitals; retail; hospitality; and resellers of Grainger products. Grainger owns a number of trademarks, including Dayton motors, Dem-Kote spray paints, and Westward tools.

Many of Grainger's customers are corporate account customers, primarily *Fortune* 1,000 companies that spend more than $5 million annually on facilities maintenance products. Corporate account customers represent about 25 percent of Grainger's total U.S. sales. Both government and corporate account customer groups typically sign multiyear contracts for facilities maintenance products or a specific category of products, such as lighting or safety equipment. In 2009, the company averaged 95,000 transactions per day.

The Grainger strategy is centered on the idea of being easy to do business with. Customers can interact with a direct sales force, interact with one of the 400 distribution outlets in the United States, or order through an e-commerce website. Released quietly during the dot.com boom, *www.grainger.com* handles some $1.5 billion, or about 25 percent of the company's U.S. business each year, a solid e-commerce success story.

The business also depends a lot on reputation, and the company has earned numerous awards, including number one on *Fortune*'s America's Most Admired Companies list for diversified wholesalers and several prominent "best places to work" awards.

Financial Highlights, Fiscal Year 2011

Improving industrial production, increased market share, and control over price, and strong e-commerce initiatives all led to another stellar year for Grainger. FY2011 revenues advanced 14 percent to $8.1 billion, while per-share earnings were ahead a full percent to $9.04 per share. During the year, the company eliminated all but $175 million of the long-term debt it incurred in 2008 for acquisitions and general purposes, leaving that scant figure against $15 billion in market capitalization. Beyond retiring the debt, the company also repurchased 1 million shares in FY2011. It's worth noting that Grainger has reduced share count 25 percent since 2004, while doubling revenues and tripling profits in that same period. The company has raised its dividend 40 years in a row, and has accelerated the rate of increase, ahead 23 percent for FY2011 alone to $2.52 per share (if only you were receiving similar raises!). For FY2012 the company raised guidance to 12 to 14 percent sales growth and EPS of $10.40 to $10.80, the midpoint of this range representing at 17 percent growth in per-share earnings.

Reasons to Buy

Grainger is far and away the biggest presence in the MRO world. Their only broad-line competitor is one-quarter their size and the rest of the market is highly fragmented. They also have the deepest catalog by far. It's estimated that 40 percent of purchases in the MRO market are unplanned, so having the broadest inventory, fastest delivery, and friendliest service is a big advantage for Grainger.

Even with its size and scope, the company estimates that it has less than 6 percent of the U.S. MRO market, leaving a large growth opportunity. International sales are less than 20 percent of the total, and Grainger has established a foothold, but not dominance, in Mexico, China, Japan, Korea, Colombia, and Puerto Rico with less than 1 percent of those markets. The company has a larger presence in Canada (and 8 percent market share), and just acquired Fabory Group, the largest MRO supplier in Europe (but still, less than 1 percent market share). Especially with so much manufacturing relocated overseas, the international opportunity looks rich for Grainger.

The share repurchases and dividend increases reflect a better-than-average orientation to shareholder value, and shareholder value is indeed one of the stated goals of the company. We find it refreshing to see it not only stated but also delivered upon.

Reasons for Caution

Grainger will always be vulnerable to economic cycles and manufacturing displacement, especially so long as it remains concentrated on U.S. soil. International expansion will help alleviate this concern. Over the past five years, the share price has reflected most of the good news, mandating either careful price shopping for the stock or reliance on incremental growth opportunities in United States and especially overseas market share. Look for price pullbacks in times of greater macroeconomic concern.

SECTOR: **Industrials**
BETA COEFFICIENT: **0.93**
10-YEAR COMPOUND EARNINGS PER SHARE GROWTH: **11.5%**
10-YEAR COMPOUND DIVIDENDS PER SHARE GROWTH: **11.0%**

	2004	**2005**	**2006**	**2007**	**2008**	**2009**	**2010**	**2011**
Revenues (Mil)	5,050	5,527	5,884	6,418	6,850	6,222	7,182	8,075
Net Income (Mil)	276	346	383	420	479	402	502	643
Earnings per share	3.02	3.78	4.25	4.94	6.09	5.25	6.81	9.04
Dividends per share	0.79	0.92	1.16	1.4	1.55	1.78	2.08	2.52
Cash flow per share	4.14	4.97	5.79	6.95	8.28	7.60	9.40	11.33
Price: high	67	72.4	80	98.6	94	102.5	139.1	193.2
low	45	51.6	60.6	68.8	58.9	59.9	96.1	124.3

W. W. Grainger, Inc.
100 Grainger Parkway
Lake Forest, IL 60045
(847) 535-0881
Website: *www.grainger.com*

AGGRESSIVE GROWTH

Harman International Industries

Ticker symbol: HAR (NYSE) ◻ S&P rating: BB- ◻ Value Line financial strength rating: B ◻ Current yield: 0.6% ◻ Dividend raises, past 10 years: 1

Company Profile

Harman International is one of the world's leading producers of audio and infotainment solutions for an increasingly mobile society. That sounds like marketing copy, but it's a true depiction of this company.

Harman, through a collection of well-known brands like JBL, Harman/Kardon, Infinity, Crown, Mark Levinson, Soundcraft, Becker, AKG, and others, controls a substantial piece of the fragmented market for home audio, professional and studio audio, and automotive markets. Normally that wouldn't get us too excited—the glory days of home audio are 30 years behind us, and professional audio is a steady-going but not particularly growing or dynamic market. What has us interested in the present and future of the company is the automotive market. Again, there's little in traditional car audio to get us very jazzed; the markets are flooded with cheap competition. However . . .

The center of interest for this company is the development of "infotainment" systems for the audio market—those integrated systems that all work together to provide sound, video, wireless communications, navigation, Internet access, and climate control on demand and in all parts of the vehicle. As Harman evolves, the integration of digital automotive electronics with personal digital devices (e.g., the iPod) offers a huge opportunity. The company is also leveraging this idea to "smart" hotel room adaptations, where you can plug in your device to get your music and tap into your chosen personal information. Major automotive manufacturers such as Tata, BMW, Geely (China–Volvo), Volkswagen, and others have been signing large long-term contracts with Harman to provide these systems.

Indeed, Harman is really an automotive company, with 73 percent of FY2011 sales coming from this business, while consumer audio is 11 percent and professional audio is 10 percent. So enjoy those JBLs in your living room, but realize that such products are not the true "drivers" of Harman's business.

Financial Highlights, Fiscal Year 2011

Harman has ridden the strengthening auto cycle to a decent FY2011 performance, with sales up 12 percent over FY2010 and earnings more than double, at $2.08 per share. A trip through the financials will show that this company is more sensitive to top-line fluctuations than most; the boom years were really boom years, and the high beta of 2.12 bears that into the stock price. As the auto markets improve and the company logs large contracts, the bottom line should improve even more. In fact, the company just inked a $2 billion renewal contract with "its largest customer" (probably BMW) and $500 million in long-term contracts with BAIC and Geely of China and Tata. Estimates call for $2.75 to $3.00 in per-share earnings on sales in the $4.2–$4.4 billion range for FY2012. The company also expects to pay off virtually all long-term debt in FY2012 with cash on hand, and recently raised the dividend from 5 cents to 30 cents annually.

Reasons to Buy

We like to invest "where the puck is going," not where it has been, and if you look at the puck destination for Harman, it is pretty compelling. The idea of integrating audio and infotainment systems in cars and other spaces with your own personal media devices makes a lot of sense. Once Harman becomes the platform supplier of choice for the major auto brands, we expect that placement will be "sticky," that is, difficult for the auto company or the consumer to switch once in place. The company has a degree of first-mover advantage in this market, and as major contracts are signed, the moat expands. Long-term contracts will also dampen the effects of the cycles. The financials seem solid and better than the Value Line "B" grade given, and we think the dividend will grow further once the debt retirement is complete.

Reasons for Caution

As plainly visible from the company's sales and earnings history, Harman is vulnerable to economic cycles and particularly those in the auto industry, and downturns in discretionary consumer audio purchases will "amplify" auto industry woes. Audio and infotainment tastes can be fickle, so the company will have to quickly embrace the latest trends. We'd also like to see the company market itself a bit more effectively to become a brand standard as "Intel inside" has in the computer industry.

SECTOR: **Consumer Discretionary**
BETA COEFFICIENT: **2.12**
10-YEAR COMPOUND EARNINGS PER SHARE GROWTH: **-3.5%**
10-YEAR COMPOUND DIVIDENDS PER SHARE GROWTH: **NM**

	2004	2005	2006	2007	2008	2009	2010	2011
Revenues (Mil)	2,711	3,030	3,248	3,551	4,112	2,891	3,364	3,772
Net income (Mil)	158	233	268	25	146	(56)	60	149
Earnings per share	2.27	3.31	3.94	4.14	2.35	(1.01)	0.85	2.08
Dividends per share	.05	.05	.05	.05	.05	.05	.05	.05
Cash flow per share	3.99	5.27	6.02	6.17	5.10	1.32	2.70	3.89
Price: high	131.7	130.5	115.9	125.1	73.8	40.3	53.4	52.5
low	66.1	68.5	74.6	69.5	9.9	9.2	28.1	25.5

Harman International Industries
400 Atlantic St.
Stamford, CT 06901
(202) 393-1101
Website: *www.harman.com*

GROWTH AND INCOME

H. J. Heinz Company

Ticker symbol: HNZ (NYSE) ❑ S&P rating: BBB+ ❑ Value Line financial strength rating: A+ ❑ Current yield: 3.6% ❑ Dividend raises, past 10 years: 8

Company Profile

H. J. Heinz Company manufactures and markets food products such as condiments and sauces, frozen food, soups, desserts, entrées, snacks, frozen potatoes, appetizers, and others for consumers and commercial customers. The company's best-known product, its ketchup, has a 60 percent market share in the United States, 70 percent in Canada, and nearly 80 percent in the UK. Condiments and sauces (including ketchup) account for approximately 42 percent of the company's revenue, with meals and snacks producing 45 percent, and infant/nutrition products making up the remainder. Ore-Ida frozen potato products, Classico pasta sauces, and SmartOnes meals are among the more well-known Heinz brands.

The Heinz portfolio includes 150 brands that hold the number one or number two market share positions in their categories, with presence on five continents and in more than 50 countries. The company sells its products through its own direct sales organizations, through independent brokers and agents, and to distributors to retailers and commercial users. The company has operations in North America, Africa, Latin America, Europe, Asia/Pacific, and the Middle East. Recently the company has made significant acquisitions in Brazil and China. About 63 percent of Heinz's sales are from overseas, and the company estimates that 18 percent of sales are from emerging markets; these markets, including China and Russia, are growing rapidly. Heinz's laboratories develop the company's recipes, which are then duplicated at one of the 79 company-owned factories or one of several leased factories. Lately the company has been experimenting with promising new packaging and balsamic-flavored ketchup and other products.

Financial Highlights, Fiscal Year 2011

Strength and acquisitions in emerging markets capped off a 9 percent revenue gain in FY2011, which led to an 11 percent gain in per-share earnings. The company has prided itself in achieving "organic" growth, that is, growth within the current product base, not dependent on acquisitions or price increases. From a recent quarterly report, CEO William R. Johnson cited "27 straight quarters of organic growth." He also cited 20 percent organic growth rates in emerging markets (with acquisitions, the total reported growth rate was 39.7 percent), a 9 percent organic growth in ketchup, and a 6 percent organic growth rate in the "top 15 brands." Such stats give insight into what Heinz does—and what it thinks about.

Reasons to Buy

The resilience of Heinz's strong brands was apparent during the recession as the company maintained growth in sales and earnings over each of the past three years, and it appears that those brands are continuing to perform well, especially in emerging markets. The company looks to be a solid and steady player in a steady industry with a growth "kicker" in the form of its international business and international expansion. Heinz has been successful recently with its new brand introductions, leveraging its Global Innovation and Quality Center. Part of the company's product development goal is to derive 15 percent of revenues from products introduced within the previous 36 months.

For investors looking for steady and solid shareholder returns, especially in the form of a strong dividend payout both current and future, Heinz is an attractive choice. Beyond that, the stock has been trading in a relatively narrow $32 to $55 trading range for twelve years—some of the growth initiatives may finally move this stock further forward in the not-too-distant future.

Reasons for Caution

Growth in emerging markets will come at a cost. Many of the brands we take for granted will require large investments in marketing to establish presence and familiarity. Heinz can also expect to see higher acquisition costs for established local brands as competitors move into this arena, and international acquisitions in particular can be tricky. Finally, higher commodity prices will continue to produce some headwinds, especially in the near term.

SECTOR: **Consumer Staples**
BETA COEFFICIENT: **0.54**
10-YEAR COMPOUND EARNINGS PER SHARE GROWTH: **1.5%**
10-YEAR COMPOUND DIVIDENDS PER SHARE GROWTH: **2.0%**

	2004	2005	2006	2007	2008	2009	2010	2011
Revenues (Mil)	8,913	8,643	9,002	10,070	10,148	10,495	10,707	11,650
Net Income (Mil)	779	750	792	845	923	915	989.5	1,075
Earnings per share	2.34	2.18	2.38	2.63	2.9	2.87	3.08	3.35
Dividends per share	1.14	1.2	1.4	1.52	1.66	1.71	1.80	1.92
Cash flow per share	3.11	3.06	3.28	3.63	3.82	3.83	4.01	4.40
Price: high	40.6	39.1	46.8	48.8	53	43.8	50.8	55.0
low	34.5	33.6	33.4	41.8	35.3	30.5	40.0	47.0

H.J. Heinz Company
One PPG Place
Pittsburgh, PA 15222
(412) 456-5700
Website: *www.heinz.com*

AGGRESSIVE GROWTH

Honeywell International, Inc.

Ticker symbol: HON (NYSE) ❏ S&P rating: A ❏ Value Line financial strength rating: A++
Current yield: 2.5% ❏ Dividend raises, past 10 years: 8

Company Profile

Honeywell is a diversified technology and manufacturing company, developing, manufacturing, and marketing aerospace products and services (31 percent of sales); control technologies for buildings, homes, and industry (40 percent); automotive products (15 percent); and specialty materials (14 percent).

Honeywell operates in four business segments: Aerospace, Automation and Control Solutions, Specialty Materials, and Transportation Systems.

The Aerospace segment primarily makes cockpit controls, power generation equipment, and wheels and brakes for commercial and military aircraft and for airports and ground operations. It also makes jet engines for regional and business jet manufacturers. Products include avionics, auxiliary power units (APUs), aircraft lighting, and landing systems. Demand for the company's aircraft equipment is driven primarily by expansion in the global jetliner fleet, particularly jets with 100 or more seats. Since 1993, the global airliner fleet has grown at a 3 percent annual pace. More recently, the company has also sold a lot of equipment into the aircraft retrofit market, as global airlines, particularly in Asia, modernize their fleets. Honeywell's Automation and Control Solutions segment is best known as a maker of home and office climate-control equipment. It also makes home automation systems; thermostats; sensing and combustion controls for heating, A/C, and other environmental controls; lighting controls; security systems and sensing products; and fire alarms. This segment produces most of the components of what is known in the trade and advertising lingo as a "smart building." The company estimates that its products are at work in some 150 million homes and 10 million commercial buildings worldwide.

The Specialty Materials operation makes a wide assortment of specialty chemicals and fibers, which are sold primarily to the food, pharmaceutical, petroleum refining, and electronic packaging industries. Petroleum refining catalysts and carbon fiber materials are among the more important and fastest-growing products in this segment.

The Transportation System segment consists of a portfolio of parts and supplies for the automotive industry. With the recent sale of its consumer automotive brands, the familiar Fram filters, Prestone antifreeze, Simoniz finishes, and Autolite spark plugs and related components, this group will now focus on OEM components such as sensors and braking systems. The consumer brand divestiture accounts for about $1 billion of the $35 billion business. International sales represent a significant and growing portion of the business, up from 41 percent of sales in 2002 to 54 percent of sales in 2011.

Financial Highlights, Fiscal Year 2011

Not too surprisingly, Honeywell is riding the wave of economic recovery and especially recovery in the air transport, construction, and energy markets to a solid financial performance. FY2011 revenues advanced about 10 percent with operating margins up more than a percentage point and earnings per share up some 35 percent from FY2010. Strength in end markets and improved capacity utilization in its operations contributed to these gains. For FY2012, the company sees solid gains albeit with a deceleration in the recovery. EPS

guidance has been raised to $4.35 to $4.55 per share, the midpoint of which would be an 11 percent gain over FY2012 on revenues of $38.5 billion, which would be about 5 percent ahead of FY2012. These figures include the $1 billion consumer auto business divestiture.

Reasons to Buy

Honeywell has outlined its key growth vectors as international ("globalization"), safety and security, energy efficiency, and energy generation. We like this rather diverse but timely set of focal points. In particular, Honeywell is positioned well with regard to the growing awareness of the value of energy efficiency. Over the next few years we see a lot of movement toward green practices in building design and use, and no one has a stronger portfolio of lighting and temperature control systems than Honeywell. Over half of the company's portfolio, across all four segments, is in the area of energy efficiency. The company also has a valuable distribution network and existing customer base in all of its businesses. The company has a solid balance sheet and participates almost exclusively in high-margin businesses, particularly with the divestiture of the consumer auto business. The company actively manages its operating leverage and cash flow, and free cash flow and investor returns have been growing at an accelerating rate recently, save for the recession setback in 2009–10. The company has been actively buying back shares and has raised its dividend significantly in recent years.

Reasons for Caution

Honeywell has a lot of competition, particularly in the aerospace and transportation sectors, and is sensitive to economic cycles, especially in these industries. Europe may also prove to be a drag. Many of the industries Honeywell sells to—in particular, the aerospace industry—are and probably will always be low-growth businesses. Finally, the company does depend on acquisitions for a portion of its growth, as it did for approximately 2 percent of its 10 percent FY2011 growth. Such dependence on acquisitions may deliver erratic results; we see HON as a fairly difficult company to manage as it is, kind of a General Electric on a smaller scale.

SECTOR: **Industrials**
BETA COEFFICIENT: **1.38**
10-YEAR COMPOUND EARNINGS PER SHARE GROWTH: **3.5%**
10-YEAR COMPOUND DIVIDENDS PER SHARE GROWTH: **6.5%**

		2004	2005	2006	2007	2008	2009	2010	2011
Revenues (Mil)		25,601	27,653	31,367	34,589	36,556	30,908	33,370	36,500
Net Income (Mil)		1,281	1,736	2,083	2,444	2,792	2,153	2,153	3,160
Earnings per share		1.49	1.92	2.52	3.16	3.75	2.85	3.00	4.05
Dividends per share		0.75	0.83	0.91	1.00	1.10	1.21	1.21	1.37
Cash flow per share		2.27	2.93	3.59	4.39	5.03	4.07	4.27	5.35
Price:	high	38.5	39.5	45.8	62.3	63	41.6	53.7	62.3
	low	31.2	32.7	35.2	43.1	23.2	23.1	36.7	41.2

Honeywell International, Inc.
101 Columbia Road
P.O. Box 2245
Morristown, NJ 07962–2245
(973) 455-2222
Website: *www.honeywell.com*

Illinois Tool Works

Ticker symbol: ITW (NYSE) ❑ S&P rating: A+ ❑ Value Line financial strength rating: A++ ❑ Current yield: 2.6% ❑ Dividend raises, past 10 years: 10

Company Profile

Illinois Tool works is a longstanding multinational conglomerate involved in the manufacture of a diversified range of industrial products, mainly components, fasteners, and other "ingredients" for other manufacturers. Customers include the automotive, machinery, construction, food and beverage, and general industrial markets. The company currently operates some 850 decentralized and modestly sized business units in 57 countries, employing approximately 61,000. Some of the products are branded and familiar, like Wolf and Hobart kitchen equipment and DeVilbiss air power tools; most are obscure and only known to others in their industries. Overseas sales account for about 58 percent of the total.

The businesses are organized into seven major segments, each contributing fairly equally to revenue:

■ Industrial Packaging includes steel, plastic, and paper products used for bundling, shipping, and protecting goods in transit. Primary brands include Acme, Signode, Pabco, and Strapex. Major end markets served are primary metals, general industrial, construction, and food/beverage.

■ Power Systems and Electronics produces equipment and consumables associated with specialty power conversion, metallurgy, and electronics. Their primary products include arc-welding equipment and consumables, solder materials, equipment and services for electronics assembly, and airport ground support equipment. Primary brands include AXA Power, Hobart, Kester, and Weldcraft.

■ Transportation includes transportation-related components, fasteners, fluids, and polymers, as well as truck remanufacturing and related parts and services. Major end markets are automotive OEM and automotive aftermarket.

■ Food Equipment produces commercial food equipment and related service, including professional kitchen ovens, refrigeration, mixers, and exhaust and ventilation systems. Major brands include

Hobart, Traulsen, Vulcan, and Wolf.
- Construction Products concentrates on tools, fasteners, and other products for construction applications. Their major end markets are residential, commercial, and renovation construction.
- Polymers and Fluids businesses produce adhesives, sealants, lubrication and cutting fluids, and hygiene products. Their primary brands include Futura, Kraft, Devcon, and Rocol.
- Decorative Surfaces produces a line of countertops, flooring, and laminates primarily for the commercial and retailing markets.

Finally, the remaining ITW brands include a cornucopia of businesses addressing a dozen or more markets. Brands well known to industrial users (and probably not many others) include Chemtronics, Magnaflux, and Texwipe.

Financial Highlights, Fiscal Year 2011

ITW is enjoying its second "re-entry" year on our *100 Best* list. The economic slowdown had hurt the company worse than we expected, so it came off the 2011 list, but we liked the recovery and put it back on last year. Based on 2011 performance and results in 2012 so far, we

think the company will stay with us for a while.

FY2011 was a very good year. The rebound in the global economy and especially in the automotive and construction sectors helped bring record results. Sales advanced 12 percent to $17.8 billion, while earnings advanced 21 percent to $1.9 billion, or $4.74 per share. Strong cash flows allowed the company to raise its dividend 10 percent and retire about 3 percent of outstanding shares, part of a long-term campaign to reduce share counts by 134 million from the 617 million shares outstanding in 2003.

ITW has been on an acquisition binge lately, digesting some 174 companies in the past five years alone. In the near term, the company expects to do some consolidating and rightsizing for some of the business, particularly in the international sector, which may result in a few sales and one-time restructuring costs. FY2012 growth should moderate into the mid single digits for revenues and about 10 percent for earnings.

Reasons to Buy

Buying shares of ITW is like buying a mutual fund of medium-sized manufacturing businesses you've probably never heard of, but would definitely like to own. The company is well diversified and serves many markets, some with end products, some with components, some in cyclical industries like automotive and construction, some in "steady-state" industries like food processing and packaging. The company has solid models for making acquisitions, and seems to do better than most conglomerates historically in choosing candidates and then managing them once they're in the fold. The company seems to do an equally good job of turning opportunity into cash flow and using that cash flow to enhance shareholder returns, as exemplified by the steady record of dividend increases each year since 1994. Finally, the balance sheet is strong, with long term debt only 11 percent of total capital and net profit margins exceeding 10 percent, both healthy for the type of business(es) ITW is engaged in.

Reasons for Caution

ITW is by nature tied to some of the more volatile elements of the business cycle, so it may not be the best pick for investors living in fear of the next downturn. Conglomerates are notoriously difficult to manage (it's hard enough to manage one business, let alone 850 of them); any sign of cracks in this structure should be taken seriously. While acquisitions are part of the growth strategy, the company, thus far, keeps them small and does not depend on acquiring other big names, but the disruptions of a big acquisition could pose problems.

SECTOR: **Industrials**
BETA COEFFICIENT: **1.18**
10-YEAR COMPOUND EARNINGS PER SHARE GROWTH: **6.0%**
10-YEAR COMPOUND DIVIDENDS PER SHARE GROWTH: **14.5%**

	2004	2005	2006	2007	2008	2009	2010	2011
Revenues (Mil)	11,371	12,922	14,055	16,169	15,869	13,876	15,870	17,787
Net income (Mil)	1,340	1,494	1,717	1,826	1,583	969	1,527	1,852
Earnings per share	2.20	2.60	3.01	3.36	3.05	1.93	3.03	3.74
Dividends per share	0.50	0.61	0.71	0.91	1.15	1.24	1.27	1.38
Cash flow per share	2.90	3.34	3.87	4.44	4.56	3.27	4.17	5.06
Price: high	48.3	47.3	53.5	60.0	55.6	51.2	52.7	59.3
low	36.5	39.3	41.5	45.6	28.5	25.6	40.3	39.1

Illinois Tool Works, Inc.
3600 West Lake Avenue
Glenview, IL 60026
(847) 724-7500
Website: *www.itwinc.com*

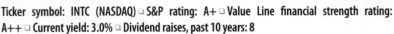

CONSERVATIVE GROWTH

Intel Corp.

Ticker symbol: INTC (NASDAQ) ❑ S&P rating: A+ ❑ Value Line financial strength rating: A++ ❑ Current yield: 3.0% ❑ Dividend raises, past 10 years: 8

Company Profile

Intel is the world's largest integrated circuit manufacturer. They produce memory, large-scale logic, networking hardware, and motherboards (among other things), but are best known for their microprocessors, first introduced 40 years ago. Their processors can be found in desktops, laptops, servers, tablets, smartphones, and in embedded applications for industrial controllers. Intel's best-known application is, of course, the personal computer, and Intel's microprocessors have always had a major share of the personal computer market. Against their early competitors in the PC space—companies such as Advanced Micro Devices (AMD), Via, Cyrix, and Motorola—Intel grew to be the major player and the standard for the application. That major share has now become a dominant position, as many of Intel's early competitors are now out of the game, and its sole remaining rival, AMD, has had some financial struggles recently. Overall, Intel commands 80 percent of the worldwide market for microprocessors, with a 95 percent share in servers and a 71 percent share in desktop PCs. Intel's shares of the

other markets in which they participate are not as dominant, but are still significant. They make some of the best-regarded products for the networking and solid-state drive (SSD) market, though other suppliers fare better in cost-sensitive installations.

In February 2011 the company acquired McAfee, a developer and marketer of security and utility software for the consumer markets.

Financial Highlights, Fiscal Year 2011

Intel's FY2011 was even stronger than their terrific rebound year in FY2010. Revenues grew 22 percent, and while net margin fell off FY2010's record high of 26.8 percent, it remains very strong at 24 percent and should remain near that in 2012. After a very strong FY2010, Intel found itself with nearly $22 billion in cash. Rather than going on a spending spree (we're looking at you, Mr. Zuckerberg), Intel's board did the right thing and committed $14 billion of it for share repurchase and raised their target for future share repurchase by an additional $20 billion. They also raised the dividend by 25 percent. The company also made major improvements to its manufacturing capacity and capability by committing nearly $11 billion to capital equipment, double their average of the past four years.

Reasons to Buy

Intel's vaunted "tick-tock" product development strategy continues to move along at what must seem to its competitors a relentless pace. The "tick" is the introduction of new manufacturing capability, providing increased performance and lower power consumption and cost through reduced feature size. The "tock" is the introduction of a new processor microarchitecture, providing performance improvements and feature addition through advances in CPU design. Every 18 months you get either a tick or a tock. This synergy of design and manufacturing improvements has worked brilliantly for Intel for the past 10 years, and Intel has a roadmap for at least the next five years of this strategy.

Last year, for the first time in history, China became the world's largest market for personal computers. Rising incomes in China have helped to make the PC far more affordable there and in other emerging markets as well. We expect this trend to accelerate as Chinese incomes rise and the currencies adjust.

The SSD market will shake out over the next year or so. The majority of the lower-tier resellers will fall by the wayside, leaving this relatively new market in the hands of the silicon developers and producers like Intel and Samsung. This should inevitably lead to an increased market share for Intel, at the cost of slightly lower margins. These products represent only 3 percent of Intel's 2011 revenue, but the margins are very good and we expect to see greatly increasing demand as prices drop.

Finally, after years of modest returns for shareholders, the company is starting to share its cash more liberally with its owners.

Reasons for Caution

Intel's current dominant position makes it very tough to grow market share in their highest-volume products. The company will need to develop their lower-power processors in order to compete successfully in the rapidly growing mobile markets. Their early mobile offerings, based on the Atom architecture, did not do well against lower-cost ARM-based cores on a performance-per-watt basis. And while the company seems to have finally put its major competitive nemesis (AMD) behind it, they must now be wary of the emergence and possible dominance of tablets and smartphones, and must fight to be included on these platforms. Also, this is still a company with 5.5 billion shares outstanding, which can apply some gravity to the share price.

SECTOR: **Information Technology**
BETA COEFFICIENT: **1.0**
10-YEAR COMPOUND EARNINGS PER SHARE GROWTH: **0.5%**
10-YEAR COMPOUND DIVIDENDS PER SHARE GROWTH: **28.0%**

	2004	**2005**	**2006**	**2007**	**2008**	**2009**	**2010**	**2011**
Revenues (Mil)	34,209	38,826	35,382	38,334	37,586	35,127	43,623	53,999
Net income (Mil)	7,516	8,664	5,044	6,976	5,292	4,369	11,692	12,942
Earnings per share	1.16	1.40	0.86	1.18	0.92	0.77	2.05	2.39
Dividends per share	0.16	0.32	0.41	0.45	0.55	0.56	0.63	0.78
Cash flow per share	1.94	2.20	1.68	1.98	1.74	1.65	2.92	3.24
Price: high	34.6	28.8	26.6	28.0	26.3	21.3	24.4	25.8
low	19.6	21.9	16.8	18.8	12.1	12.0	17.6	19.2

Intel Corporation
2200 Mission College Boulevard
Santa Clara, CA 95054–1549
(408) 765-8080
Website: *www.intc.com*

CONSERVATIVE GROWTH

International Business Machines

Ticker symbol: IBM (NYSE) ❑ S&P rating: AA- ❑ Value Line financial strength rating: A++ ❑ Current yield: 1.4% ❑ Dividend raises, past 10 years: 10

Company Profile

Big Blue is the world's leading provider of computer hardware and services. Really—we should say services and hardware. Get the drift? IBM makes a broad range of computers, mainframes, and network servers. But the company has morphed over the years into a software and services company; it is number two behind Microsoft in the software business. IBM is also an innovation and new product development leader, for years leading the world in the number of U.S. patents issued.

IBM is divided into four principal business units. The largest, at 38 percent of revenues, the Global Technology Services unit, is really an IT service, offering cloud computing, analytics, and other applications outsourcing. The Global Business Services unit (18 percent of revenues) is also a service unit but now provides its service on customer sites through consulting, application design, systems integration, and similar services. The Software unit (23 percent) supplies primarily "middleware" products that make everything in an IT environment work together. Finally, the Financing unit (2 percent) helps the company market it all.

It's not hard to see how the company has evolved from the old "Big Blue" maker of mainframes. They still produce high-margin commercial servers and enterprise-level installations, but in recent years, as a deliberate, and frankly, envied strategy, they have exited the lower-margin hardware businesses, such as consumer PCs, laptops, and hard drives.

Financial Highlights, Fiscal Year 2011

FY2011 was a story of strong high-single-digit revenue growth, with improved margins as the business shifted to relatively more profitable businesses. Revenues were up 7 percent to $106.9 billion, while per-share earnings surged 13 percent to $13.06. Global Technology Services revenue increased the company average 7 percent, while Global Business Services lagged slightly by 6 percent. The higher-margined Software business grew 11 percent. Additionally, the company noted a 19 percent revenue increase in the so-called "BRIC" countries—Brazil, Russia, India, China—a strong showing. Operating margins improved to 14.6 percent from

10–11 percent in the 2006–2008 period, again reflecting the favorable business mix shift. Cash flow continues to excel and accelerate at double-digit rates, and that cash has been used to increase the dividend continuously and substantially, while continuing to also fund strong share retirement to the tune of over 6 percent of outstanding shares in 2011. Since 2002, IBM has bought back a third of outstanding shares. The company expects to earn $20 per share by 2015.

Reasons to Buy

Once viewed as a teetering giant of the computer industry with a massive intellectual property portfolio but an uncertain product strategy, IBM has, over the past decade, successfully reinvented itself as a powerhouse in the Software and Services sector. Further, IBM seems positioned "where the puck is going" in the IT world, a fact not lost on HP and other competitors trying to emulate the business model. Not long ago, many companies felt they had to have in-house information technology departments to service their IT needs. Now, most have found that it's far more efficient to contract those services out to someone who can provide data warehousing, website development and maintenance, regional/national/global IT infrastructure, etc., without requiring a commitment in fixed assets. This is where IBM has leveraged their expertise, and as this trend continues and as businesses increase their reliance on these services, IBM benefits. As the common architecture becomes more "cloudlike," we also feel IBM will benefit.

IBM has traditionally led in the development of international IT markets, and today, international business represents about 63 percent of the total. While international has been the fastest-growing marketplace for years, U.S. growth has also resumed. They continue to innovate and are in a great position to acquire whatever technology they choose not to develop internally. They have world-class semiconductor design and production facilities and license design, manufacturing, and packaging services and products.

While all IT companies are vulnerable to economic cycles, IBM services income is largely based on long-term contracts, which are not as subject to the vagaries of the world economy as would be sales of hardware.

Finally, the company has an exceptionally strong cash and cash flow position and has shown a propensity to turn this into shareholder return, both through buybacks and a 16.5 percent annual dividend increase rate for the past 10 years.

Reasons for Caution

IBM has carved out a very large chunk of the outsourced IT business. Innovation in this area can be rapid and disruptive, and margins can shrink precipitously as a result. IBM will have to stay ahead of the curve with innovative and compelling products and defensive product strategies in order to maintain revenue growth.

Competition in the services area is heating up, with Hewlett-Packard's purchase of EDS and Oracle's acquisition of Sun Microsystems. These two moves have created competitors with strong synergies and a compelling sales pitch to new and existing customers.

Finally, IBM has a larger exposure to governments and government contracts than many of its competitors. While this can be stabilizing in hard times, this time we feel that a massive and widespread public sector belt tightening could hurt the company.

SECTOR: **Information Technology**
BETA COEFFICIENT: **0.66**
10-YEAR COMPOUND EARNINGS PER SHARE GROWTH: **10.5%**
10-YEAR COMPOUND DIVIDENDS PER SHARE GROWTH: **16.5%**

	2004	2005	2006	2007	2008	2009	2010	2011
Revenues (Mil)	96,503	91,134	91,424	98,786	103,630	95,758	99,870	106,900
Net Income (Mil)	8,448	7,934	9,492	10,418	12,334	13,425	14,833	15,600
Earnings per share	4.39	4.91	6.06	7.18	8.93	10.01	11.52	13.06
Dividends per share	0.7	0.078	1.1	1.5	1.9	2.15	2.50	2.90
Cash flow per share	8.24	8.71	9.56	11.28	13.28	13.9	16.01	17.85
Price: high	100.4	99.1	97.4	121.5	130.9	132.3	147.5	194.9
low	81.9	71.8	72.7	88.8	69.5	81.8	116.0	146.6

International Business Machines Corporation
New Orchard Road
Armonk, NY 10504
(800) 426-4968
Website: *www.ibm.com*

CONSERVATIVE GROWTH

International Paper Company

Ticker symbol: IP (NYSE) ❑ S&P rating: BBB ❑ Value Line financial strength rating: B+ ❑ Current yield: 3.2% ❑ Dividend raises, past 10 years: 3

Company Profile

International Paper Company (International Paper), incorporated in 1941, is a global paper and packaging company complemented by a North American merchant distribution system with primary markets and manufacturing operations in North America, Europe, Latin America, Russia, Asia, and North Africa.

At the end of 2011, the company operated 20 pulp, paper, and packaging mills, 142 converting and packaging plants, 18 recycling plants, and three bag facilities. Production facilities in Europe, Asia, Latin America, and South America have grown by two pulp/paper mills and twelve converting and packaging plants to include 11 pulp, paper, and packaging mills; 64 converting and packaging plants; and two recycling plants.

The company operates in three segments (with FY2011 sales in parenthesis): Industrial Packaging (60 percent), Printing Papers (28 percent), and Consumer Packaging (12 percent), with distribution and forestry divisions supporting the three product segments.

The Industrial Packaging segment produces containerboard, including linerboard, whitetop, recycled linerboard, and saturating crafto. About 70 percent of the company's production is converted into corrugated boxes and other packaging. The company also recycles a million tons of corrugated, mixed, and white paper through 21 recycling plants.

The Printing Papers segment produces uncoated printing and writing papers, including papers for use in copiers, desktop and laser printers, and digital imaging. Market pulp is used in the manufacture of printing, writing, and specialty papers; towel and tissue products; and filtration products. Pulp is also converted into nonpaper products such as diapers and sanitary napkins.

The Consumer Packaging segment produces somewhat finer materials including bleached sulfate board for making packaging for food, cosmetics, pharmaceuticals, etc.

In 2011 and early 2012, IP made two major acquisitions. It acquired a 75 percent stake in Indian paper products producer

Andhra Pradesh. Later in 2011, the company announced the acquisition of Temple-Inland for $4.3 billion, thought to be a bargain price for this $4 billion packaging materials producing competitor, which should produce about $300 million in cost-saving synergies once digested.

Financial Highlights, Fiscal Year 2011

The company has recovered nicely from a very sharp 2008–09 dip related to the recession. During that time the dividend was cut by two-thirds and the share price dropped almost 90 percent, quite a wild ride for investors. While the company did have to borrow to fund some operations, it never reported a loss even during this down cycle. In FY2011, earnings recovered to $1.29 billion on sales of $26 billion (not including Temple-Inland), both levels that far exceeded annual sales and earnings in the peak pre-recession year of 2007 at $21.9 billion in sales and $963 million in net profit. As it turns out, the company used the recession as a chance to clean house, buy some cheap assets in the form of Weyerhauser's containerboard, packaging, and recycling businesses, and emerged stronger than ever. Sales, margins, earnings, and most likely, dividends are expected to take another decent step forward in FY2012.

Reasons to Buy

We like to include a few turnaround situations, because patient investors can be amply rewarded by well-executed turnarounds. Brands, supply chains, channels, and general operational and market experience are already in place; the company just needs to prune the dead branches and make it all work. International Paper continues to be successful at turning itself around, and, like some patients finally undergoing long-awaited surgery, we think it is emerging stronger and better for the experience. The company has added to its dominance in key commodity and value-add paper and packaging markets, exited low-margin businesses, and increased operating margins substantially as a result. Acquisitions and international expansion plans bode well. Cash flow is strong, supporting continued dividend increases and, eventually, share buybacks. We think the company is well managed and is a solid player in a fairly steady industry.

Reasons for Caution

For the most part, IP is in a commodity business with a high reliance on corrugated boards and raw packaging materials. To the extent that the company can find ways to add value to its products, deliver finished paper and packaging to end consumers, and develop international markets, the company will overcome the negatives of being a commodity producer. We are also concerned that enhanced Internet experiences and devices like iPads may be reducing the amount of computer-generated printing, but that only affects a segment accounting for 28 percent of the business. More aggressive investors may not find this to be a sexy business.

SECTOR: Materials
BETA COEFFICIENT: 2.17
10-YEAR COMPOUND EARNINGS PER SHARE GROWTH: 3.0%
10-YEAR COMPOUND DIVIDENDS PER SHARE GROWTH: -5.5%

		2004	2005	2006	2007	2008	2009	2010	2011
Revenues (Mil)		25,548	24,097	21,995	21,890	24,829	23,366	25,179	26,034
Net Income (Mil)		634	513	635	963	829	378	644	1.292
Earnings per share		1.30	1.06	2.18	2.70	1.96	0.88	1.48	2.96
Dividends per share		1.00	1.00	1.00	1.00	1.00	0.33	0.40	.98
Cash flow per share		4.51	3.85	3.63	4.15	5.02	4.27	4.78	6.00
Price:	high	45	42.6	38	41.6	33.8	27.8	29.3	33.0
	low	37.1	27	30.7	31	10.2	3.9	19.3	21.5

International Paper Company
6400 Poplar Avenue
Memphis, TN 38197
(901) 419-4957
Website: *www.internationalpaper.com*

Iron Mountain Incorporated

Ticker symbol: IRM (NYSE) ❑ S&P rating: BB- ❑ Value Line financial strength rating: B ❑ Current yield: 3.5% ❑ Dividend raises, past 10 years: 3

Company Profile

The name implies security and invulnerability, and as such, Iron Mountain is the world's leading provider of secure record, document, and information-management services. Businesses that require or desire off-site, secure storage and/or archiving of data in physical or electronic form contract with IRM for whatever level of service meets their needs.

In general, IRM provides three major types of service: records management, data protection and recovery, and information destruction. All three services include both physical and electronic media.

Revenues accrue to the company through two streams—storage and services. Storage revenues consist of recurring per-unit charges related to the storage of material or data. The storage periods are typically many years, and the revenues from this service account for just over half of IRM's total revenue over the past five years. Service revenue comes from charges for any number of services, including those related to the core storage service and others such as temporary access, courier operations,

secure destruction, data recovery, media conversion, and the like.

Although its roots are in document management, the company offers digital archiving and services, which are analogous to the services done for paper, except that they are done for e-mail, e-statements, images, and other forms of electronic documents. It also includes web-based archiving of computer, server, and website data, as well as storage of backup or disaster-recovery digital media. The company sold a portion of this business to HP's Autonomy in early 2011, but continues to offer these services through partnerships. IRM also offers tailored industry-specific services for industries such as health care. The company also offers value-add services in organizing, indexing, and facilitating search through documents and records.

IRM's client base is deep and diverse. They have over 90,000 clients, including 93 percent of the *Fortune* 1,000 and over 90 percent of the FTSE 100. They have over 975 facilities in 165 markets worldwide, and they are six times the size of their nearest competitor. The company has strengthened its competitive position by acquiring some 44 smaller competitors in local markets since 1998.

Financial Highlights, Fiscal Year 2011

Iron Mountain's business has mostly flat-lined from a revenue perspective both in FY2011 and in FY2012 projections. Revenues were off about 3 percent in FY2011, partly due to currency fluctuations, partly due to softer prices for recycled paper (which the company sells a lot of through document destruction and shredding). However, margins have improved almost 3 percent in two years, and the company bought back almost 8 percent of outstanding shares in FY2011, resulting in an 8 percent earnings per share increase, and the company forecasts another such increase for FY2012. That said, increased energy prices (the company moves a lot of stuff too) may crimp these estimates. The company has raised its dividend to an indicated $1.00 per year from $0.19 in 2010 and nothing prior to that, indicating some confidence in future cash-generation potential.

Reasons to Buy

Iron Mountain's business strategy for the past 15 years has been one of becoming by far the biggest in the business with the strongest and most recognizable brand. Much of this growth and dominance has been achieved through acquisition and integration, buying smaller businesses and consolidating their operations and, more importantly, their customer base. Customers in this business tend to stay with a known quantity, and over the years, no one has become more known than IRM. This strategy has worked very well for them, and now IRM is the clear market leader. Their large, predictable revenue stream gives them the flexibility to maintain their policy of strategic acquisition while funding the resulting restructuring internally.

A common observation of IRM's critics is that paper records are dying off and most data is now generated and stored electronically, creating opportunity for competitors like IBM and EMC. This is true, but it ignores a couple of facts: Existing paper still needs to be stored for a long time, and there's a lot of it. Nearly 75 percent of IRM's revenue comes from paper storage, but this percentage is declining as IRM's customers are storing far more electronic data now.

It also ignores a number of other important points. For one, IRM's current customers would need a very good reason to split their data storage business between two vendors, one doing only electronic storage and the other doing electronic storage plus everything else as well. Second, if competitors for the electronic storage business become a problem, IRM can price their electronic storage below market and still be quite profitable. And last, for the customer base that IRM serves, this is not a burdensome expense. Changing vendors could likely cost them more than they might ever hope to save. For now, IRM has a pretty good moat.

The company is growing its overseas base, and expects stricter records keeping guidelines to help both domestic and international businesses.

Finally, it's hard to ignore the growing dividend; the payout of nearly 3 percent is quite attractive for a company with a solid future and decent growth prospects.

Reasons for Caution

Although many of its services are required for compliance to various record-keeping laws and norms, IRM is vulnerable to economic dips, high energy prices, and low recycled paper prices. Further, the company still hasn't completely found its way in the digital space, which should prove to be its biggest growth area moving forward. It remains to be seen whether digital storage and services are as profitable as their paper counterparts.

SECTOR: **Information Technology**
BETA COEFFICIENT: **0.85**
5-YEAR COMPOUND EARNINGS PER SHARE GROWTH: **11.4%**
10-YEAR COMPOUND DIVIDENDS PER SHARE GROWTH: **NM**

	2004	2005	2006	2007	2008	2009	2010	2011
Revenues (Mil)	1,817	2,078	2,350	2,730	3,055	3,014	3,127	3,027
Net Income (Mil)	94.2	114	129	153	152	195	230	255
Earnings per share	0.48	0.57	0.64	0.76	0.78	0.96	1.15	1.25
Dividends per share	—	—	—	—	—	0.75	0.19	0.88
Cash flow per share	1.32	1.52	1.69	2.01	2.19	2.55	2.75	3.25
Price: high	23.4	30.1	29.9	38.8	37.1	24.9	28.5	35.8
low	17.2	17.8	22.6	25	16.7	21.3	19.9	24.3

Iron Mountain Incorporated
745 Atlantic Avenue
Boston, MA 02111
Website: *www.ironmountain.com*

AGGRESSIVE GROWTH

Itron, Inc.

Ticker symbol: ITRI (NASDAQ) ❑ S&P rating: BB ❑ Value Line financial strength rating: B+ ❑ Current yield: Nil ❑ Dividend raises, past 10 years: NA

Company Profile

Itron is the world's largest provider of "intelligent" metering systems for residential and commercial gas, electric, and water usage. Intelligent meters, in addition to tracking raw usage over a period of time, can also measure at the point of use operating parameters such as pressure, temperature, voltage, phase, etc. This information can be extremely valuable to the supplying utility but has in the past been difficult and expensive to obtain.

Itron supplies a range of products from basic meters that are read manually to meters that act as network devices and transmit their data in real time to the managing utility and/or to the consuming customer. Products and systems are produced and sold in three groupings:

- Standard metering—basic meters that measure electricity, gas, or water flow by electrical or mechanical means, with displays but no built-in remote reading or transmission capability;
- Advanced metering—these units, depending on the country and the communications

technologies available— transmit usage data remotely through telephone, cellular, radio frequency (RF), Ethernet, or power line carrier paths. Among other value-adds, these meters transmit usage data for billing thereby eliminating the need for on-site meter reading.

- Smart metering—Smart meters collect and store interval data and other detailed info, receive commands, and interface with other devices through assorted communication paths to thermostats, smart appliances, and home network and other advanced control systems.

Itron also sells a range of software platforms for utilities and building managers for the management of the installed base and the analysis and optimization of usage and is active in developing so-called "smart grid" solutions for utilities and utility networks. The company also markets "advanced metering initiative" (AMI) contracts to utilities, where it installs devices and monitors and optimizes power usage for a utility. The company was founded in 1977 and in 2004 acquired the electric meter operations of Schlumberger, who at the time was the largest global supplier of this equipment. About 52 percent of the business comes from overseas. The company recently acquired SmartSynch, a provider of metering and communications systems using cellular technology.

Financial Highlights, Fiscal Year 2011

Although the utility infrastructure investment environment was a bit soft, FY2011 sales rang up a 7.7 percent gain, while per-share earnings charged ahead 20 percent to $3.94. For FY2012, the company projects revenues to be slightly lower, from $2.1 to $2.3 billion, as the company completes key AMI contracts. Per-share earnings are projected flat, between $3.80 and $4.20, including a $0.10 charge related to the Smart-Synch acquisition. The company announced a $100 million buyback in late 2012, which, if completed, would take a significant chunk out of outstanding shares—from 41 million to about 38.5 million, a 6 percent drop.

Reasons to Buy

Can you picture a day when you might manage your energy consumption, device by device, in your home, using your smartphone? Even if you're away from home? And the day when utilities can monitor usage in real time to shift supply of a resource like electricity that virtually cannot be stored? Where solar energy generated from one locale on a sunny day is moved to another with clouds and rain?

If you believe that the need for managed energy efficiency will only grow in the future, Itron is a good place to be. As utilities modernize, reduce costs and replace infrastructure, Itron products and networks will be in the sweet spot. Internationally, utilities are adding infrastructure, as well as replacing it, and Itron is positioned well for that, too. Worldwide, only about 12 percent of 2.5 billion meters are "smart" or "advanced."

Conceptually, these ideas make for a fine story, but as with so many similar companies they retain the question, "Yeah, but does this company make money?" In Itron's case the answer is yes; the earnings of about $4 per share and cash flows north of $5 well support the recent $40 stock price, even if the company forecasts near zero growth in the near term. Over time, this company, like the utility industry it supports, has been relatively stable for a technology stock, and at recent prices, the stock appears to be a good holding to sock away for the future.

Reasons for Caution

Companies that sell good ideas don't always grow, particularly if the size of their markets is limited or are particularly conservative about spending money; that might describe the utility industry. Energy credits and subsidies are always subject to change. Finally, as a criticism unique to this company on the *100 Best* list and most other companies we research, we found the website particularly jargony and uninformative, making it difficult to grasp what the company really sells or why it makes sense for its customers. Of course, that made us wonder how effectively their marketing and overall strategies are executed. Improve the website, please!

SECTOR: **Information Technology**
BETA COEFFICIENT: **1.62**
10-YEAR COMPOUND EARNINGS PER SHARE GROWTH: **16.0%**
10-YEAR COMPOUND DIVIDENDS PER SHARE GROWTH: **NA**

	2004	2005	2006	2007	2008	2009	2010	2011
Revenues (Mil)	399	553	644	1,464	1,909	1,687	2,259	2,434
Net income (Mil)	20.3	45.6	56.4	87.3	117.6	44.3	133.9	161.5
Earnings per share	.93	1.84	2.16	2.78	3.36	1.15	3.27	3.94
Dividends per share	—	—	—	—	—	—	—	—
Cash flow per share	2.77	2.34	2.79	4.24	4.96	2.53	4.85	5.55
Price: high	24.7	53.9	73.7	112.9	109.3	69.5	81.9	64.4
low	15.9	21.5	39.4	51.2	34.3	40.1	52.0	26.9

Itron, Inc.
2111 North Moller Rd.
Liberty Lake, WA 99019
(509) 924-9900
Website: *www.itron.com*

GROWTH AND INCOME

Johnson & Johnson

Ticker symbol: JNJ (NYSE) ❑ S&P rating: AAA ❑ Value Line financial strength rating: A++ ❑ Current yield: 3.5 percent ❑ Dividend raises, past 10 years: 10

Company Profile

With FY2011 sales of $65 billion, Johnson & Johnson is the largest and most comprehensive health-care company in the world. JNJ offers a broad line of consumer products and over-the-counter drugs, as well as various other medical devices and diagnostic equipment.

The company has three reporting segments: Consumer Health Care (23 percent of FY2011 revenues), Medical Devices and Diagnostics (40 percent), and Pharmaceuticals (37 percent). In those segments, Johnson & Johnson has more than 200 companies operating in 54 countries, selling some 50,000 products in more than 175 countries. Among Johnson & Johnson's premier assets are its well-entrenched brand names, which are widely known in the United States as well as abroad. And as a marketer, JNJ's reputation for quality has enabled it to build strong ties to commercial health-care providers.

The company has a stake in a wide variety of health segments: anti-infectives, biotechnology, cardiology and circulatory diseases, diagnostics, gastrointestinals, minimally invasive therapies, nutraceuticals, orthopedics, pain management, skin care, vision care, women's health, and wound care.

The company's vast portfolio of well-known trade names includes Band-Aid adhesive bandages; Tylenol; Stayfree, Carefree, and Sure & Natural feminine hygiene products; Mylanta; Pepcid AC; Motrin; Sudafed; Zyrtec; Neosporin; Neutrogena, Johnson's baby powder; shampoo, and oil; Listerine; and Reach toothbrushes.

The company is typically fairly active with acquisitions, acquiring small niche players to strengthen its overall product offering. In April 2011 JNJ announced a much larger buyout of the trauma devices maker Synthes for $21.3 billion, which will make the company the largest player in the trauma health market. The acquisition is still awaiting regulatory approval.

Financial Highlights, Fiscal Year 2011

Johnson & Johnson has a dominant and stable franchise in a secure and lucrative industry. We like the model of steady, recurring income from solid consumer brands such as Tylenol combined with more aggressive and lucrative ventures into pharmaceuticals and surgical products. Yet the company's earnings performance continues to be a bit softer than most investors would like, likely a victim of increased "utilization" (i.e., more efficient health-care delivery to folks who really need it), a stronger dollar, and sheer size. The usual assortment of recalls and legal challenges seem to be accelerating lately as well, although none are to the extent of the Tylenol/Benadryl/Zyrtec plant shutdown and recall of 2010. That said, revenues advanced almost 6 percent to $65 billion, while earnings per share advanced 5 percent to an even $5.00. FY2012 projections, however, call for earnings only in the $5.05–$5.10 range. Most of the growth that the company is seeing is coming from overseas, which accounts for about 45 percent of the business overall.

Reasons to Buy

Even if unexciting for the growth and momentum investor, JNJ's business remains solid and intact. Although growth is slowing a bit, earnings and cash flow are steady, and when you combine the healthy dividend and share repurchases, shareholder returns have been healthy. Acquisitions and the new drug pipeline will likely add a bit to margins. International sales continue to be a solid growth path.

As standards of medical care rise internationally and as the potential for health-care funding reform in the United States increases, JNJ's growth outside the United States is particularly appealing. Despite the size and some softness in consumer spending and improvements in utilization, the company has delivered a solid double-digit growth triple play in ten-year earnings, cash flow, and dividend growth, despite sales growth narrowly missing double digits at 9 percent. Dividends have not only been raised 10 consecutive years, but the increases are substantial, 5 to 10 percent or more each year (are your wage increases this large?). We feel that JNJ is rock solid with modest growth prospects and little long-term downside.

Reasons for Caution

While JNJ is a "steady Eddie" in a steady health-care segment, investors aren't likely to strike it rich on this company due to its size and relative steadiness of the markets it serves. Even a blockbuster drug or acquisition isn't likely to move the needle very much.

There may be some concern that regulators and litigators, now having seen JNJ as a juicy target for action, will step up these actions or, short of that, watch JNJ through a microscope, creating a distraction for management. Worse, these events could damage consumer perception and brand strength if they continue. However, we think these blemishes will likely heal and won't be contagious to long-term performance.

SECTOR: **Health Care**
BETA COEFFICIENT: **.53**
10-YEAR COMPOUND EARNINGS PER SHARE GROWTH: **12.0%**
10-YEAR COMPOUND DIVIDENDS PER SHARE GROWTH: **13.5%**

	2004	2005	2006	2007	2008	2009	2010	2011
Revenues (Mil)	47,348	50,514	53,324	61,095	63,747	61,897	61,587	65,030
Net Income (Mil)	8,509	10,411	11,053	10,576	12,949	12,906	13,279	13,867
Earnings per share	2.84	3.35	3.73	4.15	4.57	4.63	4.76	5.00
Dividends per share	1.1	1.28	1.46	1.62	1.8	1.93	2.11	2.25
Cash flow per share	3.84	4.25	4.6	5.23	5.70	5.69	5.90	6.25
Price: high	64.2	70	69.4	68.8	72.8	65.9	66.2	66.3
low	49.2	59.8	56.6	59.7	52.1	61.9	56.9	64.3

Johnson & Johnson
One Johnson & Johnson Plaza
New Brunswick, NJ 08933
(800) 950-5089
Website: *www.jnj.com*

Johnson Controls, Inc.

Ticker symbol: JCI (NYSE) □ S&P rating: BBB+ □ Value Line financial strength rating: A □ Current yield: 2.3% □ Dividend raises, past 10 years: 9

Company Profile

Johnson Controls is a fairly low-profile U.S. manufacturer with three principal businesses that just now happen to all be in favor for the first time in years. JCI is a large manufacturer of automotive parts and subassemblies; heating; ventilation, and air conditioning (HVAC); and other energy controls; and an assortment of battery technologies and products. Their products are found in over 200 million vehicles, 12 million homes, and 1 million commercial buildings. Their business operates in three segments: Automotive Experience, Building Efficiency, and Power Solutions.

Their automotive business (49 percent of FY2011 revenues, 46 percent of profits) is one of the world's largest automotive suppliers, providing seating and overhead systems, door systems, floor consoles, instrument panels, cockpits, and integrated electronics for more than 30 million vehicles each year. Customers include virtually every major automaker in the world, including newer start-ups and plants in China. The company now plans a third plant in that country. The business produces automotive

interior systems for original equipment manufacturers (OEMs) and operates in 29 countries worldwide. Additionally, the business has partially owned affiliates in Asia, Europe, North America, and South America. Building Efficiency (37 percent of revenues, 40 percent of profits) is a global leader in delivering integrated control systems, mechanical equipment, services, and solutions designed to improve the comfort, safety, and energy efficiency of nonresidential buildings and residential properties with operations in more than 125 countries. Revenues come from facilities management, technical services, and the replacement and upgrade of controls/HVAC mechanical equipment in the existing buildings and "smart buildings" market.

The Power Solutions business (14 percent of revenues, 24 percent of profits) produces lead-acid automotive batteries, serving both automotive original equipment manufacturers and the general vehicle battery aftermarket. They also offer Absorbent Glass Mat (AGM), nickel-metal-hydride, and lithium-ion battery technologies to power hybrid vehicles.

Financial Highlights, Fiscal Year 2011

After a dismal period during the 2008–09 recession, Johnson Controls is now in the right place at the right time with all three of its businesses.

A recovery in the auto industry and especially the U.S.-based auto industry, combined with greater emphasis on energy-efficient buildings and focus on new battery technologies for electric vehicles have combined to not only bring JCI out of the doldrums but to bring in steadily rising revenues and profits. The Automotive Experience group enjoyed its second consecutive double-digit revenue jump of 15 percent following an 18 percent gain in FY2010. The building efficiency group brought a 4 percent gain, a bit lower than expected because of softness in Europe. Power Systems was a bit softer—of all things, because of warmer-than-expected weather, so not so many battery replacements! Those batteries will all go belly up sooner or later. Coupled with some acquisitions, revenues rose about 19 percent to give the company its first $40 billion year. Earnings jumped about 22 percent. For 2012, the company is staying conservative because of European exposure and the uncertain end to the warm weather, and is forecasting a 6 percent revenue growth and a 14 percent growth in per-share earnings.

Reasons to Buy

As previously noted, JCI is hitting on all cylinders right now, with a resurgent automotive manufacturing climate, strong demand for energy-efficient buildings, and even stronger demand for effective battery technologies for current and future applications.

JCI will be a major participant in the coming automotive applications of lithium battery technology. They are already in the Mercedes S-class hybrid and are the exclusive suppliers to the upcoming Ford plug-in hybrid for its battery and battery controls. Johnson's joint venture with Saft Advanced Power Solutions (JCS) is also providing lithium-ion batteries to the Dodge Sprinter development program. JCI's subsidiary Varta has set up a JCS development center in Hanover, Germany, to support the European market.

Reasons for Caution

Needless to say, the automotive and building efficiency businesses can be intensely cyclical and economically sensitive; in fact, the construction industry is still somewhat in its doldrums. The beta coefficient of 1.86 reflects this cyclicity; in fact, the range between annual high and low share prices is pretty large each year—which might make some investors nervous, but also provides attractive buying opportunities.

Also, JCI is a leader in the race for the next automotive power technology, but there's no guarantee that lithium will be the clear winner. Other technologies are making progress as well, and the politics of lithium sourcing are far from settled. Finally, operating margins in the 7 percent range don't leave much room for error.

SECTOR: **Industrials**
BETA COEFFICIENT: **1.86**
10-YEAR COMPOUND EARNINGS PER SHARE GROWTH: **7.5%**
10-YEAR COMPOUND DIVIDENDS PER SHARE GROWTH: **12.0%**

		2004	2005	2006	2007	2008	2009	2010	2011
Revenues (Mil)		25,363	27,883	32,235	34,624	38,062	28,497	34,305	40,833
Net Income (Mil)		818	909	1,028	1,252	1,400	281	1,365	1,665
Earnings per share		1.41	1.5	1.75	2.09	2.33	0.47	2.00	2.42
Dividends per share		0.28	0.33	0.37	0.44	0.52	0.52	0.52	.68
Cash flow per share		2.5	2.6	2.95	3.34	3.63	1.48	3.00	3.45
Price:	high	21.1	25.1	30	44.5	36.5	28.3	40.2	42.9
	low	16.5	17.5	22.1	28.1	13.6	8.4	25.6	24.3

Johnson Controls, Inc.
P. O. Box 591
Milwaukee, WI 53201–0591
(414) 524-2375
Website: *www.johnsoncontrols.com*

Kellogg Company

Ticker symbol: K (NYSE) ❑ S&P rating: BBB+ ❑ Value Line financial strength rating: A ❑ Current yield: 3.3% ❑ Dividend raises, past 10 years: 7

Company Profile

Founded in 1906, Kellogg is the world's leading producer of breakfast cereal and a leading producer of convenience foods, including cookies, crackers, toaster pastries, cereal bars, frozen waffles, meat alternatives, pie crusts, and cones. The company's brands include Kellogg's, Keebler, Pop-Tarts, Eggo, Cheez-It, Nutri-Grain, Rice Krispies, Special K, Murray, Austin, Morningstar Farms, Famous Amos, Carr's, Plantation, and Kashi. Kellogg's cereal brands include a long list of familiar names: Corn Flakes, All-Bran Crunch, Cocoa Krispies, Corn Pops, Rice Krispies, Raisin Bran, Smart Start, Special K, Mueslix, Low Fat Granola—just to name a few. The company sells most of these brands and variations thereof in overseas markets.

The company operates in two segments: Kellogg North America (NA) and Kellogg International, with International generating about 37 percent of revenue. NA operations are further divided into Cereals, Snacks, and Frozen/Specialty categories. The company produces more than 1,500 different products, manufactured in 19 countries

and marketed in more than 180 countries around the world. The company operates manufacturing facilities in 16 countries in addition to the United States.

The company has traditionally not been too active in the acquisition space but in 2012 agreed to acquire Procter & Gamble's Pringles business for $2.7 billion, a major step into the snack foods market and, most likely, an important source of useful food processing technology patents and processes. The purchase will be mostly debt financed; that will curtail the existing and fairly aggressive share repurchase program in place.

Financial Highlights, Fiscal Year 2011

FY2011 was a mixed year. The company recorded a 6.3 percent revenue gain to $13,175 billion. But the familiar industry story of rising commodity prices hurt profits, and some company-specific issues of manufacturing problems, recalls, and resulting manufacturing plant upgrades hurt further. These factors combined to drop net income almost 2 percent, although share buybacks resulted in a gain of 5 cents per share to $3.35 per share. The company projects a 5 percent sales increase for FY2012 with a 2 to 4 percent increase in earnings—these figures would not include the Pringles acquisition.

Reasons to Buy

Kellogg owns just over a third of the U.S. market for ready-to-eat cereals, which makes them the most recognized brand and market leader in probably the most mature food category in the world. But, having invented it over a hundred years ago, they continue to respond to customer demand for new and interesting products, many with a health bent, with various new versions of Mueslix, Granola, Special K, and other brands.

Kellogg's strategy since 2001 has been to "win in cereal and expand snacks." Until 2012, this primarily referred to internal innovation; now the Pringles acquisition ups the ante considerably, and we applaud the move, which will leverage existing channels and manufacturing capacity. We like Kellogg's growth in international markets. As discretionary income rises, so does consumption of prepared foods, and the international markets will reward companies that have the right products. Special K,

for example, is growing at double-digit rates internationally and at triple-digit rates in India.

The company has a compelling history of slow but steady growth. The past year has presented some operating challenges, but we feel the company will get past them and resume its slow, steady earnings growth trajectory. The dividend is secure, and has been raised more aggressively in recent years, and it buys time to wait for the growth resumption. Although the Pringles purchase will slow share repurchases, the combination of total investor returns and safety over the long term make Kellogg an attractive box in your stock pantry.

Reasons for Caution

Particularly in a soft economy, Kellogg faces threats from generic and store-branded products, especially on the cereal aisle. Price competition is intense, and required advertising and marketing spend can further eat into profits. Growth prospects beyond the single digits for this type of company are unlikely. The company is exposed to commodity price swings, although they do tend to hedge such swings. Finally, the Pringles acquisition does bring with it some uncertainty.

SECTOR: **Consumer Staples**
BETA COEFFICIENT: **.45**
10-YEAR COMPOUND EARNINGS PER SHARE GROWTH: **8.0%**
10-YEAR COMPOUND DIVIDENDS PER SHARE GROWTH: **4.0%**

	2004	**2005**	**2006**	**2007**	**2008**	**2009**	**2010**	**2011**
Revenues (Mil)	9,614	10,177	10,907	11,776	12,822	12,575	12,397	13,175
Net Income (Mil)	891	980	1,004	1,103	1,148	1,212	1,247	1,225
Earnings per share	2.14	2.26	2.51	2.76	2.99	3.17	3.30	3.35
Dividends per share	1.01	1.06	1.14	1.24	1.3	1.43	1.56	1.67
Cash flow per share	3.15	3.39	3.41	3.78	3.99	4.35	4.48	4.55
Price: high	45.3	47	51	56.9	58.5	54.1	56	57.7
low	37	42.4	42.4	48.7	35.6	35.6	47.3	48.1

Kellogg Company
One Kellogg Square
P. O. Box 3599
Battle Creek, MI 49016–3599
(269) 961-6636
Website: *www.kelloggcompany.com*

Kimberly-Clark

Ticker symbol: KMB (NYSE) ❑ S&P rating: A ❑ Value Line financial strength rating: A++ ❑ Current
yield: 4.0% ❑ Dividend raises, past 10 years: 10

Company Profile

Kimberly-Clark develops, manufactures, and markets a full line of personal care products, mostly based on paper and paper technologies. Well known for their ubiquitous Kleenex brand tissues, KMB also is a strong player in bath tissue, diapers, feminine products, incontinence products, industrial and health-care-related paper products, and others.

The company operates in four segments: Personal Care, Consumer Tissue, K-C Professional & Other, and Health Care. The Personal Care segment provides disposable diapers, training and youth pants, and swim pants; baby wipes; and feminine and incontinence care products and related products. Brand names include Huggies, Pull-Ups, Little Swimmers, GoodNites, Kotex, Lightdays, Depend, and Poise. The Consumer Tissue segment offers facial and bathroom tissue, paper towels, napkins, and related products for household use under the Kleenex, Scott, Cottonelle, Viva, Andrex, Scottex, Hakle, and Page brands. The K-C Professional & Other segment provides paper products for the away-from-home, that is, commercial/institutional marketplace under Kimberly-Clark, Kleenex, Scott, WypAll, Kimtech, KleenGuard, Kimcare, and Jackson brand names. The Health Care segment offers disposable health-care products, such as surgical drapes and gowns, infection control products, face masks, exam gloves, respiratory products, pain management products, and other disposable medical products.

The company was founded in 1872 and is headquartered today in Dallas, Texas, with a historical, technology, and manufacturing base in the Fox River Valley in Wisconsin.

Financial Highlights, Fiscal Year 2011

FY2011 was a mixed and fairly flat year for operating performance, but "steady" isn't all bad for a company like KMB. Revenues grew 6 percent to $20.8 billion, but about half of that was due to currency benefits. Of the remaining 3 percent, approximately 2 percent came from price increases, 1 percent from volume. Earnings were again aided by ongoing cost-cutting efforts stemming from its rather bluntly named "Project FORCE"—Focus on Reducing Costs Everywhere— program. The company went further during the year to "restructure" pulp and paper operations—which meant to sell them off—and the company continues to streamline other activities. Commodity cost increases and some restructuring charges dropped net income some 14 percent from FY2010, but this drop should be viewed as temporary. For FY2012, the company expects operating profit growth in the 3–6 percent range on net revenue growth between 0 and 1 percent (a figure somewhat attenuated from expected negative currency effects). Despite restructuring and commodity costs, cash flow continues to march northward, covering the 4 percent dividend well, allowing for increases, and allowing for further share repurchases, which have averaged 3 percent of float of late.

Reasons to Buy

Kimberly-Clark has shown itself to be a steady business in all kinds of economic climates. The high yield and strong track record of raising dividends and buying back shares is a definite plus. Strong cash flow has financed these initiatives as well as funding international expansion and enhanced marketing efforts. With a dividend at 4 percent, often

higher during share price dips, and growing; share buybacks; and steady performance, the company seems to make shareholder interests a priority.

The company has stellar brands, and should do well expanding them into overseas markets, a relatively untapped frontier compared to some of its peers. Also, compared to some peers, especially Procter & Gamble, the company is less inclined to go for "glamour" markets such as cosmetics, choosing instead to add to margins through operating efficiencies and scale. Safety-oriented investors may find this approach preferable. In addition, Value Line gives the company an "A++" for financial strength and a top rating for safety, the latter of which it has maintained since 1990.

Reasons for Caution

While the paper products business is steady, it isn't easy to see where growth would come from. The company, rightly so, is targeting international expansion, but competition and currency fluctuation make the results far from certain. The cost of pulp and paper raw materials can also be highly volatile. Investors should focus on income and safety with this issue; any growth would be a plus.

SECTOR: **Consumer Staples**
BETA COEFFICIENT: **0.33**
10-YEAR COMPOUND EARNINGS PER SHARE GROWTH: **4.0%**
10-YEAR COMPOUND DIVIDENDS PER SHARE GROWTH: **9.0%**

	2004	2005	2006	2007	2008	2009	2010	2011
Revenues (Mil)	15,083	15,903	16,747	18,266	19,415	19,115	19,746	20,846
Net Income (Mil)	1,800	1,803	1,844	1,861	1,698	1,884.0	1,843	1,591
Earnings per share	3.61	3.78	3.90	4.25	4.14	4.52	4.45	3.99
Dividends per share	1.60	1.80	1.96	2.08	2.27	2.38	2.58	2.76
Cash flow per share	5.39	5.74	6.10	6.34	5.98	6.40	6.53	6.78
Price: high	69	68.3	68.6	72.8	69.7	67	67.2	74.1
low	56.2	55.6	56.6	63.8	50.3	43.1	58.3	61

Kimberly-Clark
P.O. Box 619100
Dallas, TX 75261
(972) 281-1200
Website: *www.kimberly-clark.com*

Macy's

Ticker symbol: M (NYSE) ❑ S&P rating: BBB ❑ Value Line financial strength rating: B+ ❑ Current yield: 2.0% ❑ Dividend raises, past 10 years: 5

Company Profile

Macy's is, now by far, the largest operator of department stores in the United States. The company operates under two brand names: Macy's and Bloomingdale's, and operates about 850 stores in 45 states, Puerto Rico, and Guam. Macy's has been assembled over the years from a large assortment of famed department store predecessors including Marshall Field, May, and the assortment of names once under ownership of Federated Department Stores, including Lazarus, Weinstocks, Dillard, Abraham & Straus, I. Magnin, and others. The company, in current form, was assembled after Federated emerged from bankruptcy in 1992.

In addition to department stores, Macy's operates its own credit card operations and an internal merchandising group that, among other things, develops and markets a number of familiar proprietary brands such as Charter Club, Club Room, Hotel Collection, Tommy Hilfiger, Ellen Tracy, and now the Martha Stewart Collection. The company also operates 90 specialty stores including outlets and furniture stores, and has a significant and growing online presence through

www.macys.com. The sales mix is approximately 62 percent women's clothing, shoes, and accessories, 23 percent men's and children's, and 15 percent home and miscellaneous.

Financial Highlights, Fiscal Year 2011

Macy's has ridden the economic recovery and a series of internal operational improvements to a successful new growth trajectory in a business that many had given up on. Same-store sales improved 5.3 percent in FY2011 on top of a 4.6 percent increase in FY2010. Online sales grew 40 percent, almost doubling the previous two years' growth rate. Total sales advanced about 5.5 percent to $26.4 billion, almost a full recovery to the boom years prior to the recession. Operational improvements in procurement and supply chain, combined with improved and more locally customized merchandising, grew net profit margins back to 4.7 percent after years in the 2–3 percent range, and new profits came in at a record $1.24 billion. Meanwhile, the company had reinvested its strong cash flows, more than double the earnings, in share repurchases, buying back (many at a discount, of course!) some 143 million of 546 million shares outstanding since 2005, resulting in an EPS of $2.88. The company also has repaid some $2 billion in long-term debt since FY2009, regaining investment-grade status at popular rating agencies. Earnings growth should continue into FY2012, with EPS for the year projected at $3.25 to $3.30.

Reasons to Buy

Justifiably, perhaps, most investors would perceive Macy's and the department store business to be yesterday's news, as big box retailers and the Internet have taken over. True, those players have snatched important parts of the retail business, but the department store idea has made a comeback with more affluent, brand-conscious, and experience-conscious shoppers. The stores have been upgraded, merchandise assortments made more exciting, and service has improved. Merchandise assortments have been localized and are now more exciting and edgier

and more aimed at the younger set. Department stores aren't just for grandma any longer. The company has managed its image and product well and has turned the new interest and a more scientific approach to management into solid bottom line results, and has returned more than just a few discount coupons to investors, doubling the dividend in early 2012.

Reasons for Caution

The economy, of course, is always a biggie. While it may be less true than in the recent past, department stores, Macy's included, still seem to have to throw expensive advertisements and discounts at customers pretty regularly to get them into the store; many people avoid malls and department stores altogether unless shopping a 50 percent off special or toting a card for 15 percent off for the day in hand. While Macy's is increasing its appeal to the younger set, the Internet is still a big contender here, although the growth in macys.com is encouraging.

SECTOR: **Retail**
BETA COEFFICIENT: **1.67**
10-YEAR COMPOUND EARNINGS PER SHARE GROWTH: **2.5%**
10-YEAR COMPOUND DIVIDENDS PER SHARE GROWTH: **15.0%**

	2004	2005	2006	2007	2008	2009	2010	2011
Revenues (Mil)	15,630	22,390	26,970	26,313	24,892	23,489	25,003	26,405
Net income (Mil)	689	1,111	1,147	970	543	595	867	1,238
Earnings per share	1.93	2.56	2.16	2.18	1.29	1.41	2.03	2.88
Dividends per share	1.10	1.12	1.15	1.17	1.19	1.19	1.19	1.19
Cash flow per share	4.26	3.76	4.85	5.42	4.33	4.29	4.77	5.61
Price: high	29.1	39	45	46.7	28.5	20.6	26.3	33.3
low	21.4	27.1	32.4	24.7	5.1	6.3	15.3	21.7

Macy's, Inc.
7 West Seventh St.
Cincinnati, OH 45202
(513) 579-7000
Website: *www.macys.com*

AGGRESSIVE GROWTH

Marathon Oil Corporation

Ticker symbol: MRO (NYSE) □ S&P rating: BBB □ Value Line financial strength rating: A □ Current yield: 2.2% □ Dividend raises, past 10 years: NM

Company Profile

Until 2011, Marathon Oil was a vertically integrated producer, refiner, and marketer of petroleum and natural gas products. It sold crude to other refiners, but its primary revenue stream was through the sale of its refined petroleum products to resellers and to end consumers via company-owned retail locations.

In June 2011 the company completed a split of its Exploration and Production and Oil Sands Mining businesses from its Refining, Marketing and Transportation business. The Marathon Oil we currently include on our *100 Best* list includes the E&P and Oil Sands units; the Refining & Marketing segment now goes by the name of Marathon Petroleum and trades under the ticker symbol "MPC." We would have preferred a more clearly distinguished naming. The split is similar to others in the industry like *100 Best* stock ConocoPhillips, but that company much more clearly distinguished its split-off sub as the Phillips 66 Company.

The overall strategy is to unlock shareholder value, and from a business point of view, for the E&P operation to more easily sell product into multiple channels, rather than be held captive to one distribution business. Capital requirements for production are far different from those for exploration. The risk-reward profile is much different: MRO is about half of the old company's revenue but most of the profit; the separated refining/marketing business is a very low-margin business these days.

The new company has 40 percent of its reserves in Africa, 35 percent in Canada, 18 percent in the United States, and 7 percent in Europe.

It has exploration rights/interests in the United States, Angola, Norway, Indonesia, Equatorial Guinea, Libya, Canada, and the UK. The bulk of its U.S. activities are in the Gulf Coast region. The company holds a 20 percent outside-operated interest in the Athabasca Oil Sands Project in Alberta, Canada. Oil sands mining bears no resemblance to any of Marathon's other oil production processes. Instead these operations more closely resemble a coal surface mine. Output from these operations is on the order of 30,000 barrels of synthetic crude per day, with significantly higher than normal refining costs.

Financial Highlights, Fiscal Year 2011

Analysis and comparisons are difficult since we have only a one-half year of operations in FY2011 to examine. The company earned $2.3 billion on $15.3 billion in sales in the half year; it estimates sales in the $16.8 billion range, and profits of $1.9 billion, for FY2012. Earnings are projected at $2.70 per share with a cash flow of $6.20 and a dividend of 70 cents. Naturally, the company's results are more tuned to the price of oil than in the past.

Reasons to Buy

MRO's exploration is oriented toward oil, as opposed to natural gas, and that's a good thing in today's oil and gas price environment. The new company seems "rightsized," and its track record of success should carry forward with more focus than before. How much success really remains to be seen, but a 2.2 percent yield gives us time to wait and see.

Reasons for Caution

Some analysts have expressed concern that the new company lacks the diverse revenue and profit base of its ancestor, and that the risk profile of an explorer/producer is inherently higher. True, but risk brings reward in this business. A drop in oil prices, seen as unlikely, could hurt. For now, the dividend yield lags some of its peers, like ConocoPhillips and Total S.A., also on our *100 Best* list.

SECTOR: **Energy**
BETA COEFFICIENT: **1.34**
10-YEAR COMPOUND EARNINGS PER SHARE GROWTH: **NM**
10-YEAR COMPOUND DIVIDENDS PER SHARE GROWTH: **NM**

	2004	2005	2006	2007	2008	2009	2010	2011 (half year)
Revenues (Mil)	45,135	58,596	59,917	59,389	72,128	48,456	67,113	15,282
Net Income (Mil)	1,314	3,051	4,636	3,755	3,528	1,184	2,568	2,268
Earnings per share	1.94	4.22	6.42	5.43	4.95	1.67	3.61	2.41
Dividends per share	0.52	0.61	0.77	0.92	0.96	0.96	0.99	0.30
Cash flow per share	3.65	6.01	8.85	7.56	8.08	5.38	8.80	7.30
Price: high	21.3	36.3	49.4	67	63.2	33.1	37.2	35.0
low	15	17.8	30.2	41.5	19.3	20.2	27.6	18.1

Marathon Oil Corporation
5555 San Felipe Road
Houston, TX 77056
(713) 629-6600
Website: *www.marathon.com*

McCormick & Company, Inc.

Ticker symbol: MKC (NYSE) □ S&P rating: A- □ Value Line financial strength rating: A □ Current yield: 2.3% □ Dividend raises, past 10 years: 10

Company Profile

McCormick manufactures, markets, and distributes spices, herbs, seasonings, and flavors to the global food industry. They are the largest such supplier in the world. Customers range from retail outlets and food manufacturers to foodservice businesses.

McCormick's U.S. Consumer business (59 percent of sales and 81 percent of operating profits), its oldest and largest, manufactures consumer spices, herbs, extracts, proprietary seasoning blends, sauces, and marinades. Spices are sold under an assortment of recognizable brand names: McCormick, Lawry's, Zatarain's, Thai Kitchen, Simply Asia, Clubhouse, Billy Bee, Produce Partners, Golden Dipt, Old Bay, and Mojave. Industrial customers include foodservice, food-processing businesses, and retail outlets. The Industrial segment was responsible for 41 percent of sales and 19 percent of operating profits.

Many of the spices and herbs purchased by the company, such as black pepper, vanilla beans, cinnamon, herbs, and seeds must be imported from countries such as India, Indonesia, Malaysia, Brazil, and the Malagasy Republic. Other ingredients such as paprika; dehydrated vegetables, onion, and garlic; and food ingredients other than spices and herbs originate in the United States.

The company was founded in 1889 and has approximately 7,500 full-time employees in facilities located around the world. Major sales, distribution, and production facilities are located in North America and Europe. Additional facilities are based in Mexico, Central America, Australia, China, Singapore, Thailand, and South Africa. International sales account for about 29 percent of the total. The company has recently deployed more informative print and web content with recipes and other information to spur cooking with spices. The company does a lot of R&D in the area of flavors and flavor trends, and we also like a new packaging initiative to sell prepackaged spices set to cook a particular meal called "Recipe Inspirations"; this launch has been successful.

Financial Highlights, Fiscal Year 2011

The spice and ingredient business is a fairly slow, steady business at most times, but, aided by a growing number of people eating at home to control expenses in response to the recession, McCormick had another good year in FY2011, and the stock price performed accordingly. Revenues increased 9 percent, as the company enjoyed the benefits of new products and packaging, and was largely able to pass on price increases mostly commensurate with ingredient cost increases it experienced. Earnings rose a more modest 6 percent as the company was unable to recover all cost increases. The company and most analysts expect stronger performance in FY2012, as a few small 2011 acquisitions come on line, international sales grow, more price increases take effect, and more benefits from new products accrue. The company expects another 9 percent revenue increase and a 14 percent increase in earnings per share to about $3.20 per share.

Reasons to Buy

McCormick's is about as "pure" a play as there is in this book. They make seasonings (spices/herbs/flavorings), a few specialty foods, and nothing else. They're the largest branded producer of seasonings in North America, and they're the largest private-label producer of seasonings in North America, giving them a substantial level of price protection. McCormick is not just

a producer/supplier, however—they also create new seasoning products. In fact, every year since 2005, between 13 percent and 18 percent of their industrial business sales have come from new products launched in the preceding three years. Keeping up with changing tastes requires McCormick to produce that new, hot flavor and to come up with new and interesting flavors and blends of existing seasonings. The company has also tapped existing niches, for example, reporting a 40 percent increase in flavorings sold into the Hispanic market since 2006.

On the consumer side, as amateur cooks ourselves, we have long felt that people would use more spices if they only knew how to use them. The new information outlets, and the prepackaged Recipe Inspirations meal kits will serve well to get the less experienced cooks "across the chasm" of using spices effectively in their own cooking. In our view, these initiatives, combined with continuing growth in the health-conscious segment by learning to replace fat flavoring with spice flavoring, will add to a solid business base for the company.

McCormick's sales have increased every year for the past 50 years, and the company has paid a dividend every year since 1925. In 2011, they raised the dividend for the twenty-sixth consecutive year. The profitability, stability, and defensive nature of the company and its business present an attractive combination for investors.

Reasons for Caution

Downsides include the rising cost of ingredients and the sourcing of many of these ingredients in geopolitically unstable regions. Top-line growth is likely to remain moderate except by acquisition. While earnings and share price growth have been steady, they don't add a lot of "spice" to an aggressive portfolio. That said, we don't see people's tastes in taste diminishing anytime soon.

SECTOR: **Consumer Staples**
BETA COEFFICIENT: **.43**
10-YEAR COMPOUND EARNINGS PER SHARE GROWTH: **11.0%**
10-YEAR COMPOUND DIVIDENDS PER SHARE GROWTH: **10.5%**

	2004	2005	2006	2007	2008	2009	2010	2011
Revenues (Mil)	2,526	2,592	2,716	2,916	3,177	3,192	3,339	3,650
Net Income (Mil)	214	215	202	230	282	311	356.3	380
Earnings per share	1.52	1.56	1.72	1.92	2.14	2.35	2.65	2.80
Dividends per share	0.56	0.64	0.72	0.8	0.88	0.96	1.04	1.24
Cash flow per share	2.1	2.24	2.45	2.64	2.83	3.08	3.39	3.55
Price: high	38.9	39.1	39.8	39.7	42.1	36.8	47.8	51.3
low	28.6	29	30.1	33.9	28.2	28.1	35.4	43.4

McCormick & Company, Inc.
18 Loveton Circle
P. O. Box 6000
Sparks, MD 21152–6000
(410) 771-7244
Website: *www.mccormick.com*

McDonald's Corporation

Ticker symbol: MCD (NYSE) ◻ S&P rating: A ◻ Value Line financial strength rating: A++ ◻ Current yield: 2.9% ◻ Dividend raises, past 10 years: 10

Company Profile

McDonald's Corporation operates and franchises the ubiquitous "golden arches" McDonald's restaurants. At 2011 year-end, there were approximately 33,510 restaurants in 118 countries (up from 32,737 at the end of 2010), more than 27,000 of which were operated by franchisees and 6,435 of which were operated by the company. Franchisees pay for and own the equipment, signs, and interior of the businesses and are required to reinvest in same from time to time. The company owns the land and building or secures leases for both company-operated and franchised restaurant sites.

Revenues to the company come in the form of sales from company-owned stores and rents, fees, royalties, and other revenue streams from the franchisees. The company is primarily a franchisor and has recently begun to sell off more of its company-owned stores, in the process realizing benefits to cash flow, reduced operational costs, and reduced exposure to commodities prices.

McDonald's completely dominates the fast food hamburger restaurant market segment with a 46.8 percent market share. Burger King and Wendy's are the next largest competitors, with Wendy's just recently edging out Burger King for the number two position, both with market shares in the mid-teens. In the overall fast food segment, McDonald's is still the single biggest player with a 19 percent market share by revenue, followed by Doctor's Associates, Inc. (Subway) with a 10 percent share.

An iconic brand worldwide, the company generates about 66 percent of its revenue outside the United States.

Financial Highlights, Fiscal Year 2011

McDonald's is one of many companies that issue informative summaries with their earnings press releases; we like theirs especially and will use it to summarize FY2011, this time showing comparable numbers for FY2010 in parenthesis. These figures capture the essence of MCD's success quite well:

- A global comparable sales increase of 5.6 percent (5 percent in FY2010), with positive comparable sales across all geographic segments for every quarter.
- Consolidated revenues up 12 percent (6 percent) with 8

percent (5 percent) in constant currencies to a record-high $27 billion ($24 billion).

- Combined operating margin increase of 60 basis points to 31.6 percent (90 basis points to 31.0 percent).

- Consolidated operating income increase of 14 percent (9 percent) with 10 percent (9 percent) in constant currencies, with the United States up 6 percent (7 percent), Europe up 15 percent (8 percent), with 10 percent (12 percent) in constant currencies, and APMEA up 27 percent (21 percent) (11 percent in constant currencies both years).

- Earnings per share of $5.27 (4.58), up 15 percent (11 percent) (11 percent in constant currencies both years).

- Return of $6.0 ($5.1) billion to shareholders through share repurchases and dividends paid.

Wow, quite a happy meal. Better in every respect (except perhaps U.S. operating income growth) than FY2010, a stellar year in its own right.

The reasons for their success include new menu offerings and a continuing drive to move more stores to a franchising model. The latter in particular is responsible for the operating margin increases. Rents and royalty incomes are a low-cost and

very stable revenue stream with low capital requirements, and we expect this re-franchising trend to continue even as McDonald's opens new locations. The company has also benefited from "reimaging" its stores, and plans to spend about $2.9 billion redoing about 2,400 stores and opening 1,300 new ones.

For FY2012, the company expects sales to follow a similar path, with earnings attenuated slightly by increased ingredient costs and higher tax rates.

Reasons to Buy

In the early part of the decade, McDonald's had been adding mainly company-owned stores in an effort to boost revenues. They aren't as profitable, and there were signs that people were becoming tired of the menu and more concerned about health. In 2003, McDonald's initiated a new strategy that called for increasing sales at its existing stores by expanding menu options, expanding store hours, and renovating stores. The customer base has apparently adapted quite well to all of these initiatives. The company also began franchising a higher percentage of its stores, driving revenue with reduced capital expense. The strategy has paid off handsomely—revenues have grown by 40 percent, which would be impressive on its own, but operating margins have grown from the mid-20s to the mid-30s, with most of that increase coming in the 2008–2010 time frame, and not surprisingly, net income has increased more than two and a half times in that same period. At the same time, share buybacks have reduced share counts from 1.26 billion down to about 1.0 billion. These factors have produced substantial shareholder returns, much of which is actually getting returned to shareholders, as the dividend has climbed from 24 cents per share to $2.53 per share in the 10-year period. As a result, the share price is now eight times its 2003 low.

McDonald's has an exceptionally strong international franchise, and is growing particularly well in China. Local menus continue to evolve, and the convenience that fast food provides is highly valued.

Reasons for Caution

Concerns over childhood obesity have drawn attention to dietary factors, and fast food restaurants will likely be central to most conversations on the topic. Some states are requiring the posting of signs with caloric content next to item price, but it's not clear that this will lead to a decline in sales in the near term. The company, like all in the food business, is vulnerable to ingredient price swings. The stock has also enjoyed a long-run higher compatible with the steady earnings growth, which has been closely reflected in the share price; similar growth in the near future may be harder to attain.

SECTOR: **Restaurants**
BETA COEFFICIENT: **0.41**
10-YEAR COMPOUND EARNINGS PER SHARE GROWTH: **11.0%**
10-YEAR COMPOUND DIVIDENDS PER SHARE GROWTH: **26.0%**

		2004	2005	2006	2007	2008	2009	2010	2011
Revenues (Mil)		19,065	20,460	21,586	22,787	23,522	22,745	24,075	27,008
Net Income (Mil)		2,358	2,509	2,873	3,522	4,201	4,451	4,970	5,503
Earnings per share		1.93	1.97	2.3	2.91	3.67	4.11	4.60	5.27
Dividends per share		0.55	0.67	1.00	1.50	1.63	2.05	2.26	2.53
Cash flow per share		2.88	2.98	3.43	4.06	4.85	5.2	5.95	6.75
Price:	high	33	35.7	44.7	63.7	67	64.8	80.9	101
	low	24.5	27.4	31.7	42.3	45.8	50.4	61.1	72.1

McDonald's Corporation
One McDonald's Plaza
Oak Brook, IL 60523
(630) 623-3000
Website: *www.mcdonalds.com*

CONSERVATIVE GROWTH

McKesson Corporation

Ticker symbol: MCK (NYSE) ▢ S&P rating: A– ▢ Value Line financial strength rating: A++ ▢ Current yield: 0.9% ▢ Dividend raises, past 10 years: 3

Company Profile

McKesson Corporation is America's oldest and largest health-care services company and engages in two distinct businesses to support the health-care industry. Pharmaceutical and medical-surgical supply distribution is the first and by far the largest business: The company is the largest such distributor in North America. The company delivers to approximately 40,000 pharmaceutical outlets as well as hospitals and clinics throughout North America from 28 domestic and 17 Canadian distribution facilities.

Second and not to be ignored is a technology solutions business that provides clinical systems, analytics, supply-chain management, and connectivity solutions to hospitals, pharmacies, and an assortment of health-care providers. While the distribution business, at $109 billion for FY2011, continues to provide 97 percent of the company's revenue, the information technology business is no less important and is a $3.2 billion business all by itself. McKesson's software and hardware IT solutions are installed in some 70 percent of the nation's hospitals with more than 200 beds.

The company offers products and services covering most aspects of pharmacy and drug distribution, including not only physical distribution and supply-chain services but also a line of proprietary generics and automated dispensing systems, record-keeping systems, and outsourcing services used in retail and hospital pharmacy operations.

In late 2010, the company completed a $2.16 billion acquisition of U.S. Oncology, a distributor of products targeted to the cancer-care industry. With that acquisition, McKesson became the leading supplier of materials, technology, and operational platforms to the oncological community, and that acquisition has performed well. In early 2012, the company acquired the Katz Group Canada, a major distributor supplying over 1,000 Canadian pharmacies.

Financial Highlights, Fiscal Year 2011

The McKesson business is about as close to recession-proof as one can become, and recently, aided by the U.S. Oncology acquisition, the company has resumed a moderate growth path. Revenues grew 8 percent to $121 million in FY2011 while earnings continued a nice upward run to $6.05 per share, up a generous 21 percent from the previous year. Pharmaceutical distribution is a very low-margin business, but the company has managed to raise its net profit margin incrementally from 1.1 percent in FY2008 to 1.3 percent in FY2011. Every little bit helps. Cash flow is strong, and McKesson repurchased $672 million in shares during the year, about 3 percent of outstanding shares. The company has given guidance of $6.19 to $6.39 per share for FY2012, a level that was raised twice during FY2011.

Reasons to Buy

The distribution business has proven to be rock solid and will likely continue that way. Demographics and the addition of millions to the "insured" health-care rolls will keep demand moving in the right direction. McKesson dominates its niche. Additionally, hospitals and other care providers are starting to get the memo that it is time to improve operational efficiency, and McKesson's

technology solutions are hard to ignore, although many might do so at first glance, as they are only 3 percent of the business. As most distributors do, McKesson operates on very thin margins; the expansion of technology services and generic equivalent drugs should help. The company has reduced its share count about 19 percent since 2005 and will continue to buy back shares. Earnings per share growth has accelerated in recent years.

Reasons for Caution

Some, and perhaps much, of the optimism previously mentioned has already been priced into the stock; the company will have to continue to seek growth opportunities to keep the earnings momentum going. That could result in more acquisitions, and while the U.S. Oncology buyout has worked out, that is no guarantee that all such moves will be successful. Additionally, and as mentioned, the company does operate on thin margins and as such has a low tolerance for mistakes or major changes in the health-care space that could be brought on by legislation or regulation.

SECTOR: **Health Care**
BETA COEFFICIENT: **.81**
10-YEAR COMPOUND EARNINGS PER SHARE GROWTH: **15.5%**
10-YEAR COMPOUND DIVIDENDS PER SHARE GROWTH: **5.5%**

	2004	2005	2006	2007	2008	2009	2010	2011
Revenues (Mil)	80,515	88,050	92,977	101,703	106,632	108,70	112,084	121,010
Net income (Mil)	653	737	881	1,021	1,194	1,251	1,316	1,525
Earnings per share	2.18	2.34	2.89	3.43	4.28	4.58	5.00	6.05
Dividends per share	0.24	0.24	0.24	0.24	0.48	0.48	0.72	0.80
Cash flow per share	3.02	3.30	3.99	5.03	6.03	6.37	7.18	8.40
Price: high	35.9	52.9	55.1	68.4	68.4	65	71.5	87.3
low	22.6	30.1	44.5	50.5	28.3	33.1	57.2	66.6

McKesson Corporation
One Post Street
San Francisco, CA 94104
(415) 983-8300
Website: *www.mckesson.com*

AGGRESSIVE GROWTH

Medtronic, Inc.

Ticker symbol: MDT (NYSE) ❑ S&P rating: A+ ❑ Value Line financial strength rating: A++ ❑ Current yield: 2.6% ❑ Dividend raises, past 10 years: 10

Company Profile

Medtronic is the world's largest manufacturer of implantable medical devices and is a leading medical technology company, providing lifelong solutions to "alleviate pain, restore health and extend life," primarily for people with chronic diseases. The seven business segments are (with contribution to FY2011 revenues in parenthesis):

- Cardiac Rhythm Disease Management (31 percent) develops products that restore and regulate a patient's heart rhythm as well as improve the heart's pumping function. This segment markets implantable pacemakers, defibrillators, monitoring and diagnostic devices, cardiac resynchronization devices, and minimally invasive catheter ablation equipment.
- Cardiovascular (20 percent) develops products and therapies that treat a wide range of vascular diseases and conditions. These products include coronary, peripheral, and neuro-vascular stents; stent graft systems for diseases and

conditions throughout the aorta; angioplasty technologies; and distal protection systems. The segment also develops products that are used in both arrested and beating heart bypass surgery and markets the industry's broadest line of heart valve products for replacement and repair, plus autotransfusion equipment and disposable devices for handling and monitoring blood during major surgery.

- Medtronic Spinal and Biologics (21 percent) develops and manufactures products that treat a variety of disorders of the cranium and spine, including traumatically induced conditions, deformities, herniated discs and other disc diseases, osteoporosis, and tumors. The Biologics business is the global leader in biologics regeneration and pain therapies across a variety of musculoskeletal applications including spine, orthopedic trauma, and dental.
- Neuromodulation (10 percent) employs many technologies used in heart electrical stimulation to treat diseases of

the central nervous system.
It offers therapies for movement disorders, chronic pain,
urological and gastroentero-
logical disorders, and psy-
chological diseases, including
incontinence, benign prostatic
hyperplasia (BPH), enlarged
prostate, and gastroesophageal
reflux disease (GERD).

- Diabetes (8 percent) offers
advanced diabetes manage-
ment solutions, including
insulin pump therapy, glucose
monitoring systems, and treatment management software.
- Surgical Technologies (7
percent) develops and markets
products and therapies for
ear, nose, and throat–related
diseases and certain neurological disorders; among them are
precision image-guided surgical systems.

Financial Highlights, Fiscal Year 2010 (FY2010 ends April 30, 2011)

Increased competition and higher
utilization (an industry trend; translation: cost management and defer-
ral of elective surgeries) softened
top-line growth to 1 percent to
$15.9 billion in FY2011. The com-
pany saw especially soft sales in the
Cardiac Rhythm Disease and Spinal
markets particularly in the United
States. Earnings per share also flattened, up only 2.3 percent to $3.45
per share. FY2012 EPS, affected by
a 2011 acquisition, will probably
come in at the same figure after a 4
to 6 cent per share write-off, while
revenues, also affected by the acquisition, are projected at $16.5 billion.

Dividends were increased
another 8 percent, and the company
bought back another 20 million
shares of stock, or approximately 2
percent of the outstanding float.

Reasons to Buy

Looking at the soft FY2011 results
and competition from more nimble
competitors, notably St. Jude Medical (also a *100 Best* stock) we had
considered dropping MDT from
our list—until realizing the company's twin strengths in R&D and
international markets. International
represented 43 percent of the company's business in FY2011, and
momentum in these markets is high
and increasing, especially in emerging markets, as MDT-supported
medical procedures become mainstream. International revenues are
growing at a 12 percent clip, and
emerging market growth, primarily in the "BRIC" (Brazil, Russia,
India, China) markets is 20 percent.
The R&D footprint, with 9,000
employed scientists and 9.4 percent
of revenues spent on R&D, also
bode well for the future, and there

are a number of important new products in the pipeline.

The company is a pioneer technology leader and a successful innovator in many surgical and implant technologies, including the restoration of normal brain function and chemistry to millions of patients with central nervous system disorders. The company's DBS (Deep Brain Stimulation) systems treat disorders by modulating the nervous system with electrical stimulation, chemicals, and biological agents delivered in precise amounts to specific sites in the brain and spinal cord. This system has been used successfully to treat the most severe symptoms of conditions such as Parkinson's disease, and in March 2010 Medtronic received FDA approval for techniques employing DBS devices for treatment of epilepsy.

Medtronic has enjoyed steady growth and has achieved the quintuple-play—double-digit compounded ten-year growth in revenues, earnings, cash flow, dividends, and book value. The dividend, relatively generous for a "tech" company of this sort, has tripled in seven years. The stock price has been relatively flat during this period, offering reasonable entry points.

Reasons for Caution

Medtronic may be entering the "mature" lifecycle phase in many of its product lines. meaning future growth opportunities may be harder to come by. The trend toward improved "utilization" in the United States is probably here to stay, but deferred procedures will be made up at some point. Earnings growth has clearly slowed for now, and the company has relied on small acquisitions for a lot of its growth, a somewhat riskier strategy than growing "organically." We hope that the company doesn't get too aggressive with acquisitions and instead focuses on making the most of its internally generated new products and international growth opportunities.

SECTOR: **Health Care**
BETA COEFFICIENT: **.86**
10-YEAR COMPOUND EARNINGS PER SHARE GROWTH: **13.5%**
10-YEAR COMPOUND DIVIDENDS PER SHARE GROWTH: **17.5%**

	2004	2005	2006	2007	2008	2009	2010	2011
Revenues (Mil)	10,055	11,292	12,299	13,515	14,599	15,817	15,933	15,900
Net Income (Mil)	2,270	2,687	2,798	2,984	3,282	3,576	3,647	3,660
Earnings per share	1.63	1.86	2.21	2.41	2.61	2.92	3.22	3.45
Dividends per share	0.31	0.36	0.41	0.47	0.63	0.82	0.90	0.97
Cash flow per share	2.26	2.8	2.96	3.22	3.45	3.96	4.16	4.25
Price: high	53.7	58.9	59.9	58	57	44.9	46.7	43.3
low	44	48.7	42.4	44.9	28.3	24.1	30.8	30.2

Medtronic, Inc.
710 Medtronic Parkway N. E.
Minneapolis, MN 55432–5604
(763) 505-2692
Website: *www.medtronic.com*

CONSERVATIVE GROWTH

Molex Inc.

Ticker symbol: MOLX (NASDAQ) ❑ S&P rating: NA ❑ Value Line financial strength rating: A ❑ Current yield: 2.8% ❑ Dividend raises, past 10 years: 7

Company Profile

Molex is one of the largest suppliers to the worldwide electrical and electronics manufacturing industries. They provide both industry-standard and custom parts for a balanced mix of automotive, aerospace, consumer, commercial, medical, and industrial applications. Their catalog includes over 100,000 electromechanical components, including connectors, cabling, backplanes, sockets, and switches, among others. Molex's products are sold both direct and via one of the largest distribution networks in the industry. Typical direct customers would include large ODMs (original design manufacturers) such as Foxconn, Flextronics, and SCI, as well as OEMs like carmakers who build their own product. Their two product divisions (Connectors—72 percent of sales, and Electronics—28 percent of sales) also provide custom design and contract manufacturing services. The company has over 33,000 employees and operates nearly 40 manufacturing locations in 16 countries. Sales are split roughly two-thirds in Asia and one-third in Americas/Europe. The $45 billion worldwide market for the type of interconnects that represent the bulk of Molex's revenue is well fragmented, with the top 10 suppliers accounting for just over half of the overall market. Molex owns about 8 percent of the market, and their 2011 sales revenue was about 80 percent of the market's leader, Amphenol Corporation.

Financial Highlights, Fiscal Year 2011

Coming on the heels of what was a very good rebound year in 2010, Molex's excellent FY2011 catapulted the company's outlook beyond its prerecession levels and exceeded many expectations with record revenue and earnings. This sort of performance may have been a surprise to those who don't follow this segment closely—while many market watchers keep close tabs on the fortunes of companies such as Apple, HP, and the other whales in the electronics food chain, 2011 was a very good year for the sardines. Molex's revenue rose 20 percent in the period, while net income grew a whopping 60 percent. Net margins improved nearly six percentage points to 8.3 percent of revenue, partly due to a 20 percent reduction in SG&A as a percentage of revenue. The results motivated the company to raise the dividend twice during the year, nearly 15 percent each time.

Reasons to Buy

Interconnects are the Rodney Dangerfield of high-tech: no respect, no respect at all. And while it's true that the materials and manufacturing processes for the bulk of this industry's products have been, historically, pretty low-tech, there is a subset of Molex's catalog that makes possible many of the current leading-edge designs. As devices (such as smartphones and tablets) get smaller and provide more functionality, the internal connections also have to get smaller and provide higher-speed operation. These interconnect modules, typically custom-designed for each application, are where the high margins live. They require sophisticated design and fabrication techniques, and this is where Molex excels.

The company's vision for the future is to be able to design anywhere, manufacture anywhere, and sell anywhere. Having design, manufacturing, and admin resources close to the customer is a big advantage in a rapid-turn environment, but it's also very difficult to do in the traditionally low-margin interconnect business. Molex's efforts in the area of overhead reduction over the past two years have been very encouraging—however gross margin has improved 20 percent over the period. We like their approach here, particularly in light of the fact that one of their larger customers (Hon Hai) is also one of their largest competitors.

The company's revised pricing models have generated some reduction in price erosion, and with over a third of their revenue coming from products less than three years old, maintenance of pricing power in their markets is important.

Reasons for Caution

Molex competes in a fragmented market with a large number of capable players, all looking at many of the same customers for the next big win. These high-margin design wins are a big part of market leadership, and these wins are highly sought after. Compounding the sales challenges are the issues with raw materials—gold and copper are a significant component of Molex's costs, and it appears that intelligently predicting prices on those two commodities is going to continue to be a challenge, as it has been for several years now.

SECTOR: **Industrials**
BETA COEFFICIENT: **1.20**
10-YEAR COMPOUND EARNINGS PER SHARE GROWTH: **13.6%**
10-YEAR COMPOUND DIVIDENDS PER SHARE GROWTH: **23.0%**

	2004	2005	2006	2007	2008	2009	2010	2011
Revenues (Mil)	2,247	2,549	2,861	3,266	3,328	2,582	3,007	3,587
Net income (Mil)	176	196	264	263	254	52.4	192	308
Earnings per share	0.92	1.03	1.38	1.42	1.40	0.30	1.10	1.76
Dividends per share	0.10	0.15	0.20	0.30	0.45	0.61	0.61	0.70
Cash flow per share	2.14	2.27	2.60	2.72	2.85	1.76	2.47	3.14
Price: high	36.1	30	40.1	32.3	30.6	22.4	23.7	28.5
low	27.1	23.8	25.6	23.5	10.3	9.7	17.5	18.5

Molex Incorporated
2222 Wellington Court
Lisle, IL 60532
(630) 969-4550
Website: *www.molex.com*

AGGRESSIVE GROWTH

Monsanto Company

Ticker symbol: MON (NYSE) ❑ S&P Rating: A+ ❑ Value Line financial strength rating: A ❑ Current yield: 1.6% ❑ Dividend raises, past 10 years: 7

Company Profile

Monsanto was once a major chemical company with a broad pedigree ranging from saccharine to sulfuric acid to Agent Orange and DDT. Monsanto was absorbed into Pharmacia Upjohn in 2000, which kept its pharmaceutical products and spun off the agricultural products business into a "new" Monsanto in 2002. Today's Monsanto provides a set of leading-edge, technology-based agricultural products for use in farming in the United States and overseas. The company broadly views its business as providing better-quality foods and animal feedstocks while reducing the costs of farming.

The company has two primary business segments: Seeds and Genomics, and Agricultural Productivity.

The Seeds and Genomics segment (71 percent of FY2011 revenues) produces seeds for a host of crops, most importantly corn and soybeans, but also canola, cotton, and a variety of vegetable and fruit seeds. Most of the seed products are bioengineered to provide greater yields and to be more resistant to insects and weeds. Familiar to many consumers, especially those who travel in the Midwest, is the DeKalb seed brand, but there are many others.

The Agricultural Productivity segment (27 percent) offers glyphosate-based herbicides, known as Roundup to most of us, for agricultural, industrial, and residential lawn and garden applications. Beyond this market-leading product, the division also offers other selective herbicides for control of pre-emergent annual grass and small seeded broadleaf weeds in corn and other crops. Monsanto owns many of the major brands in both seed and herbicide markets. The company also partners with other agricultural and chemical companies like Cargill, BASF, and Biotechnology, Inc. to develop other high-tech agricultural and food-processing solutions.

In recent years, the company underwent some upheaval as patents on its flagship Roundup herbicide system expired, almost immediately followed by reports that certain weeds were developing immunity to it anyhow, and cheaper foreign competitors were starting to invade its garden. Beyond that, they alienated some of their farmer base with pricing and marketing practices for their seed and herbicide systems. These reports and a sag in earnings brought the stock price from the 70s to the mid 40s. Since then, the company has taken steps to modernize its herbicide offerings and become less dependent on them, to develop the core seed businesses further, and to focus on developing markets like Latin America and China, making them less dependent on the "one trick" Roundup pony. We applaud these moves.

Financial Highlights, Calendar Year 2011

After a weak and somewhat unsettling year in FY2010, Monsanto made, and continues to make, a promising comeback. Total revenues bounced back some 13 percent to $11.8 billion. Net earnings increased 19 percent to $1.6 billion (EPS $2.93), although far short of the Roundup-centered 2009 heyday of $2.5 billion (EPS $4.41). The descent from the Roundup mountaintop is also illustrated by net operating margins, which came in at 34.2 percent, 23 percent, and 26.3 percent in FY2009, FY2010, and FY2011, respectively. Monsanto is a case study in overdependence on

a single profitable cash cow; the company appears to have learned its lesson and is moving forward. The company now projects FY2012 per-share earnings in the $3.50–$3.55 range, a continued healthy recovery.

Reasons to Buy

The expiration of the Roundup "monopoly" combined with news of its attenuated effectiveness was a double whammy, especially for a company whose profits were so dependent on the product and its combination sales with glyphosate-resistant seed stocks. The company was forced to lower product prices to keep market share. This was the bad news; the bigger picture shows Monsanto still as a market leader in technology-based agricultural products with a strong track record for innovation and a big head start on most competitors. The company is stressing its biotechnology-rich Seeds and Genomics products while the Agricultural Productivity unit brings new formulations to market and reduces costs on the glyphosate products to bring them in line with the newer, lower prices. We still feel this is a premier technology company positioned well in a sector of primary global importance—that is, agriculture—and is a good place for invested capital, especially long term.

Reasons for Caution

Clearly, Monsanto didn't anticipate the negative effects of the adverse news on the glyphosate products. The strong lock they had on their markets seemed to disappear overnight, and they were caught with their proverbial overalls down. Lesson learned, we hope. Monsanto's future success will continue to depend on agricultural innovation—but also on being the best player in competitive markets with a diverse product portfolio. While the growth statistics presented below appear very strong, technology-based cyclical companies like Monsanto, as we saw, can hit a wall pretty quickly. Monsanto is positioned well to take advantage of agricultural up-cycles, as we're in now, but if crop prices and planted acreage fall, the company may suffer in the short term. In recent years, however, these down-cycles have proved short-lived.

SECTOR: **Industrials**
BETA COEFFICIENT: **0.93**
10-YEAR COMPOUND EARNINGS PER SHARE GROWTH: **26.0%**
10-YEAR COMPOUND DIVIDENDS PER SHARE GROWTH: **36.0%**

		2004	2005	2006	2007	2008	2009	2010	2011
Revenues (Mil)		5,457	6,294	7,344	8,563	11,365	11,724	10,502	11,822
Net Income (Mil)		334	565.7	722.1	1,027	1,895	2,448	1,327	1,568
Earnings per share		0.61	1.05	1.31	1.98	3.39	4.41	2.41	2.93
Dividends per share		0.28	0.34	0.34	0.55	0.83	1.01	1.08	1.14
Cash flow per share		1.73	2.06	2.28	2.85	4.5	5.49	3.57	4.07
Price:	high	28.2	39.9	53.5	116.3	145.8	93.4	87.1	78.7
	low	14	25	37.9	49.1	63.5	66.6	44.6	58.9

Monsanto Company
800 North Lindbergh Boulevard
St. Louis, MO 63167
Phone: (314) 694-1000
Web Site: *www.monsanto.com*

NEW FOR 2013

Mosaic Company

Ticker symbol: MOS (NYSE) ❑ S&P rating: BBB ❑ Value Line financial strength rating: A ❑ Current yield: 1.0% ❑ Dividend raises, past 10 years: 1

Company Profile

We generally shy away from commodities producers. Why? Because it's hard to establish a brand or a competitive advantage. Typically the business becomes a race to the bottom, where the low-cost producer wins. But if you're the low-cost producer, you probably aren't making much money—and you probably won't stay the low-cost producer for long.

We prefer companies that have other routes to establishing—and maintaining—a competitive advantage. But there are commodities, and then there are *strategic* commodities. What do we mean by that? Well, some commodities are more important—and in more constrained supply than others. And if a company can invest itself wholly in these commodities, and establish a dominant market share and position in doing so, it will establish a competitive advantage.

That's where the Mosaic company comes in. Mosaic, formed in 2004 through a merger of Cargill's fertilizer operations with IMC Global, is the dominant world producer in the so-called "P+K"

market—that's phosphorus and potassium, for those of you who didn't take high school chemistry. And in case you're not clear on why P and K are important, they are vital fertilizer ingredients and hence vital to most of the world's agriculture production. Plants require more potassium than any other nutrient besides nitrogen, and it is vital to root system development and many processes that form plant starch and proteins. Potassium is mined and sold in its oxide form known more popularly as potash. Phosphorus is a vital component to photosynthesis for plant metabolism and growth.

Mosaic is the largest combined P+K producer in the world. About two-thirds of the business is phosphorus and a third potash. Both minerals are produced commercially in a limited number of places in the world. Mosaic has interests in the important locations in North and South America, notably Florida phosphorus mines and potash mines in Saskatchewan, Michigan, New Mexico, and Peru. Through a network of processing and packaging plants in several countries, the company sells its product in approximately 40 countries. As a percentage of FY2011 sales, the United States accounted for 35 percent, Brazil 18 percent, India 16 percent, Canada 6 percent, and the remaining 25 percent made up of most of the rest of the agricultural free world.

Financial Highlights, Fiscal Year 2011

Not surprisingly, Mosaic's fortunes are driven by what is happening in the agriculture world, and the news from down on the farm has been pretty good lately. Several factors, including increasing overseas demand for basic foodstuffs, has driven crop prices up, and when that happens, more crops are planted and farmers are willing to spend more to grow them. That's pretty simple economics, and with the world recovery from recession helping that along, Mosaic recorded an impressive 47 percent sales gain from a depressed FY2010 to achieve its second highest sales in its eight year history, only beaten slightly in FY2009. Earnings more than doubled to $1.9 billion, comparable to the prerecession boom years. Demand for P+K can fluctuate considerably depending on inventories and planting cycles, and the company so far has been conservative on guidance for FY2012, forecasting roughly

comparable earnings numbers on 10 percent sales increase. Additionally, the company bought back 20 million shares in FY2011, about 5 percent of its float, and announced a doubling in the dividend to 50 cents per share annually in early FY2012.

Reasons to Buy

Particularly for those interested in investing in commodities, we think this is some of the most fertile ground on which to stand. Demand for food will only increase over time, and Mosaic is the largest and one of only five major free world producers of P+K. The combination of prime mining sites and size and operational efficiency in its processing and distribution operations should lead to at least maintaining, if not expanding, market share. As market share expands, control of price and operating margins increases, and we expect margins to increase over time from the current 32.2 percent, already near a record high for the company. We like the strong footprint in emerging markets. The company is more actively returning cash to shareholders, and recently was reasonably priced compared to history and prospects.

Reasons for Caution

Commodity markets and commodity producers are inherently

volatile, and any reduction in planting or backup in inventory, not to mention overall global economic weakness, can drive prices down in a heartbeat. Particularly in the mining business, adjusting to these cycles can be difficult; it's a hard ship to turn.

SECTOR: **Materials**
BETA COEFFICIENT: **1.34**
10-YEAR COMPOUND EARNINGS PER SHARE GROWTH: **NM**
10-YEAR COMPOUND DIVIDENDS PER SHARE GROWTH: **NM**

	2004	**2005**	**2006**	**2007**	**2008**	**2009**	**2010**	**2011**
Revenues (Mil)	2,374	4,397	5,304	5,774	9,812	10,298	6,759	9,937
Net income (Mil)	72.3	167.6	82.6	342.5	1,962.2	1,909.7	862.8	1,942.2
Earnings per share	—	.47	.18	.80	4.38	4.28	1.93	4.34
Dividends per share	—	—	—	—	—	.20	.20	.20
Cash flow per share	—	.99	1.15	1.67	5.20	5.11	2.94	5.35
Price: high	18.6	18	23.5	97.6	103.3	62.5	76.9	59.5
low	14.8	12.4	13.3	19.5	21.9	31.2	37.7	44.9

Mosaic Company
3033 Campus Drive
Plymouth, MN 55441
(800) 918-8270
Website: *www.mosaicco.com*

NextEra Energy, Inc.

Ticker symbol: NEE (NYSE) □ Standard & Poor's rating: A- □ Value Line financial strength rating: A □ Current yield: 3.8% □ Dividend raises, past 10 years: 10

Company Profile

NextEra is really the evolved utility stalwart Florida Power & Light, which had previously changed its name to FPL Group, then NextEra in 2010. NextEra not only represents an evolution in name but also a hint to how the company does business and expects to do business in the future as a leader in clean and large-scale alternative energy sourcing for the power market.

Headquartered in Juno Beach, Florida, FPL Group's principal operating subsidiaries are NextEra Energy Resources, LLC, and the original Florida Power & Light Company, one of the largest rate-regulated electric utilities in the country. FP&L serves 4.5 million customer accounts in eastern and southern Florida. Through its subsidiaries, FPL Group collectively operates the third-largest U.S. nuclear power generation fleet.

As a nonregulated subsidiary, Next Era Energy Resources, LLC (or "NEER"), is a wholesale energy provider and a leader in producing electricity from clean and renewable fuels and, unlike many other alternative-energy driven businesses,

is a viable standalone business entity. It has 4,700 employees at 115 facilities in 26 states and has solar and wind farms, nuclear energy facilities, and gas infrastructure operations not just in Florida but in 22 states and Canada. NEER's energy-producing portfolio includes 8,569 megawatts of wind generation facilities in 17 states and Canada; 2,721 mW of nuclear generation in four facilities; 2,700 mW of traditional natural gas–fired generation; 1,168 mW in hydro and oil facilities; and 940 mW of solar projects. The subsidiary accounts for $1.85, about 40 percent, of the company's reported $4.82 per share in earnings, nearly a third of NextEra's total revenue—and nearly half of its profits—a healthy return for an alternative energy–based operation.

The company has a few small but promising nonregulated subsidiaries, offering design and consulting services for other alternative and conventional utility providers (WindLogics, and FPL Services). Its FPL FiberNet subsidiary specializes in high-bandwidth data transmission from telecommunications locations to cell phone towers, mainly in Florida, Texas, and other areas in the South. Finally, the company was named "No. 1 overall" among electric and gas utilities on *Fortune*'s 2011–12 "World's Most Admired Companies" list.

Financial Highlights, Fiscal Year 2011

Revenues in FY2011 came in about flat at $15.3 billion, while earnings per share rose slightly from $4.74 to $4.82. The company, and particularly the NEER subsidiary, suffered the effects of slightly declining power prices nationwide and some small write-downs of alternative energy assets. For FY2012, the company expects to resume earnings growth to somewhere in the $4.35–$4.65 per share range.

Reasons to Buy

For those who believe that alternative energy is the future for large-scale power generation, NextEra is the best play available. The Recovery Act of 2009 contains a number of tax incentives for the deployment and use of renewable and nuclear sources, and NextEra is well positioned to take advantage. The company continues to grow alternative energy capacity on all fronts, particularly wind and solar, and continues to make money on these efforts. All of this adds to the solid and traditional FP&L regulated utility base. Cash flow is very strong, and supports both the dividend and continued investments in alternative energy production.

Reasons for Caution

The company's FPL subsidiary is still a regulated utility, and may not always receive the most accommodating treatment. Additionally, there is some risk if wind energy production tax credits are allowed to expire in 2012—we don't think that will really happen, although some of the recent turmoil with government investments in the solar industry makes this a bit more of a wild card. The dividend yield, while still healthy for a company with future growth prospects in an up-and-coming industry, is still low by current utility standards—reflecting in part the fact that investors have already put a lot of energy into this stock and the price accounts for its prospects. Buyers should continue to look for good entry points.

SECTOR: **Utilities**
BETA COEFFICIENT: **.54**
10-YEAR COMPOUND EARNINGS PER SHARE GROWTH: **8.0%**
10-YEAR COMPOUND DIVIDENDS PER SHARE GROWTH: **6.0%**

	2004	**2005**	**2006**	**2007**	**2008**	**2009**	**2010**	**2011**
Revenues (Mil)	10,522	11,846	15,710	15,263	16,410	15,646	15,317	15,341
Net Income (Mil)	887	885	1,261	1,312	1,639	1,615	1,957	2,021
Earnings per share	2.46	2.32	3.23	3.27	4.07	3.97	4.74	4.82
Dividends per share	1.3	1.42	1.5	1.64	1.78	1.89	2.00	2.20
Cash flow per share	5.6	6.18	6.77	6.85	8.03	8.75	9.60	9.15
Price: high	38.1	48.1	55.6	72.8	73.8	60.6	56.3	61.2
low	30.1	35.9	37.8	53.7	33.8	41.5	45.3	49

NextEra Energy, Inc.
700 Universe Boulevard
Juno Beach, FL 33408
(561) 694-4697
Website: *www.investor.fplgroup.com*

AGGRESSIVE GROWTH

NIKE, Inc.

Ticker symbol: NKE (NYSE) □ S&P Rating: A+ □ Value Line financial strength rating: A++ □ Current yield: 1.3% □ Dividend raises, past 10 years: 9

Company Profile

NIKE's principal business activity is the design, development, and worldwide marketing of footwear, apparel, equipment, and accessory products. NIKE is the largest seller of athletic footwear and athletic apparel in the world, but a big part of the story is how they are extending beyond traditional footwear and apparel. Their products are sold to retail accounts, through NIKE-owned retail outlets, and through a mix of independent distributors and licensees in more than 170 countries around the world.

NIKE does no manufacturing—virtually all of their footwear and apparel items are manufactured by independent contractors outside the United States, while equipment products are produced both in the United States and abroad.

NIKE's shoes are designed primarily for athletic use, although a large percentage of these products are worn for casual or leisure purposes. Their shoes are designed for men, women, and children for running, training, basketball, and soccer use, although they also carry brands for casual wear.

NIKE sells apparel and accessories for most of the sports addressed by their shoe lines, as well as athletic bags and accessory items. NIKE apparel and accessories are designed to complement their athletic footwear products, feature the same trademarks, and are sold through the same marketing and distribution channels. All NIKE-branded products are marketed with the familiar "swoosh" logo, one of the most recognized and successful branding images in history.

NIKE has a number of wholly owned subsidiaries, or "affiliate brands," including Cole Haan, Converse, Hurley, Jordan Brand, and Umbro that variously design, distribute, and license dress, athletic, and casual footwear, sports apparel, and accessories. In FY2011, these subsidiary brands, together with NIKE Golf accounted for approximately 13 percent of total revenues.

The $20.9 billion in total FY2011 sales breaks down as follows: 51 percent NIKE brand overseas, 36 percent NIKE brand North America, and 13 percent affiliate brands. It's not hard to see the strength of the NIKE brand abroad.

Financial Highlights, Fiscal Year 2011

NIKE's sales rebounded nicely from a soft FY2010, racing ahead some 9.7 percent to the $20.9 billion figure just mentioned. Earnings per share, helped along by a 2 percent reduction in share count, jogged ahead 13.7 percent to $4.39. Forecasts call for about $23.8 billion in revenues and $4.93 to $5.00 in earnings per share, another healthy increase. The company is striving for revenues in the $28–$30 billion range by FY2015. NIKE continues to have strong cash flows and almost negligible long-term debt, $276 million against a total market capitalization of $46 billion.

Reasons to Buy

Why buy NIKE? In a word, brand. The NIKE brand and its corresponding "swoosh" are one of the most recognized—and sought after—brands in the world. It is a lesson in simplicity and image congruence with the product behind it. NIKE doesn't sit still with it; rather, they are learning to leverage it into more products outside the traditional athletic wear circuit—golf clubs, golf balls, even a new line of GPS watches and apps. Further, NIKE doesn't just limit the brand appeal to athletes: Slogans like "Just Do It" and "If you have a body, you're an athlete" emphasize the appeal and lifestyle across all segments of the population. We think this is drop-dead smart.

Of course, solid brand and brand reputation lead to category leadership and hence, higher profitability, and NIKE has finished far ahead of the pack in this area too. The brand and "moat" created by the brand seem to have nowhere to go but forward, and improved manufacturing efficiencies, strong channel relationships, and international exposure, particularly in China, all keep the company moving faster in the right direction. Despite its size, the company continues to deliver double-digit earnings, cash flow, and dividend growth, and just when revenue growth slows into the single digits, it bounces forward once again into growth rates in the teens, as is forecast for FY2012. We continue to like the combination of protected profitability through brand excellence, combined with a clean conservative balance sheet, providing a good combination of safety and growth potential.

Reasons for Caution

Three things could put hurdles in NIKE's path. The first is higher commodity input prices. Second, the company is continually in the news—and the rumor mill—for "unfair labor practices" and child labor violations in some of its foreign manufacturing plants. The company doesn't actually own or operate these plants, but the rumors can stick nonetheless. A particularly egregious violation could tarnish the brand, but there have been none to date. Finally, the stock price has run along in lockstep to the good news, so obvious buying opportunities have been hard to find. We also feel the company could return a little more cash to shareholders, although the company has bought back about 9 percent of common "B" shares since 2005.

SECTOR: Consumer Discretionary
BETA COEFFICIENT: 0.91
10-YEAR COMPOUND EARNINGS PER SHARE GROWTH: 15.0%
10-YEAR COMPOUND DIVIDENDS PER SHARE GROWTH: 16.0%

	2004	2005	2006	2007	2008	2009	2010	2011
Revenues (Mil)	12,253	13,740	14,955	16,326	18,627	19,176	19,014	20,862
Net Income (Mil)	945	1,212	1,392	1,458	1,734	1,727	1,907	2,133
Earnings per share	1.76	2.25	2.63	2.86	3.44	3.52	3.86	4.39
Dividends per share	0.37	0.48	0.59	0.71	0.88	0.98	1.06	1.20
Cash flow per share	2.37	2.64	3.2	3.43	4.15	4.25	4.61	5.19
Price: high	46.2	45.8	50.6	67.9	70.6	66.6	83.4	96.5
low	32.9	37.6	37.8	47.5	42.7	38.2	60.9	69.4

NIKE, Inc.
One Bowerman Drive
Beaverton, OR 97005
(503) 671-6453
Website: *www.nikebiz.com*

CONSERVATIVE GROWTH

Norfolk Southern

Ticker symbol: NSC (NYSE) ❑ S&P Rating: BBB+ ❑ Value Line financial strength rating: B+ ❑ Current yield: 2.8% ❑ Dividend raises, past 10 years: 10

Company Profile

Norfolk Southern Corp. was formed in 1982 as a holding company when the Norfolk & Western Railway merged with the Southern Railway. Including lines received in the split takeover (with CSX) of Conrail, the current railroad operates 20,000 route-miles of track in 22 eastern and southern states. They serve every major port on the east coast of the United States and have the most extensive intermodal network in the east.

Company business is about 31 percent coal, coke, and iron ore; 19 percent intermodal; 14 percent agricultural and consumer products; 11 percent metals and construction; and 29 percent other. Within those categories, the railroad transports the usual mix of raw materials, intermediate products such as parts, and manufactured goods.

In the late 1990s, the company split the acquisition of Northeastern rail heavyweight Conrail with rival CSX corporation, so it has considerable operations in the Northeast and Midwest in addition to its traditional southern base. The heaviest traffic corridors

are New York-Chicago; Chicago-Atlanta; Appalachian coalfields to the port of Norfolk, Virginia, and Sandusky, Ohio; and Cleveland to Kansas City. The company has a diverse base of large Midwestern factories and large and smaller southern factories and basic materials producers in the coal and lumber industry, giving a well-diversified traffic base.

The company has been an innovator in the intermodal business, that is, combining trucking and rail services—with its "Triple Crown" services, centered on the "Roadrailer," a train of coupled-together highway vans on special wheelsets. At the terminal, a cab simply backs up to the van and drives it off.

The company provides a number of logistics services and has substantial traffic to and from ports and overseas destinations. Finally, Norfolk Southern actively courts lineside customers, and reports new industries along its lines totaling $9.5 billion in investment, adding 6,800 new jobs, and most importantly for the railroad, adding 152,000 carloads of new business annually.

Financial Highlights, Fiscal Year 2011

After predictably soft years in 2008 through 2010, the company did very well in FY2011. Revenues topped $11.1 billion, a 9.4 percent increase over FY2010, driven by a 27 percent rise in coal revenues, a 19 percent increase in intermodal revenues, and a 12 percent increase in general merchandise. Aided by improved efficiencies, expense control, and share repurchases, earnings per share highballed ahead to $5.27, fully 31 percent higher than FY2010. The company continues to be highly efficient, with an industry-leading operating ratio (variable costs to revenue) now at an almost record low of 71.2 percent; maintaining volumes and this level of operating efficiency are key to the company's future. The company bought back $2 billion in stock—27 million of the 357 million shares outstanding at the end of FY2010, and increased the dividend 19 percent.

Reasons to Buy

NSC's results for FY2012 should continue the momentum established in FY2011. Analysts predict earnings per share in the $6.00 vicinity on another 7 percent revenue increase. The company recently raised its dividend again to an annual $1.88 rate, another 12 percent bump above FY2011. The company has a strong base in serving vital economic activity in a large and productive region of the United States.

This railroad has done an excellent job containing costs and sizing its physical plant for its demand. Its operating ratio (the ratio of variable to total costs) of 71.2 percent is second only to industry stalwart Union Pacific's stellar 70.6 percent. NSC has proven over the past 30 years that it can compete effectively for long-haul truck business with its intermodal offerings and has some of the most competitive service and terminal structures in the business. It has gained market share from trucks. Additionally, NSC serves some of the more dynamic and up-and-coming manufacturing markets in the United States, namely, Asian and other foreign-owned manufacturing facilities found particularly in the Southeast. The company has created a "Heartland Corridor" time freight and double-stack container routing between Chicago and the East Coast, reducing distance by 250 miles and, more importantly, transit times from four to three days. Such innovations will further assert the company's leadership. Additionally, we like the strength and diversity coming from serving the domestic and especially the foreign-owned auto industry—the company serves plants for (in alphabetical order) BMW, Chrysler, Ford, General Motors, Honda, Isuzu, Mazda, Mercedes-Benz, Mitsubishi, Nissan, Subaru, Suzuki, and Toyota.

Reasons for Caution

There are two concerns: first, the strength of the recovery and the overall economy. Recessions hurt this company. Second, much of the growth potential is in the intermodal business (trailers, containers on specialized flat cars); this business tends to be highly competitive and relatively low in margin. Additionally, higher fuel prices can hurt, but this is usually offset somewhat by increased use of rail transport as customers are looking to save on fuel costs, and also on fuel surcharges the company levies on shipments from time to time. Finally, recent share prices have reflected this success; investors should look for long-term entry points brought on by market or economic uncertainty.

SECTOR: **Transportation**
BETA COEFFICIENT: **.91**
10-YEAR COMPOUND EARNINGS PER SHARE GROWTH: **19.0%**
10-YEAR COMPOUND DIVIDENDS PER SHARE GROWTH: **9.0%**

		2004	2005	2006	2007	2008	2009	2010	2011
Revenues (Mil)		7,312	8,527	9,407	9,432	10,661	87,969	9,516	11,172
Net Income (Mil)		870	1,161	1,481	1,464	1,716	1,034	1,498	1,853
Earnings per share		2.18	2.82	3.58	3.68	4.52	2.76	4.00	5.27
Dividends per share		0.36	0.48	0.68	0.96	1.22	1.36	1.40	1.68
Cash flow per share		3.67	4.72	5.58	5.9	6.88	5.07	6.48	8.22
Price:	high	36.7	45.8	57.7	59.6	75.5	54.8	63.7	78.4
	low	20.4	29.6	39.1	45.4	41.4	26.7	46.2	57.6

Norfolk Southern
Three Commercial Place
Norfolk, VA 23510–2191
Phone: (757) 629-2680
Website: *www.nscorp.com*

Nucor Corporation

Ticker symbol: NUE (NYSE) ❑ S&P rating: A ❑ Value Line financial strength rating: A ❑ Current yield: 3.6% ❑ Dividend raises, past 10 years: 8

Company Profile

Nucor is the twelfth-largest global steel producer by shipment volumes and the largest U.S.-based producer. It is also the largest recycler in North America, recycling some 13.4 million tons of scrap steel in 2009. Their production model is unique, based on numerous mini-mills and the exclusive use of scrap material as production input. Nucor operates scrap-based steel mills in 22 facilities, producing bar, sheet, structural, and plate steel product. Production in 2011 totaled shy of the 20.4 million tons in 2008, but well ahead of the 14 million tons in the recession-peak year of 2009.

Nucor's steel mills are considered to be among the most modern and efficient in the United States. Recycled scrap steel and other metals are melted in electric arc furnaces and poured into continuous casting systems. Sophisticated rolling mills convert the various types of raw cast material into rebar and basic shapes such as angles, rounds, channels, flats, sheet, beams, plate, and other products.

The company operates in three primary businesses: Steel Mills, Steel Products, and Raw Materials.

1. The Steel Mills segment produces sheet and hot-rolled steel, including angles, rounds, flats, channels, sheet, wide-flange beams, pilings, billets, beam blanks, and plate and cold-rolled products. These products are sold to a variety of heavy manufacturing businesses and some construction. Mills are principally located in the United States, Canada, and Mexico.

2. The Steel Products segment produces materials primarily for the commercial construction industry, including steel joists and joist girders, steel deck, fabricated concrete reinforcements, fasteners, metal building and framing systems, and wire and wire mesh.

3. The Raw Materials segment gathers and sells ferrous and nonferrous metals and provides brokerage, transportation, and other handling services.

Financial Highlights, Fiscal Year 2011

Nucor has largely recovered from the deep recession trough a few years ago, which brought an approximately 50 percent reduction in volumes, revenues, profits, and even dividends. The company came off of prior years of booming demand, which not only dried up but downstream customers and distributors, in addition, cut inventories, which deepened the decline. Revenues have recovered from $11.1 billion in FY2009 and $15.8 billion in FY2010 to a more respectable $20 billion in FY2011, which was about 11 percent ahead of the more optimistic forecasts and 26 percent ahead of the previous year. Of the 26 percent, about 21 percent was from higher prices and about 5 percent from increased volumes. For FY2012, the company projects a more moderate sales increase to about $21 billion, moderated by slack European demand and a modest drawdown of inventories among distributors and end consumers, which started in late FY2011. Earnings per share increased quite dramatically from a deficit in FY2009 to 42 cents in FY2010 and $2.45 in FY2011, and are forecast in the $3.20 range for FY2012.

Reasons to Buy

As bad as things were during 2008–2010, Nucor came out of it in better shape than most of its competitors. It is known to be well managed and a good place to work. It has been very conservative with the business during strength and weakness over the past five years and continues to have low levels of debt.

With modern and smaller, more rightsized mills, Nucor is the lowest-cost producer in the world—its gross margin is 40 percent higher than the largest player in the industry. Its capital structure is solid and puts it in a better position than any of its competitors to absorb volume declines or to buy up capacity should others fail to recover quickly. Its large rapid-start capacity positions it well to take advantage of the opportunity—or to shed costs—as demand and inventory cycles occur, and it is acknowledged to be one of the best-run, most flexible, and most innovative players in the industry.

Additionally, we feel that pent-up construction demand and especially the growing need for infrastructure replacement projects bodes well for Nucor's business. We also like the healthy yield, although as we learned during the downturn, these dividends, like all dividends, can be cut. (It should be noted that while Nucor raised its dividend eight times in 10 years, it also *cut* that dividend—deeply—twice.) Nucor is a "best in class" player in a key industry, and should prosper in times of economic strength, strength in developing markets, or major infrastructure replacement cycle.

Reasons for Caution

The industry is inherently cyclical, and those who fear recessions and slowdowns, or even hints thereof, short-term investors included, should proceed with caution on this company. Nucor (and other domestic producers) still have to compete with what many claim are "dumping" practices from overseas producers, which (it is claimed) sell product in the United States below their cost in order to cripple their competition. Steel prices are critical, as is infrastructure demand from growing economies like China. Investors should watch operating margins, which have just recently retaken the 10 percent level; a protracted period below 10 percent may signal trouble ahead.

SECTOR: **Materials**
BETA COEFFICIENT: **1.09**
10-YEAR COMPOUND EARNINGS PER SHARE GROWTH: **8.5%**
10-YEAR COMPOUND DIVIDENDS PER SHARE GROWTH: **28.0%**

		2004	2005	2006	2007	2008	2009	2010	2011
Revenues (Mil)		11,377	12,701	14,571	16,593	23,663	11,190	15,845	20,024
Net Income (Mil)		1,122	1,310	1,758	1,472	1,831	(294)	134.1	778.2
Earnings per share		3.51	4.13	5.73	4.98	6.01	(0.94)	0.42	2.45
Dividends per share		0.24	0.93	2.15	2.44	1.91	1.41	1.44	1.45
Cash flow per share		4.72	5.43	7.05	6.51	7.36	0.60	2.00	4.10
Price:	high	27.7	35.1	67.6	69.9	83.6	51.1	50.7	45.8
	low	13	22.8	33.2	41.6	25.3	29.8	35.7	29.5

Nucor Corporation
1915 Rexford Road
Charlotte, NC 28211
(704) 366-7000
Website: *www.nucor.com*

GROWTH AND INCOME

Otter Tail Corporation

Ticker symbol: OTTR (NASDAQ) ❑ S&P rating: BBB- ❑ Value Line financial strength rating: B+ ❑ Current yield: 5.4% ❑ Dividend raises, past 10 years: 5

Company Profile

Otter Tail Corporation is a holding company and a mini-conglomerate operating primarily in the upper Midwest. The conglomerate is centered on and stabilized by the Otter Tail Power Company, a regulated utility serving about 130,000 customers in rural Minnesota, North Dakota, and South Dakota. The utility accounts for about 32 percent of the total business. Use of wind generation and hydro power, and lower grades of coal available in the region have driven fuel costs down to 10.4 percent of revenues, a very low figure for the industry. (By comparison, Xcel Energy, which supplies electricity to surrounding areas in North Dakota and Minnesota as well as other Great Plains locations, Colorado, and Texas, spends 50 percent of revenues on fuel.) Approximately 12 percent of power generation is from wind or hydro sources.

Beyond the utility, the company operates in five other business segments, accounting for the other two-thirds of the business:

■ Wind Energy (19 percent of revenues) produces windmill towers through a subsidiary known as DMI Industries. The company also owned a trucking company, E.W. Wylie, within this segment which specialized in hauling wind tower equipment, but this subsidiary was sold in FY2011.

■ The Manufacturing segment (21 percent of revenues) houses three smaller businesses. BTD Manufacturing is a metal stamping, fabricating, and laser-cutting shop supplying custom parts for agriculture, lawn care, health and fitness, and the RV industry. Shoremaster produces and markets residential and commercial waterfront equipment—boat lifts, docks, and marinas. T.O Plastics supplies packaging and handling products for the horticultural industry.

■ The Plastics segment (11 percent of revenues) has two operations supplying commercial and utility-grade PVC and other plastic pipe and accessories.

■ Construction (17 percent) is a residential, commercial, and industrial installer of electric, fiber optic, HVAC, water, and wastewater systems primarily in the Midwest.

Otter Tail divested itself of two other substantial businesses in 2011: Idaho Pacific Holdings, a maker of dehydrated potato products for the snack food and food service industries, formerly 7 percent of total revenue, and its Health Services Segment, which integrated and sold diagnostic medical imaging and patient monitoring equipment, representing 9 percent of the total.

Overall, the company has 3,155 employees, and most operations are centered in the upper Midwest.

Financial Highlights, Fiscal Year 2011

FY2011 was a transition year for the company highlighted by the sale of the three larger businesses. With the sales, reported revenues actually declined a fraction to $1.08 billion and earnings, spearheaded by a noncash write-off related to the acquisitions, fell to 45 cents a share, although the loss from discontinued operations was 85 cents, suggesting a running EPS rate of $1.30. The company expects to return to stability and profitability, with FY2012 revenues up as much as 13 percent and earnings returning to the $1.00 to $1.40 level, which would be the best level since the 2008–09 recession.

Reasons to Buy

If one were to look at the assortment of Otter Tail businesses, without the Otter Tail name attached, one might jump to the conclusion that this was a Berkshire Hathaway portfolio. Aside from the utility, the company operates small niche players in relatively simple, understandable businesses, all well managed with a trusting corporate parent. The utility anchors the portfolio much as Mid-American Energy anchors Berkshire's—but there is no railroad analogous to Burlington Northern Santa Fe, at least as of yet.

We like this combination of safety and income with the other relatively solid businesses. We generally like the recent restructurings and the current business portfolio, and the yield exceeding 5 percent gives investors plenty of return while awaiting growth in the other businesses. We also like Otter Tail's involvement in—and use—of wind power. The plastics and construction businesses also support another key strategic area in our minds— infrastructure replacement.

One should note that cash flow far and away exceeds earnings as reported, and is expected to recover well north of $3.00 per share in FY2012 and beyond, so the dividend appears well covered for now. Otter Tail is a good way to participate in several well-managed businesses while getting a decent current return, and is the only "small cap" stock on our *100 Best* list, for those wanting to add a bit of small cap flavor to their portfolios. It is indeed like a "small town" company in contrast to "big city" corporate America.

Reasons for Caution

The dividend isn't presently covered by current earnings, a caution flag in any business, although at least for now it is amply covered by cash flow. The utility is stable but not likely to be helped along by population growth. The other businesses are all positive now but always will be economically sensitive, and the wind power business may face headwinds if subsidies dry up and cheap natural gas continues to rule the day. We compared Otter Tail to Berkshire Hathaway, but should note that Berkshire, by contrast, is more diversified, and has much larger "anchor" businesses.

SECTOR: **Energy**
BETA COEFFICIENT: **1.05**
10-YEAR COMPOUND EARNINGS PER SHARE GROWTH: **-6.5%**
10-YEAR COMPOUND DIVIDENDS PER SHARE GROWTH: **2.0%**

	2004	2005	2006	2007	2008	2009	2010	2011
Revenues (Mil)	882	1,046	1,105	1,239	1,311	1,040	1,118	1,078
Net income (Mil)	40.9	52.9	50.8	54.0	35.1	26.0	13.6	16.4
Earnings per share	1.50	1.78	1.88	1.78	1.09	0.71	0.38	0.45
Dividends per share	1.10	1.12	1.15	1.17	1.19	1.19	1.19	1.19
Cash flow per share	2.88	3.35	3.39	3.55	2.81	2.76	2.82	2.39
Price: high	27.5	32	31.9	39.4	46.2	25.4	25.4	23.5
low	23.8	24	25.8	29	15	18.5	18.2	17.5

Otter Tail Corporation
P.O. Box 496
Fergus Falls, MN 56538
(866) 410-8780
Website: *www.ottertail.com*

AGGRESSIVE GROWTH

Pall Corporation

Ticker symbol: PLL (NYSE) ❑ S&P rating: BBB ❑ Value Line financial strength rating: A ❑ Current yield: 1.4% ❑ Dividend raises, past 10 years: 7

Company Profile

Okay, raise your hand if you've heard of Pall Corporation. Anyone? No? Well, neither had we, until we found this company in 2010 in a search for quality industrial suppliers that were number one or two in their markets.

Pall supplies filtration, separation, and purification technologies for the removal of solid, liquid, and gaseous contaminants from a variety of liquids and gases. Its products are used in thousands of industrial and clinical settings: removal of contaminants from gas reagents in every semiconductor production facility in the world, removal of bacteria and virus spores from water in hospitals and other clinical settings, and detection of bacteria in blood samples. Its products range in scale from simple in-line filters sold 100 to the carton up to entire graywater treatment systems with capacities up to 150,000 gallons/day.

Pall's product and customers fall into two broad categories: Life Sciences (40 percent of the FY2011 business) and Industrial (60 percent). The Life Sciences category breaks down further into Blood/Medical (16 percent) and

Biopharma (24 percent). The company's Life Sciences technologies are used in the research laboratory, pharmaceutical, and biotechnology industries; in blood centers; and in hospitals at the point of patient care. Certain medical products improve the safety of the use of blood products in patient care and help control the spread of infections in hospitals. Pall's separation systems and disposable filtration and purification technologies are critical to the development and commercialization of chemically synthesized and biologically derived drugs and vaccines.

The Industrial segment includes General Industrial (39 percent of sales), Aerospace & Transportation (11 percent), and Microelectronics (10 percent). Industrial markets include, but aren't limited to consumer electronics, municipal and industrial water, fuels, chemicals, energy, and food and beverage markets. As an example, Pall sells filtration solutions to the wine, beer, soft drink, bottled water, and food ingredient markets. Additionally, the company sells filtration and fluid monitoring equipment to the aerospace industry for use on commercial and military aircraft, ships, and land-based military vehicles to help protect critical systems and components. Pall also sells filtration and purification technologies for the semiconductor, data storage, fiber optic, advanced display, and materials markets.

Pall is the leader in almost all of these markets. International sales account for 69 percent of the total.

Financial Highlights, Fiscal Year 2011

The pickup in industrial production, as well as R&D, in the wake of the recession has helped Pall considerably, as has a strengthening in international markets. Total revenues advanced 14 percent to $2.7 billion, while improving margins drove earnings ahead some 31 percent. FY2011 appears to be a particularly strong year, but FY2012 earnings are also projected to grow at a healthy clip, 19 percent to be exact, to $3.20 per year. The company projects earnings growth in the 10–12 percent range out to 2016. A recent 20 percent dividend increase and a strong cash flow indicate healthy future cash returns for investors.

Reasons to Buy

We like companies with a dominant position in their marketplaces or market niches, and we like industrials with a diversified customer base. The company sells into the medical, biopharma, energy, and water process technologies; aerospace; and microelectronics spaces, among others. These sectors will continue to show consistency and strength over time. Further, Pall's products are consumables used consistently within the lab and manufacturing processes they sell into; they do not depend greatly on capital spending decisions and are relatively less sensitive to economic cycles. Seventy-five percent of Pall's sales are repeat-purchased consumables; this makes the company a little more recession proof. We also like the company's strong international footprint.

Reasons for Caution

While its presence in the consumables side of the business attenuates the effects of economic cycles somewhat, the company is still sensitive to economic downturns. The recent strength in the business and business model has been noticed by others, too. This may attract more competition (or who knows, a takeover bid?) from the likes of 3M or someone similar. The strength has also been reflected in the share price; new investors should look to buy on dips.

SECTOR: **Industrials**
BETA COEFFICIENT: **1.17**
10-YEAR COMPOUND EARNINGS PER SHARE GROWTH: **9.5%**
10-YEAR COMPOUND DIVIDENDS PER SHARE GROWTH: **3.0%**

	2004	2005	2006	2007	2008	2009	2010	2011
Revenues (Mil)	1,771	1,902	2,017	2,250	2,572	2,392	2,402	2,741
Net Income (Mil)	152	141	146	128	217	196	241	315
Earnings per share	1.20	1.12	1.16	1.02	1.76	1.64	2.03	2.67
Dividends per share	0.36	0.40	0.44	0.48	0.51	0.58	0.64	.70
Cash flow per share	1.90	1.86	1.97	1.81	2.60	2.44	2.90	3.60
Price: high	29.8	31.5	35.6	49	43.2	37.3	44.7	59.5
low	22	25.2	25.3	33.2	21.6	18.2	31.8	39.8

Pall Corporation
2200 Northern Boulevard
East Hills, NY 11548
(516) 484-5400
Website: *www.pall.com*

Patterson Companies, Inc.

Ticker symbol: PDCO (NASDAQ) ❑ S&P rating: not rated ❑ Value Line financial strength rating: A ❑ Current yield: 1.7% ❑ Dividend raises, past 10 years: 3

Company Profile

Patterson Companies is a value-added distributor operating in three segments—Dental Supply, Veterinary Supply, and Medical Supply. Dental Supply (about 65 percent of sales) provides a complete range of consumable dental products, equipment, and software; turnkey digital solutions; office design and setup; and value-added services to dentists and dental laboratories primarily for the North American market. Veterinary Supply (20 percent) is the nation's second-largest distributor of consumable veterinary supplies, equipment, diagnostic products, vaccines, and pharmaceuticals to companion-pet veterinary clinics. Medical Supply (15 percent) distributes medical supplies and assistive products, primarily for rehabilitation and sports medicine, globally to hospitals, long-term-care facilities, clinics, and dealers.

Patterson has one-third of the Dental Supply market. Their main competitors are HSIC (Henry Schein), which also has about a one-third share and Dentsply (a former *100 Best* stock, but removed from the 2013 list because we didn't

see the need for two companies in this business), with the remaining share fragmented among a number of smaller players. As one of the lead dogs, Patterson has the clout to negotiate a number of exclusive distribution deals. It is sole distributor for the industry's most popular line of dental chairs, and also has an exclusive on the CEREC 3D dental restorative system, an increasingly popular alternative to traditional dental crowns. Patterson is also the leading provider of digital radiography systems, which create instant images of dental work, superior to the images generated by traditional X-ray equipment.

Patterson's veterinary business, Webster Veterinary, is the second-largest distributor of consumable veterinary supplies to companion-pet veterinary clinics. Its line also includes equipment and software, diagnostic products, and vaccines and pharmaceuticals.

Financial Highlights, Fiscal Year 2011

The soft economy claimed even dental services as a victim, with patients deferring elective and even not-so-elective procedures, and dentists contracting their inventories. This scenario hasn't fully reversed as of early FY2012; particularly with supply-chain contraction effects, dental services are truly a lagging economic indicator. FY2011 sales grew at an unspectacular 2.4 percent rate, while net profits actually declined slightly. That said, PDCO actually managed to drill out a 2 percent gain in earnings per share. Why? Because of an active share buyback program, which retired some 16 million of 121 million shares in 2011 alone. This is a significant share repurchase, and bodes well for per-share earnings and, likely, dividend increases as the company redirects improved cash flows to that purpose. To wit, the company announced a 17 percent dividend increase to $0.56 per share in early FY2012, but guided earnings to $1.90 to $1.94, essentially flat taking into account the presently soft business conditions.

Reasons to Buy

We think that, eventually, dental procedures (and inventory replenishment) will return to normal levels. While there have been some improvements in the art of long-term dental care, such as more widespread fluoride use, we see the need for replacement crowns, as well as more expensive and material-intensive implant restorations, continuing if not growing as the population ages and as dental care becomes a bigger industry overseas.

The aforementioned CEREC 3D is an imaging and milling system that allows the dentist to take an image of the area to be restored and in less than 30 minutes produce a crown, inlay, or other device that is then fitted to the patient's existing dental structure. It's a compelling proposition for high-volume offices where patient throughput is at a premium and the equipment can be fully utilized. Sales of this high-ticket item have been very good and generate ongoing supplies revenue. Patterson's exclusive license to this product is a powerful foot in the door for new accounts.

We like the company's moves into the companion-pet veterinary and rehabilitative markets, both of which are driven by a growing and profitable demographic. Today the company is primarily focused on the North American market, with promised 24- to 48-hour delivery for most items. They have established an international beachhead with the Patterson Medical group in the UK and France, and intend to leverage this presence to expand the dental and veterinary businesses; thus far international expansion remains more an opportunity—a good one—than a reality.

The company has really made a statement toward increasing shareholder returns through buybacks and the 2009 initiation and subsequent growth in the dividend. Notably, the company has also been named to the *Forbes* list of America's 100 Most Trustworthy Companies.

Reasons for Caution

Competition in this arena is strong, growth is slowing, and operating and net margins have softened a bit since the middle of the last decade.

Unless the company more clearly taps into global growth, the industries it supports are not really growth industries—that said, a recovery to more normal volumes should bode well. Finally, while the share repurchase was aggressive and generally favorable, the company did consume some existing cash reserves to pull it off; it wasn't entirely from free cash thrown off by the business.

SECTOR: **Health Care**
BETA COEFFICIENT: **.86**
10-YEAR COMPOUND EARNINGS PER SHARE GROWTH: **14.5%**
10-YEAR COMPOUND DIVIDENDS PER SHARE GROWTH: **NM**

	2004	2005	2006	2007	2008	2009	2010	2011
Revenues (Mil)	2,421	2,615	2,798	2,998	3,094	3,237	3,415	3,500
Net Income (Mil)	95	198	208	225	200	212	225	215
Earnings per share	1.32	1.43	1.51	1.69	1.70	1.78	1.91	1.95
Dividends per share	0	0	0	0	0	0.10	.42	0.50
Cash flow per share	1.60	1.68	2.05	1.88	2.00	2.04	2.20	2.45
Price: high	43.7	53.8	38.3	40.1	37.8	28.3	32.8	39.9
low	29.7	33.4	29.6	28.3	15.8	16.1	24.1	26.2

Patterson Companies, Inc.
1031 Mendota Heights Road
St. Paul, MN 55120–1419
(651) 686-1775
Website: *www.pattersondental.com*

AGGRESSIVE GROWTH

Paychex, Inc.

Ticker symbol: PAYX (NASDAQ) ❑ S&P rating: not rated ❑ Value Line financial strength rating: A ❑ Current yield: 4.2% ❑ Dividend raises, past 10 years: 8

Company Profile

Paychex, Inc. provides payroll, human resource, and benefits outsourcing solutions for small to medium-sized businesses. Founded in 1971, the company has more than 100 offices and serves over 564,000 clients, mostly small to medium businesses with 10 to 200 employees in the United States and an additional 1,900 clients in Germany. The company has two sources of revenue: service revenue, paid by clients for services, and interest income on the funds held by Paychex for clients.

Paychex offers a portfolio of services and products, which includes:

■ Payroll processing
■ Payroll tax administration services
■ Employee payment services
■ Regulatory compliance services (new-hire reporting and garnishment processing)
■ Comprehensive human resource outsourcing services
■ Retirement services administration
■ Workers' compensation insurance services
■ Health and benefits services
■ Time and attendance solutions
■ Medical deduction, state unemployment, and other HR services and products

The company's products are marketed primarily through its direct sales force, the bulk of which is focused on payroll products. In addition to the direct sales force, the company utilizes its relationships with existing clients, CPAs, and banks for new client referrals. Approximately two-thirds of its new clients come via these referral sources.

Larger clients can choose to outsource their payroll and HR functions, or to run them in-house using a Paychex platform. For those clients the company offers what they call "Major Market Services" (MMS) products, which can be run locally or on a web-hosted environment.

In addition to traditional payroll services, Paychex offers complete "full-service" HR outsourcing solutions; custom-built solutions including payroll, compliance, HR, and employee benefits sourcing and administration; outsourcing management; and even professionally trained onsite HR representatives. The company also manages retirement plans and other benefits, including pretax "cafeteria" plans, and has a subsidiary insurance agency offering property and casualty, workers' comp, health, and auto policies to an employer's employee base. About 21,000 of the 564,000 clients utilize the full Human Resource Services offering.

Financial Highlights, Fiscal Year 2011

Paychex's business lagged the general economy somewhat, and as such, FY2010 was the softest year. The company's revenues are driven by payroll numbers, payroll activity, and the "float"—the interest earned on money held before paychecks are cashed and before tax payments are made to tax collecting authorities—which can be 30 to 90 days depending on the type of tax and the arrangement with the employer. With interest rates paid on cash deposits near all-time lows (a byproduct of the recession), revenue and profit increases have been held at bay.

FY2011 saw a modest 4.3 percent gain in revenues to $2.1 billion, with a more generous 8 percent increase in net earnings. The generous dividend continues to consume about 87 percent of earnings, so there wasn't much left over for share buybacks or even dividend

increases during the past few years. The company has three primary growth strategies: first, offer a more complete service, such as HR; second, acquire other smaller companies offering similar local services; and third, create more "cloudlike" services to enable clients to switch from homegrown to Paychex solutions. With three moderately sized acquisitions—SurePayroll, ePlan Services, and Icon Time Systems—under its belt in FY2011–12, PayChex expects FY2012 revenue growth in the 7–9 percent range and earnings growth of 5–7 percent.

Reasons to Buy

Paychex's primary market is companies with fewer than 100 employees. This is one of the primary reasons that Paychex lost clients—many small businesses, being undercapitalized, simply went out of business during the recession. That trend has turned around with the economy, and beyond that, the cost of switching and a generally good client relationship has made for a loyal client base. We think the trend to outsource payroll and HR activities will not only continue but accelerate as easier, Internet-based solutions come more into favor. The company is conservatively run and is well financed. It carries zero long-term debt and should have little difficulty funding the generous dividend, even at its current payout level of 80 to 90 percent of earnings. Fragmentation in the market and Paychex's extremely strong financial position will allow the company to continue to grow market share through acquisition. As business activity has heated up and competition waned, the company has been able to tack on a few small price increases. Finally, sooner or later short-term interest rates must tick upward; when that happens the company will once again be able to profit from the float. We would expect dividend increases to resume at that point if not before. As it is, PAYX has one of the highest yield percentages on our *100 Best* list.

Reasons for Caution

This company will always be vulnerable to economic swings, and did hit the "slow growth" wall in 2009 with only a slow recovery. The company's acquisition strategy makes sense, as those acquisitions will increase market share, but they do come with costs and risks. Finally, while most analysts consider the dividend payout secure, it does account for a substantial fraction of the company's cash flow, and increases may be hard to come by for the immediate future. Also, with such a high yield and relatively low growth, near-term share appreciation might be difficult.

SECTOR: **Information Technology**
BETA COEFFICIENT: **0.85**
10-YEAR COMPOUND EARNINGS PER SHARE GROWTH: **10.5%**
10-YEAR COMPOUND DIVIDENDS PER SHARE GROWTH: **18.8%**

		2004	2005	2006	2007	2008	2009	2010	2011
Revenues (Mil)		1,294	1,445	1,675	1,887	2,066	2,083	2,001	2,084
Net Income (Mil)		303	369	465	515	576	534	477	516
Earnings per share		0.8	0.97	1.22	1.35	1.56	1.48	1.32	1.42
Dividends per share		0.47	0.51	0.61	0.79	1.20	1.24	1.24	1.24
Cash flow per share		0.95	1.14	1.4	1.54	1.82	1.72	1.56	1.67
Price:	high	39.1	43.4	42.4	47.1	37.5	32.9	32.8	33.9
	low	28.8	28.8	33	36.1	23.2	20.3	24.7	25.1

Paychex, Inc.
911 Panorama Trail South
Rochester, NY 14625–0397
(585) 383-3406
Website: *www.paychex.com*

PepsiCo, Inc.

Ticker symbol: PEP (NYSE) ❑ S&P rating: A ❑ Value Line financial strength rating: A++ ❑ Current yield: 3.1% ❑ Dividend raises, past 10 years: 10

Company Profile

PepsiCo is a global beverage, snack, and food company. It manufactures, markets, and sells a variety of salty, convenient, sweet, and grain-based snacks, carbonated and non-carbonated beverages, and foods in approximately 200 countries, with its largest operations in North America (United States, Canada, and Mexico); the UK; and now, Russia. You'll recognize most of the major PepsiCo brands—which range widely from the familiar Pepsi Cola—and are likely to show up in abundance in your refrigerator and kitchen cupboard at any given time.

PepsiCo is organized into four business units, as follows:

■ Frito-Lay North America (20 percent of FY2011 sales, 29 percent of profits) makes and distributes the too-familiar snack brands—Fritos, Doritos, Lay's, Cheetos, Tostitos, Ruffles, SunChips, and various dips and spreads to go with these products.
■ Quaker Foods North America (4 percent, 7 percent) came to Pepsi in 2001 and sells Quaker Oats, Aunt Jemima, Cap'n Crunch, Life cereal, Rice-A-Roni, and Near East, to name a few.
■ PepsiCo Americas Beverages (33 percent, 28 percent), the flagship business, includes PepsiCo Beverages North America and all of the Latin American beverage businesses, and brings to market Tropicana and Gatorade products, in addition to several familiar soft drink brands like Pepsi, Mountain Dew, Sierra Mist, and 7UP outside the United States.
■ PepsiCo International includes all PepsiCo businesses in the UK, Europe, Asia, the Middle East, Latin America, and Africa. The international business accounts for about 42 percent of sales and 29 percent of profits. Of sales, Europe is about 20 percent; Asia, the Middle East, and Africa is 11 percent; and Latin America rounds it out with another 11 percent. These units distribute U.S.-branded products but also many that are formulated and branded for local markets, e.g., Sabritas and Gamesa for the Mexican market.

Many of PepsiCo's brand names are over 100 years old, but the corporation is relatively young. PepsiCo was founded in 1965 through the merger of Pepsi-Cola and Frito-Lay. PepsiCo now has at least 18 brands that generate over $1 billion in retail sales. The top two brands are Pepsi-Cola and Mountain Dew, but beverages constitute less than half of Pepsi's sales. It is primarily a snack company, with beverages coming in second. Frito-Lay brands alone account for more than half of the U.S. snack chip industry. Note also that the snack businesses are relatively more profitable and contribute a larger share of the company's total profits.

PepsiCo began its international snack food operations in 1966. Today, with operations in more than 40 countries, it's the leading multinational snack chip company, with more than a 25 percent market share of international retail snack chip sales. Brand Pepsi and other Pepsi-Cola products—including Diet Pepsi, Pepsi-One, Mountain Dew, Slice, Sierra Mist, and Mug brands—account for nearly one-third of total soft drink sales in the United States, a consumer market totaling about $60 billion. Pepsi-Cola also offers a variety of noncarbonated beverages, including Aquafina bottled water, Lipton ready-to-drink tea, and Frappuccino ready-to-drink

coffee through a partnership with Starbucks.

PepsiCo acquired Tropicana, including the Dole juice business, in August 1998 and now markets these products in 63 countries. Tropicana Pure Premium is the third-largest brand of all food products sold in grocery stores in the United States. Gatorade, acquired as part of the Quaker Oats Company merger in 2001, is the world's leading sports drink.

At the beginning of FY2011, the company completed the acquisition of 60 percent of Wimm-Bill-Dan, a major branded food and beverage company in the Russian market for $3.8 billion, giving PepsiCo a 77 percent stake in the company, with plans to purchase all remaining shares eventually.

The company has been undergoing a modest restructuring to reduce costs, improve efficiency, and strengthen its brands, especially overseas. Areas of focus include supply-chain efficiencies and an additional $500 million of annual advertising spend; in addition the company is investing in international and especially emerging markets like Brazil, China, India, and Russia. Sales in international markets, once the domain of rival Coke, have tripled to $22 billion in five years and now account for 42 percent of Pepsi's sales. The company is also turning up the innovation machine to produce healthier products in a "Global Nutrition Group" formed last year.

Financial Highlights, Fiscal Year 2011

Strategic shifts, new investments, and rising commodity costs kept the fizz out of Pepsi's earnings in FY2011. Per-share earnings rose a modest 2 percent to $3.98 per share, almost entirely accounted for by share count reduction, on a relatively healthy revenue growth of 14.8 percent, although some of that was driven by Wimm-Bill-Dan and other acquisitions. While the performance looks tepid (and many called for the head of CEO Indra Nooyi and did succeed in creating a new "president" position to share leadership with her), it really represents a deliberate strategy to build international markets and operating efficiencies. These initiatives, combined with an unfavorable currency environment, have the company guiding for only another 2 percent earnings notch on a 3 percent gain in revenues for FY2012. During this "flat spot" the company continues to raise its dividend and plans to repurchase about 2 percent of its shares; it expects completion of these new initiatives and resumption of earnings growth in FY2013.

Reasons to Buy

PepsiCo continues to offer a compelling combination of earnings, dividend, and cash flow growth potential with a strong measure of safety. The food business adds some diversification, channel strength, and profitability that rival Coke does not have.

The company is taking an aggressive approach to geographical expansion and brand recognition, and expects continued solid growth in international markets. That combined with new operational efficiencies should bode well for the long term; in the meantime the current flat spot may be a good time to invest with a nice dividend yield to hold investors over until these initiatives bear fruit.

Reasons for Caution

PepsiCo will need to move quickly to retain the health-conscious market. They have many new and reformulated products in the works that use healthier ingredients and reduced levels of sodium and trans fats, but the competition for this segment is intense. The Global Nutrition Group should address this challenge. While Pepsi is investing heavily in international markets, there is no guarantee that they will displace Coke, although the food offering will help get attention and valuable shelf space. Finally, the food business may be a drag depending on which way commodity prices run; for instance, most snack products are heavily influenced by corn prices.

SECTOR: **Consumer Staples**
BETA COEFFICIENT: **.51**
10-YEAR COMPOUND EARNINGS PER SHARE GROWTH: **10.5%**
10-YEAR COMPOUND DIVIDENDS PER SHARE GROWTH: **12.0%**

	2004	2005	2006	2007	2008	2009	2010	2011
Revenues (Mil)	29,261	32,562	35,137	39,474	43,251	43,232	57,938	66,504
Net Income (Mil)	4,174	4,078	5,065	5,543	5,142	5,946	6,320	6,379
Earnings per share	2.44	2.39	3.00	3.34	3.21	3.77	3.91	3.98
Dividends per share	0.85	1.01	1.16	1.43	1.60	1.75	1.89	2.03
Cash flow per share	3.14	3.65	3.95	4.38	4.30	4.84	5.47	5.83
Price: high	55.7	60.3	66	79	79.8	64.5	68.1	71.9
low	45.3	51.3	56	61.9	49.7	43.8	58.8	58.5

PepsiCo, Inc.
700 Anderson Hill Road
Purchase, NY 10577–1444
(914) 253-3055
Website: *www.pepsico.com*

Perrigo Company

Ticker symbol: PRGO (NASDAQ) ❑ S&P rating: not rated ❑ Value Line financial strength rating:
B++ ❑ Current yield: 0.3% ❑ Dividend raises, past 10 years: 9

Company Profile

Perrigo is the world's largest manufacturer of over-the-counter pharmaceutical products for the store-brand market. They also manufacture generic prescription pharmaceuticals, nutritional products, and active pharmaceutical ingredients (APIs).

The company operates in four segments: Consumer Healthcare, Nutritionals, Rx Pharmaceuticals, and API. Consumer Healthcare is by far the largest segment, generating about 61 percent of Perrigo's revenue in 2011, while Nutritionals brings in 18 percent, Rx Pharma 12 percent, and API 6 percent.

The company's success depends on its ability to manufacture and quickly market generic equivalents to branded products. It employs internal R&D resources to develop product formulations and manufacture in quantity for its customers. It also develops retail packaging specific to the customer's needs.

If you have bought a store-branded over-the-counter medication, like ibuprofen or cough medicine in the past year, there's a good chance (a 70 percent chance, in fact) that it was made by Perrigo.

The company's Consumer Healthcare business produces and markets over 2,400 store-brand products in 12,000 individual SKUs to approximately 800 customers, including Walmart, CVS, Walgreens, Kroger, Target, Safeway, Dollar General, Costco, and other national and regional drugstores, supermarkets, and mass merchandisers. Walmart is its single largest customer and accounts for 23 percent of Perrigo's net sales. The retail market for the branded equivalents of Perrigo's most widely used products is over $12 billion.

The Nutritionals segment is relatively new as a standalone segment and includes store-brand infant formula, vitamins, and minerals. This operation moved forward with a recent distribution partnership for U.S.-manufactured baby formula to be distributed in China. The company is pursuing similar partnerships in other regions.

The Rx Pharma operations produce generic prescription drugs (in contrast to the over-the-counter drugs produced in the Consumer Healthcare segment), obviously benefiting when key patented drugs run past their patent protection. Rx

Pharma markets approximately 300 generic prescription products, many of them topicals and creams, with over 620 SKUs, to approximately 120 customers, while the API division markets an assortment of active ingredients to other drug manufacturers as well as for the company's own products, including a number of active ingredients that we'd have trouble spelling correctly, so won't even try. The company's products are manufactured in nine facilities around the world. Its major markets are in North America, Mexico, the UK, and China. About 33 percent of sales are overseas, and, interestingly, Walmart accounts for 22 percent of sales, mostly over-the-counter health-care products.

Financial Highlights, Fiscal Year 2011

Perrigo posted another healthy sales increase in FY2011, up some 21.5 percent at $2.8 billion from FY2010, although this included the effects of some smaller acquisitions. Earnings per share climbed 28 percent to a record $3.64. For FY2012, the company is giving guidance for a 13 percent earnings-per-share increase to $4.10. Gross and operating margin expansion have been a key part of the growth story. The consumer store-branded products market is large and secure but relatively low margin, so the company has been putting more

focus on the Rx and API businesses. Operating margins have risen from the low teens in mid-decade to the mid-teens in 2008 and 2009, 19.4 percent in FY2010, 21.5 percent in FY2011, and are projected to go up another notch to 22.5 percent in 2012. Although there have been some signs of competitive pressure in the over-the-counter segments, the company still appears to dominate its niches and to be able to exert some control over prices.

Reasons to Buy

Perrigo is a real success story of solid niche dominance (store-branded medications) with a couple of high-growth, high-margin businesses mixed in. Steady growth in sales combined with a steady growth in margins have a multiplicative effect, and the company has enjoyed well-above-average profit growth in this industry.

Not only does the company dominate a niche—it is a growing niche. People are becoming more sensitive to their own health-care costs and spending in general and are opting more often for the store brand; after all, 200 mg of ibuprofen is 200 mg of ibuprofen. And this all sits on top of the demographic tailwind of the aging population.

The company continues to successfully bring both new generic over-the-counter and generic prescription drugs to market. New generics for Pravacid, Mucinex, and a store-branded version of Allegra will help, as will the new ventures for baby formula and other products in China. With its 70 percent market share of the private-label OTC market, Perrigo is in a position to capture the larger share of any future generic rollout opportunities.

The company is well funded to capitalize on future opportunities with strong cash flow and a strong balance sheet for a company still in its strong growth phase.

Reasons for Caution

There are some risks in the generic pharmaceutical industry; among them are patent infringement lawsuits and manufacturing problems. The company has had a few lawsuits but fortunately none of the manufacturing problems experienced by rival Johnson & Johnson; a major hiccup could put a dent in the company's business. Competition has been heating up as others see the niche opportunities. Also, the stock price has followed the story upward, which makes investors vulnerable to any short-term hiccup in the growth story. New investors should choose buying opportunities carefully.

SECTOR: Health Care
BETA COEFFICIENT: 0.66
10-YEAR COMPOUND EARNINGS PER SHARE GROWTH: 25.0%
10-YEAR COMPOUND DIVIDENDS PER SHARE GROWTH: NM

		2004	2005	2006	2007	2008	2009	2010	2011
Revenues (Mil)		898	1,024	1,366	1,447	1,822	2,007	2,269	2,765
Net Income (Mil)		67.5	37.9	74.1	78.6	150	176	263	341
Earnings per share		0.93	0.49	0.79	0.84	1.58	1.87	2.83	3.64
Dividends per share		0.13	0.16	0.17	0.18	0.21	0.22	0.25	0.27
Cash flow per share		1.35	0.77	1.41	1.46	2.35	2.67	3.69	4.78
Price:	high	25	19.9	18.7	36.9	43.1	61.4	67.5	104.7
	low	15.6	12.8	14.4	16.1	27.7	18.5	37.5	62.3

Perrigo Company
515 Eastern Avenue
Allegan, MI 49010
(269) 673-8451
Website: www.perrigo.com

CONSERVATIVE GROWTH

Praxair, Inc.

Ticker symbol: PX (NYSE) ❑ S&P rating: A ❑ Value Line financial strength rating: A ❑ Current yield: 1.9% ❑ Dividend raises, past 10 years: 10

Company Profile

Praxair, Inc. is the largest producer of industrial gases in North and South America and the second-largest supplier of industrial gases in the world. The company, which was spun off to Union Carbide shareholders in June 1992, supplies a broad range of atmospheric, process, and specialty gases; high-performance coatings; and related services and technologies.

Praxair's primary products are atmospheric gases—oxygen, nitrogen, argon, and rare gases (produced when atmospheric air is purified, compressed, cooled, distilled, and condensed) and process and specialty gases—carbon dioxide, helium, hydrogen, and acetylene (produced as by-products of chemical production or recovered from natural gas). Customers include makers of primary metals, metal fabricators, petroleum refiners, and producers of chemicals, health-care products, electronics, glass, pulp and paper, and environmental products.

The gas products are sold into the packaged-gas market and the merchant market. In the packaged-gas market, bulk gases are packaged into high-pressure cylinders and either delivered to the customer or to distributors. In the merchant market, bulk gases are liquefied and transported by truck to the customer's facility.

The company also designs, engineers, and constructs cryogenic and noncryogenic gas supply systems for customers who choose to produce their own atmospheric gases on-site. This is obviously a capital-intensive delivery solution for Praxair, but results in lower delivered cost to the customer and higher returns for Praxair, as all operational costs are paid by the customer. Contracts for these installations can run to 20 years.

Praxair Surface Technologies is a subsidiary that applies wear-, corrosion-, and thermal-resistant metallic and ceramic coatings and powders to metal surfaces in order to resist wear, high temperatures, and corrosion. Aircraft engines are a primary market, but it serves others, including the printing, textile, chemical, and primary metals markets, and provides aircraft engine and airframe component overhaul services.

Financial Highlights, Fiscal Year 2011

Praxair followed the familiar story of most of the industrial world into a soft FY2009, and has followed that world back to a degree of prosperity. Beyond 2009, the company has turned steady growth and modestly growing margins into good results. FY2011 revenues came in at $11.3 billion, a nice 12.3 percent gain from FY2010, and earnings per share, helped along by share repurchases and effective cost controls, gained 41 percent to $5.45 per share. The company's performance has been steady and growing since, with one analyst describing FY2012 Q1 performance meeting revenue and earnings targets to the penny as a "golf clap" quarter—on its way to a guided top line in the $11.6–11.9 billion range and EPS between $5.75 and $5.90.

Reasons to Buy

It's nice to own a few "golf clap" stocks in companies that show high margins, steady growth, and no surprises. Par, par, birdie, par—not a bad round, and Praxair is the sort of company that can deliver that.

Praxair is the largest gas provider in the emerging markets of China, India, Brazil, and Mexico. Praxair China now has 15 wholly owned subsidiaries and at least 10 joint ventures. Asian markets account for 8 percent of Praxair's

sales, and these markets are growing steadily.

The petroleum industry is recovering heavier and heavier crude oil sources, such as the tar sands in Alberta. To refine these sources at existing facilities requires the input of greater and greater volumes of hydrogen. While hydrogen for refining is now one of Praxair's largest growth markets, in reality it serves a broad industrial base—broader than many of its competitors, and a broad geographic base as well. The company has stepped up its shareholder returns and has a particularly admirable track record of dividend growth, from 46 cents per share in 2003 to a projected $2.20 in 2012, and has added $1.5 billion to its share repurchase program, enough to retire about 4 percent of outstanding shares.

Reasons for Caution

The company no longer has to deal with the effects of an Air Products-Airgas merger, but consolidation of smaller players by Praxair's competitors may force Praxair to follow suit at some point. As hydrocarbon energy products are feedstock for many of Praxair's products, the company is sensitive to increases in energy prices, although the recent decline in natural gas prices—an important feedstock—bodes well shorter term. Finally, the markets have recognized Praxair's recent score card and have given it a low handicap in the form of a high share price—new investors should look for favorable entry points at times when industrial production and manufacturing sectors look weak.

SECTOR: **Materials**
BETA COEFFICIENT: **0.84**
10-YEAR COMPOUND EARNINGS PER SHARE GROWTH: **11.0%**
10-YEAR COMPOUND DIVIDENDS PER SHARE GROWTH: **19.0%**

	2004	**2005**	**2006**	**2007**	**2008**	**2009**	**2010**	**2011**
Revenues (Mil)	6,594	7,656	8,324	9,402	10,796	8,956	10,118	11,252
Net Income (Mil)	607	726	988	1,177	1,335	1,254	1,195	1,672
Earnings per share	2.10	2.20	3.00	3.62	4.19	4.01	3.84	5.45
Dividends per share	0.6	0.72	1.00	1.20	1.50	1.60	1.80	2.00
Cash flow per share	3.94	4.61	5.25	6.18	8.63	6.85	6.95	8.95
Price: high	46.2	54.3	63.7	92.1	77.6	86.1	96.3	111.7
low	34.5	41.1	50.4	58	53.3	53.3	72.7	88.6

Praxair, Inc.
39 Old Ridgebury Road
Danbury, CT 06810–5113
(203) 837-2354
Website: *www.praxair.com*

The Procter & Gamble Company

Ticker symbol: PG (NYSE) ❑ S&P rating: AA- ❑ Value Line financial strength rating: A++ ❑ Current yield: 3.1% ❑ Dividend raises, past 10 years: 10

Company Profile

Procter & Gamble dates back to 1837, when William Procter and James Gamble began making soap and candles in Cincinnati, Ohio. The company's first major product introduction took place in 1879 when it launched Ivory soap. Since then, P&G has continually created a host of blockbuster products and has some of the strongest, most recognizable consumer brands in the world.

P&G is a uniquely diversified consumer products company with a strong global presence. P&G markets its broad line of products to nearly 5 billion consumers in more than 180 countries.

The company is a recognized leader in the development, manufacturing, and marketing of quality laundry, cleaning, paper, personal care, food, beverage, and health-care products, including prescription pharmaceuticals.

To understand Procter, it's worth a look at how the company is now organized. As of mid-FY2011, there are two Global Business Units: Beauty and Grooming and Household Care. Within these two units are six reportable segments: Beauty (24 percent of sales, 22 percent of

profits), Grooming (10 percent, 13 percent), Health Care (14 percent, 16 percent), Fabric Care & Home Care (30 percent, 28 percent), Baby Care & Family Care (19 percent, 19 percent), and Snacks and Pet Care (4 percent, 2 percent). The 300 brands sold under these segments are eminently familiar but too numerous to list and categorize; here are a few: Gillette, Tide, Always, Whisper, Pro-V, Olay, Duracell, Ariel, Crest, Pampers, Pantene, Vicks, Bold, Dawn, Head & Shoulders, Cascade, Iams, Zest, Bounty, Braun, Comet, Scope, Old Spice, Charmin, Tampax, Downy, Cheer, and Prell.

Total FY2011 sales were $82.5 billion, with 63 percent of that coming from overseas. The company also manufactures locally for the largest international markets.

The company will complete the sale of its Pringles snack foods division to Kellogg (another *100 Best* stock) in 2012, pretty much completing its exit from the food and snacks business.

Financial Highlights, Fiscal Year

The $82.5 billion in FY2011 revenues represented a decent 4.6

percent rate of growth over FY2010, but only brought the company back to where it was in FY2008. The dip was partly due to the recession, which strengthened generic competition, but also was a result of sales of large chunks of its food and coffee operations (Jif, Folgers, etc.) to J. M. Smucker (another *100 Best* pick) and others. Per-share earnings came in at $3.93, an 11 percent jump aided by the retirement of 80 million shares, a 3 percent drop in share count. The company recently announced some restructuring moves (mostly organizational simplifications, designed to reduce advertising spend and overhead) and combined with decent core sales and operating performance and strength in international markets, projects sales in the $87 billion range for FY2012 but has guided earnings lower into the $3.93–$4.03 per share range due to charges from the Pringles sale and higher commodity costs.

Reasons to Buy

Regardless of developments in the world economy, people will continue to shave, bathe, do laundry, and care for their babies, and P&G is the global leader in baby care, feminine care, fabric care, and shaving products. Everyone should consider at least one defensive play in their portfolio, and P&G deserves to be at the top of the list.

P&G is extending its reach to capture share in channels and markets that are currently underserved. Developing markets are a huge opportunity, representing 86 percent of the world's population, and P&G feels it can be a leader in many product categories. Emerging markets already represent 32 percent of their revenue, up from 20 percent in 2002. P&G is also broadening its distribution channels to pursue opportunities in drug and pharmacy outlets, "convenience" stores, export operations, and even e-commerce.

In a move that will reduce operating and some marketing and advertising costs significantly, the company has departed from its traditional model of managing brands as wholly separate businesses with brand-specific advertising budgets, products research labs, and so forth. Synergies from combining ads and ad strategies alone should get more bang for the buck and reduce total costs across the company's many portfolios. Recent cost-cutting moves (which are expected to save $10 billion annually by 2016) will grow the profit base faster than the moderately strong growth in the sales base—all a good combination. In short, we like the brand, marketplace, and financial strength; sure and steady dividend growth; and short- and long-term prospects.

Reasons for Caution

The recent recession made consumers much more price conscious, and many switched to generics. That switch has reversed to a degree, but it may take a long time to get everybody back on board, if the company can do it at all. The company has dealt with that to a degree by introducing some "low-end" sub-brands to its mix. Rising commodity costs can affect P&G, and the expansion into the health and beauty business brings more exposure to often-fickle consumer tastes and shorter brand life than the company may be used to.

SECTOR: **Consumer Staples**
BETA COEFFICIENT: **.45**
10-YEAR COMPOUND EARNINGS PER SHARE GROWTH: **9.5%**
10-YEAR COMPOUND DIVIDENDS PER SHARE GROWTH: **11%**

		2004	2005	2006	2007	2008	2009	2010	2011
Revenues (Mil)		51,407	56,741	68,222	76,476	83,503	79,029	78,938	82,559
Net Income (Mil)		6,481	7,257	8,684	10,340	12,075	11,293	10,946	11,797
Earnings per share		2.32	2.53	2.64	3.04	3.64	3.58	3.53	3.93
Dividends per share		0.93	1.03	1.15	1.28	1.45	1.64	1.80	1.97
Cash flow per share		3.18	3.51	3.51	4.25	4.97	4.65	4.87	5.21
Price:	high	57.4	59.7	64.2	75.2	73.8	63.5	65.3	67.7
	low	48.9	51.2	52.8	60.4	54.9	43.9	39.4	57.6

The Procter & Gamble Company
1 Procter & Gamble Plaza
Cincinnati, OH 45202
(513) 983-1100
Website: *www.pg.com*

AGGRESSIVE GROWTH

Ross Stores, Inc.

Ticker symbol: ROST (NASDAQ) ❑ S&P rating: BBB+ ❑ Value Line financial strength rating: A ❑ Current yield: 1.0% ❑ Dividend raises, past 10 years: 10

Company Profile

Ross Stores is the second-largest off-price retailer in the United States. Ross and its subsidiaries operate two chains of apparel and home accessories stores. As of 2011 the company operated a total of 1,055 stores, of which 988 were Ross Dress for Less locations in 27 states and Guam and 67 were dd's DISCOUNTS stores in four states. Just over half the company's stores are located in three states—California, Florida, and Texas.

Both chains target value-conscious women and men between the ages of 18 and 54. Ross's target customers are primarily from middle-income households, while the dd's DISCOUNTS target customers are typically from lower- to middle-income households. Merchandising, purchasing, pricing, and the locations of the stores are all aimed at these customer bases. Ross and dd's DISCOUNTS both offer first-quality, in-season, name-brand and designer apparel, accessories, and footwear for the family at savings typically in the 20–60 percent range off department store prices (at Ross) or 20–70 percent off (at dd's DISCOUNTS). The stores also offer discounted home fashions and housewares, educational toys and games, furniture and furniture accents, luggage, cookware, and at some stores jewelry.

Ross's strategy is to offer competitive values to target customers by offering a well-managed mix of inventory with a strong percentage of name brands and items of local and seasonal interest at attractive prices.

Financial Highlights, Fiscal Year 2011

Not surprisingly, the recession was nothing but good news for this company, bringing newly cost-conscious customers by the busload. Sales rose 20 percent from 2007 to the depth of the recession in 2009. But did they fall off when the economy started to recover? No. Not yet, anyway. And it doesn't look like they will anytime soon.

FY2010 sales kept the growth pace at $7.9 million, 9.5 percent ahead of FY2009, and FY2011 marched ahead another 9 percent to just short of $8.6 billion. Same store sales, the real measure of retail success, advanced 5 percent in both of these years. The earnings story is as good if not better, with earnings per share of $2.84 in FY2011 compared to 95 cents in 2007. It's little wonder that the stock price has pretty much quadrupled over that period. For FY2012, the company projects a return to more modest, but still healthy growth rates, with same-store sales up 1 to 2 percent and earnings in the $3.12–$3.27 range.

Reasons to Buy

The recession helped Ross gain mainstream appeal across a wider set of customers. While some of those customers will "defect" back to full-price retail stores as things improve, a greater number have shown that they will continue to shop at the stores. At the same time, the company was successful with operational improvements begun in 2009 to improve merchandising and inventory management, which led to better stocking of a more favorable mix of goods and improved inventory turnover. These marketplace and operational improvements have led to the financial success one would expect and then some, and the company continues to improve its inventory management and should see greater profitability almost regardless of the economic environment.

The company plans to expand the formula into the Midwest and into other regions, which should be a good match for the offering. The company operates in only 27 states, suggesting in itself a growth opportunity, and overseas? No immediate plans, but why not?

Ross has increased dividends regularly, but to date the increases have been small and the payout has stayed low as a percentage, favoring internal growth, share repurchases, and resulting price appreciation as a return for investors. That may change; there is plenty of room in the cash flow to increase the payout, and the company has almost no long-term debt.

Reasons for Caution

The stock continues to trade at an all-time high, and there are questions about Ross's ability to acquire the same quantity and quality of merchandise as the economy picks up and full-price retailers begin to see higher levels of foot traffic. Such inventory follows a cycle, and if full-price retailers cut back on orders, there is less for everyone—and if the economy picks up, they will sell more, so less for Ross. Upshot: Inventory management improvements at full-price retailers could make things tougher for the company.

SECTOR: **Retail**
BETA COEFFICIENT: **0.70**
10-YEAR COMPOUND EARNINGS PER SHARE GROWTH: **15.5%**
10-YEAR COMPOUND DIVIDENDS PER SHARE GROWTH: **23.0%**

	2004	**2005**	**2006**	**2007**	**2008**	**2009**	**2010**	**2011**
Revenues (Mil)	4,240	4,944	5,570	5,975	6,486	7,184	7,866	8,575
Net Income (Mil)	180	200	241	261	305	443	555	650
Earnings per share	0.60	0.68	0.85	0.95	1.77	1.77	2.32	2.84
Dividends per share	.09	.11	.13	.16	.20	.25	.35	.45
Cash flow per share	.93	1.08	1.26	1.42	1.76	2.45	3.03	3.65
Price: high	16.4	15.7	15.9	17.6	20.8	25.3	33.3	49.2
low	10.5	11.2	11.1	12.2	10.6	14	21.2	30.1

Ross Stores, Inc.
4440 Rosewood Dr.
Building 4
Pleasanton, CA 94588–3050
(925) 965-4400
Website: *www.rossstores.com*

AGGRESSIVE GROWTH

Schlumberger Limited

Ticker symbol: SLB (NYSE) ◻ S&P rating: A+ ◻ Value Line financial strength rating: A++ ◻ Current yield: 1.6% ◻ Dividend raises, past 10 years: 6

Company Profile

Schlumberger Limited is the world's leading oilfield services company. It provides technology, information solutions, and integrated project management services with the goal of optimizing reservoir performance for its customers in the oil and gas industry. Founded in 1926, today the company has a large international footprint, employing more than 113,000 people in 80 countries.

The company operates in two business segments:

Schlumberger Oilfield Services is, at 93 percent of revenues and 99 percent of profits, by far the largest segment and supplies a wide range of products and services. Within the Oilfield Services segment, three groups broadly characterize the deliverables of the segment. The Reservoir Characterization Group is mostly a consulting service, applying technologies toward finding, defining, and characterizing hydrocarbon deposits. The Drilling Group, not surprisingly, does the actual drilling and creation of wells for production, while the Reservoir Production Group completes and services the well for production

and to maintain and enhance productivity through its life. The company not only provides physical on-site services but also substantial consulting, modeling, information management, and project management around these activities. In short, SLB Oilfield Services offers a full outsourcing supply chain for oil and gas field development and production.

The smaller Distribution Operations segment operates in the refining, petrochemical mining, and power generation industries. Schlumberger manages its business through 28 "GeoMarket" regions, which are grouped into four geographic areas: North America; Latin America; Europe, Commonwealth of Independent States, and Africa; and Middle East and Asia. The GeoMarket structure provides a single point of contact at the local level for field operations and brings together geographically focused teams to meet local needs and deliver customized solutions.

The company made the bigticket acquisition of oil services giant Smith International, which was integrated into the operations and financials during FY2011.

Financial Highlights, Fiscal Year 2011

Although affected by a crosscurrent of macroeconomic and pricing conditions in FY2011, the company did well, although much of the "growth" was related to the Smith acquisition. Revenues came in at $39.5 billion, well ahead of the $27.4 billion in FY2010. On paper, this is a 43 percent growth rate; without Smith the figure is closer to 8 percent, still healthy. Per share earnings may be a better barometer of continuing performance, since about 175 million shares were issued to buy Smith. EPS rose from $2.70 in FY2010 to $3.51, a 30 percent rise.

Oil prices continue to rise, bringing strength in demand and pricing to the Oilfield Services business. The overseas business has been particularly strong, with about a 10 percent estimated rise in rig count. Working against this success is the collapse of natural gas prices in the United States; it remains to be seen how this will affect the industry and revenues in the near term. The company also faces possible headwinds from the economic slowdown in Europe and a slackening of growth in China.

SLB is buying back about 30 million shares a year—about 2 percent of the total float—and just raised its dividend 10 percent. FY2012 projections are a bit uncertain but call for $45 billion in revenues, up 14 percent, and $4.90 per share in earnings, up almost 40 percent, so obviously the stronger oil prices and resulting oilfield service needs represent the stronger wind current.

Reasons to Buy

The first page of Schlumberger's 2009 annual report began with: "The age of easy oil is over." Written many months before the explosion of BP's deepwater platform in the Gulf of Mexico and the ensuing spill, the sentence seems prescient and is perhaps the most succinct statement of Schlumberger's advantages in the E&P business. Its expertise is most valuable in the most technically challenging projects, such as the several recent sub-salt offshore finds in Brazil, West Africa, and the Gulf of Mexico.

Unlike a lot of players in the oil business, it has been prudent with its money. Income from the boom years has been used to fund selected acquisitions of companies that operate only in its core business segment. It has also plowed money back into the company in the form of increased spending on R&D; Schlumberger invests more each year in R&D than all other oilfield services companies combined. The company has also accelerated the return of some cash to shareholders in the form of dividends and share buybacks.

Reasons for Caution

Naturally, Schlumberger is vulnerable to the ups and downs of the oil and gas industry. The current dip in natural gas prices—if it starts to really eat into production—could become a firm "down" story. The company also faces the traditional risks of oil drilling—particularly offshore drilling—that culminated in the BP disaster of 2010. Finally, the share price has already taken a strengthening oil market into account, so new investors will have to watch closely for worthwhile entry points.

SECTOR: **Energy**
BETA COEFFICIENT: **1.35**
10-YEAR COMPOUND EARNINGS PER SHARE GROWTH: **15.5%**
10-YEAR COMPOUND DIVIDENDS PER SHARE GROWTH: **8.0%**

	2004	2005	2006	2007	2008	2009	2010	2011
Revenues (Mil)	11,480	14,309	19,230	23,277	27,163	22,702	27,447	39,540
Net Income (Mil)	1,236	2,022	3,747	5,177	5,397	3,142	3,408	3,954
Earnings per share	1.03	1.67	3.04	4.18	4.42	2.61	2.70	3.51
Dividends per share	0.38	0.41	0.48	0.7	0.81	0.84	0.84	1.00
Cash flow per share	2.16	2.86	4.51	5.94	6.42	4.70	4.55	6.05
Price: high	34.9	51.5	74.8	114.8	112	71.1	84.1	95.6
low	26.3	31.6	47.9	56.3	37.1	35.1	54.7	54.8

Schlumberger Limited
5599 San Felipe, 17th Floor
Houston, TX 77056
(713) 375-3535
Website: *www.slb.com*

AGGRESSIVE GROWTH

Seagate Technology

Ticker symbol: STX (NYSE) ❑ S&P rating: BB+ ❑ Value Line financial strength rating: B++ ❑ Current yield: 3.3% ❑ Dividend raises, past 10 years: 4

Company Profile

About 30 years ago, you could buy a 5 megabyte hard disc drive from a major computer manufacturer like IBM or HP. It was about the size of a washing machine, cost several thousand dollars, and made little grunting noises as it operated that would drive R2D2 into a frenzy.

Today, you can store about 200,000 times the information—1 terabyte—on a hard drive measuring about 2.5 by 3 inches, about 7mm thick, that makes no noise whatsoever, retrieves information almost instantly, and never breaks. These hard drives fit into laptops, netbooks, or even smaller devices, and you scarcely know they're even there. Or they can be assembled into racks and arrays to provide huge storage capability for enterprise servers and data centers, even major hubs in the "cloud."

At the heart of the evolution, as well as a dominant force in producing these devices today, is Seagate Technology—the world's largest producer of computer hard disk drives and related storage media. Seagate offers a range of internal (that is, built-in) and external (packaged standalone) drive devices for enterprise, client

(PC and similar), and noncomputer environments, such as DVRs, video game consoles, and the like.

Computer hard disc drives have become a high-volume commodity. Seagate will ship somewhere around 210 million drives in FY2012. Roughly 70 percent of those are for "client" applications—PCs, notebooks, external storage for PCs, workstations, and similar. About 18 percent are for the noncomputer market—DVRs, games, and so forth—leaving about 12 percent for enterprise storage applications.

So why would we be interested in a commodity business, one that the majority of its volume has traditionally supported a mature, if not declining, PC industry? In an industry known for intense price competition and one where brand has meant less and less as time goes on?

The reasons are fairly simple. First—as has happened with other commodity industries in the past like oil refining, agricultural processing, and others—the industry eventually consolidates from many smaller players into a few larger, more powerful ones. During the PC boom, numerous small, nameless, mostly Asian manufacturers got on the bandwagon, creating oversupply and driving prices down. As prices dropped and profits disappeared, and as OEMs like HP and Dell wanted more reliable sourcing, the weak hands left the market. Now—particularly after Seagate's 2011 purchase of Samsung's hard drive business—two companies pretty much control the market: Seagate and Western Digital.

The second factor driving long-term profitability is the forthcoming change in the computing landscape toward cloud computing. While the cloud may temper client demand somewhat, those cloud server centers will need huge amounts of larger, more profitable storage devices. Innovation will once again drive this business, and Seagate is in a good position to lead this innovation. Seagate is also leading the way in solid-state hard drive (SSHD) technology, which will replace mechanical drives in many applications with simpler, more energy-efficient units.

These two factors, plus the more short-term supply disruption due to the 2011 Thailand floods, have raised average selling prices some 22 percent, from $55 to $67 per unit sold. This drops pretty much straight to the bottom line, and the demand, supply, and inventory situation along with the long-term supply contracts being signed with OEMs suggest that hard drives

will be more of a seller's market in years to come.

Financial Highlights, Fiscal Year 2011

We've given some of the reasons why, now here are some of the numbers, which are on a notable—stunning, really—upward trajectory. After years of up and down performance typical for a commodity producer, Seagate reported, yet again, declining revenues and profits for FY2011. That fiscal year actually ended in June 2011. Revenues dropped 4 percent from FY2010, and profits dropped a far more significant 68 percent on drastically reduced margins and costs related to the Thailand floods, after a strong FY2010, which followed a losing year in FY2009. Typical commodity cycle, right? The floods and further industry consolidation shifted the picture, and since mid-2011 the company has performed superbly, with solid long-term contracts, higher selling prices, and a projected stable margin of 18.5 percent compared to the 14.2 percent of FY2011. The company expects to report revenue in the $15.5 billion range for FY2012, 40 percent ahead of FY2011, and expects to hit a $20 billion annual rate in the following year. The business bump is driving profitability and cash flow, and a lot of that cash is being used to buy back shares—about 10 percent in FY2011 alone, and the company authorized another $2.5 billion for FY2012. Per share earnings are estimated to rise from $1.09 to $6.10 in FY2012 to $8.35 in FY2013. To help convince you that what you're seeing is real, the company also raised the dividend from 15 cents annually in FY2011 to a $1.00 annual rate.

Reasons to Buy

We've already shared most of the "buy side" story—a shift to a suppliers' market with Seagate and Western Digital in charge, larger long-term contracts, higher value-add technology, and an evolving computing and network architecture that should drive more high-value demand. The company seems to be capitalizing on these trends well and is willing to return some of the proceeds to shareholders.

Reasons for Caution

What still remains to be seen is how permanent the change in the supply and demand balance really is. This industry is noted for its "dreaded diamonds"—where scant supply triggers over-ordering, which eventually triggers overproduction—into a softening market; on top of that, the excess orders get cancelled, supply balloons, and prices drop. With only two suppliers and a healthy and broadening technology demand, most don't see this happening this time around. But one must always question the "it's different this time" viewpoint. This will, by nature, be a more volatile play than most on the *100 Best Stocks* list, but we do think that volatility will decline from years past.

SECTOR: **Information Technology**
BETA COEFFICIENT: **2.28**
10-YEAR COMPOUND EARNINGS PER SHARE GROWTH: **19.0%**
10-YEAR COMPOUND DIVIDENDS PER SHARE GROWTH: **NM**

	2004	2005	2006	2007	2008	2009	2010	2011
Revenues (Mil)	6,224	7,553	9,208	11,380	12,708	9,805	11,395	10,971
Net income (Mil)	529	707	840	822	1,415	(231)	1,609	511
Earnings per share	1.06	1.41	1.60	1.40	2.63	(0.47)	3.14	1.09
Dividends per share	.20	.26	.32	.40	.42	.27	—	.18
Cash flow per share	2.07	2.46	2.52	3.13	4.63	1.42	5.08	2.98
Price: high	21.7	21.5	28.1	28.9	25.8	18.5	21.6	18.5
low	10.1	13.8	19.2	20.1	3.7	3	9.8	9

Seagate Technology
P.O. Box 309, Ugland House
Grand Cayman, Cayman Islands
(831) 438-6550
Website: *www.seagate.com*

Sigma-Aldrich Corporation

Ticker symbol: SIAL (NASDAQ) ❑ S&P rating: A+ ❑ Value Line financial strength rating: A ❑ Current yield: 1.1% ❑ Dividend raises, past 10 years: 10

Company Profile

Sigma-Aldrich is a manufacturer and reseller of the world's broadest range of high-value-add chemicals, biochemicals, laboratory equipment, and consumables used in research and large-scale manufacturing activities. The company sells over 167,000 chemicals and manufactures about a third of the items itself, comprising about 60 percent of sales. It also stocks over 45,000 laboratory equipment items. Most of the company's 97,000 customer accounts are research institutions that use basic laboratory essentials such as solvents, reagents, and other supplies. The company also sells chemicals in large quantities to pharmaceutical companies, but no single account provided more than 2 percent of Sigma-Aldrich's total sales. Sigma-Aldrich's business model is to provide its generic and specialized products with expedited (in most cases, next-day) delivery. The company sells in 165 countries and obtains about 65 percent of its sales internationally.

Sigma-Aldrich operates four business units, each catering to a separate class of customer and product. Research Essentials sells common lab chemicals and supplies such as biological buffers, cell culture reagents, biochemicals, solvents, reagents, and other lab kits to customers in all sectors. Research Specialties sells organic chemicals, biochemicals, analytical reagents, chromatography consumables, reference materials, and high-purity products. Research Biotech provides "first to market products" to high-end biotech labs, selling immunochemical, molecular biology, cell signaling, genomic, and neuroscience biochemicals. Fine Chemicals fills large-scale orders of organic chemicals and biochemicals used for production in the pharmaceutical, biotechnology, and high-tech electronics industries.

The company's biochemical and organic chemical products and kits are, used in scientific and genomic research, biotechnology, pharmaceutical development, the diagnosis of disease, and as key components in pharmaceutical and other high-technology manufacturing. Research applications account for about 70 percent of sales. Most of Sigma-Aldrich's customers are life science companies, university and government institutions, hospitals, and general manufacturing industry.

Financial Highlights, Fiscal Year 2011

Sigma-Aldrich is on a mid- to high-single-digits growth trajectory. The 10 percent top-line growth shown in FY2011 is augmented by the acquisition of biopharmaceutical supplier BioReliance, which accounted for about half the year's sales gains and about 5 percent of the reported 19 percent gain in profits. FY2012 will be another year of steady growth, with mid-single-digit gains to about $2.7 billion in sales, with EPS growing to about $4.00 per share.

Reasons to Buy

Sigma has been a very steady performer in a high-value-add segment of the chemical and health-care business. The company is big enough and broad enough to maintain its top-dog position in this lucrative niche, and has a good brand and sterling reputation both in domestic and international markets. For investors, it is a safe, steady grower in a solid business in a solid industry.

Reasons for Caution

The company's growth is tied to the state of research in the chemical and bio/pharmaceutical industries, and, while steady, economic and political factors can create doubts from time to time. Rapid growth in existing businesses isn't likely; when a company depends on acquisitions to grow, that brings some risks with it. While Sigma gets high marks for regular dividend raises, a company in this industry with such a steady business and cash flow could pay out a little more to shareholders.

SECTOR: **Industrials**
BETA COEFFICIENT: **.88**
10-YEAR COMPOUND EARNINGS PER SHARE GROWTH: **13.5%**
10-YEAR COMPOUND DIVIDENDS PER SHARE GROWTH: **14.5%**

	2004	**2005**	**2006**	**2007**	**2008**	**2009**	**2010**	**2011**
Revenues (Mil)	1,409	1,667	1,798	2,039	2,201	2,148	2,271	5,505
Net Income (Mil)	233	258	276	311	342	347	384	457
Earnings per share	1.67	1.88	2.05	2.34	2.65	2.80	3.12	3.72
Dividends per share	0.26	0.38	0.42	0.46	0.52	0.58	0.64	0.72
Cash flow per share	2.23	2.55	2.74	3.09	3.6	3.61	3.95	4.59
Price: high	30.8	33.6	39.7	56.6	63	56.3	67.8	76.2
low	26.6	27.7	31.3	37.4	34.3	31.5	46.5	58.2

Sigma-Aldrich Corporation
3050 Spruce Street
St. Louis, MO 63103
(314) 771-5765
Website: *www.Sigma-Aldrich.com*

GROWTH AND INCOME

J. M. Smucker Company

Ticker symbol: SJM (NYSE) □ S&P rating: NA □ Value Line financial strength rating: A+ □ Current yield: 2.4% □ Dividend raises, past 10 years: 10

Company Profile

"With a name like Smucker's, it has to be good!" This ad jingle says it all about this eastern Ohio-based firm, a leading manufacturer of jams, jellies, and other processed foods for years. Thanks in large part to divestitures from the Procter & Gamble food division and other companies, it has grown itself into a premier player in the packaged food industry.

Smucker manufactures and markets products under its own name, as well as under a number of other household names like Crisco, Folgers, Jif (why not sell the peanut butter if they sell the jelly?), Laura Scudder's, Hungry Jack, Eagle, and Pillsbury, among others. The company also produces and distributes Dunkin' Donuts coffee and produces an assortment of cooking oils, toppings, juices, and baking ingredients. The company has had good success in revitalizing such brands as Folgers and Jif through improved marketing, channel relationships, and better overall focus on the success of these brands. Overall, the company aims to sell the "number one" brand in the various markets it serves. Operations are centered in the United States, Canada, and

Europe, with about 10 percent of sales coming from overseas.

Even as a $5.6 billion a year enterprise, the company still retains the feel of a family business, with brothers Tim and Richard Smucker sharing the CEO responsibilities as chairman and president respectively.

Financial Highlights, Fiscal Year 2011

Smucker continues to produce strong results, and the integration of the coffee and peanut butter businesses is going well. Revenues expanded almost 12 percent during the year, although there were some signs of slowing as price increases, driven by ingredient cost increases, were rejected to a degree by some consumers in favor of generic brands and more frugal consumption habits—a trend we've seen through the industry. Likewise, the ingredient cost increases hurt the bottom line, which was essentially flat from 2010. The company has been buying back some shares since a twofold increase related to the P&G acquisitions in 2008—between 2 and 5 percent of shares outstanding since then—so earnings per share increased about 3 percent during FY2011. Cash flows remained strong, over $7 per share, supporting the dividend, buybacks, and the share price.

Reasons to Buy

This is a very well-managed company with an excellent reputation in its markets. In recent years, it has a proven track record in buying and revitalizing key brands, the most prominent being former Procter & Gamble food brands and International Multifoods brands. We expect this trend to continue. Additionally, the company is trying out new initiatives for packaging and delivering foods, including "jar-free" peanut butter and healthier fare in certain categories, which should add to its competitive lead and to margins. We view the slowdown in revenue and profit growth as temporary; the base for steady growth is well established—and international growth will help—over the long term. Steady and safe: Smucker is the peanut butter and jelly sandwich of the investing landscape.

Reasons for Caution

In the food business, commodity costs can drive short-term performance and should be watched, although strong brands don't fail because of commodity costs. For the long term, however, while the brands are strong, companies like Smucker must always worry about generic competition and the increased buying power of mega-channel players like Walmart. Future earnings could be attenuated somewhat by advertising spend and other costs.

SECTOR: **Consumer Staples**
BETA COEFFICIENT: **0.60**
10-YEAR COMPOUND EARNINGS PER SHARE GROWTH: **13.0%**
10-YEAR COMPOUND DIVIDENDS PER SHARE GROWTH: **9.0%**

		2004	2005	2006	2007	2008	2009	2010	2011E
Revenues (Mil)		2043.9	2154.7	2148.0	2524.8	3757.9	4605	4,826	5,650E
Net Income (Mil)		150.1	155.1	164.6	178.9	321.4	494	566.5	565E
Earnings per share		2.60	2.65	2.89	3.15	3.77	4.15	4.79	4.95E
Dividends per share		1.02	1.08	1.14	1.22	1.31	1.40	1.68	1.88
Cash flow per share		3.52	3.97	3.94	4.42	3.73	5.60	7.06	7/25E
Price:	high	53.5	51.7	50	64.3	56.7	62.7	66.3	80.3
	low	40.8	43.6	37.2	46.6	37.2	34.1	53.3	61.2

The J. M. Smucker Company
One Strawberry Lane
Orrville, OH 44667
(330) 682-3000
Website: *www.smuckers.com*

Southern Company

Ticker symbol: SO (NYSE) ❑ S&P rating: A ❑ Value Line financial strength rating: A ❑ Current yield: 4.3% ❑ Dividend raises, past 10 years: 10

Company Profile

Through its four primary operating subsidiaries Georgia Power, Alabama Power, Mississippi Power, and Gulf Power, Southern Company serves some 4.4 million customers in a large area of Georgia, Alabama, Mississippi, northern Florida, and parts of the Carolinas. The company also wholesales power to other utilities in a wider area.

The revenue mix is balanced: 38 percent residential, 31 percent commercial, 18 percent industrial, and 13 percent other. The service area includes the Atlanta metropolitan area and a large base of modern manufacturing facilities like the many Asian-owned manufacturing facilities, including large auto plants, in the region. The fuel mix is more diverse and less vulnerable to price fluctuations than some, with 55 percent coal, 24 percent oil and gas, 14 percent nuclear, 2 percent hydroelectric, and 5 percent purchased. That said, with its high percentage of coal-fired plants, SO must work to stay up with environmental regulations and pay close attention to transportation costs. Additionally, the company plans to deploy two of 40 worldwide copies of the new and more efficient Westinghouse AP1000 nuclear reactors for its massive Vogtle power station in Georgia, purchased with an $8.3 billion loan guarantee from the U.S. Department of Energy. These plants, which serve as a showcase for the industry, are under construction and on track, and received their operating license from the Nuclear Regulatory Commission in February 2012. They are expected to come on line in 2016.

The company also has engaged in telecommunications services, operating as a regional wireless carrier in Alabama, Georgia, southeastern Mississippi, and northwest Florida and operating some fiberoptic networks collocated on company rights of way. The company also provides consulting services to other utilities.

Financial Highlights, Fiscal Year 2011

A slow return to prosperity in the manufacturing-intensive service area continues. FY2011 revenues advanced 1.2 percent to $17.7 billion, while earnings per share moved ahead a healthier 8.4 percent to $2.57. The majority of the business depends on regular, and typically formulaic rate relief, so the slow, steady pace of revenue and earnings growth will likely continue. FY2012 EPS is now guided in the $2.58–$2.70 range, which, especially with the strong cash flow, adequately supports the dividend and the typical 7-cents-per-year raise. We expect this well-entrenched pattern to continue.

Reasons to Buy

Southern serves a growing, diverse, and economically stable customer base, and operates in a cooperative regulatory environment. The main appeal of this stock lies almost entirely in its dividend, which has been raised slowly but steadily for years. The percent plus or minus return won't put you into a yacht, but if you've already got one, it will certainly help you keep it. The solid history and relationship with local regulatory bodies makes the dividend and its annual raises look

secure for the future. The stock price, too, has been very stable over time with one of our lowest beta coefficients of 0.28.

In today's environment the new nuclear facilities do add some risk, but we feel this is a good economic move for the future.

Reasons for Caution

Electric utilities are always subject to rate and other forms of regulation, and one never knows what will happen in that arena. Additionally, utilities are always vulnerable to capital costs and the attractiveness of alternative fixed-income investments, and are sensitive to rising interest rates, especially if they rise quickly. SO is more exposed to coal prices and rail freight rates for its transport than most, and these have fluctuated a bit more in recent years. Recently, the stock price has hit new highs, adding to risk should interest rates rise; new investors should pick good entry points.

SECTOR: **Utilities**
BETA COEFFICIENT: **0.28**
10-YEAR COMPOUND EARNINGS PER SHARE GROWTH: **2.0%**
10-YEAR COMPOUND DIVIDENDS PER SHARE GROWTH: **2.5%**

	2004	**2005**	**2006**	**2007**	**2008**	**2009**	**2010**	**2011**
Revenues (Mil)	11,902	13,554	14,356	15,353	17,127	15,743	17,456	17,657
Net Income (Mil)	1,589	1,621	1,608	1,782	1,807	1,912	2,040	2,268
Earnings per share	2.06	2.13	2.10	2.28	2.25	2.32	2.37	2.57
Dividends per share	1.42	1.48	1.54	1.6	1.66	1.73	1.80	1.87
Cash flow per share	3.65	4.03	4.01	4.22	4.43	4.25	4.30	4.85
Price: high	34	36.5	37.4	39.3	40.6	33.8	38.6	46.7
low	27.4	31.1	30.5	33.2	29.8	30.8	30.8	35.7

Southern Company
30 Ivan Allen Jr. Boulevard NW
Atlanta, GA 30308
(404) 506-5000
Website: *www.southerncompany.com*

CONSERVATIVE GROWTH

Southwest Airlines, Inc.

Ticker symbol: LUV (NYSE) ❑ S&P rating: BBB- ❑ Value Line financial strength rating: B+ ❑ Current yield: 0.2% ❑ Dividend raises, past 10 years: 0

Company Profile

Southwest Airlines provides passenger air transport, operating almost exclusively in the United States. At the end of FY2010, the company served 73 cities in 38 states with point-to-point, rather than hub-and-spoke, service. The company serves these markets almost exclusively with 548 Boeing 737 aircraft.

The company is one of the largest in the United States and is the world's largest by number of passengers flown, which should give an idea of their business model—low-cost, shorter flights, and maximum passenger loads. Indeed, the average trip is 885 miles and the average fare is $130.27, one of the lowest in the industry. The business model is one of simplicity—no-frills aircraft, no first-class passenger cabin, limited interchange with other carriers, no on-board meals, simple boarding and seat assignment practices, direct sales over the Internet (84 percent of revenues are booked this way), no baggage fees—all designed to provide steady and reliable transportation, with one of the best on-time performances in the industry, and to maximize asset utilization with minimal downtime, crew disruptions, and other upward influences on operating costs. The company has long used secondary airports—such as Providence, Rhode Island, and Manchester, New Hampshire, to serve Boston and the New England area; Allentown, Pennsylvania, and East Islip, New York, to serve the New York/New Jersey area; and Chicago Midway to reduce delays and costs. This strategy has worked well.

Most of what we have just said reflects the business of the original Southwest Airlines. In 2011, the company announced the acquisition of AirTran Holdings, a medium-sized Florida-based discount carrier. With 140 aircraft, again mostly 737s, AirTran brings a similar operational footprint but expands service to mainstream airports, particularly Atlanta, Orlando, the D.C. area, and other destinations in the eastern half of the United States.

We expect the combined carrier to continue the simple, straightforward value proposition that has been a customer favorite for years. Recently Southwest has embarked on a few initiatives to squeeze out some extra revenue without alienating the core passenger group, mostly targeted to business travelers. One is Business Select, which offers priority boarding, priority security, bonus frequent flyer credit, and a free beverage for an upgrade fee. The company also sells "one-off" early boarding for a small fee. Although the company has avoided the cost and complexities of offering international flights, they are expanding partnerships and experimenting with through flights, now to Mexico, and likely soon to other destinations.

Financial Highlights, Fiscal Year 2011

Aided by an economic recovery, diminished capacity with other carriers, and we think a wise decision to eschew the baggage fees charged by most other carriers, Southwest enjoyed a banner year from a revenue perspective, with total revenues up 29 percent, moved along by a record-high load factor of 80.9 percent (that is, the percent of seats filled) and a series of modest price increases, which have stuck this time due to lack of competitive pressure and a public acceptance of rising fuel prices. As the fuel price "thing" is real (fuel costs increased 56 percent from FY2010), operating margins did take a hit, dipping from 14 percent to 9 percent, and earnings dropped from $550 million to $330 million. While we've always been negative on airlines because of

fuel price volatility and inability to control price, it seems that Southwest is setting itself up for a strong performance if fuel prices stabilize, better yet, if they drop. Margins for FY2012 are expected to return to 11 percent, and AirTran will climb on board, indicating earnings, as forecast, at $620 million, or about 80 cents per share. Of course, it depends on what really happens with fuel prices, and for that matter, customer demand.

Reasons to Buy

Those who have read *100 Best Stocks* for the past two years have heard us say we'd never put an airline on the list. Why? Because airlines are extremely competitive with little to no control over prices, and with the major cost components of fuel, airport fees, and union labor, have little to no control over their costs. In other words, the exact opposite of what you'd want to see in a business you own.

However, Southwest has continually proved to be the exception. The value proposition is the envy of the industry, and we're frankly surprised that no one else has been able to emulate it (United and Delta, among others, have tried). The airline realizes that what customers want is no-hassle transportation at best-possible prices—and yes, no bag fees—and has been able to do that better than anyone else for years. Good management, efficient operation, and excellent marketing make it possible. The value proposition and business model have been accepted by a greater portion of the flying public, and now the company is expanding coverage. Larger market share in a larger market—we like that. When that happens, not being able to control price becomes more of a problem for the competition than it is for Southwest. We think this is a stock people have forgotten about after its glory days decades ago.

Reasons for Caution

The acquisition of AirTran and a modest de-simplification of the "Rapid Rewards" frequent flyer program to provide international rewards and sell points to third parties gave us some pause, but both have gone well and the core business model seems intact. The company is less hedged against fuel prices than it was in 2008, so a prolonged fuel and commodity spike could hurt, as could a double-dip recession. We continually fear that some other airline may successfully invade Southwest's niche (which shows no sign of happening at present) or that Southwest forgets what got it this far (also, no sign, although the AirTran acquisition did cause us to grab our armrest a bit tighter). Investors should watch for any sign that Southwest is straying from its successful, industry-leading business model.

SECTOR: **Transportation**
BETA COEFFICIENT: **1.08**
10-YEAR COMPOUND EARNINGS PER SHARE GROWTH: **-3.5%**
10-YEAR COMPOUND DIVIDENDS PER SHARE GROWTH: **3.0%**

		2004	2005	2006	2007	2008	2009	2010	2011
Revenues (Mil)		6,530	7,584	9,086	9,861	11,023	10,350	12,104	15,658
Net income (Mil)		313	469	592	471	294	140	550	330
Earnings per share		0.38	0.57	0.72	0.81	0.40	0.19	0.73	0.42
Dividends per share		0.02	0.02	0.02	0.02	0.02	0.02	0.021	.02
Cash flow per share		0.95	1.18	1.41	1.40	1.41	1.21	1.02	1.35
Price:	high	17.1	17	18.2	17	16.8	11.8	14.3	13.9
	low	12.9	13	14.6	12.1	7.1	4	10.4	7.1

Southwest Airlines, Inc.
P.O. Box 36661
2702 Love Field Drive
Dallas, TX 75235
(214) 904-4000
Website: *www.southwest.com*

St. Jude Medical, Inc.

Ticker symbol: STJ (NYSE) ❑ S&P rating: A ❑ Value Line financial strength rating: A ❑ Current yield: 2.4 percent ❑ Dividend raises, past 10 years: 1

Company Profile

St. Jude Medical, Inc. designs, manufactures, and distributes cardiovascular medical devices for cardiology and cardiovascular surgery, including pacemakers, implantable cardioverter defibrillators (ICDs), vascular closure devices, catheters, and heart valves. The company has four main business segments:

■ The Cardiac Rhythm Management (CRM) portfolio (responsible for about 69 percent of sales) includes products for treating heart rhythm disorders as well as heart failure. Its products include ICDs, pacemaker systems, and a variety of diagnostic and therapeutic electrophysiology catheters. The company also develops catheter technologies for the Cardiology/Vascular Access therapy area. Those products include hemostasis introducers, catheters, and a market-leading vascular closure device. Many products in this portfolio use RF (radio frequency) and other leading technologies for rhythm management, ablation, and other advanced cardiovascular problems.

■ The Cardiovascular segment (20 percent) has been the leader in mechanical heart valve technology for more than 25 years. St. Jude Medical also develops a line of tissue valves, vascular closures, and valve-repair products for various cardiac surgery procedures.

■ The company's Neuromodulation segment (7 percent) produces implantable devices and drug delivery systems for use primarily in chronic pain management and in treatment for certain symptoms of Parkinson's disease and epilepsy.

■ The Atrial Fibrillation business (14 percent) markets a series of products designed to map and treat atrial fibrillation and other heart rhythm problems.

St. Jude Medical products are sold in a highly targeted niche market in more than 100 countries.

Financial Highlights, Fiscal Year 2011

The cardiac care business is by nature really two businesses. The cardiac surgery business is critical and almost completely immune to economic cycles; when you need it you need it. The largest segment, Cardiac Rhythm Management, which essentially makes pacemakers and related products, is a bit more discretionary and vulnerable to expense cuts on the part of patients and care providers and contractions in the inventory pipeline. As a result, CRM segment revenue actually declined in late FY2011. Still, the company managed a 9 percent gain in the top line overall, with a somewhat disappointing 8 percent gain in per-share earnings to $3.26 per share. The company just raised FY2012 guidance to between $3.44 and $3.49 per share. The company expects stronger long-term growth in the three business segments outside of CRM, particularly as a series of new products comes on line. St. Jude has become much more aggressive in producing shareholder returns, paying dividends for the first time in FY2011 at a substantial 86 cents per year rate, and continuing to retire shares. Share counts have dropped 14 percent since 2004, even with various acquisitions.

Reasons to Buy

Both the Neuromodulation and Atrial Fibrillation segments have grown rapidly and seem well positioned for growth in at least the 15 percent range. The techniques employed in neuromodulation are growing quickly in the field as a preferred treatment for long-term pain management. St. Jude (and others) see this as a disruptive technology, potentially replacing drug and physical therapy regimens and offering improved lifestyle at a reduced cost. These two businesses serve as solid growth "kickers," complementing the flatter CRM and cardiovascular segments.

St. Jude has a consistent track record of steady growth and relative earnings and share-price stability. The company easily scores a triple play with double-digit ten-year compounded growth in sales, earnings, and cash flows, and we expect this to continue—and now it pays a reasonable dividend to boot.

Reasons for Caution

While much of St Jude's growth is driven by market fundamentals and organic innovation, some of it is also delivered through acquisition, and some of the recent acquisitions have been expensive. The company could also be slowed by a general belt tightening, the medical device excise tax, and further legislative action and uncertainty in the medical field. Finally, as other surgical and cardiac equipment providers have shown us, errors can be very costly in this business.

SECTOR: **Health Care**
BETA COEFFICIENT: **.77**
10-YEAR COMPOUND EARNINGS PER SHARE GROWTH: **20.0%**
10-YEAR COMPOUND DIVIDENDS PER SHARE GROWTH: **NM**

	2004	2005	2006	2007	2008	2009	2010	2011
Revenues (Mil)	2,294	2,915	3,302	3,779	4,363	4,681	5,165	5,612
Net Income (Mil)	410	394	548	652	807	838	995	1,074
Earnings per share	1.1	1.04	1.47	1.85	2.31	2.43	3.01	3.26
Dividends per share	—	—	—	—	—	—	—	0.84
Cash flow per share	1.38	1.42	2.05	2.48	2.92	3.24	3.70	4.35
Price: high	42.9	52.8	54.8	48.1	48.5	42	43	54.2
low	29.9	34.5	31.2	34.9	25	28.9	34	32.1

St. Jude Medical, Inc.
One Lillehei Plaza
St. Paul, MN 55117
(651) 766-3029
Website: *www.sjm.com*

Starbucks Corporation

Ticker symbol: SBUX (NASDAQ) ❑ S&P rating: A- ❑ Value Line financial strength rating: A+ ❑ Current yield: 1.1% ❑ Dividend raises, past 10 years: 3

Company Profile

Starbucks Corporation, formed in 1985, is the leading retailer, roaster, and brand of specialty coffee in the world. The company sells whole bean coffees through its retailers, its specialty sales group, and super-markets. The company has 7,634 company-owned stores in the Americas and 1,461 in international markets, in addition to 4,776 licensed stores worldwide. Retail coffee shop sales constitute about 91 percent of its revenue. These figures reflect the effects of a modest downsizing campaign in 2010 and 2011, in which a number of poorly performing stores were closed, an unusual but necessary move in the retail industry. Note also that the company does not franchise its stores—all are either company owned or operated by licensees in special venues like airports, college campuses, and other places where access is restricted. The company enters international markets primarily through partnerships but then often buys out its partner, as it did in 2011 to acquire a remaining 30 percent of a China distributorship it did not own. Recently, it signed a major 50-50 joint venture deal to enter India.

Starbucks also has joint ventures with Pepsi-Cola and Dreyer's to develop bottled coffee drinks and coffee-flavored ice creams. All channels outside the company-operated retail stores are collectively known as specialty operations.

The company's retail goal is to become the leading retailer and brand of coffee in each of its target markets through product quality and by providing a unique Starbucks experience, which the company defines as a third place beyond home and work. The "experience" is built upon superior customer service and a clean, well-maintained retail store that reflects the personality of the community in which it operates, thereby building a high degree of customer loyalty.

The company's specialty operations strive to develop the Starbucks brand outside the company-operated retail store environment through a number of channels, with a strategy to reach customers where they work, travel, shop, and dine. The strategy employs various models, including licensing arrangements, foodservice accounts, and other initiatives related to the company's core businesses.

In its licensed retail store operations, the company leverages the expertise of its local partners, and shares Starbucks operating and store-development experience. As part of these arrangements, Starbucks receives license fees and royalties and sells coffee, tea, and related products for resale in licensed locations.

The company just ended a long-term arrangement with Kraft Foods for distribution of its products into grocery chains and similar. Most likely the company plans to approach the grocery retail market more aggressively and with more products inside and outside the coffee space, including single-serving products and other coffee- and non-coffee-based beverages.

Financial Highlights, Fiscal Year 2011

Macroeconomic factors combined with a bloated costs structure to bring a pretty dreary 2009 financial and stock price performance; at one point the stock had dropped 80 percent from its highs set just three years prior. This turned out to be a classic buying opportunity, as revenues were off only 6 percent and earnings 15 percent from previous years. Was the "trendy" Starbucks star finally fading? Was a substantial base of clients about to defect to McDonald's to sip coffee on plastic chairs with vanloads of screaming kids in the background? We never

really thought so, and we were right. Boy, were we right.

We were actually surprised that the recession cut into the business as much as it did, for we've thought Starbucks to be one of those little luxuries people could afford no matter what. That wasn't entirely the case, as same-store comps were dropping 5 or 6 percent during the height of the downturn. Since then, comps have come roaring back, and the company reported FY2010 revenues some $1 billion ahead of the previous year, with earnings of $1.28 well ahead of the previous year's $0.80. The company continued along that path in FY2011, with revenues up another billion to $11.7 billion and earnings per share up another 19 percent to $1.52. Margins increased a healthy 1.4 percent to 23.9 percent and are projected to rise to 24.5 percent due to operational efficiencies and ventures into the single-cup brewing market; these gains are projected to lead to $1.85 per share in FY2012 on $13.2 billion in revenues. All told, the business model is picking up steam.

Reasons to Buy

With founder Howard Shultz back at the helm, the company seems to be hitting on all cylinders again. We never thought the downturn to be permanent; the company's stores continue to be more than coffee shops and really that "third place" where professionals, students, moms, and other prosperous people will meet and dole out a few bucks for quality drinks. The "third place" aura creates a lot of the brand strength and, in our view, represents the company's true strength—well beyond the quality of the coffee itself. The company has a steadily (and profitably) growing presence in Europe, Japan, and China. New single-cup ventures and the new Blonde light-roast products are promising and will broaden appeal to larger customer segments. The once-perceived McDonald's "threat" appears to be largely over, although some of the smaller niche players—Peet's, Caribou, Green Mountain—are also gaining strength. The company is well managed, has an extremely strong brand, has solid financials, and is making an ever-stronger international footprint.

Reasons for Caution

There is continued fear—although little has happened to justify it—that coffee drinkers may learn to get along without the $5 latte and become just $1.50 drippers. As we saw at the end of the 2000 decade, over-saturation is also a risk. But our bigger fear as we write this is that the stock price may be more like the $5 latte (or perhaps a $10 or $15 latte) than the $1.50 tall drip—a 25 percent run up in FY2012 Q1 alone may prove to be too hot to handle. While Starbucks is an exceptional story for the long term, it's worth waiting for an attractive price.

SECTOR: **Restaurant**
BETA COEFFICIENT: **1.2**
10-YEAR COMPOUND EARNINGS PER SHARE GROWTH: **21.0%**
10-YEAR COMPOUND DIVIDENDS PER SHARE GROWTH: **NM**

	2004	2005	2006	2007	2008	2009	2010	2011
Revenues (Mil)	5,294	6,369	7,787	9,412	10,383	9,774	10,707	11,700
Net Income (Mil)	392	495	519	673	525	598	982	1,174
Earnings per share	0.48	0.61	0.73	0.87	0.71	0.8	1.28	1.52
Dividends per share	0	0	0	0	0	.23	0.52	.88
Cash flow per share	0.85	1.09	1.28	1.54	1.46	1.53	2.00	2.28
Price: high	32.1	32.5	40	36.6	21	24.5	31.3	46.5
low	16.5	22.3	28.7	19.9	7.1	21.3	21.3	30.8

Starbucks Corporation
2401 Utah Avenue South
Seattle, WA 98134
(206) 447-1575
Website: *www.starbucks.com*

Stryker Corporation

Ticker symbol: SYK (NYSE) □ S&P rating: A+ □ Value Line financial strength rating: A++ □ Current yield: 1.62% □ Dividend increases, past 10 years: 9

Company Profile

Stryker Corporation was founded in 1941 by Dr. Homer H. Stryker, a leading orthopedic surgeon and the inventor of several orthopedic products. The company now ranks as a dominant $8 billion player in a $12 billion global orthopedics industry. The Reconstructive segment, formerly known as "Orthopedic Implants," comprising about 45 percent of FY2011 sales, has a significant market share in such "spare parts" as artificial hips, prosthetic knees, implant products for other extremities, and trauma products.

The MediSurg unit, about 38 percent of sales, develops, manufactures, and markets worldwide powered and computer-assisted surgical instruments, endoscopic surgical systems, hospital beds, and other patient care and handling equipment.

The Neurotechnology & Spine segment, a large part of which was acquired from Boston Scientific in 2010, accounts for 17 percent of sales and sells spinal reconstructive and surgical equipment, neurovascular surgery, and craniomaxilofacial products.

Stryker's revenue is split roughly 60/40 among implants and equipment and 63/37 domestic and international. The company recently announced a cut of 1,000 jobs, or 5 percent of the workforce, to offset the impact of the Medical Device Excise Tax contained in the new 2010 health-care law. Thus far this has been one of the more noted responses to the new law.

Financial Highlights, Fiscal Year 2011

Stryker reported FY2011 sales of $8.3 billion, which was helped along by acquisitions but still represented a healthy increase over FY2010's $7.3 billion. Per-share earnings were $3.72, 13 percent ahead of FY2010. For FY2012, the company is guiding for a revenue increase in the 4 percent range with earnings up about 10 percent after digesting the restructuring. After a temporary dividend cut in FY2009, Stryker has been actively raising its dividend to almost double its previous 2008 high, and looks to continue to be active on this front and with share repurchases.

Reasons to Buy

Stryker's top line is driven largely by elective surgeries, and 2009 turned out to be the year for delaying whatever medical procedures could be delayed. Many consumers decided to wait and see how the medical care legislation would turn out, and some were simply deciding to hold on to their cash until economic conditions improved. The good news for Stryker is twofold: Medical care reform did not significantly increase the cost to consumers of implant surgeries, and those dodgy hips aren't getting any better and eventually will need to be replaced. In the meantime, the surgical equipment niches are healthy, and the likely comeback in more elective orthopedic surgeries bodes well, particularly with Stryker's dominant market share. We see Stryker as a health-care products company with relatively less entrenched competition than many others. We also see an acceleration in shareholder returns through dividends and buybacks.

Reasons for Caution

Ongoing scrutiny of health-care costs and continued reliance on acquisitions to fuel growth bring risks to the company, but we don't think the risks are excessive. The down cycle in discretionary or elective medical procedures has hung on a little longer than most had expected but should end sooner rather than later.

SECTOR: **Health Care**
BETA COEFFICIENT: **.87**
10-YEAR COMPOUND EARNINGS PER SHARE GROWTH: **21.0%**
10-YEAR COMPOUND DIVIDENDS PER SHARE GROWTH: **28.5%**

	2004	2005	2006	2007	2008	2009	2010	2011
Revenues (Mil)	4,262	4,872	5,406	6,001	6,718	6,723	7,320	8,307
Net Income (Mil)	586	644	778	1,017	1,148	1,107	1,330	1,448
Earnings per share	1.43	1.57	1.89	2.44	2.78	2.77	3.30	3.72
Dividends per share	0.09	0.11	0.11	0.22	0.33	0.50	0.63	.72
Cash flow per share	2.08	2.49	2.85	3.33	3.87	3.75	4.40	5.05
Price: high	57.7	56.3	55.9	76.9	74.9	52.7	59.7	65.2
low	40.3	39.7	39.8	54.9	35.4	30.8	42.7	43.7

Stryker Corporation
P.O. Box 4085
Kalamazoo, MI 49003–4085
(616) 385-2600
Website: *www.strykercorp.com*

Suburban Propane Partners, L.P.

Ticker symbol: SPH (NYSE) ❑ S&P rating: BB ❑ Value Line financial strength rating: B+ ❑ Current yield: 7.8% ❑ Dividend raises, past 10 years: 10

Company Profile

You probably know this company best for its propane distribution business and the white sausage-shaped tanks dotting the landscape, especially in rural areas, and for the trucks serving them. Suburban Propane Partners, L.P., through its subsidiaries, engages in the retail marketing and distribution of propane, fuel oil, and refined fuels, and to a lesser extent, in the marketing of natural gas and electricity in the United States.

At about 70 percent of the business, the Propane segment is the largest segment, and engages in the retail distribution of propane to residential, commercial, industrial, and agricultural customers, as well as wholesale distribution to large industrial end users. The Fuel Oil and Refined Fuels segment engages in the retail distribution of fuel oil, diesel, kerosene, and gasoline to residential and commercial customers for use primarily as a source of heat in homes and buildings, primarily in the East, while the Natural Gas and Electricity segment markets those commodities to residential and commercial customers in the deregulated energy markets of New York and Pennsylvania.

Suburban Propane Partners, L.P. is also involved in selling and servicing heating, ventilation, and air conditioning (HVAC) units that consume its fuels. As of September 2011, the company served approximately 750,000 residential, commercial, industrial, and agricultural customers through approximately 300 locations in 30 states, concentrated in the East and West coast regions of the United States, including Alaska.

Financial Highlights, Fiscal Year 2011

Call it bad luck if you want, but while Suburban is in an inherently steady business, the past few years have brought on an unusually negative environment for the company. Suburban emerged from the recession, which dampened demand and particularly demand from industrial customers, only to find itself operating against unusually warm winters, record-low natural gas prices, and continued low new housing starts. Add to that a rise in input costs (a lot, but not all, propane is a by-product of oil refining) and you get a fairly perfect storm of negative events. As a result, while higher prices did support a modest 4.7 percent revenue growth, FY2011 net profits were flat, and more worrisome, net earnings per unit (SPH is a master limited partnership, not a common stock per se; the differences are probably not important to most investors) of $3.24 fell short of the annual distribution. Worse yet, warm 2012 winter weather brought a weak first quarter, and current projections call for cash flow (not net earnings) only slightly in excess of the distribution. Correspondingly, the company dipped into cash reserves to make the current distribution; those reserves dropped from $149 million to $89 million by the end of FY2011. The bottom line is—if the fundamentals don't improve, the company will probably be forced to cut the distribution.

Reasons to Buy

The main draw with companies like Suburban Propane is the high, steady, and often growing dividend. The current yield of 7.8 percent, with relatively little volatility in what is usually a fairly steady business, is salivating in an environment where a 2 to 4 percent yield is considered attractive. The company is willing to pay out almost all of its earnings in a favorable environment, and is willing to dip into assets to sustain the payout when necessary, indicating the true priority of owner interests.

The question, of course, is whether the cash payout is sustainable. We think the core business model is still relatively safe, and any upside (lower temperatures, higher natural gas prices) should stabilize the cash flow situation. Moreover, even if the company cuts the distribution, say by a third, it would still be paying about $2.30 a unit, which would be a healthy 5.2 percent yield at today's unit price. So while there is risk, we don't think the downside risk is too severe; moreover, current unit prices, which take today's scenario into account, may represent a buying opportunity, and a return to a more favorable climate may even provide a small opportunity for price appreciation. It all depends on how you feel about the long-term stability of the core business. Obviously, we think it's a "businessperson's risk" that's worth taking in the interest of achieving above-market yields from a company with utility-like fundamentals.

Reasons for Caution

The concern, of course, is whether warm weather is here to stay (we're not so sure) and whether natural gas prices will continue to stay so low (we don't think so). One structural concern we do have is the softness in the building industry, particularly in building large homes (McMansions) in outlying areas (exurbs). Apparently the company was getting some new business from the trend of building big outside of traditional gas utility service areas; propane became the logical heating choice. For many reasons, we doubt if large-scale exurban construction will resume anytime soon, If the current negative environment continues, we're concerned, of course, about how long Suburban can maintain its business model and its payout. We're also concerned about the balance sheet and the recent cash drawdown. That all said, even after a possible large cut in the payout, the company still appears to be a worthwhile candidate.

SECTOR: Utilities
BETA COEFFICIENT: 0.40
10-YEAR COMPOUND EARNINGS PER SHARE GROWTH: 9.5%
10-YEAR COMPOUND DIVIDENDS PER SHARE GROWTH: 5.0%

		2004	2005	2006	2007	2008	2009	2010	2011
Revenues (Mil)		1,307.3	1,620.2	1,661.6	1,439.6	1,574.2	1,143.2	1,136.7	1,191
Net Income (Mil)		28.9	(9.1)	90.7	123.3	111.2	165.2	115.2	115
Earnings per share		.96	(.29)	2.84	3.79	3.39	4.99	3.26	3.24
Dividends per share		2.41	2.45	2.50	2.69	3.14	3.28	3.37	3.41
Cash flow per share		2.17	.92	4.09	4.66	4.26	5.55	4.13	4.25
Price:	high	35.7	37.4	39.2	49.6	42.6	47.7	57.2	59.0
	Low	27.6	23.5	26	35.1	20.4	31	39.2	40.3

Suburban Propane Partners, L.P.
240 Route 10 West
Whippany, NJ 07981
(973) 887-5300
Website: *www.suburbanpropane.com*

CONSERVATIVE GROWTH

Sysco Corporation

Ticker symbol: SYY (NYSE) ❑ S&P rating: A+ ❑ Value Line financial strength rating: A++ ❑ Current yield: 3.6% ❑ Dividend raises, past 10 years: 10

Company Profile

Sysco is the leading marketer and distributor of food, food products, and related equipment and supplies to the foodservice industry. The company distributes fresh and frozen meats, prepared entrées, vegetables, canned and dried foods, dairy products, beverages, and produce, as well as paper products, restaurant equipment and supplies, and cleaning supplies. The company might be familiar for its "institutional" number-ten-sized cans of food found in many high-volume kitchens, but the product line and customer base is much larger, including many specialty and chain restaurants, lodges, hotels, hospitals, schools, and other distribution centers across the country. If you eat out at all, you've most likely consumed Sysco-distributed products.

Sysco was founded in 1969 with the goal of becoming a national foodservice network. By 1977, the company had become the largest foodservice supplier in North America, a position they have retained for more than 30 years. They have over 400,000 customers and conduct business in more than 100 countries.

Sysco operates 186 distribution facilities across the United States, Canada, and Ireland and distributes 1.3 billion cases of food annually. Their 90 Broadline facilities supply independent and chain restaurants and other food preparation facilities with a wide variety of food and nonfood products. They have 14 hotel supply locations, 31 specialty produce facilities, 21 SYGMA distribution centers (specialized, high-volume centers supplying to chain restaurants), 17 custom-cutting meat locations, and two distributors specializing in the niche Asian foodservice market.

The company also supplies the hotel industry with guest amenities, equipment, housekeeping supplies, room accessories, and textiles.

Most people are unaware of just how many times during the day they cross paths with Sysco's products and services. Sysco's distribution facilities provide over 400,000 different food and related products (including 40,000 with Sysco brands) to over 400,000 restaurants, hotels, schools, hospitals, retirement homes, hotels, and other locations where food is prepared.

Sysco is by far the largest company in the foodservice distribution industry. The company estimates that it serves 17.5 percent of a $220 billion market, and is more than twice the size of the nearest competitor.

Financial Highlights, Fiscal Year 2011

The restaurant industry is climbing out of its recessionary dip, and that led to a record $39.7 billion in FY2011 sales, 6 percent ahead of FY2010. Some of this gain, it should be noted, owes to food price inflation, not volumes. That inflation, plus fuel price increases, also affected costs, resulting in a near flat earnings performance. For FY2012, continued improvements in the restaurant and hospitality climate, expense controls, and absorption of commodity increases all work together toward a forecasted 4 percent revenue gain, and a 9 percent gain in earnings, which should lead to a continuation of the roughly 5 to 10 percent annual increase in the dividend.

Reasons to Buy

Sysco continues to be a dominant player in a niche that won't go away anytime soon. While near-term commodity prices may add some cost pressure, the value of the franchise and near-term sales should

remain unchanged; we think the worst is over for the recession and that any such recurrence in the future should only temporarily slow the business.

Sysco keeps margins high by selling products under its own label, a strategy it began a year after its founding. Its private-label business carries an estimated 24 percent gross margin, or 10 percent more than it earns on national brands. This is a very healthy figure in the food industry.

Sysco's recent investments in technology continue to bear fruit, and we like to see innovation in an industry not known for innovation. Improvements in routing and inventory management have allowed the company to increase its shipment frequency by 10 percent with 4 percent fewer people, all while using 10 percent less fuel. Shipments per man-hour are up 15 percent, cases per trip are up 2 percent, and errors are down 3 percent, according to the company.

The company dominates a highly fragmented industry and could increase that domination through acquisition; it has the financial strength to do so. In sum, this is a steady and safe company with a healthy payout to customers and has experienced some price dips, giving good buying opportunities.

Reasons for Caution

Although the trend is slowing, the recession got many folks away from the habit of eating out, and restaurants and hotels are buying less food and fewer supplies and equipment. Many restaurants disappeared altogether, although we expect the better times to reverse that trend to a degree. Investors seeking rapid growth might want to look somewhere outside of this steady and rather unsexy business.

SECTOR: **Consumer Staples**
BETA COEFFICIENT: **.71**
10-YEAR COMPOUND EARNINGS PER SHARE GROWTH: **10.5%**
10-YEAR COMPOUND DIVIDENDS PER SHARE GROWTH: **15.5%**

	2004	2005	2006	2007	2008	2009	2010	2011
Revenues (Mil)	29,335	30,282	32,628	35,042	37,522	36,853	37,243	39,323
Net Income (Mil)	907	961	855	1,001	1,106	1,056	1,181	1,153
Earnings per share	1.37	1.47	1.35	1.6	1.81	1.77	1.99	1.96
Dividends per share	0.48	0.58	0.66	0.72	0.82	0.93	0.99	1.03
Cash flow per share	1.87	2.03	1.92	2.23	2.46	2.44	2.67	2.62
Price: high	41.3	38.4	37	36.7	35	29.5	32.6	32.6
low	29.5	30	26.5	29.9	20.7	19.4	27	25.1

Sysco Corporation
1390 Enclave Parkway
Houston, TX 77077–2099
(281) 584-1458
Website: *www.sysco.com*

Target Corporation

Ticker symbol: TGT (NYSE) ❑ S&P rating: A+ ❑ Value Line financial strength rating: A ❑ Current yield: 2.1 percent ❑ Dividend raises, past 10 years: 10

Company Profile

Target is the nation's second-largest general merchandise retailer, and specializes in general merchandise at a discount in a large-store format. The company now operates 1,768 stores in 49 states, including 251 "Super Targets," which also carry a broad line of groceries. The greatest concentration of Target stores is in California (14 percent), Texas (9 percent), and Florida (7 percent), with a combined total of about 30 percent of the stores. There is another concentration in the upper Midwest. With the sale of Marshall Field and Mervyn's in 2004, the company has focused completely on discount retail in store locations and on the Internet.

Target positions itself against its main competitor, Walmart, as a more upscale and trend-conscious "cheap chic" alternative. The typical Target customer has a higher level of disposable income, which the company courts by offering brand-name merchandise in addition to a series of largely successful house brands like Michael Graves and Archer Farms. The company's revenues come from retail sales and credit card operations. Target is one of the few retailers that still finances its in-house credit operations. Although in-house credit operations have given the company some problems in tougher times, bad debt write-offs have dropped sharply, and the credit card unit began contributing to earnings once again.

Target is in the midst of a 125-store expansion into Canada, leveraging the acquisition of a series of store sites there. The company is also investing domestically in its food lines, which now account for 17 percent of total sales.

Financial Highlights, Fiscal Year 2011

Target took some lumps during the recession, but the strong value proposition of quality for less resonated well with most customers. Revenues logged about a 4 percent gain, with earnings per share rising about 7 percent to $4.15 per share, despite small write-offs from the credit side. FY2012 is off to a good start, with guidance raised about 7 percent early in the year. The company expects earnings in the $4.55–$4.75 range before charges mostly related to the Canada startup. Cash flows continue strong, at about $7.50 per share for FY2011.

Reasons to Buy

Helped along by a reversal in fortunes in the credit business, Target recovered relatively quickly from the downturn. Moreover, Target has some of the highest customer satisfaction numbers in the industry. The company continues to take share away from specialty retailers in home lines, clothing, children's items, and other areas. People like the Target brand and associate it with quality and good taste at a reasonable price, and more recently have come to make regular and frequent visits to the store because of the grocery department.

Target is also introducing a new store format called PFresh, which is very much like their Super Target in terms of items, but in a smaller format. They will carry 90 percent of the grocery items that a Super Target carries, but the space devoted to the grocery area will be about 40 percent smaller. Grocery traffic may not require the amount of space that has been allocated in the Super Targets, and a "deli" atmosphere may in fact be more conducive to impulse sales.

Better economic conditions should improve Target's market share. Trend data indicates that Target performs better than its competitors during periods of economic growth. Share counts have dropped from 911 million in 2003 to about 670 million recently. Further, the company recently authorized a $5 billion share buyback program. The company also "eyes" a $3 dividend by 2017, suggesting a 22 percent dividend growth rate between now and then.

Reasons for Caution

Target is up against some very tough competitors in Walmart, Costco, and others. Also, these two competitors are growing their international presence, while Target, other than Canada, has none and has no plans for growth outside the United States. Target may also experience some of the challenges of U.S. companies expanding into Canada; the Canadian government just announced a "cultural review" to "assure a minimum level of Canadian content." The company will likely survive this review, but it may slow up the expansion and add cost. We also see some risk in the grocery business, as groceries are very low margin and the company hasn't really figured out how to make the grocery offering complete with meats and fresh produce. Gross margins have dipped slightly recently, probably a result of the larger grocery footprint.

SECTOR: **Retail**
BETA COEFFICIENT: **0.89**
10-YEAR COMPOUND EARNINGS PER SHARE GROWTH: **10.5%**
10-YEAR COMPOUND DIVIDENDS PER SHARE GROWTH: **13.5%**

	2004	2005	2006	2007	2008	2009	2010	2011
Revenues (Mil)	46,839	52,620	59,490	63,367	64,948	63,435	67,390	69,800
Net Income (Mil)	1,885	2,408	2,787	2,849	2,214	2,488	2,830	2,835
Earnings per share	2.07	2.71	3.21	3.33	2.86	3.3	3.88	4.15
Dividends per share	0.3	0.38	0.42	0.56	0.6	0.66	0.84	1.10
Cash flow per share	3.53	4.37	4.98	5.51	5.37	5.9	6.98	7.40
Price: high	54.1	60	60.3	70.8	59.6	51.8	60.7	61
low	36.6	45.6	44.7	48.8	25.6	25	46.2	45.3

Target Corporation
1000 Nicollet Mall
Minneapolis, MN 55403
(612) 370-6735
Website: *www.target.com*

Teva Pharmaceutical Industries, Ltd.

Ticker symbol: TEVA (NASDAQ) □ S&P rating: A- □ Value Line financial strength rating: A □ Current yield: 2.1% □ Dividend raises, past 10 years: 10

Company Profile

Teva was founded in Jerusalem in 1901 as Salomon, Levin and Elstein, Ltd., a small wholesale drug business that imported medicines, loaded them onto the backs of camels and donkeys, and distributed them to customers throughout the area. Teva is now among the top 15 pharmaceutical companies in the world and is the largest generic pharmaceutical company.

The company develops, manufactures, and markets generic and proprietary pharmaceuticals and active pharmaceutical ingredients.

Teva's generic portfolio is extensive—in the United States. Teva USA markets nearly 400 generic pharmaceuticals in 1,300 dosage levels. Its innovative drug line is far smaller, but includes some widely prescribed and very profitable medications, including Copaxone (for the treatment of multiple sclerosis) and Azilect (for early- and late-stage Parkinson's disease). The company also makes and markets a line of respiratory products for asthma, allergic rhinitis, and chronic obstructive pulmonary disease, and another line of women's health products including traditional and emergency oral contraceptives. Finally, the company also makes biopharmaceutical products including white blood cell stimulating factors for oncology and human growth hormone for children with growth hormone deficiency, among others.

The company has more than 60 manufacturing and marketing facilities worldwide, with the bulk of its operations located in Europe, the United States, and Israel. More than 56 percent of Teva's sales are in North America and 85 percent in North America and Western Europe combined. The company is headquartered in Israel and shares trade as American Depository Receipts in the United States.

During the past two years and especially of late, the company has gone through a bit of a strategic shift to put more emphasis on proprietary branded, as opposed to generic, medicines. The company apparently felt too much competition in the generic segment. They made a few smaller acquisitions, then a big one, acquiring Cephalon in late 2011 for $6.8 billion, a maker of cancer, sleep disorder, and other drugs. A new CEO and a greater emphasis on developing markets rounds out the shift.

Financial Highlights, Fiscal Year 2011

Competition and a slowdown in new generic offerings led to a softening growth rate, which had been on a steady 20 percent trajectory for years. Revenues grew 14 percent to $18.3 billion, while earnings growth slowed considerably into the 7 percent range. The company has raised the low end of its guidance to the $4.70–$4.80 range for FY2012, and still projects a resumption of a 19 percent top-line growth and about 11 percent on the bottom line.

Reasons to Buy

Teva is still a major player in the generic industry and will expand its offerings in the proprietary drug market. The company has the R&D and market muscle to make a good go with a mixed product line, and we expect that it will return to something close to previous growth rates. Teva was once the purest generics play; now we would suggest Perrigo, another *100 Best* stock,

for dominance in that market. The company, which had been adding to share counts to make acquisitions, has now announced a $3 billion share repurchase program, and continues to raise its dividend in attractive increments.

Last year we noted that the dominance of the MS drug Copaxone was on the wane, and that has indeed become the case as orally administered drugs have entered the market. In the bigger picture, we were surprised at the strategic shift and the imperatives that brought it on, and recognize that such shifts can be disruptive and not always successful, especially as the company puts more resources into an already crowded proprietary drug market and does a lot of that through a major acquisition. Still, this company has proven to be well managed and directed toward relatively strong growth opportunities in this market, and the recent disruptions—and the possible entering of a more mature phase—may provide a buying opportunity and a chance to capitalize on more income for more patient investors.

SECTOR: **Health Care**
BETA COEFFICIENT: **.30**
5-YEAR COMPOUND EARNINGS PER SHARE GROWTH: **29.0%**
5-YEAR COMPOUND DIVIDENDS PER SHARE GROWTH: **26.0%**

		2004	2005	2006	2007	2008	2009	2010	2011
Revenues (Mil)		4,799	5,250	8,400	9,408	11,085	13,899	16,121	18,350
Net Income (Mil)		691	1,072	1,867	1,952	2,374	3,029	4,134	4,415
Earnings per share		1.42	1.59	2.3	2.38	2.86	3.37	4.54	4.95
Dividends per share		0.16	0.27	0.3	0.39	0.49	0.60	0.74	.89
Cash flow per share		1.94	2.13	3.03	3.22	3.37	4.45	5.70	6.10
Price:	high	34.7	45.9	44.7	47.1	50	56.9	64.9	57.1
	low	22.8	26.8	29.2	30.8	35.9	41.1	47	35

Teva Pharmaceutical Industries, Ltd.
5 Basel Street
P.O. Box 3190
Petach Tikva
Israel 49131
(215) 591-8912
Website: ***www.tevapharm.com***

AGGRESSIVE GROWTH

NEW
FOR 2013

Tiffany & Co.

Ticker symbol: TIF (NYSE) ⸱ S&P rating: not rated ⸱ Value Line financial strength rating:
A ⸱ Current yield: 1.7% ⸱ Dividend raises, past 10 years: 10

Company Profile

As a variant on the old cliché goes, "If you have to ask who they are, you can't afford them." But when it comes to investing, it's perfectly okay to ask, and we're here to provide the answer, so here goes . . .

Tiffany is a jeweler and specialty retailer principally offering jewelry (accounting for 91 percent of FY2011 sales) but also timepieces, sterling silver goods (e.g., silver spoons), china, crystal, fragrances, stationery, leather goods, and other personal items. The design of both product and packaging is distinctive, with a historic tradition and elegant simplicity that sets it apart. Ditto for the stores and catalog. Tiffany is probably the world's most recognized general jewelry brand (aside from Rolex and similar brands in the watch business) and the company has a sizeable presence in other countries.

In fact, some 50 percent of sales are from outside the Americas. Just to give some figures, there are 87 stores in the United States, seven in Mexico, five in Canada, and three in Brazil. Notably, the multistory flagship store on Fifth Avenue in New York City accounts for about 10 percent of Tiffany's business alone, albeit much of it from visiting foreign tourists craving the experience (and weak dollar).

Now, moving to Asia, which accounts for 21 percent of sales, there are 16 stores in China, 14 in Korea, 7 in Taiwan, 5 in Australia, 4 in Singapore, 2 in Macau, and 2 in Malaysia. Oh, yes—what about Japan? Japan is so large it is accounted for as a separate region, with 17 percent of the business and 51 stores. Do the Japanese appreciate quality and elegant simplicity? You bet!

Finally, we come to Europe, which represents 12 percent of sales with 10 stores in the UK, 6 in Germany, 3 in France, 2 in Spain, 2 in Switzerland, and 1 each in 4 other countries. Beyond Europe, the company also does business in the Middle East, Russia, and elsewhere through distributors.

In addition to retailing a broad line of luxury goods, Tiffany also designs and manufactures much of its branded jewelry. The Tiffany cachet raises margins on these items without significantly diluting brand strength, while at the same time driving store visits higher.

Clearly, the company is a bastion for wealthy consumers, but it also works hard to attract so-called "aspirational" consumers seeking moderately priced, say, $100–$300, items with that Tiffany cachet and experience. Internationally, and particularly in Asia, Tiffany appeals to the very wealthy, and the average selling price of items in Asia runs 8 to 10 times the average price of items sold in the Americas.

Financial Highlights, Fiscal Year 2011

The stronger economy and a return to relatively freer spending habits by the rich spurred an 18 percent sales gain to $3.6 billion, while earnings rose 23 percent to $3.60 per share excluding nonrecurring items. While the 18 percent sales growth translates to only 15 percent without currency translation, the company did report a very healthy 13 percent gain in same-store sales. For FY2012, the company plans to open 24 stores, a greater than 10 percent increase in the store footprint, in a deliberate strategy to increase physical presence and strengthen the brand. Even with the new stores, the company expects sales growth to moderate to somewhere in the 10 percent range, and has given an EPS forecast in the range of $3.95–$4.05, the midpoint of which would represent an 11 percent rise. Beyond FY2012, the company has repeated its objectives of achieving 10 to 20 percent sales growth annually with earnings growth "in the mid teens."

Reasons to Buy

Tiffany is a classic branding story, where brand image supports the product and the product supports the brand image. People buy Tiffany because it is Tiffany, and because they are attracted to the distinctive cachet and elegant simplicity. While the company is working to offer more moderately priced items for the "aspirational" market, we don't expect it to lower quality and damage the brand prestige—although this is always a risk. We are very strong on the company's international footprint and the ability to grow sales and leverage the brand, particularly in Asia. The company has been raising its dividend steadily and at a growing rate.

Reasons for Caution

Tiffany makes things out of gold and silver, and the escalating price of these commodities isn't news. However, many, particularly in Asia, buy jewelry because it is made of gold and silver, and thus is a store of value. So here is one rare case where rising commodity prices can increase demand, and in any case the company is able to pass on cost increases to an understanding clientele. That said, rising prices may leave aspirational customers at the door. Naturally, the company is somewhat exposed to economic cycles, particularly economic circumstances that affect the rich, as the last recession clearly did. We also do see some risk that the company may go too far catering to the aspirational base, only to lower product quality and put a dent in its cachet, as has happened to Mercedes and other high-end brands in the past.

SECTOR: **Retail**
BETA COEFFICIENT: **1.81**
10-YEAR COMPOUND EARNINGS PER SHARE GROWTH: **10.0%**
10-YEAR COMPOUND DIVIDENDS PER SHARE GROWTH: **20.5%**

	2004	2005	2006	2007	2008	2009	2010	2011
Revenues (Mil)	2,204	2,395	2,648	2,938	2,860	2,709	3,085	3,600
Net income (Mil)	210	254	254	322	294	266	378	459
Earnings per share	1.42	1.75	1.60	2.33	2.33	2.12	2.93	3.60
Dividends per share	0.23	0.30	0.38	0.52	0.66	0.68	0.95	1.12
Cash flow per share	2.20	2.56	2.74	3.50	3.44	3.21	4.13	4.85
Price: high	45.2	43.6	41.3	57.3	50	44.5	65.8	84.5
low	27	28.6	29.6	38.2	18.8	16.7	35.6	54.6

Tiffany & Co.
727 Fifth Ave.
New York, NY 10022
(212) 755-8000
Website: *www.tiffany.com*

CONSERVATIVE GROWTH

NEW FOR 2013

Time Warner, Inc.

Ticker symbol: TWX (NYSE) ❑ S&P rating: BBB ❑ Value Line financial strength rating: B++ ❑ Current yield: 2.9% ❑ Dividend raises, past 10 years: 6

Company Profile

We'd be willing to bet that all of you, our readers, have made a big, glaring goof at one time during your lives. A mistake that caused pain, grief, embarrassment, and startled looks from the people around you. Anything from a bad investment to a drinking binge to a big traffic ticket. It took a while to recover. But you did, you learned from the mistake, and moved on to do much bigger, better things and to laugh about it in the end. It's a common human experience.

Time Warner proved itself to be quite human in the late 1990s, too. It tried to buy the Internet. It bought Netscape, then followed this gaffe by buying America Online (AOL) in what at the time amounted to David buying Goliath. It changed its name to "AOL Time Warner" and proceeded to destroy one of history's largest chunks of shareholder value. Finally, in 2009, Time Warner got rid of AOL (and spun off Time Warner Cable too) and cleaned house with an extraordinary (for our *100 Best* list, anyway) one-for-three reverse split—and went back to being a premier media and content company. To heck with

trying to own the last mile of its distribution. Leave that headache for someone else.

So now we have a focused $29 billion media giant (okay, so that's down from $47 billion in AOL and cable days) aimed squarely at producing and distributing media in both traditional and innovative ways. The company operates in three main segments:

- Film and TV Entertainment (44 percent of revenues) including Warner Bros. Pictures and New Line Cinema. Warner Bros produces about 22 feature films a year and distributes hundreds of others;
- Networks (47 percent), which feeds a variety of content to an assortment of media devices and includes such brands as HBO, Cinemax, TNT, Turner Classic, CNN, Cartoon Network, Boomerang, and others;
- Publishing (13 percent) which includes legacy magazine businesses such as *Time*, *Sports Illustrated*, *People*, and others, 21 magazines in the United States and 70 magazines internationally in all.

The details of these businesses and sub-businesses expands far further than described here; suffice it to say TWX has a huge presence in the creation and distribution of many forms of media. The company is quite dedicated to innovation, and the use of innovations to get more content to more people in more places at more times than ever before. A new "TV Everywhere" initiative is one example. The company lists its innovations right behind its home page (tabs are "Our Content," "Our Company," and "Our Innovations"), speaking to the importance of finding new ways to do things. Platforms like HBO GO are designed to deliver content to tablets and smartphones as well as traditional devices. At the end of 2011, the company announced that all of its magazine properties are available as apps for Apple and Android-based platforms.

Financial Highlights, Fiscal Year 2011

Time Warner is still gaining its feet after the AOL debacle, and is right-sizing its operations to maximize efficiency. Sales gains have been moderate, in fact about 8 percent in FY2011, with net profits up a decent 12 percent during the same period. The real "What's up, Doc?" appears in the "common shares outstanding" line, which declined via buybacks from 1.099 billion to 974

million—10 percent—in FY2011 alone (the figure was about 1.5 billion in 2005). Further, the company just authorized another $4 billion repurchase, and this comes on top of an almost 3 percent dividend, which was also hiked 10 percent in early FY2012. FY2012 guidance is for low double-digit growth in sales and earnings, to $3.12–$3.19 per share.

Reasons to Buy

Time Warner has taken its medicine and we think it is unlikely to repeat past mistakes. As the Internet universe expands, and as people have smart devices capable of receiving anything anywhere anytime, we think the demand for content will only go up, and TWX has some of the great properties and brands, such as CNN, HBO, and TBS, to leverage as platforms to develop and deliver this content. The stock price has been flat in the wake of the hard reset, apparently waiting to see what's next; we think it could start to march northward once it proves its focus and some of the new delivery methods; that is, once content really becomes ubiquitous and people start to use it ubiquitously. We love the idea of a real-time tablet version of *Sports Illustrated* or *People*, for instance. In the meantime, a 3 percent dividend pays well to await this inflection.

Reasons for Caution

The content business is very competitive, and tastes change frequently. You never know what some of the big moguls, like Rupert Murdoch of News Corp, or Sumner Redstone of Viacom will come up with next. TWX is aimed at an older crowd than the edgier Viacom, with its Comedy Central, MTV, and Nickelodeon brands. The magazine businesses are losing money and need to find their new groove. Finally, there's good reason to question whether "TV Everywhere" is what people really want. And of course, we would frown on any other big acquisitions, especially outside the core industry.

SECTOR: **Entertainment**
BETA COEFFICIENT: **1.11**
10-YEAR COMPOUND EARNINGS PER SHARE GROWTH: **26.0%**
10-YEAR COMPOUND DIVIDENDS PER SHARE GROWTH: **NM**

	2004	2005	2006	2007	2008	2009	2010	2011
Revenues (Mil)	42,089	43,652	44,224	46,482	46,894	25,785	26,888	28,940
Net income (Mil)	3,209	2,905	5,114	4,051	3,574	2,079	2,578	2,886
Earnings per share	2.04	1.86	3.63	2.97	2.88	1.74	2.25	2.71
Dividends per share	—	0.30	.063	0.71	0.75	0.75	0.85	0.94
Cash flow per share	6.23	4.12	6.75	7.07	6.83	2.66	3.20	3.91
Price: high	59.7	58.9	66.8	69.5	50.7	33.5	34.1	38.6
low	46.2	45.3	47.1	45.5	21	17.8	26.4	27.6

Time Warner Inc.
One Time Warner Center
New York, NY 10019
(212) 484-6000
Website: *www.timewarner.com*

Total S.A. (ADRs)

Ticker symbol: TOT (NYSE) ❑ S&P rating: AA- ❑ Value Line financial strength rating: A++ ❑ Current yield: 6.2% ❑ Dividend raises, past 10 years: 5

Company Profile

Total S.A. (S.A. is short for Société Anonyme, which is the French equivalent of "incorporated") is the fifth-largest publicly traded oil and gas company in the world. Headquartered in France and primarily traded on the French CAC stock exchange, the company has operations in more than 130 countries. Total is vertically integrated with upstream operations engaged in oil and gas exploration and downstream operations engaged in refining and distribution of petroleum products; the company also has a chemicals subsidiary.

Upstream activities are geographically well diversified, with exploration occurring in 40 countries and production occurring in 30 of them. Many of the E&P projects are done through partnerships to spread risk. The largest production regions are (in production-volume sequence) in the North Sea, North Africa, West Africa, and the Middle East, with smaller operations in Southeast Asia and North and South America. Liquids account for about 61 percent of production, while natural gas is 39 percent. The company is a leader in the emerging

liquefied natural gas (LNG) market for export. The company has had good results in the exploration and production side, somewhat better than the industry, with production up 6 percent, led by a 19 percent increase in gas output.

Downstream operations are also worldwide and centered in Europe. Operations include interests in 25 refineries worldwide, with 11 refineries and 85 percent of total refining capacity in Europe. Total also operates 16,425 service stations, again weighted toward Europe and North Africa. The downstream presence is also growing in Asia/Pacific (including China), Latin America, and the Caribbean. The company is currently building a new major refinery in Saudi Arabia to come on line in 2013.

The company has made numerous small acquisitions in recent months. Of note is the 2011 purchase of a 60 percent interest in solar equipment maker SunPower. The company also made headlines in the first quarter of 2012 with news of a gas leak in its Elgin Well Head Platform in the North Sea. That leak was at first thought to be along the lines of the BP Deepwater

Horizon spill in the Gulf of Mexico but has been kept under control as the appropriate relief wells and seals are put into place.

Financial Highlights, Fiscal Year 2011

Although oil production was off a bit from FY2010 (9 percent to be exact), price increases and acquisitions drove a 23 percent increase in revenues and a 14 percent increase in net earnings, to about $7.05 per ADR with cash flows of $11.40 per ADR. Total pays dividends in euros, so following dollar-denominated dividends from year to year can be tricky, but weeding out this anomaly, dividend growth has been a healthy 19 percent over the past 10 years and looks to continue at a healthy pace.

Reasons to Buy

Total S.A. is a solid energy sector play with many of the features that make "big energy" attractive—namely strong cash flows, high dividend yields, and demand that isn't going away anytime soon. Companies with a price-to-cash-flow ratio under 5, implying a 20 percent annual cash return, aren't easy to find. In addition, Total provides a stronger international play than other energy picks on our list. The company has a dominant position in Europe, which, albeit not growing, is a steady market, producing plenty of cash flow while allowing the company to dabble in more promising markets like China and others in Asia Pacific and Latin America. Energy prices, at least at this writing, are on the rise, and Total is well positioned to take advantage of higher prices for their production as well as recent strength in the refining business. Finally, those believing that the dollar will weaken longer term, particularly against the euro, will like the fact that the dividend is paid in euros, which would translate favorably to ever-cheaper dollars.

Reasons for Caution

The Elgin episode, combined with general European economic uncertainty, brought the stock price down to recessionary levels. The Elgin event served as a reminder of what can happen in this industry, while European economic speed bumps may hurt this company more than some of its multinational brethren. We also remain cautious on investing in foreign companies because of differences in management style and accounting rules; they aren't necessarily bad but are difficult to understand and follow. Typically, we prefer U.S. companies that do a lot of business overseas. We feel the strengths of Total overcome these concerns.

SECTOR: **Energy**
BETA COEFFICIENT: **0.99**
10-YEAR COMPOUND EARNINGS PER SHARE GROWTH: **15.5%**
10-YEAR COMPOUND DIVIDENDS PER SHARE GROWTH: **19.0%**

	2004	**2005**	**2006**	**2007**	**2008**	**2009**	**2010**	**2011**
Revenues (Mil)	153,375	144,689	167,188	167,149	236,087	157,014	186,131	229,331
Net income (Mil)	11,118	14,302	15,463	16,718	18,205	11,626	14,006	15,910
Earnings per share	4.49	6.41	6.82	7.35	8.55	5.31	6.24	7.05
Dividends per share	2.19	1.83	2.10	2.81	3.10	3.28	2.93	3.12
Cash flow per share	7.42	9.72	9.60	10.73	12.42	9.49	11.25	11.40
Price: high	55.3	69	73.8	87.3	91.3	66	67.5	64.4
low	43.8	51.9	58.1	63.9	42.6	42.9	43.1	40

TOTAL, S.A.
2, Place de la Coupole
La Defense 6 92400 Courbevole, France
(713) 483-5070 (U.S.)
Website: *www.total.com*

Tractor Supply Company

Ticker symbol: TSCO (NASDAQ) ❏ S&P rating: not rated ❏ Value Line financial strength rating: A+ ❏ Current yield: 0.5% ❏ Dividend raises, past 10 years: 2

Company Profile

Tractor Supply Company is the largest operator of retail farm and ranch stores in the United States. Their focus is on the needs of recreational farmers and ranchers and those who enjoy the rural lifestyle, as well as tradesmen and small businesses. They operate retail stores, many in a "big-box" format, under the names Tractor Supply Company and Del's Farm Supply. Their stores are located in towns outside major metropolitan markets and in rural communities, thus far mostly in the eastern two-thirds of the United States. Representative merchandise includes supplies for pets, horses, and other farm animals; equipment maintenance products; hardware and tools; lawn and garden equipment; and work and recreational clothing and footwear. Tractor Supply is to farm, rural, and pet supply stores what Home Depot was once to lumber yards—a more complete, price-competitive, and convenient "big box" reformatting of the business—only TSCO thus far has no real competition.

Tractor Supply stores typically range in size from 15,500 square feet to 18,500 square feet of inside selling space and additional outside selling space. As of December 2011, they operated 1,085 retail farm and ranch stores in 44 states. Del's Farm Supply operates 27 stores, primarily in the Pacific Northwest, offering a wide selection of products (primarily in the horse, pet, and animal category) targeted at those who enjoy the rural lifestyle. The company does not plan to grow Del's significantly beyond its current size.

For FY2011, sales were divided between the following segments: livestock and pet products (40 percent); seasonal products like mowers and snow blowers (21 percent); hardware, tool, truck, and towing products (23 percent); clothing and footwear (10 percent); and agriculture (6 percent). Tractor Supply Company also sells a subset of its store goods online.

The company plans continued growth in store count to about 2,100, including about 300 new stores in the West. There is also a new initiative to create a series of higher-margin, smaller-format stores.

Financial Highlights, Fiscal Year 2011

Tractor did quite well in FY2011, with sales plowing ahead 16 percent and earnings per share rising at an even faster rate to $3.01, partly on the back of a full percentage point improvement in operating margins to 10.2 percent. The company will play a same-store sales gain in the 3–5 percent range, further margin gains from price mix optimization and operational improvements, plus an additional million or so of 71 million shares retired, into projected earnings per share of $3.40–$3.50 per share in FY2012. Cash flows are strong and growing and should bring further dividend increases and share repurchases, and the company has virtually no long-term debt.

Reasons to Buy

TSCO serves a growing, specialized niche in geographies often ignored by other retailers. They carry a specialized mix of merchandise that occupies a broad space—part big-box hardware, part garden shop, and part feed store. Their unique target market nonetheless has broad geographic distribution, giving TSCO room for growth, and thus far, no real competition has emerged in their niche to temper that growth. The fact that TSCOs biggest growth opportunity is in the outdoor-oriented West also bodes well.

TSCO carries a higher percentage of house brands than you would find at a typical hardware retailer. They earn higher gross margins on these products and build loyalty in the process. The business is unique, and for a retailer, has a wide "moat."

Reasons for Caution

TSCO's growth could eventually attract competition, just as Home Depot's success attracted Lowe's and others. The sooner they can build out to their target size, the better they will be able to protect margins. Following the story, the stock has performed extremely well in the past three years, so investors may want to choose their entry points carefully.

SECTOR: **Retail**
BETA COEFFICIENT: **0.80**
10-YEAR COMPOUND EARNINGS PER SHARE GROWTH: **23.0%**
10-YEAR COMPOUND DIVIDENDS PER SHARE GROWTH: **NM**

	2004	**2005**	**2006**	**2007**	**2008**	**2009**	**2010**	**2011**
Revenues (Mil)	1,739	2,068	2,370	2,703	3,008	3,207	3,638	4,232
Net Income (Mil)	64.1	85.7	91	96.2	81.9	115.5	168	223
Earnings per share	0.79	1.05	1.11	1.20	1.10	1.58	2.25	3.01
Dividends per share	—	—	—	—	—	—	0.28	.43
Cash flow per share	1.19	1.52	1.65	1.97	1.99	2.52	3.27	4.25
Price: high	22.9	28.3	33.8	28.8	23.6	27.3	49.5	88.6
low	5.11	6.6	19.4	17.5	13.4	14.3	24.6	68.5

Tractor Supply Company
200 Powell Place
Brentwood, TN 37027
(615) 440-4000
Website: *www.tractorsupply.com*

Union Pacific Corporation

Ticker symbol: UNP (NYSE) ❑ S&P rating: A- ❑ Value Line financial strength rating: A ❑ Current yield: 2.2% ❑ Dividend raises, past 10 years: 7

Company Profile

Union Pacific has been a familiar name and logo in the railroad business since its inception during the Civil War. With about 32,000 miles of track covering 23 states in the western two-thirds of the United States, today's Union Pacific Railroad, the primary subsidiary of the Union Pacific Corporation, describes itself as "America's Premier Railroad Franchise."

With 25,000 customers, a large number in today's era of trainload-sized shipments, UP has a more diversified customer and revenue mix than the other rail companies, including the other three of the "big four" railroads: BNSF, Norfolk Southern, and CSX. Energy (mostly coal from the Powder River Basin area of Wyoming) accounts for 22 percent of revenues; Intermodal (trucks or containers on flatcars), 17 percent; Agricultural, 18 percent; Industrial, 17 percent; Chemicals, 15 percent; and Automotive, 8 percent of FY2011 revenues.

The company has long been an innovator in railroad technology, including motive power, communications and technology automation, physical plant, community relations,

and marketing. The company operates with one of the lowest operating ratios in the industry, 70.6 percent, meaning that operating costs account for 70.6 percent of total costs, allowing a good contribution to the substantial fixed costs of owning and running a railroad. This success has translated to continued strong operating margins, which of course have helped earnings and cash flows.

The company also invests a lot in marketing and community relations. One example is the steam-powered excursion train program, where the company operates excursions on selected lines. The company has planned a major series of excursions and exhibits related to the celebration of the railroad's 150th anniversary during 2012. Such public relations efforts may seem fairly ordinary for a major U.S. corporation, but for the railroad industry, these activities stretch the envelope, hence our noting them here.

Railroads have quietly been learning to use technology to improve operations and deliver better customer service. New tools can track shipments door to door using GPS-based technology, and the railroad will accept shipments and manage them door to door, even over other railroads or with other kinds of carriers. Customers can check rates and route and track shipments online. These services, combined with high fuel prices, have led to a continuing migration from trucks back to rail and intermodal rail services.

Financial Highlights, Fiscal Year 2011

Moved forward by strong freight demand, pricing and operational improvements, UP posted record results in FY2011. Revenues were up 15 percent to $19.6 billion, while per-share earnings, aided in part by a 2.5 percent reduction in share count, were up some 33 percent to $6.72. The net profit margin of 16.8 percent is remarkably high for a railroad, and a full five percentage points ahead of comparable figures in the 2006–2009 time frame, reflecting a strong bias toward operating efficiency. These trends should continue in FY2012, with western U.S. shale oil and gas "fracking" activities adding some traffic, to produce revenue gains in the 10 percent range and per-share earnings gains in the 20 percent range to something close to $8.00. The company has been aggressively returning cash to investors, with substantial dividend raises in recent years, including two increases in FY2010 and a current per-share payout more than double that in 2008. Additionally, the

company has retired 14 percent of its shares since 2006 and is on track to do more in that area.

Reasons to Buy

It's hard not to like a company that grows earnings 11.5 percent and dividends 13 percent on a mere 4 percent compounded increase in revenue over the past 10 years. UP has managed its business well to become more efficient and at the same time more "user friendly" to its customers and to the general public. As fuel prices increase and new short- and long-distance intermodal services move higher-valued goods more quickly and cost effectively than trucks, we see a steady shift toward this business. The company has a solid and diverse traffic base, and continues to have a good brand and reputation in the industry.

Reasons for Caution

Railroads are and will always be economically sensitive. They are also vulnerable to negative publicity. A single event like a derailment or spill can put them in the public eye in a bad way, or worse, tangle them up in regulation and unplanned costs. Finally, railroads are and always will be extremely capital intensive, meaning high fixed costs for physical plant and equipment. A decline in volumes or even a shift to other transportation requirements can be costly and hard to recover from.

SECTOR: **Transportation**
BETA COEFFICIENT: **1.18**
10-YEAR COMPOUND EARNINGS PER SHARE GROWTH: **11.5%**
10-YEAR COMPOUND DIVIDENDS PER SHARE GROWTH: **13%**

		2004	2005	2006	2007	2008	2009	2010	2011
Revenues (Mil)		12,215	13,578	15,578	16,283	17,970	14,143	16,965	19,557
Net income (Mil)		758	809	1,606	1,856	2,338	1,826	2,780	3,292
Earnings per share		1.45	1.70	2.96	3.46	4.54	3.61	5.53	6.72
Dividends per share		0.60	0.60	0.60	0.68	0.93	1.08	1.31	1.71
Cash flow per share		3.39	3.78	5.15	6.09	7.40	6.47	8.68	10.23
Price:	high	34.8	40.6	48.7	68.8	85.8	66.7	95.8	107
	low	27.4	29.1	38.8	44.8	41.8	33.3	60.4	77.7

Union Pacific Corporation
1416 Dodge St.
Omaha, NE 68179
(402) 271-5777
Website: *www.up.com*

UnitedHealth Group

Ticker symbol: UNH (NYSE) ❏ S&P rating: A- ❏ Value Line financial strength rating: A+ ❏ Current yield: 1.2% ❏ Dividend raises, past 10 years: 4

Company Profile

UnitedHealth Group is the parent company of a number of health insurers and service organizations. They are the second-largest publicly traded health insurance company in the United States, with over $100 billion in revenue reported in 2011.

The company has reorganized and rebranded part of its business and now operates in two major business segments: UnitedHealthcare and Optum. UnitedHealthcare provides traditional and Medicare-based health benefit and insurance plans for individuals and employers, covering approximately 26 million Americans with about 400 national employer accounts and many more smaller employer accounts. The company estimates that it serves over half of the *Fortune* 100 companies list. The company, mainly through this unit, has been an active acquirer of other familiar health-care and insurance brands, including Oxford Health in 2004, PacifiCare in 2005, Sierra Health Plans and Unison Health Plans in 2008, AIM Health-care Services in 2009, and more recently an assortment of small mostly Medicare-related providers. The UnitedHealthcare Medicare

and Retirement business, formerly known as Ovations, serves about 9 million seniors—one in five Medicare beneficiaries. Taken together, these operations generated approximately 77 percent of UNH's overall revenue in 2011 and 85 percent of profits.

The remainder of the company's revenue comes from its health services businesses, which it markets under the Optum brand umbrella. This segment, which touches some 65 million customers, delivers service through three separate businesses. OptumHealth is an "information and technology" based health solution, deploying mostly remote telesupport for well care, mental health, ongoing disease management, and substance abuse programs. The OptumRx business is a pharmacy benefits provider, while OptumInsight is a relatively new management information, analytics, and process-improvement arm providing an assortment of services for health plans, physicians, hospitals, and life science research, formerly marketed under the "Ingenix" brand. Of the total Optum-branded business of $28.7 billion, Rx accounts for the lion's share at $19.3 billion, while OptumHealth weighs in at $6.7 billion and OptumInsight at $2.6 billion. Although these numbers may seem small in the context of UNH's total $101.9 billion annual revenue footprint, they are sizeable businesses when looked at individually. The Optum umbrella brand is gaining in prominence, and even has its own unique web presence at *www.optum.com*. Together, the two business units serve about 78 million individuals in the United States and in 18 other countries.

Financial Highlights, Fiscal Year 2011

United posted solid results in FY2011, ahead of forecast and well ahead of FY2011. Revenues grew 8 percent to $101.9 billion, while per-share earnings, helped along by utilization and other cost management efforts, rose 15.3 percent to $4.73 per share. The company recently raised FY2012 guidance to $109–$110 billion in revenues and $4.80–$4.95 per share in earnings, figures which again could prove conservative. The company bought back 16 million shares in FY2011, approximately 1.5 percent of its float, and has posted large dividend increases during the past two years after a previous history of almost insignificant dividends.

Reasons to Buy

The company is one of the most solid and diverse enterprises in the health insurance industry. Health insurers such as Aetna, included on our *100 Best* list, seem to be getting past many of the fears of reform and other contrary public opinion; these companies simply pass costs through, and attempts to manage costs and improve utilization are paying off. Meanwhile, like Aetna, UNH brings a fair amount of innovation to the marketplace, primarily through its Optum offerings. Even slight efficiency improvements can help the bottom line substantially, and if price competition eventually dictates lower premiums, those adjustments will lag cost-side improvements.

The scale of UNH's operation gives it tremendous leverage when negotiating for the services of health-care providers. Hospitals and physicians are strongly motivated to join UNH's network, as doing so will provide assurance of steady referrals.

Finally, the company, through increased dividends and share buybacks, seems to have turned the corner in terms of looking after shareholder returns.

Reasons for Caution

Since 2007, the company has paid over $3 billion in fines, legal costs, and settlements pertaining to legal actions brought against them by various private and public agencies. The company is still legally exposed as a result of some actions taken by previous management with regard to Medicare payment rates. Current management appears to be serious about cleaning up the messes left behind, but the investor should be aware of this risk of additional litigation. The company is vulnerable to shifts in public opinion and to new regulation, as well as economic downturns, which can hurt employer participation. The company also has demonstrated a fairly aggressive acquisition strategy—good, mostly so far, but it comes with risks.

SECTOR: **Health Care**
BETA COEFFICIENT: **0.91**
10-YEAR COMPOUND EARNINGS PER SHARE GROWTH: **22.5%**
10-YEAR COMPOUND DIVIDENDS PER SHARE GROWTH: **51.5%**

	2004	2005	2006	2007	2008	2009	2010	2011
Revenues (Mil)	37,218	45,365	71,542	75,431	81,186	87,138	94,155	101,862
Net Income (Mil)	2,587	3,300	4,159	4,654	3,660	3,822	4,633	5,142
Earnings per share	1.97	2.48	2.97	3.42	2.95	3.24	4.10	4.73
Dividends per share	0.02	0.03	0.03	0.03	0.03	0.03	0.41	0.61
Cash flow per share	2.30	2.76	3.59	4.35	3.86	4.20	5.25	5.86
Price: high	44.4	64.6	62.9	59.5	57.9	33.3	38.1	53.5
low	27.7	42.6	41.4	45.8	14.5	16.2	27.1	36.4

UnitedHealth Group
9900 Bren Street
Minnetonka, MN 55343
(952) 936-1300
Website: *www.unitedhealthgroup.com*

CONSERVATIVE GROWTH

United Parcel Service

Ticker symbol: UPS (NYSE) ◻ S&P rating: AA- ◻ Value Line financial strength rating: A ◻ Current yield: 2.9% ◻ Dividend raises, past 10 years: 10

Company Profile

Welcome back, UPS. We took you off the *100 Best Stocks* list in one of our early programs to weed out multiple companies on our list doing the same thing. We saw FedEx and UPS converging on the same business from different directions—FedEx being an air company getting ever more into the ground business; UPS being a ground business taking to the air. That convergence is still the case. And both companies continue to build international capabilities, invest in technology to track shipments, and to provide logistics services beyond basic assortments of transportation services.

So why are we adding UPS back to the list? Three reasons. First, with the continued expansion of e-commerce, and now the gradual demise of the U.S. Postal Service in the works, we foresee dramatic increases possible in the small package and document shipping business. Second, with its recent announcement of the acquisition of the Dutch-based carrier/forwarder TNT, UPS appears to be serious about becoming a global logistics enterprise. Third, and we may have undervalued it earlier, UPS has

gone a long way to return cash to shareholders, doubling its dividend and retiring almost 20 percent of its stock in nine years.

Particularly after the $6.8 billion TNT acquisition, which will strengthen UPS's footprint in Europe, Asia, and Latin America, UPS will add to its position as the world's largest air and ground package carrier. (That acquisition is still in the approval stage at the time of this writing.) Before the merger, the company derived about 56 percent of revenues from U.S. package operations, 26 percent from international, and 18 percent from an assortment of bundled logistics and supply-chain services and solutions. After the merger, the company expects to get about 36 percent of revenue from outside the United States.

The company operates 527 aircraft and almost 100,000 ground vehicles, most of the familiar brown "package car" variety. They serve over 200 companies with an assortment of priority to deferred services. Once thought to be old fashioned and adverse to innovation, the company has invested in sophisticated package tracking systems and links for customers to tie into them. A new service called "My Choice" allows a customer to control the timing of deliveries mid-service—so no more waiting half a day at home for a delivery that might come anytime (hallelujah!), a nice perk for a consumer waiting for an e-commerce shipment as well as a savings for the company, avoiding multiple delivery attempts.

Financial Highlights, Fiscal Year 2011

The expansion of e-commerce and a strong holiday season led to a record-setting FY2011. Revenues climbed 7.2 percent to just over $53 billion, while per-share earnings, helped along by a 22 million share buyback, climbed 19 percent to $4.25 per share. The company noted higher unit volumes, revenue per shipment, and intra-Asia demand as drivers for the increase, as well as the afore-mentioned e-commerce gains in the domestic market. These forces were strong enough to offset higher fuel costs and a less favorable mix. As FY2012 opens, the company notes a bit more softness in the mix—customers are deferring shipments and using lower-priority services, but still forecasts earnings in the $4.75 to $5.00 per share range—excluding effects from the TNT acquisition.

Reasons to Buy

The "fastest ship in the shipping business" is now getting a lot bigger

and appears to be positioning itself to be the standard logistics provider of the world. That bodes well for scale and for market share, while there are many forces in play that should work to increase volumes. Of course, as volumes increase, so do economies of scale—and thus margins—so we feel that after years of fairly unexciting share price performance, these shares could start to take to higher altitudes. In the meantime, current cash flow generation and cash returns are healthy enough to bide the time until that happens. The company just approved another $500 million for share buybacks and raised the dividend almost 10 percent to $2.28 annually.

Reasons for Caution

Even with the TNT acquisition, UPS will have to battle hard for market share particularly in lucrative Asia-U.S. lanes and others, as is typical for this industry. Competition for lucrative markets can be intense. There could be some bumps along the way with the TNT acquisition. Of about 400,000 employees, 62 percent are union, so labor relations and pension funding (which is in good shape now) both bear watching. Of course, fuel prices and the state of the global economy are big factors in UPS's success in any short-term scenario.

SECTOR: Transportation
BETA COEFFICIENT: 0.84
10-YEAR COMPOUND EARNINGS PER SHARE GROWTH: 4.5%
10-YEAR COMPOUND DIVIDENDS PER SHARE GROWTH: 12.5%

		2004	2005	2006	2007	2008	2009	2010	2011
Revenues (Mil)		36,582	42,581	47,547	49,692	51,466	45,297	49,545	53,105
Net income (Mil)		3,238	3,870	4,202	4,369	3,581	2,318	3,570	4,213
Earnings per share		2.85	3.47	3.86	4.11	3.50	2.31	3.56	4.25
Dividends per share		1.12	1.32	1.52	1.64	1.77	1.80	1.88	2.08
Cash flow per share		4.23	5.03	5.56	5.91	5.42	4.09	5.43	6.20
Price:	high	89.1	85.8	84	79	75.1	59.5	73.9	77
	low	67.5	66.1	65.5	68.7	43.3	38	55.6	60.7

United Parcel Service
65 Glenlake Parkway NE
Atlanta, GA 30328
(404) 828-6000
Website: *www.ups.com*

CONSERVATIVE GROWTH

United Technologies Corporation

Ticker symbol: UTX (NYSE) ❑ S&P rating: A ❑ Value Line financial strength rating A++ ❑ Current yield: 2.4% ❑ Dividend raises, past 10 years: 10

Company Profile

United Technologies is a diversified provider of mostly high-technology products to the aerospace and building systems industries throughout the world. With diversified conglomerate producers of complex products like UTX, it helps to have a high-level understanding of how the business breaks down. With that in mind, we'll divide UTX into three basic business lines by FY2011 sales. Commercial and industrial business were 58 percent of sales, its commercial aerospace sales were 22 percent, and its military aerospace sales came in at 20 percent. Sales outside the United States amounted to about 61 percent. UTX operates six primary subsidiary companies, which include, in order of decreasing share of FY2011 revenues:

■ Pratt & Whitney (23.4 percent of FY2011 revenues)—Large and small commercial and military jet engines, spare parts and product support, specialized engine maintenance and overhaul and repair services for airlines, air forces, and corporate fleets; rocket engines and space propulsion systems; and industrial gas turbines.

■ Otis (21.6 percent)—Design and manufacture of elevators, escalators, moving walkways, and shuttle systems, and related installation, maintenance, and repair services; modernization products and service for elevators and escalators.

■ Carrier (20.9 percent)—Heating, ventilating, and air conditioning (HVAC) equipment for commercial, industrial, and residential buildings; HVAC replacement parts and services; building controls; commercial, industrial, and transport refrigeration equipment.

■ Sikorsky (12.9 percent)—Design and manufacture of military and commercial helicopters; fixed-wing reconnaissance aircraft; spare parts and maintenance services for helicopters and fixed-wing aircraft; and civil helicopter operations.

■ Hamilton Sundstrand (10.8 percent)—Aircraft electrical power generation and distribution systems; engine and flight controls; propulsion systems; environmental controls for aircraft, spacecraft, and submarines; auxiliary power units; product support, maintenance, and repair services; space life support systems; industrial products including mechanical power transmissions, compressors, metering devices, and fluid handling equipment.

- UTC Fire and Security (10.3 percent)—Security and fire protection systems; integration, installation, and servicing of intruder alarms, access control, and video surveillance and monitoring; response and security personnel services; installation and servicing of fire detection and suppression systems.

The company has announced an $18.4 billion acquisition of commercial and defense aerospace materials maker Goodrich Corp to be added to the Sundstrand portfolio. This will change the weightings of the six independent businesses going forward, although to avoid issuing more shares, the company has committed to sell some existing businesses—many from the Sundstrand portfolio—to cover the acquisition cost.

Financial Highlights, Fiscal Year 2011

FY2011 saw a healthy growth in revenues, earnings, and earnings per share. Revenues grew 7 percent to just over $58 billion, while earnings per share, helped along by share buybacks, grew 15.8 percent to $5.49 per share. FY2012 will see the addition of another $3 billion in revenues from the acquisition on top of another $2.3 billion or so in "organic" revenue growth. Earnings are likely to stay flat owing mostly to acquisition costs. The company projects substantially higher sales and earnings for FY2013, as acquisition costs will be behind it and cost synergies will begin to take hold.

Reasons to Buy

UTC is a classic conglomerate play. The separate and loosely related or unrelated businesses buffer each other in line with what's happening in the economy, both in the private and public sectors. During the recession, the defense and aerospace technology segments performed, while business fell off in more economically sensitive businesses and products like jet engines and elevators; as the economy picks up, the sensitive businesses carry the load. That's the way this sort of company works, and in the case of UTX, it has worked well. Unlike many of its competitors, United Technologies maintains a global presence, which benefits from global and emerging market infrastructure and other construction, and even from defense spending by other countries. The company's brands, particularly Otis, are well known and very well supported worldwide. And like *100 Best* stock Honeywell, UTX has a broad portfolio of products geared toward improving energy efficiency, which will be a significant growth market for several years to come.

The company continues to deliver shareholder return through share buybacks and healthy and regular dividend increases. We also like the fact that UTX is trying to digest Goodrich without increasing share count.

Reasons for Caution

The stability of the public sector portion of the business may diminish as Congress wrestles with the budget deficit and the Iraq and Afghanistan wars wind down. The company does supply a lot of materials for the new F-35 fighter program, as an example. The rest of the business is still sensitive to construction, and construction may not be out of the woods yet. Finally, like all conglomerates, UTX is a very complex business to manage, and a slipup in one division, as with the problems on the A380 Airbus engines, can be damaging. The Goodrich acquisition also adds a measure of uncertainty, although it fits well with the existing businesses.

SECTOR: **Industrials**
BETA COEFFICIENT: **1.03**
10-YEAR COMPOUND EARNINGS PER SHARE GROWTH: **12.5%**
10-YEAR COMPOUND DIVIDENDS PER SHARE GROWTH: **15.0%**

		2004	2005	2006	2007	2008	2009	2010	2011
Revenues (Mil)		37,445	42,725	47,740	54,759	58,681	52,920	54,326	58,190
Net Income (Mil)		2,788	3,069	3,732	4,224	4,689	3,829	4,373	4,979
Earnings per share		2.76	3.03	3.71	4.27	4.9	4.12	4.74	5.49
Dividends per share		0.7	0.88	1.02	1.28	1.55	1.54	1.70	1.87
Cash flow per share		3.68	4.09	4.79	5.5	6.38	5.43	6.22	6.97
Price:	high	53	58.9	67.5	82.5	77.1	70.9	79.7	91.8
	low	40.4	48.4	54.2	61.8	41.8	37.4	62.9	66.9

United Technologies Corporation
One Financial Plaza
Hartford, CT 06103
(860) 728-7912
Website: *www.utc.com*

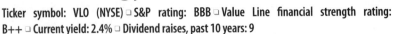

NEW FOR 2013

Valero Energy

Ticker symbol: VLO (NYSE) ❑ S&P rating: BBB ❑ Value Line financial strength rating: B++ ❑ Current yield: 2.4% ❑ Dividend raises, past 10 years: 9

Company Profile

Valero Energy is the largest independent oil refiner and marketer in the United States. The company owns 16 refineries and operates a network of 6,800 retail combined gasoline stations and convenience stores throughout the United States, UK and Ireland, and Canada.

Most of the 16 Valero refineries are located in the United States, centered in the South and on the Texas Gulf Coast with others in Memphis, Oklahoma, and on the West Coast. Others are located in the Caribbean, Quebec, and Wales in the UK. The refinery network was mostly assembled through a series of acquisitions from Diamond Shamrock in 2001; El Paso Corporation in the early 2000s; and, more recently, the Pembroke (Wales) refinery from Chevron in 2011. The refining operations produce the full gamut of hydrocarbon products—gasoline, jet fuel, diesel, asphalt, propane, base oils, solvents, aromatics, natural gas liquids, sulfur, hydrogen, and middle distillates. The company is strictly focused on downstream operations and owns no oil wells or production

facilities. Instead, they purchase a variety of feedstocks on the open market and can adjust those purchases to market conditions, while using contracts and hedging tools to manage input prices to a degree. About 63 percent of feedstocks are purchased under contracts, with the remainder on the spot market. Most of these refineries are legacy operations and have been in place for many years, as far back as 1908. The company has invested heavily in upgrading these refineries to improve capacity, efficiency, and environmental compliance.

The company operates about 6,800 stores under the Valero brand name through a mix of company-owned and franchise arrangements. About 4,000 of these outlets are in the United States, and 1,000 in the UK and Ireland. Most of these stores are operated under franchise arrangements; in addition there are about 1,000 stores owned and operated by the company under the "Corner Store" branding and an upgraded assortment of merchandise and Valero-branded fuel. The company operates another 880 outlets under the "Ultramar" brand in Canada. The company also operates a network of wholesale and commercial product outlets and a network of 10 ethanol processing plants. Bulk sales to other retail, commercial distributors, and large end customers like airlines and railroads are also important.

Financial Highlights, Fiscal Year 2011

Throughput margin per barrel (known as the "crack margin" in the industry) rose from $7.80 to $9.30 in FY2011. Operating expenses remained roughly unchanged, yielding an operating income per barrel of $3.96 vs. $2.45 in FY2010. This margin creates significant earnings leverage, some $1.6 billion in increased refining margins. Sales increased from $81.3 billion to $125.1 billion. That's about a 54 percent increase, but a lot of that was based on price increases. Refining unit volume increased about 14 percent. The leverage really became evident with per-share earnings, which rose 228 percent from $1.62 to $3.69. Price fluctuations can make FY2012 predictions difficult, but analysts are predicting a fairly steady-state year with revenues and earnings roughly consistent with FY2011.

The company repurchased about 12 million shares in FY2011, about 2 percent of its float, and has authorized another $3.46 billion for share repurchases.

Reasons to Buy

The profitability of this business, like other refining businesses, depends on the supply and cost of feedstocks and the wholesale and retail prices of finished products. Both are determined by spot and futures markets, which are in turn sensitive to supply and demand, which are in turn driven by macroeconomic events and market emotions. In addition, the availability of refining capacity is also a factor; when markets get tight, it is extremely difficult to put another refinery on the ground to handle demand. As a result, Valero's fortunes, like other refiners, can change quickly.

We like Valero's leading position in the refining business, and having 16 well-distributed and largely successful operating refineries on the ground already is a good thing. We also like the branding, abundance, look, and feel of the retail presence, and the focus this company has on the refining and marketing side of the business. The recent trend in the industry is to split large integrated companies into separate exploration and production (E&P) and downstream operations; Conoco-Phillips and Marathon (both *100 Best* stocks) have done it. But Valero is already there and entrenched, and future splits from the likes of Chevron, ExxonMobil, and others may make new refining assets available "for cheap." The recent acquisition of Sunoco by a private equity firm also signals that some are finding value in refining and marketing assets. Finally, the company has ample cash flow to continue share repurchases and to, probably, hike the dividend; we see decent shareholder returns down the road.

Reasons for Caution

The refining business in particular is inherently volatile and complex, and what may appear today as an advantageous input and output pricing profile might disappear in a minute. Gross, operating, and net margins are very thin, typically in the 1–2 percent range. The effects of these swings are obvious just in examining the company's eight-year history below. While we believe that the company has taken some steps to reduce the volatility, it is difficult to eliminate completely. Refiners also endure the headline risk of refinery mishaps, a few of which have already come Valero's way in recent years.

SECTOR: **Energy**
BETA COEFFICIENT: **1.43**
10-YEAR COMPOUND EARNINGS PER SHARE GROWTH: **2.5%**
10-YEAR COMPOUND DIVIDENDS PER SHARE GROWTH: **16.0%**

	2004	**2005**	**2006**	**2007**	**2008**	**2009**	**2010**	**2011**
Revenues (Bil)	54.6	82.1	91.8	94.5	118.3	87.3	81.3	125.1
Net income (Mil)	1,804	3,975	5,251	4,565	(1,131)	(352)	923	2,097
Earnings per share	3.33	6.75	8.30	7.72	(2.16)	(0.65)	1.62	3.69
Dividends per share	0.19	0.30	0.48	0.57	0.60	0.20	0.30	0.60
Cash flow per share	4.62	7.77	10.81	11.04	0.67	1.91	4.10	6.52
Price: high	23.9	58.6	70.8	75.7	71.1	26.2	23.7	31.1
low	11.4	21	46.8	47.7	13.9	16.3	15.5	16.4

Valero Energy Corporation
One Valero Way
San Antonio, TX 78249
(210) 345-2000
Website: *www.valero.com*

AGGRESSIVE GROWTH

Valmont Industries

Ticker symbol: VMI (NYSE) ❑ S&P rating: BBB- ❑ Value Line financial strength rating: B++ ❑ Current yield: 0.6% ❑ Dividend raises, past 10 years: 10

Company Profile

Valmont Industries was founded in 1946 as a supplier of irrigation products and became one of the classic post-war industrial success stories, growing along with the need for increased farm output. They were early pioneers of the center-pivot irrigation systems, which enabled much of that growth and which now dominates the high-yield agricultural business. These machines remain a mainstay of its product line. But the company has expanded to make such familiar infrastructure items as light poles, cell phone towers, and those familiar high-tension electric towers that crisscross the landscape. Valmont products and product lines now include:

■ Engineered Infrastructure Products (29 percent of FY2011 revenues)—lighting poles, including decorative lighting poles, guard rails, towers, and other metal structures used in lighting, communications, traffic management, wireless phone carriers, and other utilities. Products are available as standard designs and engineered for custom applications as needed for industrial, commercial, and residential applications. If you've ever sat at a stop light and wondered how a single cantilevered arm could support four 400-pound traffic signals, these are the folks to ask.

■ Utility Support Structures (23 percent)—This segment produces the very large concrete and steel substations and electric transmission support towers used by electric utilities. This has been Valmont's most profitable operation over the last few years, due mainly to increased volumes in a period of declining costs.

■ Irrigation (25 percent)— Under the "Valley" brand name, Valmont produces a wide range of equipment, including gravity and drip products, as well as its center-pivot designs, which can service up to 500 acres from a single machine. Valmont also sells its irrigation controllers to other manufacturers.

■ Coatings (11 percent)— Developed as an adjunct to its other metal products businesses, the coatings business now provides services such as galvanizing, electroplating, powder coating, and anodizing to industrial customers throughout the company's operating areas.

Financial Highlights, Fiscal Year 2011

The long-lead-time nature of Valmont's business suggested a somewhat delayed response to the economic recovery, but that recovery appears to be in full force now. Revenues of $2.7 billion in FY2011 were 35 percent ahead of FY2010, although some of that increase was due to the acquisition of UK infrastructure products maker Delta plc. Earnings per share increased about 42 percent. The company is enjoying the benefits of a return to infrastructure construction and replacement, in addition to an agricultural boom. Forward revenue projections call for another 10 percent growth on the top line, with earnings in the $7.30–$7.60 range, which would represent a roughly 25 percent increase over FY2010.

Reasons to Buy

We continue to view Valmont as a key infrastructure play. America's infrastructure needs to be replaced, as does infrastructure in much of the developed world. And as for the less developed world, that infrastructure is needed in the first place. We think, long term, that Valmont is in the right place to capture a decent share of this replacement business, including electric utility infrastructure. The original irrigation business should also do well as agriculture and farm commodity prices strengthen. Valmont has retained market share and remains the leader among the four dominant U.S.-based players in the large-scale irrigation market. The company's continued emphasis on growth into new geographies should pay dividends as India and China begin to build infrastructure and adopt more modern agricultural methods. So far, Valmont has had very little penetration in those two countries.

Reasons for Caution

Many Valmont products are purchased by public sector and government agencies, and these agencies will be scrutinizing purchases to a greater degree than in the past. Escalating raw materials costs may also hurt, especially in a reduced-demand, softer-pricing environment that might ensue from contracting government purchases. The company may be slowed a bit by troubles in Europe, and the recent Delta plc acquisition increases exposure to those troubles. Finally, we would like to see a little more shareholder return; while dividends are raised regularly, they remain small with respect to the share price, and share buybacks haven't happened on a large scale. However, it should be noted that the company only has 26.4 million shares outstanding to begin with. All that said, the cash position indicates better future cash returns for patient investors.

SECTOR: **Industrials**
BETA COEFFICIENT: **1.51**
10-YEAR COMPOUND EARNINGS PER SHARE GROWTH: **16.0%**
10-YEAR COMPOUND DIVIDENDS PER SHARE GROWTH: **8.5%**

		2004	2005	2006	2007	2008	2009	2010	2011
Revenues (Mil)		1,031	1,108	1,281	1,500	1,907	1,787	1,975	2,661
Net Income (Mil)		26.9	40.2	61.5	94.7	132.4	155	109.7	155
Earnings per share		1.10	1.58	2.38	3.63	5.04	5.70	4.15	5.95
Dividends per share		0.32	0.34	0.37	0.41	0.50	0.58	0.65	0.72
Price:	high	28	35.3	61.2	99	120.5	89.3	90.3	116
	low	19.3	21.3	32.8	50.9	37.5	37.5	65.3	73

Valmont Industries
1 Valmont Plaza
Omaha, NE 68154
(402) 963-1000
Website: *www.valmont.com*

Verizon Communications, Inc.

Ticker symbol: VZ (NYSE) □ S&P rating: A- □ Value Line financial strength rating: A+ □ Current yield: 5.3% □ Dividend raises, past 10 years: 6

Company Profile

Verizon operates two telecommunications businesses: Domestic Wireless, which provides wireless voice and data services, and Wireline, which provides voice, broadband data and video, Internet access, long-distance, and other services, and which owns and operates a large global Internet Protocol network. The wireless business represents about 63 percent of the total (up from 57 percent last year); wireline is about 37 percent of the total by revenues. As we'll get to shortly, the company's data and cloud computing business is one of the more exciting prospects.

In the consumer space, the Wireline segment also supplies Verizon's Fiber-to-the-Home (FiOS) broadband data infrastructure. One of Verizon's largest investments, FiOS provides a very high bandwidth link to the Internet, easily surpassing DSL and even cable. Over this network, Verizon can provide hundreds of HD video streams, high-speed data, and voice all simultaneously. This service competes head to head with AT&T's (a *100 Best* stock) U-verse and Comcast's (another *100 Best* stock) Xfinity services among others.

The Domestic Wireless segment is served by Verizon Wireless, which is a joint venture between Verizon Communications, Inc. and Vodafone. Verizon Communications owns a 55 percent share in the business, and Vodafone 45 percent. Verizon wireless is now the largest wireless carrier in the United States, and operates in 19 countries outside the United States as well. The wireless side of the business has been rolling out the new "LTE Mobile Broadband" network, a leading-edge 4G network designed to be 10 times faster than the standard 3G network, and now available in some 200 U.S. cities. Shortly after this December 2010 introduction, Verizon also began marketing Apple iPhone and iPad products and services for the first time in February 2010. Both rollouts are going well, although the high cost of subsidizing iPhones has made that business less profitable in the short term. In early 2012, the company also announced a joint venture with Coinstar (Redbox) to distribute on-demand video.

Adding hardware products and wireless capacity hasn't been the only growth strategy employed at Verizon. The company continues to grow its footprint in cloud computing, with the 2011 acquisition of IT and cloud services provider Terremark Worldwide, and a small but interesting partnership with a company called eMeter, which markets devices to automatically read and transmit energy usage for utilities using Verizon's wireless network. The company is leveraging its investment in the 4G LTE network for corporate customers, recently announcing the availability of secure "Private IP" networks to the commercial base. So if you're a bank and want to locate an ATM in the middle of nowhere, with wireline service not available or not cheap, you can do it quickly and with the security of a private wired network. It's not hard to see where this LTE-powered cloud ecosystem is headed.

Financial Highlights, Fiscal Year 2011

After a somewhat soft 2010, FY2011 revenues resumed a modest growth path, up 4 percent over FY2010. Hampered somewhat by costly subsidies for Apple products, earnings did not follow suit, dipping slightly from $2.21 per share to $2.16 per share. However, both revenues and profitability showed strength toward the year end, as revenues and profits

for wireless, FiOS, and business data services all were strong, and with a portion of the subsidy and LTE network buildout expenses behind it, profits appeared to be on the rise. Projections call for another 4-plus percent revenue growth (a substantial growth on a $110 billion base) and a 15 percent rise in earnings per share to approach $2.50 per share.

Reasons to Buy

Verizon offers a nice combination of stability and income with a play in the growth of the "new economy" and supporting technology. It appears that earnings may have hit a low inflection point in their growth path and should start outpacing top-line growth. We especially like the new cloud and wireless data services for the commercial market, which offer good promise and significant leverage of existing investments, and new services in the consumer space, like the new video-on-demand venture, also bear watching. With the high dividend and share buybacks, the company seems to keep shareholder interests in mind. The brand is strong and its reputation hasn't suffered some of the hits for poor-quality service that archrival AT&T has experienced.

Reasons for Caution

The telecommunications business is always capital intensive, and Verizon, like others, must spend heavily just to keep up with technology and competition. While current cash flows are strong, this scenario doesn't combine well with a business where competition has cut into margins slightly and where dividend payouts have risen from 50 percent to 80 percent of earnings since 2002. Getting a solid return on new capital investments is thus critical, and one slipup could be costly for shareholders. The business environment is extremely competitive, and Verizon's sheer size may hamper its flexibility to compete. Also, one should consider that Verizon shares ownership of the wireless business with Vodaphone; the shared ownership could cause problems or result in an expensive buyout for Verizon.

SECTOR: **Telecommunications Services**
BETA COEFFICIENT: **0.54**
10-YEAR COMPOUND EARNINGS PER SHARE GROWTH: **-2.0%**
10-YEAR COMPOUND DIVIDENDS PER SHARE GROWTH: **2.0%**

		2004	2005	2006	2007	2008	2009	2010	2011
Revenues (Mil)		71,283	74,910	88,144	93,469	97,354	107,808	106,585	110,875
Net Income (Mil)		7,261	7,151	6,021	6,854	7,235	6,805	6,256	6,115
Earnings per share		2.59	2.56	2.54	2.36	2.54	2.4	2.21	2.16
Dividends per share		1.54	1.62	1.62	1.65	1.78	1.87	1.93	1.96
Cash flow per share		7.64	7.24	7.07	7.4	7.65	7.7	7.60	7.70
Price:	high	42.3	41.1	38.9	46.2	44.3	34.8	36	40.3
	low	34.1	29.1	30	35.6	23.1	26.1	26	32.3

Verizon Communications, Inc.
140 West Street
New York, NY 10007
(212) 395-1000
Website: *www.verizon.com*

Visa Inc.

Ticker symbol: V (NYSE) ◻ S&P rating: A+ ◻ Value Line financial strength rating: A ◻ Current yield: 0.7% ◻ Dividend raises, past 10 years: 3

Company Profile

If we wrote about a company with a steady 37 percent net profit margin and a global brand that was in the business of collecting small fees on every one of billions of transactions worldwide; a company that required almost no capital expenditures, plant, and equipment, or inventory; a company that brought in more than $1.2 million per employee in revenue and $486,000 per employee in net profit; a company growing earnings 20 to 30 percent a year; a company with a time-tested business model and absolutely zero long-term debt—would you believe that it existed? Not to mention a company with a share price that rose from $74 to $118 in our standard one-year April 2011 to April 2012 measurement period.

It's all true. And the company, formed in a 2007 reorganization and taken public in 2008, is Visa. Yes, the same Visa whose emblem has traditionally appeared on a majority of the world's credit cards—and now debit cards. The company operates the world's largest retail electronic payment network, providing processing services; payment platforms; and fraud-detection services for credit, debit, and commercial payments. The company also operates one of the largest global ATM networks with its PLUS and Interlink brands.

For years, Visa has been synonymous with credit and credit cards, but in recent years it has become more of a digital currency company, stitching together consumers, retailers, banks, and other businesses in a giant global network; really, Visa is a global payments technology business that not only develops and supplies the technology but also collects fees upon its use.

The shift from traditional cash and check forms of payment to debit cards and other digital forms is growing at about a 12 percent annual rate, driven by the security and convenience of these transactions as well as a shift away from consumer debt more to "paid for today" debit transactions. Debit transactions are projected to soon account for more than half the company's overall business volume. One interesting development on this front is a new strategic alliance with Intel to link internal mobile-device hardware with Visa's "payWave" mobile payment technology; the idea is to eventually (and we think sooner rather than later) enable fast, easy, secure "mobile wallet" transactions through individual mobile devices.

More than its rivals, Visa derives a significant percentage of transaction volume, about 35 percent, from overseas. International volumes are growing faster than in the United States, with global transaction volumes up some 14 percent in FY2011 as part of an overall 11.6 percent worldwide volume increase.

Financial Highlights, Fiscal Year 2011

FY2011 was a banner year, as the share price advance indicates. Growth in global transaction volumes and the dollars per transaction (which grew 17 percent worldwide and 23 percent abroad) drove a 14 percent top-line growth to $9.2 billion, and a 23 percent bottom-line growth. A 3 percent reduction in share count amplified the net profit growth into a 28 percent growth in earnings per share. The company recently authorized another $500 million share repurchase program, and projects FY2012 revenue growth in "the low double digits" and earnings growth "in the high teens."

Reasons to Buy

Simply, it would be hard to come up with a better business model—a company that develops and sells the network, and collects fees every time it's used? It would be like Microsoft collecting fees every time a file is created and saved, or a relatively unique e-mail platform that charges fees for every message. Visa is in a great position to not only capitalize on overall world economic growth, as most companies should be, but also to capitalize on a shift in this growth toward electronic payments. Indeed, the "mobile wallet" concept, where consumers can pay for things with a mobile device that reads a bar-code-like QR (quick response), is very promising. With cellular providers recently abandoning a competitive platform under development, Visa stands in exactly the right place to benefit from this evolution. Overall, while Visa isn't a monopoly (MasterCard, American Express, and Discover are competitors), it has the strongest franchise, technology leadership, and pricing power at its back.

Reasons for Caution

The somewhat monopolistic power and pricing practices of credit card processors has come under public fire and government scrutiny, and mandates to limit transaction fees may hurt growth somewhat. Also, transaction processors are vulnerable to economic cycles, and a double-dip or protracted recession would hurt revenues. Finally, although Visa and others have driven payment technology for years, it is still possible that the mobile wallet opportunity may be capitalized on elsewhere in the industry, leaving credit card providers out of the loop. However, that doesn't look likely right now.

SECTOR: **Financials**
BETA COEFFICIENT: **0.72**
10-YEAR COMPOUND EARNINGS PER SHARE GROWTH: **NM**
10-YEAR COMPOUND DIVIDENDS PER SHARE GROWTH: **NM**

	2004	2005	2006	2007	2008	2009	2010	2011
Revenues (Mil)	—	—	—	—	6,263	6,911	8,065	9,188
Net income (Mil)	—	—	—	—	1,700	2,213	2,966	3,650
Earnings per share	—	—	—	—	2.25	2.92	3.91	4.99
Dividends per share	—	—	—	—	0.21	0.44	0.53	0.67
Cash flow per share	—	—	—	—	2.50	3.22	3.86	5.34
Price: high	—	—	—	—	89.6	89.7	97.2	103.4
low	—	—	—	—	43.5	41.8	64.9	67.5

Visa, Inc.
P.O. Box 8999
San Francisco, CA 94128
(415) 932-2100
Website: *www.visa.com*

Waste Management, Inc.

NEW FOR 2013

Ticker symbol: WM (NYSE) ❑ S&P rating: BBB ❑ Value Line financial strength rating: A ❑ Current yield: 4.2% ❑ Dividend raises, past 10 years: 8

Company Profile

Perhaps by now you've dismissed all the companies on the 2012 *100 Best Stocks* list as "garbage" stocks. That's your choice, not our call. But if you've tagged Waste Management as a "garbage" company, you've got it mostly right.

Waste Management is the largest and steadiest hand in the North American solid waste disposal industry. Like most large waste firms, WMI has grown over time by assembling smaller, more local companies into a nationally branded and highly scaled operation with a notable amount of innovation on several fronts in the core business.

The business is divided into three segments:

- Collection, which accounts for 57 percent of the business, includes the standard dumpster and garbage truck operations. The company has over 600 collection operations, some on long-term contract with municipalities and businesses. Innovations include a landfill-to-gas-liquification project that produces 13,000 gallons of fuel per day for WMI's trucks,

online dumpster ordering, and the "Bagster" small-scale disposal units now sold through retail home-improvement outlets.

- Landfill (18 percent of revenues). The company operates 270 landfills across North America, servicing its own collection operations and other collection service providers. Among these sites, there are 131 landfill-gas-to-energy conversion projects producing fuel for electricity generation—currently 540 megawatts of power, enough to power 400,000 homes.

- Waste to energy, recycling, and transfer (28 percent). These operations perform specialized material recovery and processing into useful commodities. There are 345 transfer stations set up for the collection of various forms of waste, including medical, recyclables, and e-waste. A wholly owned subsidiary, Wheelabrator Technologies, operates 17 waste-to-energy plants and five electric generating facilities producing electric power for about

900,000 homes, in addition to the gasification projects at the landfills. The company has also pioneered single-stream recycling, where physical and optical sorting technologies sort out unseparated recyclable materials. Single-streaming has greatly increased recycling rates in municipalities where it is used, and provides a steady revenue stream in recovered paper, glass, metals, etc. for the company. The company also further refines these materials into industrial inputs, e.g., glass or plastic feedstocks in certain colors. The company recycles 7 million tons of commodities annually today and expects to grow that figure to 20 million by 2020.

Financial Highlights, Fiscal Year 2011

FY2011 results were negatively affected to a degree by the absorption of a few acquisitions and soft recycled commodity prices. Revenues grew about 7 percent to $13.4 billion, while earnings, hemmed in by the above-mentioned costs and material prices, stayed almost flat at $2.14 per share. For FY2012, the company expects to get past most of the integration costs, and is projecting EPS in the $2.22–$2.30 per share range. The company

also announced a 6-cent dividend increase to $1.42 per share annually, and a $500 million share buyback authorization. WMI has reduced share count approximately 20 percent, to 460 million, since 2004.

Reasons to Buy

"Strategic" waste collection, particularly with the high-value-add material recovery operations that have become core to WMI's business, is not only here to stay but also will only become more important to residential, industrial, and municipal customers as time goes on. WMI exhibits a lot of innovation in an industry not particularly known for innovation. Additionally, the 4 percent dividend and share repurchase efforts make up for a relatively unexciting stock performance over the years; we feel that WMI could break out of the doldrums as material recovery becomes an even more strategic and profitable enterprise. In the past 10 years, earnings have nearly doubled, while the share price is only up a third. This among other considerations makes WMI a relatively safe bet, and indeed, the beta is only 0.55, a "sleep at night" stock in an economic storm. This may be a garbage company, but it is by no means a garbage stock.

Reasons for Caution

Acquisitions do fuel a lot of the growth, and the recycling

operations, while cool and sexy, aren't always profitable, especially when competing material prices, like natural gas these days, are soft. Additionally, any waste company runs the risk of going afoul of environmental regulations; WMI has largely steered clear of trouble thus far, but there are no guarantees. Growth may be difficult to handle if regulations become more stringent.

SECTOR: **Services**
BETA COEFFICIENT: **0.55**
10-YEAR COMPOUND EARNINGS PER SHARE GROWTH: **2.5%**
10-YEAR COMPOUND DIVIDENDS PER SHARE GROWTH: **68%**

		2004	2005	2006	2007	2008	2009	2010	2011
Revenues (Mil)		12,516	13,074	13,363	13,310	13,388	11,791	12,515	13,375
Net income (Mil)		820	877	994	1,080	1,087	988	1,011	1,007
Earnings per share		1.41	1.55	1.82	2.07	2.19	2.00	2.10	2.14
Dividends per share		0.75	0.85	0.88	0.98	1.08	1.16	1.28	1.36
Cash flow per share		3.78	4.05	4.35	4.68	4.74	4.43	4.64	4.85
Price:	high	31.4	31	35.6	41.2	39.3	34.2	37.3	36.7
	low	25.7	26.8	30.1	32.4	24.5	22.1	31.1	27.8

Waste Management, Inc.
1001 Fannin, Suite 4000
Houston, TX 77002
(713) 512-6200
Website: *www.wm.com*

Wells Fargo & Company

Ticker symbol: WFC (NYSE) ❑ S&P rating: AA- ❑ Value Line financial strength rating: A ❑ Current yield: 0.6% ❑ Dividend raises, past 10 years: 6

Company Profile

Wells Fargo & Company is a diversified financial services company, providing banking, insurance, investments, mortgages, and consumer finance from more than 11,000 offices and other distribution channels, including mortgage, investment management, commercial banking, and consumer finance branches across all 50 states, Canada, the Caribbean, and Central America.

The business is divided into three segments. First and largest is Community Banking, which provides traditional banking and mortgage services in all 50 states through a combination of branches, ATMs, and online services. Wholesale Banking provides commercial banking, capital markets, leasing, and other financing services to larger corporations. Wealth, Brokerage and Retirement provides financial advisory and investment management services to individuals.

As of 2011, Wells Fargo had $1.3 trillion in assets, loans of $750 billion, and shareholder equity of $140 billion. Based on assets, they are the third-largest bank holding company in the United States.

They have 267,000 employees, or "team members," as they prefer to call them. The company expanded its footprint and market share—which is close to 10 percent of all U.S. banking services—considerably with the 2009 acquisition of Wachovia.

Financial Highlights, Fiscal Year 2011

Like all big banks, Wells hit the skids in 2008–09 with a substantial hit in earnings per share and concerns about asset quality. Since then the company has rebounded more successfully than its larger brethren. Loan losses and nonperforming assets have dropped significantly and the so-called "tier 1" ratio, a measure of equity to total assets, has improved from 8.30 percent to 9.46 percent, fairly healthy by banking standards. Earnings per share grew 28 percent to $2.82 (up from a recession low of $0.70 in FY2009) and are projected to grow to $3.25 in FY2012. This adequately supports a return of the dividend north of $1 per share upon regulatory approval, and also supports continued improvement in the equity ratios.

Reasons to Buy

We've continually recognized Wells for their (relatively) conservative positions and cautious behaviors during the mortgage free-for-all. They had less exposure overall than most and were able to spot trouble earlier than many others. They've been more aggressive than others in getting rid of bad assets, modifying loans, and getting the banking crisis behind it. As an example, they've modified some 725,000 mortgage loans, achieving a triple-play of improving asset quality, reducing future write-downs and foreclosed properties, and improving both public image and confidence.

As a result, we're looking at a bank that today is in far better shape than many of its peers. In fact, with the removal of financial services firm Northern Trust from our *100 Best* list, Wells is now the only financial services company on that list. Wells has a solid brand reputation and value (number two worldwide according to a BrandFinance study). Especially as the macroeconomic environment improves, we think WFC is well positioned to take advantage. We do think shareholders will be rewarded with an attractive dividend restored eventually.

Reasons for Caution

"Headline risk" continues to abound in the banking industry. Any sign of trouble on the mortgage front will obviously hurt, although the recent settlement of the "robosigning" case reduces this risk somewhat. The company has been profiting from the difference between retail and wholesale interest rates, but if wholesale interest rates, i.e., Fed funds and commercial paper, start to rise, the profit recovery could be jeopardized. The company has been building equity not only by writing off bad loans but also by selling stock, and share counts have continued to rise after a large bump related to the Wachovia acquisition, and were up 150 million to 5.35 billion in FY2011, not our favored direction.

SECTOR: **Financials**
BETA COEFFICIENT: **1.31**
10-YEAR COMPOUND EARNINGS PER SHARE GROWTH: **5.5%**
10-YEAR COMPOUND DIVIDENDS PER SHARE GROWTH: **11.5%**

		2004	**2005**	**2006**	**2007**	**2008**	**2009**	**2010**	**2011**
Loans (Bil)		269.6	296.1	306.9	344.8	843.8	758	734	750
Net Income (Mil)		7,014	7,670	8,480	8,060	2,655	12,275	11,632	15,025
Earnings per share		2.05	2.25	2.49	2.38	0.7	1.75	2.21	2.82
Dividends per share		0.93	1	1.12	1.18	1.3	0.49	0.20	0.48
Price:	high	32	32.4	37	38	44.7	31.5	34.3	34.3
	low	27.2	28.8	30.3	29.3	19.9	7.8	23	22.6

Wells Fargo & Company
420 Montgomery Street
San Francisco, CA 94163
(415) 396-0523
Website: *www.wellsfargo.com*

CONSERVATIVE GROWTH

Whirlpool Corporation

Ticker symbol: WHR (NYSE) ❑ S&P rating: BBB- ❑ Value Line financial strength rating: A ❑ Current yield: 3.1% ❑ Dividend raises, past 10 years: 2

Company Profile

Whirlpool is the world's leading home appliance manufacturer in a $120 billion global industry. The company manufactures appliances under familiar and recognized brand names in all major home appliance categories including fabric care (laundry), cooking, refrigeration, dishwashers, water filtration, and garage organization. Familiar brand names include Whirlpool but also Maytag, Kitchen Aid, Amana, Jenn-Air, and international names Bauknecht, Brastemp, and Consul. The Whirlpool brand itself is the No. 1 global appliance brand. About 49 percent of Whirlpool's sales come from overseas, and that percentage has increased two percentage points in each of the past two years.

In an industry not known for innovation, Whirlpool has striven to be an innovation leader in its industry. This has manifested itself both in new products and product platforms and in manufacturing and supply-chain efficiencies, such as a global platform design for local manufacture of washing machine products, recalling similar achievements in the auto industry.

A recent supply-chain refinement initiative yielded $10 million in annual savings. Such gains are key in this competitive, price-sensitive industry. The company also has initiatives to build lifetime brand loyalty and product quality, improve energy efficiency, and to expand in key developing markets such as Brazil (where the Brastemp brand is sold) and India. The company is the number one appliance manufacturer in Latin America.

Financial Highlights, Fiscal Year 2011

Like most other manufacturing corporations, Whirlpool is enjoying the economic recovery. That said, unit sales decreased slightly in FY2011, although revenues were slightly higher, up 1.6 percent, from FY2010 mostly due to currency conversion and energy tax credits. Sales, however, were 7.4 percent higher than FY2009. The unit volume decrease was partly attributed to tweaks in the product/price mix, with price increases in certain markets and more emphasis on premium brands. Although price increases and productivity improvements normally would help the bottom line, it was largely static due to increases in the price of materials and some restructuring costs, which knocked about a percentage point off of operating margins. Even so, the company earned $8.95 per share with an especially healthy cash flow of $16.54 per share (the company strongly believes in managing cash flow and especially free cash flow). The company expects another modestly flat year in FY2012 as more restructuring costs hit, with earnings in the $6.50–$7.50 range.

Reasons to Buy

We like market leaders, particularly companies not content to sit on their laurels and reap increasingly lean cash flows while others close in around them. Whirlpool has used the recession and ensuing recovery as a wake-up call and an opportunity to streamline its businesses and to put some real strategic thought into how to drive its brand assortment and international portfolio to achieve better results. As the company finishes some of the restructuring initiatives, absorbs cost increases through price-mix adjustments, and continues to build critical mass in overseas markets, we would expect it to resume a solid growth path in

sales and especially earnings. Cash flows and investor returns are solid. More than most, the management team is a plus with a recognizable pragmatic and strategic approach to managing this business.

Reasons for Caution

By nature, the appliance business is highly competitive and cyclical. In addition, consumers with more disposable income have of late been opting for fancier, more expensive foreign brands, like Bosch and LG, a trend that could hurt if it continues. We believe that Whirlpool is countering this trend by adding elegance, advertising, and channel support for its top-tier brands and products; that plus a reversal of customer preferences toward American brands as seen to a degree in the auto industry should help. Commodity costs, labor issues, quality issues, and shifts in consumer preferences are perpetual risks. Finally, the share price has been relatively volatile for a mature business, probably reflecting differing views at differing times about the success of this economically sensitive company. The price swings probably represent good buying opportunities.

SECTOR: **Consumer Durables**
BETA COEFFICIENT: **1.95**
10-YEAR COMPOUND EARNINGS PER SHARE GROWTH: **3.0%**
10-YEAR COMPOUND DIVIDENDS PER SHARE GROWTH: **2.5%**

	2004	**2005**	**2006**	**2007**	**2008**	**2009**	**2010**	**2011**
Revenues (Mil)	13,220	14,317	18,080	19,408	18,907	17,099	18,366	18,666
Net income (Mil)	406	422	486	647	418	328	707	699
Earnings per share	5.90	6.19	6.35	8.10	5.50	4.34	9.10	8.95
Dividends per share	1.72	1.72	1.72	1.72	1.72	1.72	1.72	1.93
Cash flow per share	12.70	12.71	13.26	16.32	13.90	11.37	16.91	16.54
Price: high	80	86.5	96	118	98	85	118.4	92.3
low	54.5	60.8	74.1	72.1	30.2	19.2	71	45.2

Whirlpool Corporation
2000 M-63
Benton Harbor, MI 49022
(269) 923-5000
Website: *www.whirlpoolcorp.com*

▼ **Appendix A: Performance Analysis:** *100 Best Stocks You Can Buy 2012*

ONE YEAR GAIN/LOSS, APRIL 1, 2011–APRIL 1, 2012

Company	Symbol	Price 4/1/2011	Price 4/1/2012	% change	Dollar gain/loss, $1,000 invested
3M	MMM	$97.21	$85.69	-11.9%	($118.51)
Abbott	ABT	$52.04	$59.69	14.7%	$147.00
Aetna	AET	$41.38	$47.82	15.6%	$155.63
Air Products	APD	$95.52	$88.26	-7.6%	($76.01)
Alexander & Baldwin	ALEX	$52.70	$48.12	-8.7%	($86.91)
Allergan	AGN	$79.56	$94.65	19.0%	$189.67
Amgen	AMGN	$56.85	$65.59	15.4%	$153.74
Apache	APA	$133.37	$93.65	-29.8%	($297.82)
Apple	AAPL	$350.13	$605.23	72.9%	$728.59
Archer Daniels Midland	ADM	$37.02	$30.75	-16.9%	($169.37)
AT&T	T	$31.12	$30.54	-1.9%	($18.64)
Automatic Data Processing	ADP	$54.36	$54.49	0.2%	$2.39
Baxter	BAX	$56.90	$58.03	2.0%	$19.86
Becton, Dickinson	BDX	$85.94	$74.79	-13.0%	($129.74)
Bed, Bath & Beyond	BBBY	$56.13	$69.41	23.7%	$236.59
Best Buy	BBY	$31.22	$22.04	-29.4%	($294.04)
Campbell Soup	CPB	$33.59	$33.01	-1.7%	($17.27)
CarMax	KMX	$34.70	$31.31	-9.8%	($97.69)
Caterpillar	CAT	$115.41	$105.89	-8.2%	($82.49)
Chevron	CVX	$109.44	$100.78	-7.9%	($79.13)
Church & Dwight	CHD	$41.24	$50.11	21.5%	$215.08
Cincinnati Financial	CINF	$31.68	$33.87	6.9%	$69.13
Clorox	CLX	$69.66	$70.23	0.8%	$8.18
Coca-Cola	KO	$67.46	$71.94	6.6%	$66.41
Colgate-Palmolive	CL	$84.35	$97.21	15.2%	$152.46
Comcast	CMCSA	$26.21	$29.50	12.6%	$125.52
ConocoPhillips	COP	$78.89	$73.63	-6.7%	($66.68)

▼ **Appendix A: Performance Analysis:** *100 Best Stocks You Can Buy 2012* (con't)

ONE YEAR GAIN/LOSS, APRIL 1, 2011–APRIL 1, 2012

Company	Symbol	Price 4/1/2011	Price 4/1/2012	% change	Dollar gain/loss, $1,000 invested
Costco Wholesale	COST	$80.89	$86.32	6.7%	$67.13
CR Bard	BCR	$106.75	$96.03	-10.0%	($100.42)
CVS/Caremark	CVS	$36.22	$43.43	19.9%	$199.06
Deere	DE	$97.50	$79.47	-18.5%	($184.92)
Dentsply	XRAY	$37.55	$39.44	5.0%	$50.33
Dominion Resources	D	$46.42	$50.28	8.3%	$83.15
Duke Energy	DUK	$18.65	$20.41	9.4%	$94.37
DuPont	DD	$56.79	$52.02	-8.4%	($83.99)
Ecolab	ECL	$52.76	$61.61	16.8%	$167.74
ExxonMobil	XOM	$87.98	$82.95	-5.7%	($57.17)
Fair Isaac	FICO	$39.88	$42.02	5.4%	$53.66
FedEx	FDX	$95.67	$88.03	-8.0%	($79.86)
Fluor	FLR	$69.94	$58.10	-16.9%	($169.29)
FMC	FMC	$79.89	$92.68	16.0%	$160.10
General Mills	GIS	$38.58	$38.70	0.3%	$3.11
Google	GOOG	$544.10	$624.60	14.8%	$147.95
Grainger, W.W.	GWW	$151.60	$213.18	40.6%	$406.20
Harris	HRS	$53.13	$44.42	-16.4%	($163.94)
Heinz	HNZ	$51.23	$52.65	2.8%	$27.72
Hewlett-Packard	HPQ	$40.37	$24.57	-39.1%	($391.38)
Honeywell	HON	$61.24	$58.07	-5.2%	($51.76)
Illinois Tool Works	ITW	$58.41	$54.82	-6.1%	($61.46)
IBM	IBM	$170.58	$202.80	18.9%	$188.88
International Paper	IP	$30.88	$32.97	6.8%	$67.68
Iron Mountain	IRM	$31.85	$29.65	-6.9%	($69.07)
Johnson & Johnson	JNJ	$65.72	$63.54	-3.3%	($33.17)
Johnson Controls	JCI	$41.00	$32.57	-20.6%	($205.61)
Kellogg	K	$57.27	$53.24	-7.0%	($70.37)

▼ **Appendix A: Performance Analysis:** *100 Best Stocks You Can Buy 2012* (con't)

ONE YEAR GAIN/LOSS, APRIL 1, 2011–APRIL 1, 2012

Company	Symbol	Price 4/1/2011	Price 4/1/2012	% change	Dollar gain/loss, $1,000 invested
Kimberly-Clark	KMB	$66.06	$74.35	12.5%	$125.49
Lubrizol	LZ	$106.68	$134.97	26.5%	$265.19
Marathon Oil	MRO	$27.02	$29.70	9.9%	$99.19
McCormick	MKC	$49.12	$53.70	9.3%	$93.24
McDonald's	MCD	$76.09	$96.97	27.4%	$274.41
McKesson	MCK	$83.01	$90.48	9.0%	$89.99
Medtronic	MDT	$41.75	$37.51	-10.2%	($101.56)
Monsanto	MON	$68.04	$77.07	13.3%	$132.72
NextEra Energy	NEE	$56.57	$62.08	9.7%	$97.40
NIKE	NKE	$82.32	$108.80	32.2%	$321.67
Norfolk Southern	NSC	$74.68	$67.44	-9.7%	($96.95)
Northern Trust	NTRS	$49.99	$45.70	-8.6%	($85.82)
Nucor	NUE	$46.96	$41.57	-11.5%	($114.78)
Oracle	ORCL	$35.96	$28.50	-20.7%	($207.45)
Otter Tail	OTTR	$23.38	$21.18	-9.4%	($94.10)
Pall Corporation	PLL	$58.44	$59.12	1.2%	$11.64
Patterson	PDCO	$34.71	$32.89	-5.2%	($52.43)
Paychex	PAYX	$32.71	$30.83	-5.7%	($57.47)
Pepsi	PEP	$68.89	$65.06	-5.6%	($55.60)
Perrigo	PRGO	$90.36	$104.14	15.3%	$152.50
Praxair	PX	$106.42	$112.03	5.3%	$52.72
Procter & Gamble	PG	$64.90	$65.81	1.4%	$14.02
Ross Stores	ROST	$36.85	$59.06	60.3%	$602.71
Schlumberger	SLB	$89.75	$68.38	-23.8%	($238.11)
Sigma-Aldrich	SIAL	$70.58	$70.96	0.5%	$5.38
J. M. Smucker	SJM	$75.07	$79.25	5.6%	$55.68
Southern Co.	SO	$39.04	$44.74	14.6%	$146.00
Southwest Airlines	LUV	$11.75	$7.94	-32.4%	($324.26)

▼ Appendix A: Performance Analysis: *100 Best Stocks You Can Buy 2012* (con't)

ONE YEAR GAIN/LOSS, APRIL 1, 2011–APRIL 1, 2012

Company	Symbol	Price 4/1/2011	Price 4/1/2012	% change	Dollar gain/loss, $1,000 invested
St. Jude Medical	STJ	$53.44	$38.58	-27.8%	($278.07)
Staples	SPLS	$21.14	$15.53	-26.5%	($265.37)
Starbucks	SBUX	$36.20	$61.67	70.4%	$703.59
Stryker	SYK	$53.70	$55.43	3.2%	$32.22
Suburban Propane	SPH	$56.21	$42.79	-23.9%	($238.75)
Sysco	SYY	$28.91	$29.31	1.4%	$13.84
Target	TGT	$49.10	$57.43	17.0%	$169.65
Teva Pharmaceutical	TEVA	$45.73	$44.19	-3.4%	($33.68)
Total S.A.	TOT	$64.23	$47.77	-25.6%	($256.27)
Tractor Supply	TSCO	$61.87	$98.38	59.0%	$590.11
Union Pacific	UNP	$103.47	$108.84	5.2%	$51.90
UnitedHealth	UNH	$49.23	$58.05	17.9%	$179.16
United Technologies	UTX	$89.58	$79.80	-10.9%	($109.18)
Valmont	VMI	$105.30	$118.06	12.1%	$121.18
Verizon	VZ	$37.78	$37.26	-1.4%	($13.76)
Visa	V	$78.12	$123.16	57.7%	$576.55
Wells Fargo	WFC	$29.11	$32.84	12.8%	$128.13

▼ Appendix B: Dividend and Yield, by Company

Company	Symbol	2011 Dividend	2011 Yield %	2012 Dividend	2012 Yield %	Dividend Raises, Past 10 Years
3M Company	MMM	$2.10	2.3%	$2.36	2.6%	10
Abbott Laboratories	ABT	$1.92	3.9%	$2.04	3.4%	10
Aetna	AET	$0.60	1.6%	$0.70	1.5%	2
Allergan	AGN	$0.20	0.3%	$0.20	0.2%	1
Amgen	AMGN	$0.56	1.0%	$1.44	2.1%	2
Apple Inc	AAPL					
Archer Daniels Midland	ADM	$0.64	1.8%	$0.70	2.2%	10
AT&T	T	$1.72	5.6%	$1.76	5.7%	9
Automatic Data Processing	ADP	$1.44	2.8%	$1.58	2.9%	10
Baxter International	BAX	$1.24	2.3%	$1.34	2.4%	10
Becton, Dickinson	BDX	$1.64	2.0%	$1.80	2.1%	10
Bed, Bath & Beyond	BBBY					
Campbell Soup	CPB	$1.16	3.5%	$1.16	3.5%	9
Carmax, Inc	KMX					
Caterpillar	CAT	$1.76	1.6%	$1.84	1.7%	10
Chevron	CVX	$2.88	2.7%	$3.60	3.0%	10
Church & Dwight	CHD	$0.68	1.7%	$0.96	2.0%	6
Cincinnati Financial	CINF	$1.60	4.8%	$1.61	5.7%	10
Clorox Company	CLX	$2.20	3.1%	$2.40	3.5%	9
Coca-Cola	KO	$1.88	2.8%	$2.04	2.8%	10
Colgate-Palmolive	CL	$2.32	2.9%	$2.38	2.5%	10
Comcast	CMCSA	$0.44	1.7%	$0.65	2.2%	3
ConocoPhillips	COP	$2.64	3.3%	$2.64	3.7%	10
Costco Wholesale	COST	$0.80	1.1%	$0.96	1.2%	8
CVS/Caremark	CVS	$0.48	1.4%	$0.65	1.5%	10
Deere & Co.	DE	$1.40	1.4%	$1.84	2.3%	9
Dominion Energy	D	$1.96	4.4%	$2.11	4.1%	8

▼ Appendix B: Dividend and Yield, by Company (con't)

Company	Symbol	2011 Dividend	2011 Yield %	2012 Dividend	2012 Yield %	Dividend Raises, Past 10 Years
DuPont	DD	$1.64	3.0%	$1.72	3.1%	4
Eastman Chemical	EMN			$1.04	2.0%	1
ExxonMobil	XOM	$1.76	2.1%	$2.28	2.2%	10
Fair Isaac	FICO	$0.08	0.3%	$0.08	0.2%	2
FedEx	FDX	$0.48	0.5%	$0.52	0.6%	9
Fluor Corporation	FLR	$0.48	0.7%	$0.60	1.1%	2
FMC Corporation	FMC	$0.60	0.7%	$0.72	0.7%	5
General Mills	GIS	$1.12	3.1%	$1.22	3.1%	7
Grainger, W.W.	GWW	$2.16	1.5%	$3.20	1.5%	10
Harman International	HAR			$0.30	0.6%	1
Heinz	HNZ	$1.80	3.7%	$1.92	3.6%	8
Honeywell	HON	$1.32	2.2%	$1.49	2.5%	8
IBM	IBM	$2.60	1.6%	$3.40	1.4%	10
Illinois Tool Works	ITW	$1.36	2.5%	$1.44	2.5%	10
Intel	INTC			$0.84	3.0%	8
Int'l Paper	IP	$1.04	3.4%	$1.05	3.2%	3
Iron Mountain	IRM	$0.76	2.4%	$1.00	3.5%	3
Itron	ITRI					
Johnson & Johnson	JNJ	$2.16	3.6%	$2.44	3.8%	10
Johnson Controls	JCI	$0.64	1.5%	$0.72	2.3%	9
Kellogg	K	$1.64	3.0%	$1.72	3.3%	7
Kimberly-Clark	KMB	$2.80	4.3%	$2.96	4.0%	10
Macy's	M			$0.80	2.0%	5
Marathon Oil	MRO	$1.00	1.9%	$0.68	2.2%	
McCormick & Co.	MKC	$1.12	2.3%	$1.24	2.3%	10
McDonald's	MCD	$2.44	3.2%	$2.80	2.9%	10
McKesson	MCK	$0.72	0.9%	$0.80	0.3%	3

▼ Appendix B: Dividend and Yield, by Company (con't)

Company	Symbol	2011 Dividend	Yield %	2012 Dividend	Yield %	Dividend Raises, Past 10 Years
Molex	MOLX			$0.80	3.6%	10
Monsanto	MON	$1.12	1.5%	$1.20	1.6%	7
Mosaic	MOS			$0.50	1.0%	1
NextEra Energy	NEE	$2.10	3.8%	$2.40	3.8%	10
NIKE, Inc.	NIKE	$1.24	1.6%	$1.44	1.3%	9
Norfolk Southern	NSC	$1.60	2.3%	$1.88	2.8%	10
Nucor Corp.	NUE	$1.44	3.1%	$1.46	3.6%	8
Otter Tail Corporation	OTTR	$1.20	5.2%	$1.19	5.4%	5
Pall Corporation	PLL	$0.68	1.2%	$0.80	1.4%	7
Patterson	PDCO	$0.48	1.5%	$0.60	1.7%	3
PayChex	PAYX	$1.24	3.9%	$1.28	4.2%	8
PepsiCo	PEP	$1.92	2.9%	$2.15	3.1%	10
Perrigo	PRGO	$0.28	0.4%	$0.32	0.3%	9
Praxair	PX	$2.00	2.0%	$2.20	1.9%	10
Procter & Gamble	PG	$1.92	3.1%	$2.25	3.1%	10
Ross	ROST	$0.44	1.2%	$0.56	1.0%	10
Schlumberger	SLB	$1.00	1.1%	$1.10	1.6%	6
Seagate	STX			$1.00	3.3%	4
Sigma-Aldrich	SIAL	$0.72	1.1%	$0.80	1.1%	10
J. M. Smucker	SJM	$1.76	2.4%	$1.92	2.4%	10
Southern Company	SO	$1.84	4.8%	$1.96	4.3%	10
Southwest Airlines	LUV	$0.02	0.2%	$0.02	0.2%	0
St. Jude Medical	STJ	$0.84	1.6%	$0.92	2.4%	1
Starbucks	SBUX	$0.52	1.4%	$0.68	1.1%	3
Stryker Corporation	SYK	$0.72	1.2%	$0.85	1.2%	9
Suburban Propane	SPH	$3.40	6.0%	$3.41	7.8%	10
Sysco	SYY	$1.04	3.7%	$1.08	3.6%	10

▼ Appendix B: Dividend and Yield, by Company (con't)

Company	Symbol	2011 Dividend	2011 Yield %	2012 Dividend	2012 Yield %	Dividend Raises, Past 10 Years
Teva Pharmaceutical	TEVA	$0.68	1.7%	$0.79	2.1%	10
Tiffany	TIF			$1.16	1.7%	10
Time Warner	TWX			$1.04	2.9%	6
Total S.A.	TOT	$3.16	5.1%	$2.61	6.2%	5
Tractor Supply Company	TSCO	$0.28	0.5%	0.5%	$0.80	2
Union Pacific	UNP	$1.52	1.5%	$2.40	2.2%	7
UnitedHealth	UNH	$0.48	1.1%	$0.65	1.2%	4
United Parcel Service	UPS			$2.28	2.9%	10
United Technologies	UTX	$1.82	2.1%	$1.92	2.4%	10
Valero	VLO			$0.60	2.4%	9
Valmont Industries	VMI	$0.68	0.6%	$0.72	0.6%	10
Verizon	VZ	$1.96	5.1%	$2.00	5.5%	6
Visa	V	$0.60	0.8%	$0.88	0.7%	4
Waste Management	WM			$1.42	4.2%	8
Wells Fargo	WFC	$0.28	0.9%	$0.88	0.6%	7
Whirlpool	WHR			$2.00	3.1%	2

▼ Appendix C: Dividend and Yield, by Descending Yield

Company	Symbol	2011 Dividend	2011 Yield %	2012 Dividend	2012 Yield %	Dividend Raises, Past 10 Years
Suburban Propane	SPH	$3.40	6.0%	$3.41	7.8%	10
Total S.A.	TOT	$3.16	5.1%	$2.61	6.2%	5
AT&T	T	$1.72	5.6%	$1.76	5.7%	9
Cincinnati Financial	CINF	$1.60	4.8%	$1.61	5.7%	10
Verizon	VZ	$1.96	5.1%	$2.00	5.5%	6
Otter Tail Corporation	OTTR	$1.20	5.2%	$1.19	5.4%	5
Duke Energy	DUK	$1.00	5.4%	$1.00	4.8%	6
Southern Company	SO	$1.84	4.8%	$1.96	4.3%	10
PayChex	PAYX	$1.24	3.9%	$1.28	4.2%	8
Waste Management	WM			$1.42	4.2%	8
Dominion Energy	D	$1.96	4.4%	$2.11	4.1%	8
Kimberly-Clark	KMB	$2.80	4.3%	$2.96	4.0%	10
Johnson & Johnson	JNJ	$2.16	3.6%	$2.44	3.8%	10
NextEra Energy	NEE	$2.10	3.8%	$2.40	3.8%	10
ConocoPhillips	COP	$2.64	3.3%	$2.64	3.7%	10
Heinz	HNZ	$1.80	3.7%	$1.92	3.6%	8
Molex	MOLX			$0.80	3.6%	10
Nucor Corp.	NUE	$1.44	3.1%	$1.46	3.6%	8
Sysco	SYY	$1.04	3.7%	$1.08	3.6%	10
Campbell Soup	CPB	$1.16	3.5%	$1.16	3.5%	9
Clorox Company	CLX	$2.20	3.1%	$2.40	3.5%	9
Iron Mountain	IRM	$0.76	2.4%	$1.00	3.5%	3
Abbott Laboratories	ABT	$1.92	3.9%	$2.04	3.4%	10
Kellogg	K	$1.64	3.0%	$1.72	3.3%	7
Seagate	STX			$1.00	3.3%	4
Int'l Paper	IP	$1.04	3.4%	$1.05	3.2%	3

▼ **Appendix C: Dividend and Yield, by Descending Yield** (con't)

Company	Symbol	2011 Dividend	2011 Yield %	2012 Dividend	2012 Yield %	Dividend Raises, Past 10 Years
General Mills	GIS	$1.12	3.1%	$1.22	3.1%	7
PepsiCo	PEP	$1.92	2.9%	$2.15	3.1%	10
Procter & Gamble	PG	$1.92	3.1%	$2.25	3.1%	10
Whirlpool	WHR			$2.00	3.1%	2
Chevron	CVX	$2.88	2.7%	$3.60	3.0%	10
Intel	INTC			$0.84	3.0%	8
Automatic Data Processing	ADP	$1.44	2.8%	$1.58	2.9%	10
McDonald's	MCD	$2.44	3.2%	$2.80	2.9%	10
Time Warner	TWX			$1.04	2.9%	6
United Parcel Service	UPS			$2.28	2.9%	10
Coca-Cola	KO	$1.88	2.8%	$2.04	2.8%	10
Norfolk Southern	NSC	$1.60	2.3%	$1.88	2.8%	10
3M Company	MMM	$2.10	2.3%	$2.36	2.6%	10
Medtronic	MDT	$0.88	2.2%	$0.97	2.6%	10
Colgate-Palmolive	CL	$2.32	2.9%	$2.38	2.5%	10
Honeywell	HON	$1.32	2.2%	$1.49	2.5%	8
Illinois Tool Works	ITW	$1.36	2.5%	$1.44	2.5%	10
Baxter International	BAX	$1.24	2.3%	$1.34	2.4%	10
J. M. Smucker	SJM	$1.76	2.4%	$1.92	2.4%	10
St. Jude Medical	STJ	$0.84	1.6%	$0.92	2.4%	1
United Technologies	UTX	$1.82	2.1%	$1.92	2.4%	10
Valero	VLO			$0.60	2.4%	9
Deere & Co.	DE	$1.40	1.4%	$1.84	2.3%	9
Johnson Controls	JCI	$0.64	1.5%	$0.72	2.3%	9
McCormick & Co.	MKC	$1.12	2.3%	$1.24	2.3%	10
Archer Daniels Midland	ADM	$0.64	1.8%	$0.70	2.2%	10
Comcast	CMCSA	$0.44	1.7%	$0.65	2.2%	3

▼ Appendix C: Dividend and Yield, by Descending Yield (con't)

Company	Symbol	2011 Dividend	Yield %	2012 Dividend	Yield %	Dividend Raises, Past 10 Years
Marathon Oil	MRO	$1.00	1.9%	$0.68	2.2%	
Union Pacific	UNP	$1.52	1.5%	$2.40	2.2%	7
Amgen	AMGN	$0.56	1.0%	$1.44	2.1%	2
Becton, Dickinson	BDX	$1.64	2.0%	$1.80	2.1%	10
Target Corporation	TGT	$1.00	2.0%	$1.20	2.1%	10
Teva Pharmaceuticals	TEVA	$0.68	1.7%	$0.79	2.1%	10
Church & Dwight	CHD	$0.68	1.7%	$0.96	2.0%	6
Eastman Chemical	EMN			$1.04	2.0%	1
Fair Isaac	FICO	$0.08	0.3%	$0.08	2.0%	2
Macy's	M			$0.80	2.0%	5
Praxair	PX	$2.00	2.0%	$2.20	1.9%	10
Caterpillar	CAT	$1.76	1.6%	$1.84	1.7%	10
Patterson	PDCO	$0.48	1.5%	$0.06	1.7%	3
Tiffany	TIF			$1.16	1.7%	10
Monsanto	MON	$1.12	1.5%	$1.20	1.6%	7
Schlumberger	SLB	$1.00	1.1%	$1.10	1.6%	6
Aetna	AET	$0.60	1.6%	$0.70	1.5%	2
CVS/Caremark	CVS	$0.48	1.4%	$0.65	1.5%	10
Grainger, W.W.	GWW	$2.16	1.5%	$3.20	1.5%	10
IBM	IBM	$2.60	1.6%	$3.40	1.4%	10
Pall Corporation	PLL	$0.68	1.2%	$0.08	1.4%	7
NIKE, Inc.	NIKE	$1.24	1.6%	$1.44	1.3%	9
Costco Wholesale	COST	$0.80	1.1%	$0.96	1.2%	8
Stryker Corporation	SYK	$0.72	1.2%	$0.85	1.2%	9
UnitedHealth	UNH	$0.48	1.1%	$0.65	1.2%	4
Fluor Corporation	FLR	$0.48	0.7%	$0.60	1.1%	2
Sigma Aldrich	SIAL	$0.72	1.1%	$0.80	1.1%	10

▼ Appendix C: Dividend and Yield, by Descending Yield (con't)

Company	Symbol	2011 Dividend	2011 Yield %	2012 Dividend	2012 Yield %	Dividend Raises, Past 10 Years
Mosaic	MOS			$0.50	1.0%	1
Ross	ROST	$0.44	1.2%	$0.56	1.0%	10
FMC Corporation	FMC	$0.60	0.7%	$0.72	0.7%	5
Visa	V	$0.60	0.8%	$0.88	0.7%	4
FedEx	FDX	$0.48	0.5%	$0.52	0.6%	9
Harman International	HAR			$0.30	0.6%	1
Valmont Industries	VMI	$0.68	0.6%	$0.72	0.6%	10
Wells Fargo	WFC	$0.28	0.9%	$0.88	0.6%	7
Tractor Supply Company	TSCO	$0.28	0.5%	$0.80	0.5%	2
McKesson	MCK	$0.72	0.9%	$0.80	0.3%	3
Perrigo	PRGO	$0.28	0.4%	$0.32	0.3%	9
Allergan	AGN	$0.20	0.3%	$0.20	0.2%	1
Southwest Airlines	LUV	$0.02	0.2%	$0.02	0.2%	0
Apple Inc	AAPL					
Bed, Bath & Beyond	BBBY					
Carmax, Inc	KMX					
Itron	ITRI					